Praise for *Inequality in*

"Uncommonly balanced and fully accessible."

Publishers Weekly

"A well-researched and insightful perspective on economic inequality and its conflict with American ideals."

Booklist

"A welcome addition to American politics classes. Caliendo's textbook covers an array of important topics within the broad field of American income inequality …. In addition to providing foundational definitions, Caliendo's textbook offers an excellent introduction to the drivers of income inequality, with a particular focus on racial income inequality."

Political Science Quarterly

"*Inequality in America* introduces students to otherwise somewhat closed scholarly debates on inequality and its pertinent issues. The richly textured coverage of vital public policy questions related to inequality and its data-driven foundation are the strengths of the book. Students will find the format of the book appealing. Interesting features such as the "Representing" sections of each chapter help hone the respective chapters' themes and coverage. Moreover, the 'What Can I do?' section in each chapter offers very useful and empowering strategies for students to take up as they try to negotiate the many challenges that confront their generation."

James Taylor, **University of San Francisco**

"*Inequality in America* is an important addition to an introductory course in American government. It is clearly written and accessible to students, while thoughtfully addressing the complex institutionalization of inequality, and its effects, in the United States. Though there are texts that address racial politics more generally, this book is unique in its specific focus on the systemic nature of inequality and its focus on the intersections of race, poverty, and gender."

Catherine Paden, **Simmons University**

"*Inequality in America* is a thorough and comprehensive review of the state of race- and socioeconomic-status-based inequality from a multidisciplinary perspective. The author includes a great mix of political science, history, economics, and sociology. I highly recommend this book for anyone teaching an undergraduate course on U.S. inequality."

S. *Michael Gaddis*, The Pennsylvania State University

Inequality in America

Why does inequality have such a hold on American society and public policy? And what can we, as citizens, do about it? *Inequality in America* takes an in-depth look at race, class, and gender-based inequality across a wide range of issues from housing and education to crime, employment, and health. Caliendo explores how individual attitudes can affect public opinion and lawmakers' policy solutions. He also illustrates how these policies result in systemic barriers to advancement that often then contribute to individual perceptions. This cycle of disadvantage and advantage can be difficult—though not impossible—to break. "Representing" and "What Can I Do?" feature boxes highlight key public figures who have worked to combat inequality and encourage students to do the same.

The third edition has been thoroughly revised to include the most current data and cover recent issues and events such as Trump Administration policies, the #MeToo movement, and US Supreme Court decisions affecting issues of racial representation and voting rights. Concise and accessible, *Inequality in America* paves the way for students to think critically about the attitudes, behaviors, and structures of inequality.

New to the Third Edition

- Considers the heightened discussion of racial reckoning that has been occurring since the summer of 2020.

- Covers the disproportional effect to communities of color of the Covid-19 global pandemic and related recession.

- Takes an early glimpse into Biden Administration priorities compared to Trump Administration policies on education, immigration, housing, and urban development.

- Updates feature boxes, including a spotlight on US Representative Alexandria Ocasio-Cortez and Bryan Stevenson of the Equal Justice Initiative.

- Discusses the January 6, 2021 riot at the US Capitol, the #MeToo and #TimesUp Movements, and much more.

Stephen M. Caliendo is Dean of the College of Arts and Sciences and Professor of Political Science at North Central College. He is the author, co-author, or co-editor of multiple books, including *The Routledge Companion to Race and Ethnicity* and *Race Appeal: How Candidates Invoke Race in U.S. Political Campaigns.*

Inequality in America

Race, Poverty, and Fulfilling Democracy's Promise

THIRD EDITION

Stephen M. Caliendo

Routledge
Taylor & Francis Group

NEW YORK AND LONDON

Third edition published 2022
by Routledge
605 Third Avenue, New York, NY 10158

and by Routledge
2 Park Square, Milton Park, Abingdon, Oxon, OX14 4RN

Routledge is an imprint of the Taylor & Francis Group, an informa business

© 2022 Taylor & Francis

First edition published by Westview Press, 2012
Second edition published by Westview Press, 2017 and Routledge, 2018

Library of Congress Cataloging-in-Publication Data
A catalog record has been requested for this book

ISBN: 978-0-367-48834-5 (hbk)
ISBN: 978-0-367-48833-8 (pbk)
ISBN: 978-1-003-04304-1 (ebk)

DOI: 10.4324/9781003043041

Typeset in Minion Pro
by KnowledgeWorks Global Ltd.

For all those who work tirelessly for a more equitable world

Contents

2 *Income and Wealth*   43

3 *Housing*   75

4 *Education*   93

9 *Affirmative Action*   187

Conclusion: The Space Between Power and Powerlessness   205

List of Illustrations

List of Feature Boxes

Acknowledgments

The first week of March, 2020 was the original target for getting the complete manuscript of this edition to my editor. I knew that publishing a book in a presidential election year would be complicated: It would be available for fall 2020 courses, but it would be quickly outdated if the incumbent president were to lose the election. As my deadline neared, though, the news reports were drifting away from coverage of the Democratic nominating contest for President of the United States and more toward a unique virus that was proving to be quite contagious. As early indicators pointed to racial and ethnic disparities in both contracting and dying from Covid-19, I knew that I needed to wait for more information—both about the virus and about the pending election—before sending this edition to print. As it turned out, Joe Biden prevailed in securing both the Democratic Party nomination and the White House, but what transpired throughout 2020 and, indeed, in the early weeks of 2021—worldwide protests and racial reckoning following more high-profile killings of unarmed African Americans by law enforcement and a racially motivated resistance to the presidential election results, culminating in a white-supremacist-infused riot leading to forced entry into and deadly destruction at the US Capitol—were deeply relevant to the narrative of this book. I am sorry this is late, but I am glad I waited.

In 2013, when I first set out to write a concise story about racial and economic inequality in the United States (both historical and contemporary), I foresaw the challenges that would come with distilling so much information into a relatively short book. As I began the process, it struck me how deeply indebted I am to the scholars, activists, and journalists who supplied me with information (directly and indirectly). Political scientists, sociologists, anthropologists, criminal justice scholars, geographers, nutritionists, physicians, critical theorists, and education scholars have conducted rigorous empirical studies and laid the theoretical foundations that have advanced the state of knowledge in areas related to these issues.

I am also thankful for the extensive social network connections that I have developed over the years. Through my presence on Facebook and Twitter, in particular, as well as interactions through the Facebook page and Twitter feed that I maintain with my collaborator, Dr. Charlton McIlwain at New York University, under the auspices of the Project on Race in Political Communication, I became aware of a number of helpful articles, books, and data sources. Since the first edition was published, the book's Facebook page (https://facebook.com/InequalityRoutledge/) has been a valuable resource for compiling and sharing studies and news stories related to racial, economic, and gender inequality on a daily basis, serving as a live update to the content in this book. I learn much from the posts that are shared to that page, and I hope that you, as a reader, will "like" the page so that items of interest to you continue to populate your feed and stimulate your thinking about these issues.

My work on the first edition was supported by a grant from the North Central College Faculty Professional Development Committee, a portion of which supplied stipends to members of my dedicated team of undergraduate research assistants for that initial offering: Christopher Bilbro, David Depino, Jaclyn French, Emily Goodfellow, Collin Kee, Nicholas Lopez, Ingeborg Moran, Tanvi Potdukhe, Will Robinson, Pooja Sahai, Meghan Steinbeiss, Carley Timmerman, and, in particular, Kendall Bilbro, Ricky Brown, and Liz Hasseld. Besides conducting research and document retrieval, they each read the manuscript carefully and provided a student's perspective, which I greatly appreciate.

For the third edition, I benefitted once again from a highly energetic and generous volunteer team of undergraduate, multi-disciplinary research assistants at North Central College. Zaina Abdin, Lyndsay Brennan, Amelia Caliendo, Madeline Derango, Molly Dunbar, Elle Fortman, Julie Gotsch, Daniel Kim, Diamond Lee, Emily Nayder, Vincent Olejniczak, Jayne Peters, Kevin Phelan, Alexis Reese, Soile Talmadge, Kaylyn Walsh, and Elizabeth Watson, all contributed valuable feedback and new content in the fall of 2018 and 2019 to help me to keep pace with current data and scholarship. In the winter of 2020/2021, I benefited immensely from the talents of a former student, Mark Jenkins, who took over senior research assistance for the entire project, marking up every chapter and identifying the most current information possible so that this edition is as fresh as it can be by the time it made it to your hands. I cannot begin to thank him enough for his time, energy, and talent.

I have also received input from professors from across the nation who have assigned the book in their courses—political science, English, communication, social work, and interdisciplinary studies among them—or otherwise provided guidance. I wish to extend my gratitude to Dr. Jennifer Jackson, Dr. Gregory Lynch, Professor Tom Cavenagh, and Dr. Richard Guzman at North Central College; Dr. Tomeka Robinson and Dr. Philip Dalton at Hofstra University; Dr. Andra Gillespie at Emory University, and Dr. Nadia Brown, Dr. Rosalee Clawson, and Dr. Keith Shimko at Purdue University. Their influence runs throughout this volume, and the book is stronger as a result. My professional network continues to grow and inspire me. In particular, I am indebted to the National Conference of Black Political Scientists (NCOBPS), whose members are honest yet supportive, as well as welcoming, and brilliant. It is impossible for me to approximate how much my interactions with NCOBPS members and attendance at the annual meeting affect my thinking, research, and writing.

I wish to thank my patient and encouraging editor from the first two editions, Ada Fung, for years of guidance and, indeed, friendship. Jennifer Knerr has been an absolute saint throughout the process of preparing the third edition, putting up with my constant delays (however well meaning). I would also like to thank Jacqueline Dorsey, editorial assistant at Routledge, Sarahjayne Smith, project editor, and Preksha Sharma, copyeditor, for their hard work on this edition. I would like to thank the reviewers of this edition, as well as the previous editions; their feedback is extremely helpful, and the book is stronger as a result of their input. Any inadequacies that remain are my own.

Finally, I remain indebted to my family for their continuing love and devotion. Seemingly routine conversations with my wife, Jillian, have resulted in changes to this book throughout the years, as she pushes me to see things differently and explain things more clearly. My oldest daughter, Amelia, now a college junior studying sociology, psychology, and gender and sexuality studies, worked as a research assistant on this edition. My twin "tweens," Gianni and Stella, shape the way I see the world every day with their curiosity about my work and the state of injustice in the world generally. I am truly fortunate to have so many wonderful friends, family members, students, and colleagues in my life. Those blessings have made this book possible.

Introduction: The Politics of Inequality

THE MEN WHO DESIGNED THE US SYSTEM OF GOVERNMENT IN THE latter part of the eighteenth century present a frustrating paradox to current students of American politics. The Founding Fathers brilliantly devised a structure of government that would last, relatively unchanged, for well over 200 years (and counting). They were deeply flawed, however, with respect to their inability to reconcile the sweeping promises they articulated in the founding documents with the reality of widespread and brutal inequality that characterized the nation at that time. We celebrate the Founding Fathers by honoring their birthdays, displaying them on our currency, and studying them in our classrooms. But we need to qualify our admiration because their personal lives and public actions did not fully reflect their rhetoric and broader beliefs. In short, American democracy is at once vibrant because of their vision and imperfect because of their blind spots.

If we are interested in improving American democracy—in making "a more perfect union," as then-Senator Barack Obama said in his popular 2008 speech on race in America[1]—we are wise to redirect our attention from the individuals who designed the system and occupied key positions in it, to the *system* itself—the key assertion of this book. We will seek to understand how individual actors (both ordinary citizens and political elites) operate within a system that has largely constrained attempts to rectify what many recognize as injustices.

Inequality in America comes in multiple forms, though this volume focuses primarily on two: poverty and racism. But as we will see, it is

DOI: 10.4324/9781003043041-1

impossible to disentangle other types of inequality from issues related to race and economics. Although I do not specifically address inequality related to sexual orientation or physical ability, for example, these factors (and more) are very real and meaningful challenges that affect millions of Americans on a daily basis. While I recognize the interaction among these forces at certain points and address gender in Chapter 8, I mostly focus on the distinct and interrelated elements of race and poverty and the intricacies of the legacy of inequality that has come to characterize American government and politics in its first two centuries.

Poverty and the Myth of Meritocracy

On the surface, understanding poverty appears simple: some have the financial resources they need and some do not. If we want to understand how one of the wealthiest nations in the world can also be home to so much poverty, however, we need to examine the assumptions that accompany the realities of statistics about poverty. These assumptions help explain why ordinary Americans (the vast majority of whom are not wealthy) are willing to tolerate the existence of widespread income and wealth inequality, as well as abject poverty.

A decade ago, broadcaster Tavis Smiley and scholar Cornel West launched an 18-city "poverty tour" to call attention to these issues. The tour culminated in the publication of a book, *The Rich and the Rest of Us*,[2] in which the authors lay out a vision for understanding poverty in a more complete (and complicated) way. Subtitled "A Poverty Manifesto," their book serves as a call to action. They ask Americans to eschew the "lies about poverty that America can no longer afford" (e.g., that poverty is a character flaw, that minorities receive the bulk of government entitlements, and that poverty is uniquely urban),[3] and they advocate for public policies that are designed to lead to economic justice. Their work is powerful because it taps into Americans' shared core values, such as egalitarianism and justice. But other core values, such as individualism, are harder to reconcile with policies that promote economic redistribution. Together, we will explore the spaces where there is commonality and the areas where there is friction between liberals and conservatives, Democrats and Republicans on issues relating to racial and economic inequality.

Residing at the core of these differences is the notion of meritocracy, the belief that those who have success earned it while those who do not, did not.[4] Few would deny that Americans start out life with an unequal chance of financial success. But understanding how injustice is perpetuated requires an understanding of how inequality at birth often manifests in a lifetime of advantage or disadvantage.

In November 2010, Meghan McCain,[5] a noted blogger, television personality, and daughter of the late former US senator (and 2008 Republican nominee for president) John McCain, used her space on *The Daily Beast* blog to criticize former Alaska governor (and 2008 Republican vice presidential nominee) Sarah Palin for calling the Bush family "blue bloods" (a reference to their upper-class status). McCain, who considers herself a Republican, charged that such divisiveness within the party was counterproductive. But her response illustrates some core assumptions that most Americans hold about social class in the United States. In her blog entry, McCain ignores institutional factors that constrain poor Americans' chances of becoming blue bloods while enabling the children of wealthy Americans to follow in their parents' footsteps. She writes:

> I actually had to Google what the meaning of "blue bloods" was, although I could surmise that it was some kind of knock against education and coming from a family of some success. Yes, in essence that is what this statement meant. Families that work hard and achieve a long line of successful people are "blue bloods" and thus, [Palin] implied the opinions of said people are jaded and elitist, even if that family lineage has a long history of public service and leadership within [the] Republican Party.

As McCain admits later in the piece, she reacted to Palin's accusation personally because she grew up with tremendous privilege. Rather than recognizing that her privilege was unearned (it was a function of her parents' success, not her own work), she dismisses Palin's comment as inappropriate because "blue bloods" is a derogatory term for "families that work hard and achieve a long line of successful people." Here McCain invokes the myth of meritocracy; she believes that hard work leads to economic success (often through education), and she incorrectly (and perhaps unintentionally) suggests that each generation starts from scratch in its achievements.[6] It is certainly possible that members of each generation of a privileged family work hard in their own right,[7] but the lack of recognition of the head start that subsequent generations have (compared to those who begin life in poverty) is startling. Further, it reflects our collective socialization that urges us to accept the legitimacy of the American political and economic systems. We are taught to believe that those who are financially successful (as well as those who have access to excellent educational institutions) are fully deserving of that privilege, whereas those who are not must have acted badly at some point and, therefore, deserve their poverty. As we will see, however, such a generalization is harmful because it obscures systemic factors that contribute to poverty (and wealth).

This dynamic was very clearly at work in the 2016 presidential campaign, as millions of poor, primarily white, voters from rural areas of the country (in addition to more affluent Whites from suburban areas of the country) put their trust in billionaire real estate mogul and reality television star Donald Trump. On the surface, it should seem curious that millions of working-class Americans would throw their support behind a person who has never struggled economically a day in his life. There are no easy explanations, but one element is that Mr. Trump represented for millions of Americans a pushback against the cultural elite. That is, even though he is wealthy, he spoke to workers, has created jobs for workers, and openly criticized political correctness and other aspects of a cosmopolitan America that many find offensive.[8] His opponent in that election, former US Senator and former Secretary of State Hillary Clinton, embodied that elite class; though she was raised of modest means in a Chicago suburb, most of her adult life was spent in the public sphere. By the time she ran for president, she epitomized "establishment" politics, and the alternative was alluring.

As we will discover throughout the book, social class is more than income or wealth. Although it is rooted in economic stability, class encompasses a set of norms that involve many aspects of everyday life, from clothing to love to the value of education, and even the way we use and appreciate humor.[9] Wealthy as he is, rural, white Americans[10] found in Donald Trump a fellow American who shared their values and understood their struggles. He promised to help re-establish the American middle class, and they were willing to give him a chance.

Despite our national folklore, America does indeed have a class system that affects individuals' ability to achieve the American Dream. While it is not an officially designated system with titles (such as in Great Britain)[11] or clearly identified and accepted as a rigid caste system (such as in India),[12] Americans clearly recognize differences based on economic circumstances and customs that serve to organize society.[13] Class structure in the

United States is disproportionately (though not solely) based on wealth.[14] For that reason, we will address the concept of poverty as opposed to the broader concept of class. Economic and racial inequality will be our primary focus; we will explore the reasons that they exist and the myriad paths to reduce such inequality.

Irrespective of class designations—most Americans believe themselves to be in the middle class,[15] so such labels may carry little useful meaning— we will see that the data characterizing the distribution of income and wealth in the United States clearly reveal a large gap between the rich and the poor. That gap has been growing rapidly over the past 30 years, and, as we will see in Chapter 2, the number of Americans who reside in the middle is shrinking.

This notion of class differences came into sharp focus late in the summer of 2011 when the Occupy Wall Street (OWS or Occupy) movement was born with the launch of a website and a social media campaign, calling attention to the historically high and expanding degree of economic inequality in the United States. Protests began in Lower Manhattan on September 17, 2011, and rallies and demonstrations quickly spread to other cities in the United States and around the globe. The Occupy slogan, "We Are the 99 Percent," refers to the dramatic accumulation of wealth by the top 1 percent of Americans (see Chapter 2).

The mantle was carried even more visibly in the 2016 and 2020 presidential election, as US senator Bernie Sanders of Vermont ran strong campaigns for the Democratic nomination, rooted in the call to rectify economic inequality. Both Occupy and the Sanders campaign were successful in calling attention to an issue that was largely ignored by the media (and thus most of the American public) for nearly 50 years. As a result of Occupy, the 2012 presidential candidates were forced to address the issue, and America became positioned for a frank discussion about whether such trends are consistent with our fundamental shared values. Energized by the relative success of the Sanders campaigns (he lost the nomination to Hillary Clinton, but not before winning twenty-one states and Puerto Rico[16] in 2016, and he lost to former Vice President Joe Biden in a much more crowded field in 2020), young Americans in particular appear eager to continue the discussion and find unique ways to create meaningful change to bring about greater economic justice.

Given our history, we cannot consider these economic factors without also considering race. Race and poverty are not interchangeable demographic markers in the United States: there are wealthy people of color, and there are poor whites. However, poverty is disproportionately African American and Hispanic/Latinx[17] in America, and issues that uniquely face persons of color are often present irrespective of economic success.

Racial and Economic Inequality Through the Lens of Political Science

The first half of the twenty-first century marks a critical period in the racial history of the United States. By many projections, persons who identify as white[18] will become a numerical minority in the next few decades.[19] Barack Obama's election to the presidency in 2008 marked a milestone that just a generation earlier many Americans never expected they would see. Yet the racial tension that surfaced in the shadow of that election, including during his re-election campaign in 2012,[20] increased awareness of police brutality against African American men (which spawned the Black Lives Matter movement[21]) and contributed to Donald Trump's campaign in 2016.[22] Widespread and high-profile social unrest in the summer of 2020 served as a sober reminder that America's deep racial divisions persist.

In the days after the 2008 presidential election, the term *post-racial* entered the public sphere in a meaningful way. With an image of civil rights legend Jesse Jackson weeping openly in Chicago's Grant Park while the newly elected president gave his acceptance speech as a cultural backdrop, many Americans—white Americans in particular—believed that the history of racial oppression had come to a dramatic close. After all, the most powerful person in the nation was African American. Those who had been skeptical of racism's legacy in the first place believed that the event was simply a bright marker of what they had been saying for decades—racism ended in the 1960s when Jim Crow segregation was abolished legally. On the other hand, those who recognized that racism was more than racial animosity took comfort in the symbolism, if only momentarily.

The belief that America is characterized by a post-racial identity dramatically cuts against the lived experiences of generations of persons of color in America. America's poorest and most economically vulnerable citizens are still distinctly black (African American) and brown (Latinx and Hispanic). Further, inequality between middle- and upper-class whites and those who hover near the poverty line has increased dramatically in the past generation, suggesting the existence of "two Americas"[23] with little evidence of inequality being reversed in the near future. The emergence of the Covid-19 pandemic and the resulting economic recession has only contributed to this dynamic.

This book documents inequality through the lens of political science. We will examine racial and economic inequality with particular attention to how public policy and power dynamics in America are influenced by— and perpetuate—disparities in income and wealth, housing, education, crime, immigration, employment opportunities, and health. The reasons for this inequality are complicated, but answers on the political left and right often center on "common sense" or other simplistic frameworks. Potential solutions, however, require a sophisticated understanding of the systems and institutional constraints that set parameters for the attitudes and behaviors of the mass public and political elites alike. In the following chapters, we will explore this complexity with an eye to the achievement of increased equality.

Striving for more equality is not a value-neutral proposition. Equality is a core value for Americans, but that does not mean we are unified with respect to what it means or how to achieve it. In considering this dynamic, it is helpful to think about the difference between objectivity and neutrality.

Scholars and journalists both strive for objectivity—the conscious effort to be attentive to one's biases when analyzing a situation. But in many ways, this goal can never be fully realized. Striving toward neutrality, however, particularly with respect to inequality, is undesirable. Few of us would approach this book with the attitude, "Equality—I can take it or leave it." To the contrary, this subject tends to inflame passions. Many Americans have risked and indeed have given their lives in the name of social justice. The friction, as we will see, most often arises when we consider what equality looks like and, if we decide that we have fallen short of achieving it, how to remedy that failure.

This book, like all books, is not without bias because this author, like everyone else, is not without bias. The first lesson of politics is to acknowledge that we all have lived experiences and ideas that shape not only who we are but also how we view the world. This unique perspective (or bias) is a natural part of discussing issues of public concern. Bias is not problematic; ignoring or (worse) refusing to acknowledge bias is both dangerous and unproductive. The key is to be as reflective and transparent about that bias as possible and to work toward minimizing the effects of our preconceptions as we seek to learn and grow.

The baseline assumption in this discussion is twofold: (1) there is racial and economic inequality in America, and (2) inequality is inconsistent with the tenets of democracy that undergird our nation's founding principles. There are legitimate arguments against these premises. For instance, some would argue that inequality is not structural or related to race— that individuals of all races and ethnicities have, can, and do succeed in America, and that the values of hard work and persistence adequately explain economic discrepancies. By this logic, if poverty is disproportionately of color in America, it must be either biologically rooted or the result of a culture within African American and Hispanic/Latino communities that encourages laziness, criminality, drug use, and other destructive behaviors. Those who subscribe to such a perspective have no interest in resolving inequality through political channels because they do not perceive the problem as being systemic in nature. For them, this book will be irrelevant. I start from the position that poverty is neither biologically determined nor a result of cultural or behavioral choices. To the contrary, America's history of structural, persistent, and infectious racism has served as bedrock for inequality for the past 400 years.[24]

Both left and right in American politics broadly acknowledge this assertion, and solutions are proposed from across the ideological spectrum. As will become clear throughout this book, leaders and interest groups from both liberal/progressive and conservative traditions wish to rectify this historic oppression, though they approach it in very different ways. While neutrality is not a goal in these pages, some degree of partisan and ideological variety is desirable. Accordingly, efforts toward greater racial and economic equality proposed by individuals from differing perspectives are highlighted. Each reader will decide which approaches seem the most feasible or attractive, but meaningful movement toward a more socially just nation will incorporate a wide variety of ideas.

This book contains both progressive and conservative biases—a position that is increasingly difficult to find in our ideologically stratified public discourse. It is progressive in the sense that it recognizes that inequality has existed on a mass scale in the United States throughout its history, is systemic, and contradicts the underlying core values of the nation as a whole. It is conservative in the sense that it issues no explicit call for radical change to address those injustices. Assumptions about the legitimacy of American governmental institutions and norms go largely unaddressed throughout the book. The message is that there are multiple ways to address inequality, and none should be dismissed because they do not coincide with our personal political beliefs. If we are to ever fulfill America's promise, we must do so in an intellectually collaborative way. The examples in this book strive to model that assertion.

Defining Inequality

It is important to consider what *inequality* means in this context. The relationship between race (and ethnicity) and economic inequality forms the core concern of this text. In a capitalist system, some individuals will acquire, accumulate, or otherwise possess more wealth than others. Accordingly, reducing inequality does not entail allotting the same amount of possessions, money, and debt to each individual. Rather, it refers to the dramatic (and increasing) gap between the wealthiest and poorest Americans, and the disproportionate levels of poverty (and its corresponding characteristics, such as incarceration, illiteracy, health disparities, etc.) in communities of color.

By a number of measures (explained in detail in Chapter 2), the gap between those who have been able to earn money and accumulate wealth and those who struggle to make ends meet has increased dramatically. Part of America's political culture, dating back to the nation's founding, involves a belief in rugged individualism. We herald the person who achieves financial success without coming from a wealthy family. While few could find fault in such a sentiment, the other side of that coin features a lack of compassion for impoverished Americans.

To many Americans, poverty is an abstract concept that refers to others. Most do not believe themselves to be poor,[25] even those who might be considered so by objective measures.[26] Racism—another prominent symptom of "othering" in American culture—is a central (though not sole) culprit in the continued existence of inequality, but perhaps not in the way that is often suggested. Scholars who study race tend to reserve the term *racism* for systemic elements that perpetuate white privilege and power. To understand what this means (and how it works), let us consider it alongside the related concepts of bigotry and prejudice.

All three of these terms—*racism, bigotry,* and *prejudice*—relate to psychological elements of Americans' daily lives, but racism also refers to the ways that institutions, culture, and social systems reflect the historic oppression of persons of color in America and perpetuate inequality as a result. As will become clear in the following pages, decisions that were made at the time of the nation's founding, as well as those made since, have contributed to the construction of a complex system that was originally designed purposefully to disadvantage African Americans and Native Americans. Although much of our collective conscious-level attitudes about racial equality have progressed, this system continues to operate in ways that privilege whites and disadvantage persons of color. This is what scholars refer to as systemic racism, institutional racism, structural racism, or simply racism.

In colloquial use, however, *racism* or *racist* is often used to refer to overt and often hostile race-based animosity that resides at the level of individual citizens (rather than systems). Scholars often refer to this as racial bigotry.[27] Race-based bigotry can work in all directions. Whereas racism has a clear component of systemic power and therefore can only work to advantage whites, individual-level bigotry can include hostility toward persons of a race different from one's own. For example, if an African American supervisor continually berates or disadvantages white employees compared to black employees, we might say that he or she is bigoted. If an Asian American person has disdain for Latinos, that is bigotry (and is likely rooted in racism because of deeply held negative predispositions about Latinos). If a white person is a member of the Ku Klux Klan, he or she is a bigot. In short, what we generally call "racist" is more precisely defined as racial bigotry.

Bigotry is usually explicit, but prejudice often is not. It can be embarrassing to realize that we have biases related to race, ethnicity, gender, or anything else, but most of us can recall a time when such prejudices surfaced. When we are stressed, scared, deprived of sleep, or otherwise in a position to have our social filters compromised, these deep-seated associations can surface.[28] Consider the frustration we often experience when we encounter a poor driver. Attributing the tendency to drive poorly to a person's gender or race (or any characteristic that is different from our own) but not in others (when the person looks like us) reveals a subconscious bias, or prejudice.[29]

Another way to think about the difference between prejudice and bigotry is considering how we react to racist jokes. If we tell racist jokes or if we laugh when we hear them, we are bigoted. However, simply understanding why the joke might be considered funny reveals prejudice—even if we consciously resist manifesting that prejudice in our behavior. If a joke about Italian Americans contained a punch line that centered on intoxication, most folks would not get the joke because there is no stereotype about Italians drinking heavily. If, however, the same joke centered on Irish Americans, for whom that stereotype exists, most would recognize its humor (revealing prejudicial beliefs) even if they did not laugh (which would reveal bigotry).

In other words, most of this sort of prejudice lies beyond our consciousness. There is a rich body of scholarly literature dedicated to exploring the related concepts of implicit association[30] and symbolic racism.[31] As far back as the 1970s, researchers were conceptualizing and testing ways to measure (through sophisticated survey questions) subconscious prejudicial attitudes. More recently, the Project Implicit researchers at Harvard University[32] have demonstrated that most individuals hold subconscious associations about members of racial and ethnic groups (as well as groups based on other characteristics).[33] Research involving physiological indicators promises to reveal even more about these latent prejudices.[34] Experimenters have been busy measuring brain activity, heart rate, sweat on participants' hands, and a host of other variables to determine how race-based stimuli affect the body, and what those reactions may tell us about deeply held biases.

Racism is related to both implicit and explicit prejudice, and all three relate to the persistence of inequality in America. Few would disagree with the assertion that America was founded on racist principles. The superiority of Europeans over Native Americans and Africans was assumed in the nation's earliest years, and the defining document—the Constitution—explicitly dehumanizes African Americans and excludes Native Americans from considerations of representation.[35] The Fourteenth Amendment reversed the Three-Fifths Compromise relating to African Americans, and subsequent laws and court rulings have reflected (and contributed to) a shift in racial attitudes for many, but the structures relating to economics and opportunity have shifted much more slowly. This has resulted in a cycle of perception and reality that has been difficult to interrupt. For example, as explained in Chapter 5, incarceration rates for Latinos and African Americans are disproportionately higher than for whites, leading to a perception that members of those groups are predisposed to criminality. The reality, of course, is much more complicated. Incarceration rates do not necessarily reflect actual rates of crimes committed (or even arrests). Further, street crime is related to poverty, which is related to economic opportunity, which is related to educational access, which is related to housing, which is related to income and wealth, which is related to race and ethnicity.

This is why the term *racism* as commonly used today is counterproductive to finding real solutions to racial and economic inequality. Calling someone a racist inevitably leads to a denial (e.g., "I don't use the n-word" or "I have black friends"). Because most Americans are not bigoted, and because whites are particularly sensitive to accusations of racism, this exchange leads to a dead end with respect to the role that race continues to play in American political culture. Whites tend to believe that racism is either (1) a thing of the past or (2) something that is a problem for overt bigots. This inability to deal honestly with race and inequality is a significant barrier to the political solutions necessary to move forward.

Hegemony and Intersectionality

The concept of cultural hegemony refers to a largely invisible, overarching set of assumptions that pervade a culture. The power of the concept resides in the notion that while there is an accepted hierarchy that structures a culture, it is so widespread and understood that we generally do not even think about it. This results in a troubling cycle: inequality is perpetuated as a given, and at the same time we are not encouraged to think about it. Sociologists and political scientists who study culture and power work to understand how the hegemonic order continues to structure and reinforce inequality, while activists and educators often seek to make those structures visible, which is seen as the first step toward eroding their effects. This book is a combination of those efforts, seeking to understand hegemony by highlighting its effects. Bear in mind that economic and racial inequality are only two elements of America's cultural hegemonic order.

Intersectionality refers to the complicated ways that forms of discrimination and otherness interact to create advantage and disadvantage in a culture.[36] Stemming from a critical theory approach to understanding the politics of inequality, intersectionality acknowledges the limitations of addressing any type of inequality from one's own perspective without being attentive to how that perspective may not be universal. In other words, white feminists are unlikely to question their own privilege (as whites in a racist system) if they do not have heightened consciousness about how race intersects with gender in a society where both classifications have power associated with them. Similarly, African American men who are working for racial justice may not consider their own privilege in a patriarchal system unless they are mindful of where power intersects. The combination is not always additive or even multiplicative. For instance, it is true that white is the privileged race in the United States, and men are the privileged gender. However, it is not always the case that African American women are more disadvantaged than African American men. In some contexts that may be true, but in others (such as with respect to suspicion of crime), black males may be at a greater disadvantage than both black women and white men. To understand how systemic inequality functions, we must keep these dynamics in mind.

The Politics of Inequality

Some of the most interesting and thoughtful work on inequality is written by sociologists. While their findings and theories are represented throughout these pages, this book attempts to help the reader understand the politics of poverty and racial inequality. We will consider how power, government, and public policy issues interact to at once affect and reflect inequality in America. In a nation that was launched with a document that espouses equality for all (the Declaration of Independence), why are we still struggling with these issues more than two centuries later? Where is there space for agreement about solutions? Can liberals and conservatives in America agree on strategies to reduce inequality? Who is working on these issues?

At the core of this exploration is the concept of representation. As explained in the next chapter, the Framers established a democracy in which public officials are elected to stand in for the will of citizens as decision makers. This arrangement—called a republic—means that simple majority rule does not always prevail. As we will discover, this was quite intentional, as the Framers feared tyranny of the majority as well as tyranny of the minority. One result, however, has been that a small minority of wealthy, mostly white and male Americans have had disproportionate access to power throughout our history. That does not necessarily mean that the rights of the poor, women, people of color, and other minorities will not be respected, but generation after generation of such leadership causes skepticism and even cynicism among citizens who do not see themselves reflected in what sociologist C. Wright Mills called "the power elite."[37] Together we will examine how actors in the political system are constrained by institutional factors within a system that was deliberately designed to produce only small, incremental changes.

As a final caveat, the reader is encouraged to try to minimize the tendency we have to personalize and individualize blame for the injustice that is outlined in the following pages. That became more challenging since 2016, as the emergence of explicit demonstrations[38] of racial and ethnic bigotry—including deadly riots in Charlottesville, Virginia and at the nation's Capitol on January 6, 2021—began to be more visible. Not only is it counterproductive to engage in the politics of blame, but it is outside the realm of what social and behavioral science can generally explain. Political scientists are more interested in the *effects* of attitudes, behaviors, and structures rather than the *intent* of actors. While it can be tempting to try to catch someone being racist, for instance, it is more thoughtful and productive to understand that racism afflicts every American, at least (and perhaps most importantly) subconsciously, and to consider the effects of those psychological dynamics on public policy and the effort to bring about more economic and racial equality in the United States.

Structure of the Book

This book focuses on one aspect of American government and politics and encourages the reader to think more deeply about the complexities that have led to contemporary racial and economic inequality in the United States. The Notes contain ample references and can be used as a resource for drilling down more deeply into the rich areas of academic research that are too briefly considered in the following pages. Whenever possible, I provide URLs for access to online information.

Further, this book is primarily structured around the notion of representation. Accordingly, each chapter features "Representing" boxes that highlight a particular individual or organization working toward economic and/or racial justice on behalf of the American people. These boxes are designed to be inspirational and to reveal the variations in ideological grounding among those who are seeking to promote change. Similarly, the "What Can I Do?" boxes offer some suggestions about how young

Americans can make a difference in myriad ways. Often students leave a course that centers on inequality with a sense of helplessness. While the reality of widespread and deeply rooted injustice in the United States can be sobering, it need not be debilitating. This brief introduction is intended to offer an entry point into deeper reflection and scholarly examination of these issues so that future generations will see marked improvements in these areas.

1

. . . .

Representation and the Roots of Inequality

THE FRAMERS ESTABLISHED THE UNITED STATES AS A REPUBLIC (as opposed to a direct democracy) not simply because of logistics. They offered theoretically grounded arguments about the benefits of this type of system, which allows citizens to choose representatives to make decisions in government. As we examine the roots and perpetuation of inequality in America, we need to focus on the ways that the system, to differing degrees throughout our history, has allowed relatively few to achieve economic, political, and social success. As political and social equality has waxed and waned, how has representative democracy played a part? As economic inequality has increased, to what extent is a failure of the system to blame? In this chapter, we will explore the intersection of the government and interest groups as we begin to unpack the complexities of the ways representation works in the United States.

Defining (In)Equality

The concept of equality is not a modern creation; philosophers dating back to antiquity have wrestled with important questions of rights, personhood, and social power. While space does not permit even a cursory overview of those treatments here, it is important to be clear about how "equality" (and, by extension, "inequality") is treated in these pages. This book primarily focuses on economic inequality, but it also explores how social and especially political inequality is related to financial disparity. However, it is important to understand that injustice related to race, gender, and sexual orientation is problematic in its own right, not simply

DOI: 10.4324/9781003043041-2

because of resultant economic disadvantage. Nonetheless, I emphasize the contemporary and historic relationships among social, political, and economic status. For example, while it is empirically accurate to note that the majority of poor Americans are white, because most Americans are white, that is a statistical artifact; poverty in America is disproportionately of color. That reality should not obscure the challenges that white Americans face on a daily basis while living in poverty, but it complicates the picture in an important way. People of color face obstacles that whites with similar socioeconomic status often do not. These latter types of inequality (social, as it relates to our relationships with one another, and political, as it relates to access to power in terms of representation in government) are also examined in this book.

It is important to distinguish between equality of opportunity and equality of outcome with respect to economics.[1] Few voices in American discourse argue for equality of outcome. Rather, those who are concerned about economic inequality point out that many individuals in the United States are disadvantaged from birth. As a result, the ideal of a meritocratic system is undermined because those who achieve success do so either because they had a head start or in spite of significant barriers. If everyone started off with the same opportunity (and did not face structural impediments along the way), inequality of outcome could be acceptable. Put another way, most Americans agree that personal responsibility and initiative are required to achieve success. The disagreement often arises between those who believe that inequality of outcome is largely related to structural inequality of opportunity and those who believe that it is the result of personal failure. That debate is not fully addressed in this book, though it will become clear that systemic disadvantage constrains opportunities for many Americans and puts pressure on the convenient argument that the poor are struggling economically because of character flaws, laziness, bad choices, or other individual-level characteristics.

On the other hand, the idea of social and political equality is often discussed with respect to outcome—in contemporary society, most agree that fundamental rights need not be earned. As a result, equality of opportunity is the same as equality of outcome in this context: African Americans ought not to be denied the right to vote; Latinos ought not to be prevented from owning homes; women ought not to be kept from certain professions; and so forth. But this issue is also more complicated than it might initially appear.[2] Further, it is important to consider the more common term "equality" in juxtaposition to the less common but increasingly invoked term "equity." In short, "equality" in process means treating everyone the same, even if they are starting from very different places and, thus, have very different needs. "Equity" refers to making sure that everyone has what they need to prosper, even if that means treating differently situated individuals or communities different.[3] In a representative democracy, it is the responsibility of our elected leaders to know when and how to invoke equitable policies to fulfil democracy's promise.

As we will see, the concept of representation is complex. Are we to argue, for example, that for women to have equal political rights, they must comprise an equal (50 percent) number of state legislators or US representatives? Or would equality in this regard mean proportionality (in which case, women would hold slightly more seats than men in Congress)? Or by equal do we mean that the interests women have (to the extent that they can be identified as such) are represented, even if by men, in those political bodies? While these are all worthwhile discussions, they lie beyond the scope of this book. From time to time I will highlight these dilemmas, but for the most part, readers are invited to make their own decisions about what types of equality are most appropriate and under what circumstances and when equity is the more appropriate approach. Similarly, readers are encouraged to find ways to address inequality—to the extent that it is considered to be problematic—that are consistent with their own values and beliefs. This book is designed to heighten consciousness by pointing out the places where the realities of twenty-first-century American life are seemingly inconsistent with the core principles outlined by the Framers.

Democracy's Promise: America's Founding Principles

The political reasons that led to the American Revolution are many, and we need to briefly consider some of the most important philosophical principles that guided the Framers as they envisioned a new nation—an experiment in democracy—and drafted a system that they hoped would foster those ideals. In this context James Madison's writing is central. Madison, the "Father of the Constitution," contributed a number of essential elements to that document (see Box 1.1), but his ideas about power dynamics

Box 1.1. *Representing:* James Madison

The fourth president of the United States, and one of the most important intellectual leaders of America's founding, is a complex historical figure. Not only did he grow up with tremendous privilege on a tobacco plantation in Virginia, but his family's wealth did not stem from the American myth of hard work and fair play. His father inherited wealth and married into a wealthy family, and his wealth was perpetuated through plantation slave labor.

Yet within that privileged context, Madison (perhaps unintentionally) contributed ideas that would ultimately support the struggle of descendants of enslaved persons and other oppressed communities in the United States. He did not argue for an end to slavery but insisted on a strong central government that would provide a contrast to the states' rights position that Confederate states adopted during the Civil War and then during the Jim Crow era of legalized racial segregation in the American South. His belief in fundamental human rights, many of which are codified in the Bill of Rights—the first ten amendments to the US Constitution—are at odds with the lived reality that he and his contemporaries (including Thomas Jefferson) imposed on enslaved persons, Native American Indians, and white women. Yet the broad principles that are encapsulated by those ideas have driven not only movements for women's suffrage and black civil rights, but also the rights of a wide range of groups and associations that lack power or support, such as the Jehovah's Witnesses, the Ku Klux Klan, communists, LGBTQ Americans, and the criminally accused.

Characterizing Madison's representation as substantive, as described in this section, would be improper because many of the groups who have benefited from his ideas did not exist in his time. But the codification (in law and judicial interpretation) of those principles has resulted in support for minority groups far beyond those that were competing for power and consideration in the eighteenth and early nineteenth centuries. In this way, Madison is important to the struggle for racial and economic equality today even though he did not fight for those causes in his day (and very well may not have been willing to do so if he were alive today).[5]

between majority and minority factions provide a unique insight into not only the concerns of the Framers at that time, but also the ways that contemporary American government and culture is equipped to deal with inequality.

In *Federalist 10*,[4] for instance, Madison argues that representative democracy is best suited to deal with what he expected would be an enduring dilemma—how to respect the will of the majority while protecting the rights of the minority. Sometimes called "Madison's dilemma," the concern is unique to a system of government where the interests of citizens matter in a meaningful way. In authoritarian regimes, rulers can impose their will on the citizenry, often with perceived legitimacy, with the only consequences coming in the form of a coup d'état. In a democracy, however, each citizen's "opinions and passions" must be permitted to surface without interference. Otherwise the liberty on which the Revolution was based would be meaningless. However, such differences in opinions have the potential to destroy the republic, which is what Madison referred to as the "violence of faction."

That is simple enough, but we need to examine Madison's distinction between majority and minority faction. As disruptive as faction could be in and of itself, one could argue that a healthy political community should include rigorous discussion and debate. Madison was more concerned about tyranny, which he feared would result if one faction consistently had its way against the other. Minority faction was less of a concern to Madison because of the principle of majority rule. That is, if a small group of citizens or elected officials wished to impose their will on the masses, they would most likely be outvoted by the majority. Majority tyranny presented a greater concern, but Madison argued that the very structure of a republic (in particular, a large republic)—along with the specific safeguards built into the Constitution, he and his co-authors would later argue—would lead to a system that would slow people's passions and protect minority rights.

This problem was relevant in the eighteenth century, and even more so today. The extension (and later protection) of political rights to African Americans and white women, as well as vast waves of immigration, greatly diversified the polity. As a result, there are more factions, and it appears, at least to the casual observer, that a small minority (the very wealthy) has disproportionate power over the majority. But recall that Madison did not expect this to be a problem. What happened?

Representation: Elected Officials

Representation is a concept that appears to be straightforward, but on closer examination is actually quite complicated. What does it mean to "represent" a person or a group of people or an idea? If a Pittsburgher wears her Steelers jersey on a Sunday afternoon in the fall, she is representing her favorite team, or maybe even her hometown. If a student's institutional affiliation is printed on his nametag at an academic conference, he is representing his college or university. In these ways, representation is symbolic and is not particularly important to the lives of others. On the other hand, if a student is selected to represent her residence hall on the university council, she might make decisions that can influence the lives of others in her dormitory. In that situation, variations in how she chooses to understand the concept of representation can result in very different outcomes. Now let us consider a somewhat ridiculous, yet hopefully memorable, hypothetical scenario to demonstrate two prominent theories of representation.

Prior to elections for residence hall council, the administration expressed concerns about students' low energy level during morning classes. The solution: doughnuts. The university president decided that the best way to invigorate students for morning classes would be to infuse them with sugar by offering free doughnuts in classroom buildings. The only problem is that the university's bakery could not offer a variety of doughnuts in such large quantities. Consequently, the hall council would have to choose between cake or jelly-filled doughnuts.

Two candidates threw their hats in the ring. Jessica was a sophomore biochemistry major with a 3.8 GPA. She was in a number of clubs and participated in intramural athletics. Michael was a junior English major with a 3.4 GPA. He was on the swim team and active in campus ministry. During the campaign, Jessica favored cake doughnuts because they were denser and "stuck to your ribs" better. Michael, a fitness nut, noted that since jelly came from fruit, jelly doughnuts would be the better choice. When all the votes are tallied, Michael wins by a 12 percent margin. However, before he cast his vote for a doughnut at the council meeting, he conducted a poll in the residence hall to learn what his constituents thought. As it turned out, nearly 60 percent of respondents preferred cake doughnuts.

Michael now has a dilemma of representation. If he perceives himself as a *delegate*,[6] he will vote for cake doughnuts. Even though he knows in his heart that jelly would be better for the students, he believes that his job is to do what they would do if they could be there themselves. If he perceives himself as a *trustee*, however, he will vote for jelly doughnuts—not because he is indifferent to his constituents' wishes, but because he believes that he knows best and feels that the students knew his views on doughnuts when they elected him. Even though they clearly selected him for other reasons, they would not be surprised or disappointed if he voted his conscience. Besides, if they did not like his vote, they could choose to not re-elect him next year.

So, which would we prefer? In our silly example, most of us would say that Michael should act as a delegate. He clearly knows what his constituents want, and he has no (or very little valid) additional information at his disposal. This is an example of what social scientists refer to as *directive* or *restrictive governance*.[7] On the other hand, it is relatively easy to imagine the practical limits of such a preference. Many of the decisions that government officials make on a daily basis are not particularly salient (relevant to our lives), and many others are very technical. If a member of Congress would take a poll to find out whether her constituents favored or opposed a reduction in the capital gains tax, there would very likely be a lot of "don't know" answers or "non-attitudes."[8] In such an instance, we might very well prefer that our leaders act as trustees—a scenario that is sometimes referred to as *permissive governance*.

Even this level of complexity, though, does not adequately capture the reality of contemporary politics. Yet another dimension has to do with the degree to which the individuals selected to represent us are equipped to do so. At the federal level, at least, most elected officials are wealthier[9] and better educated[10] than the average citizen. In many ways, then, their personal interests ("opinions and passions," to use Madison's language) can be expected to differ from ours. That does not mean, however, that they must (or will) vote for their own personal interests at the expense of the rest of us. They could choose cake doughnuts because they know that is what we prefer, or they could choose jelly doughnuts because information they have (which we may not) indicates they are better for us. Elected officials who ignore the will of their constituents on a regular basis, at least in theory, will have difficulty at the ballot box in subsequent elections. (As we will see, however, that is not the case with appointed officials.) But that does not ensure that our elected officials will share what are perceived to be important characteristics with their constituents. Can those officials represent their constituents effectively?

Not necessarily. Political scientists differentiate between *symbolic* (or *descriptive*) *representation* and *substantive representation*.[11] The former refers to the degree to which representatives have characteristics (e.g., race, gender, wealth, ideology) that reflect their constituencies, while the latter has to do with whether they vote consistently with constituents' interests, even if they do not look like those whom they represent (see Box 1.2). This distinction is relevant to understanding why millionaires can be elected

Box 1.2. *Representing:* David Yassky

In 2006, US representative Major Owens (D-NY), who is African American, decided to retire from his seat representing a Brooklyn district where the majority of voters (about 60 percent) were African American. Four candidates competed for the Democratic Party nomination in the district (which was almost certain to choose a Democrat in the general election), one of whom, David Yassky, was white.

The seat had been held by an African American member since the 1960s, but the existence of four candidates led to uncertainty as to whether it would remain black. In the midst of the campaign, Yassky was referred to as a "colonizer" by Owens and further criticized by some African American leaders as trying to take away one of the seats that had come to symbolize important political gains for African Americans in the Congress. There were suggestions that Yassky, if elected, would seek to join the Congressional Black Caucus (CBC). In a strategy letter to CBC members, former member of Congress (and one of the CBC's founders) William Clay wrote that "it is critical that the Congressional Black Caucus remains an all-black organization," pushing the discussion about symbolic and substantive representation into the contest. When the counting was over, however, it did not matter. Yassky finished second (26.2 percent) to Yvette Clarke (31.2 percent), with the other two candidates attracting 22.9 percent and 19.6 percent of the vote.

The results were different in Tennessee that year, however. In a district that has a majority of African Americans and had been held for two generations by African Americans, Democrat Steve Cohen, who is white, won his party's nomination in a 15-candidate contest (13 of whom were African American) and went on to represent the congressional district that includes Memphis. Cohen did not seek to join the CBC.[15]

and subsequently presumed to provide appropriate representation to hundreds of thousands (or, in the case of most US senators, millions) of individuals who struggle economically. It is why the US Senate—which currently has three African American members[12]—can be considered to be representative of a diverse populace. And it is why a body like the US Congress, comprised overwhelmingly of men,[13] can be presumed (correctly or incorrectly) to be attentive to the interests of women, who comprise more than half of the nation's population. As long as officials take the "opinions and passions" of their constituents into consideration—even if those do not match their own—they can be substantively representative, even if they are not symbolically representative. However, one could certainly argue that a lack of symbolic representation can be concerning, particularly because there is a widespread and historic absence by members of particular groups in some positions.[14]

Representation: The Courts

So far our discussion has centered on elected officials. But many of the people who represent us in government are appointed. Some of those appointments are limited in their power, but others, such as members of the federal judiciary, are quite powerful. In all cases, though, the concept of representation is similar, its manifestation can be quite different. While bureaucrats at a number of agencies (Health and Human Services, Housing and Urban Development, etc.) can have direct relevance to issues relating to racial and economic inequality, the judicial branch has arguably been the most important tool for members of historically disadvantaged groups to achieve public policy success. As we will see, the courts have, on occasion, made decisions in favor of minority interests that elected officials would have had a hard time making (for fear of reprisal at the ballot box). In this way, the courts illustrate Madison's belief that the protection of minority rights is an essential element of democracy.

Although Alexander Hamilton famously referred to the judiciary as the "least dangerous" branch of the federal government,[16] the power of judicial review has resulted in a system wherein the last word on a particular issue is often handed down from appeals courts. Because courts can declare laws passed by Congress and signed by the president to be unconstitutional (and thus void), there are often concerns that such activism is undemocratic. That is only true, however, if we define democracy as majority rule. The 535 members of the US Congress and the president of the United States must appeal to the majority (or at least a plurality[17] of their constituents) to win a seat and keep it. This is particularly true with members of Congress, who have no term limits, and specifically members of the House of Representatives, who face election every two years. As a result, it is very difficult for members to routinely take unpopular positions.

Members of the federal judiciary, however, serve life terms (though they can be impeached and removed from office for particularly egregious behavior) and are not elected. This design is a function of the Framers' desire to allow one branch of government to make decisions that are immune from direct public pressure. If we understand democracy to mean respect for majority will and protection of minority rights, it is more appropriate to refer to judicial action that cuts against popular opinion as being counter-majoritarian, rather than undemocratic.

The US Supreme Court often abstains from making overtly political decisions if it can avoid it,[18] but every governmental decision affects people and is a reflection of power differences in society. In that way, everything the Court does is political, and even what the Court does *not* do is political. Unlike the legislative and executive branches, members of the judiciary cannot technically set their own agendas; they must wait until a case comes before them, and even then, they are somewhat limited in terms of the scope of the decision they can make. However, because the Supreme Court cannot possibly entertain arguments for the several thousand cases that are petitioned to be heard each term, the justices' choices of which to hear and which to deny (thus rendering the lower court decision as final) are also a political action.

As we consider the various types of inequality that exist in America today, we will be attentive to times when court decisions have contributed to or challenged inequality. At this point, though, it is important to consider some Supreme Court decisions that directly relate to the notion of representation.

One Person, One Vote

Fundamental to the broadest notions of democratic theory is the idea that each citizen has an equal chance to influence government. As always, however, the devil is in the details. What does "equal" mean? Certainly it does not mean that each citizen has the same amount of money to donate each year to political campaigns. At a minimum, it means that each citizen gets the same amount of power at the voting booth. This can be achieved in a number of ways, but in the United States, we have settled on the one person, one vote model that was clearly affirmed by the Supreme Court in *Baker v. Carr*[19] and *Reynolds v. Simms*.[20]

In *Baker v. Carr* (1962), the Court considered whether it could address a political question such as the one brought forward by Charles Baker, a Tennessee man who complained that the state had not been dutiful in redrawing US House district borders following each census, even though there was significant movement within the state. At the time the case was filed, the district in which Baker lived (near Memphis) had nearly ten times the population of some of Tennessee's rural districts. Consequently, Baker argued that he had less representation than someone who lived in a less populated district. The Court ruled that such questions were appropriate for courts to decide (a departure from earlier rulings), which opened the door for similar questions in the following years.

In *Reynolds v. Simms* (1964), the Court was asked to decide the constitutionality of an Alabama law that state legislative districts could not cross county borders. Consequently one state senate district had about 41 times the population of another by the time the suit was filed. Although that number is very large, it was not unusual at the time for districts to vary greatly in population, as many rural districts featured sparse population and state laws regarding redistricting that were in place before urbanization led to vastly disproportionate representation for areas with higher populations. In *Reynolds*, the Court established the one person, one vote principle, which means that the power of each of us to affect government by having our representatives be responsive must be relatively equal.[21]

It might seem surprising that it took 175 years into the nation's existence under the current Constitution to officially establish a fundamental principle of democracy. Such is the nature of the way our brain processes information. For instance, it also seems ridiculous to many of us that it took the same amount of time to pass a federal law that prohibited states from excluding citizens from voting based on their race, or that it took 133 years to guarantee white women the right to vote. It is only because we take these rights as common sense today that we can be critical of past generations for not acting sooner, but, conversely, it is because the actions were taken that we now see those rights as non-negotiable. It is difficult to predict what standards future generations will have that will cause them to judge us harshly. We are still, for instance, not settled on the one person, one vote standard in practice. While few would argue that anyone should be in a district with a few thousand people while someone else in the same state should be in a district with a few million, the mechanism we use to count citizens—the census—is imperfect, and questions remain about who in fact is counted.

Everybody Counts

The Constitution requires a census every ten years, and because the US House of Representatives has members from states in proportion (roughly) to the size of their population, a process of reallocation of House seats and subsequent redrawing of district boundaries follows. Put another way, it would be impossible to appropriately apply the Court's standards from *Reynolds v. Simms* without a clear picture of how many people live in each state and where (within the state) they live.

After the 2000 census, Utah lost a House seat as a result of a decline in population over the previous decade. Believing that the loss was due to the Census Bureau's process of "imputation" in some states, which involves estimating population by way of statistical procedures when questions remain after all attempts to contact citizens have been exhausted,[22] officials in Utah sued[23] to have the imputed numbers removed from the allocation. The Court rejected Utah's arguments, effectively affirming the process of imputation.

Imputation matters in this context because citizens who have less power are more likely to be difficult to count in the census than those who have access to power. These hard-to-count groups include renters (as opposed to homeowners), racial and ethnic minorities,[24] and homeless persons. If we can assume similarities in at least some characteristics based on geography (a proposition that I will question in a later section), then an undercounting of citizens in this category could result in less formal representation for them in government. If we consider the cyclical effects of reduced representation for Americans who are already struggling, we understand how these seemingly obscure questions come to life.

The 2020 census faced a number of unique challenges that, as of the writing of this edition, have yet to be fully addressed. First the Trump Administration signaled as early as 2017 that it would make good on campaign promises to deter illegal immigration by adding a question to the census questionnaire asking people to indicate their citizenship status. Experts worried that such a question would discourage participation, which would have had an effect on both congressional districting and allocation of federal funds.[25] The question was blocked by the US Supreme Court in 2019,[26] but the Covid-19 pandemic, which surfaced in February 2020, added another hurdle to accurate data collection. In February 2021, the Census Bureau announced that its work would be delayed, throwing the timeline for redistricting for the 2022 federal elections into question.[27] The reappointment process was concluded on April 30, 2021,[28] and the redistricting process began.

Symbolic Representation and Racial Minority Voting

Compared to many other nations, the United States is characterized by one of the largest gaps in voter turnout between rich and poor citizens.[29] The reasons for this are not straightforward, but at least some of it is likely attributable to race. In this section, we explore the importance of electing members of racial minority groups to public office and the related issue of voter turnout by and suppression of minorities.

After the Civil War, a number of African Americans achieved elected office, particularly in areas where the majority of citizens were nonwhite. After Reconstruction, however, the efforts to disenfranchise black Americans by way of literacy tests, white primaries, grandfather clauses, and poll taxes in the South made it difficult for blacks to run for office. As northern urban centers attracted black citizens during the Great Migration (1910–1930), African Americans began to concentrate in cities, which eventually led to electoral victories. In 1965 Congress passed and the president signed the Voting Rights Act, which abolished Jim Crow–era voter suppression and mandated federal oversight of elections in states with a history of such activity. With the passage of the Voting Rights Act, African American members of the United States Congress from Atlanta, Houston, Memphis, and New Orleans joined representatives from urban areas in the North, such as New York, Chicago, Detroit, Philadelphia, and St. Louis (as well as Los Angeles). The overwhelming majority of black elected officials today are still selected from so-called majority-minority districts.

To understand the importance and history of majority-minority districts to representing the interests of black and Latino voters, it is helpful to broaden our definitions of *majority* and *minority*. In the Madisonian sense, we can limit our understanding to the mathematical conceptualizations with which we are already familiar. A majority is 50 percent plus one. Anything less than 50 percent is a minority. But political scientists use these terms to refer to power, as well. Perhaps the most vivid example is the system of apartheid in South Africa, which, from 1948 to 1994, legally established whites as the dominant social, economic, and political group, even though they comprised only 10 percent of the population. In that situation, it does not make sense to talk about "the minority white" government in South Africa because whites comprised a power majority. Similarly, women are considered a "minority" in the United States because they have been disproportionately denied access to the levers of power (though they constitute a majority of the total population).[30]

Turning back to the first approach, majority-minority districts are those in which a numerical majority of voting-age citizens are non-white. Some of these districts do not have a clear numerical majority in terms of racial or ethnic groups (e.g., the plurality may be African American and the percentage of Hispanics combine to form more than 50 percent of the population), but the designation is meaningful because the majority of the citizens in the area are not a part of the racial group that disproportionately has access to power in the nation.

The establishment of majority-minority districts is linked both to the notion of symbolic representation discussed earlier in this chapter and to the historic reality that white voters generally do not vote for candidates of color.[31] Accordingly, the idea is that in order to make sure that people of color are represented in the legislatures, states that have a significant number of blacks, Hispanics, or Asians can draw district lines for the House of Representatives—by use of the concentration in housing patterns (discussed in Chapter 3)—such that a majority of the voters are non-white, with the expectation that they will elect a non-white person to represent them.

The Supreme Court has upheld majority-minority districts, though their utility is subject to criticism from several perspectives. For example, a number of states redrew congressional district lines with attention to this issue after the 1990 census (see Figure 1.1). Five white voters in North Carolina argued that the oddly shaped boundary of the Twelfth District (stretching some 160 miles, much of which was down an interstate highway) violated their rights because it took race into account at the expense of creating a cohesive geographical district.[32] The Supreme Court held that racially gerrymandered districts should be judged by the legal standard of "strict scrutiny" to determine whether a citizen's rights are violated on the basis of race. For a law to satisfy this standard, it must be deemed to have been made to further a compelling government interest and be narrowly tailored to achieve that interest. In other words, while it is permissible to draw majority-minority districts, a state must be attempting to avoid violation of the Voting Rights Act of 1965 (VRA), and the district lines should be drawn in a way that takes other factors besides race into consideration so that white voters' interests are also protected. Justice Sandra Day O'Connor wrote the opinion of the Court in this case; she argued that the district violated the Fourteenth Amendment rights of the white voters who brought suit. O'Connor affirmed the importance of states taking race into consideration as they draw district lines, but argued that the boundary in this particular case, while created with intentions to guarantee the rights of the minority (African Americans) in North Carolina, ultimately violated the rights of the majority (whites). Further, she argued in the opinion that African Americans might also be offended by the district as drawn because doing so makes tacit assumptions about them based on their race that would be considered to be impermissible in other contexts:

A reapportionment plan that includes in one district individuals who belong to the same race, but who are otherwise widely separated by geographical and political boundaries, and who may have little in common with one another but the color of their skin, bears an uncomfortable resemblance to political apartheid. It reinforces the perception that members of the same racial group—regardless of their age, education, economic status, or the community in which the live—think alike, share the same political interests, and will prefer the same candidates at the polls. We have rejected such perceptions elsewhere as impermissible racial stereotypes.[33]

FIGURE 1.1. Challenged Congressional Districts in the 1990s

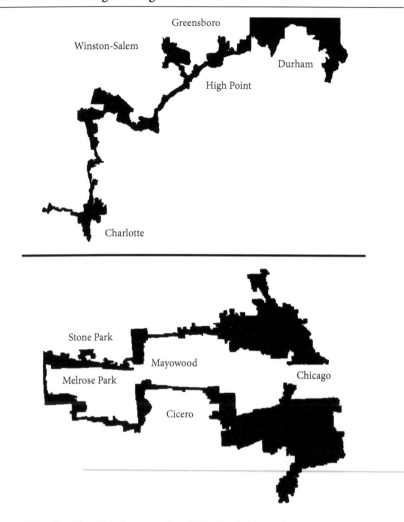

A. "I-85" District: The 12th Congressional District in North Carolina, post–1990 census. This district was designed to create a majority-minority district for African Americans. These lines were overturned in *Shaw v. Reno* (1993).

B. "Ear Muff" District: 4th Congressional District in Illinois, post–1990 Census. This district was designed to create a majority-Hispanic district without diluting African American voting in nearby districts. These lines were upheld upon challenge because they were deemed to be "narrowly tailored" to addressing a compelling state interest (of not violating the Civil Rights Act of 1965).

Source: Peter S. Wattson, "How to Draw Redistricting Plans that Will Stand Up in Court," State of Minnesota Senate, 2000, http://www.senate.leg.state.mn.us/departments/scr/REDIST/Draw/Draw992web.htm. Reprinted by permission from Election Data Services, Inc.

Yet exit polls show that African Americans, as well as Latinos from certain backgrounds, while not monolithic entities, do tend to vote similarly[34] and view their interests as linked (if not across racial and ethnic boundaries, at least within them).[35]

Voting by African Americans and Latinos, however, cannot be taken for granted. There have been significant efforts to disenfranchise African Americans throughout American history. Voting was prohibited to slaves, and many states—particularly those in the South—took extraordinary efforts (e.g., literacy tests, poll taxes, white primaries, grandfather clauses) to keep blacks from voting during the Jim Crow era.[36] Much of that changed after passage of the Voting Rights Act of 1965 (VRA),[37] but recent elections have seen renewed concerns about racial minority voters being inappropriately purged from voting rolls,[38] reportedly being stopped at police checkpoints on the way to the polls,[39] facing disproportionate ballot challenges,[40] and being asked to wait in unusually long lines in some urban precincts.[41] In 2013, the US Supreme Court heard a challenge by Shelby County, Alabama, to sections of the VRA that required nine states (and portions of six others) to obtain US Department of Justice clearance prior to making any changes in their election procedures. The Court agreed that the provisions of the law (which was reauthorized by Congress in 2006) requiring clearance were unnecessary at this time. Writing for a 5–4 majority, Chief Justice John Roberts argued that "our country has changed" and that these states are being unfairly punished for their mistreatment of racial minority voters in the past. Justice Ruth Bader Ginsburg disagreed, noting that the Justice Department blocked over 700 changes between 1982 and 2006, which suggested to her that there was still reason for concern about the targeting of minority voters.[42] The *Shelby* decision paved the way for more states to introduce laws that make voting more difficult (such as those that require voters to show valid identification).[43] The decision left open the possibility of Congress's writing legislation to require clearance, as long as the rationale was based on current evidence of discrimination.

During the 2020 presidential campaign, President Trump repeatedly told groups of supporters that the only way he could lose the election is if there was cheating[44] (a claim he also made in 2016).[45] As results of the election became clear, he doubled down on that message, arguing that illegal votes were counted in urban areas (specifically those in states that he lost: Detroit, Michigan; Atlanta, Georgia; and Philadelphia, Pennsylvania),[46] thus racializing his claims. He and his surrogates repeatedly promised that there was clear evidence of widespread voter fraud, but more than 60 lawsuits were dismissed,[47] as no evidence ever surfaced. The accusation of dishonesty by African Americans voters and officials in urban centers is rooted in a long history of racial stereotypes,[48] and it served as fuel for the eventual insurrection and riot at the Capitol Building on January 6, 2021,[49] where an overwhelmingly white crowd brandishing weapons and symbols of white supremacy[50] broke into the building in an attempt to interrupt the joint session of Congress that was counting the electoral votes. Five people died as a result of the riot.

The structure of the Electoral College, which rewards less-populated states, in combination with population patterns, has relevance to the ways that the major political parties view their chances of winning the presidency. Only once since 1988 has a Republican presidential candidate won the plurality of the popular vote; Republican candidates have won three of the eight contests that have been held (2000, 2004, and 2016). In 2016, Hillary Rodham Clinton won approximately 3 million more votes than Donald Trump, though she lost the Electoral College vote 306 to 232; in 2020, Joe Biden earned more than 7 million more votes than Donald Trump and beat him by the same Electoral College margin.[51]

In short, though it is not democratic in the traditional sense of majority rule, people do have a say in the way that presidents are elected. Whether this structure is conducive to electing presidents who will be attentive to issues of racial and economic inequality, however, is another question. The Electoral College, however, is not the only mechanism that sets the United States apart from other democracies in terms of electoral systems.

The American Anomaly

In many ways, the dilemma of symbolic representation that persists is a result of the relative uniqueness of the way we elect officials in the United States, where geography tends to matter more than political attitudes.[52] Without a comparative perspective, it is easy to lose sight of explanations for and potential solutions to inequality in America. The way that we conceptualize and operationalize representation is an important component of the way we think about government officials' responsibilities and responsiveness to our collective needs. We are constrained by the system in which we were raised, and we generally believe that it is the only way to "do" democracy. A thorough discussion of different types of democratic governance is not possible here, but we will consider a few of our idiosyncrasies that are most relevant to understanding representation of majority and minority interests.

Americans generally think about voting as a choice between two individuals for one position. Because we have a two-party system in the United States, that choice is usually between a Democrat and a Republican. We understand that primary elections or other selection mechanisms (such as the congressional party caucus) can be used to determine what candidate represents each of those parties in the general election, but for the most part, we view elections like tennis matches—someone will win and someone will lose. That sort of electoral system, known as single member district plurality (SMDP),[53] tends to lead to two-party competition (or a system where only two parties have a reasonable chance to control a branch of government). In a pluralistic society, such as the United States, each of the parties is thus left attempting to appeal to a broad range of interests so as to cobble together a coalition that will lead to electoral success. The result is that poor Americans do not have a party dedicated to representing their interests. Rather, Democrats have been successful in attracting union workers and racial minorities, whereas Republicans have attracted working-class whites in rural areas. Of course, both parties must also be responsive to the wealthier members of their coalitions, and because the wealthy are more likely to be active (not to mention donate funds to electoral campaigns), it is difficult for the poor to have proportionate influence over either party, and thus the government.

Most democracies feature electoral systems that encourage multiple parties. Most prominent among these is proportional representation (PR), whereby voters choose parties, rather than individuals, to serve them in public office. As opposed to the winner-take-all (or first-past-the-post) nature of SMDP, each party that receives a minimum level of support is awarded seats in the legislature in proportion to the votes it receives. For instance, if there are 100 seats available, and Party X receives 51 percent of the vote, Party Y receives 32 percent of the vote, and Party Z receives 17 percent of the vote, Party X would get 51 seats, Party Y would get 32 seats, and Party Z would get 17 seats. In an SMDP system, there would be 100 districts drawn, with one member selected from each. If this electoral result occurred in each district, Party X would end up with all 100 seats. While such an outcome is unlikely, what is equally unlikely is that Party Z would ever get a seat in an SMDP system, and if it did find some natural constituency in a limited regional area, the elected member would have no power in a legislature dominated by Parties X and Y. As a result, voters who support Party Z would be best served by voting for candidates from Party X or Y, which means that those parties would have to broaden their focus to appeal to those citizens. That scenario, of course, quite neatly describes the Democratic and Republican parties in the United States.

The result is that these two parties, who must attract broad coalitions to assemble a numerical majority, are generally unable or unwilling to address the needs of power minorities in the United States. As noted earlier, elected officials, particularly at the federal level, are disproportionately white and male, and they are better educated and wealthier than the average American.[54] While district lines can be redrawn to increase symbolic representation on the basis of race and ethnicity, there is no way to rectify the gender disparity in elected bodies within the confines of our current system. After all, housing in the United States is not segregated by gender but by socioeconomic status. As discussed further in Chapter 8, women, then, are unable to have their underrepresentation addressed through political or legal action beyond prohibition of overt discrimination. Because of these unique characteristics, we must bear in mind that our system of elections (rather than simply voter preference) contributes to the under-representation of minorities.

This dynamic came into focus during the 2016 presidential elections, as the Electoral College, which gives disproportionate voice to voters in rural states, selected Donald Trump as president, even though nearly 3 million more voters cast ballots for Hillary Clinton. (This was only the fifth time in history that the winner of the popular vote was not elected president, but it was the second time in five presidential elections.) While rural voters are advantaged by the system, the campaign revealed that many of them do not feel represented in general. As one voter from Kentucky noted, "A lot of us in rural areas … think people are talking down to us. What ends up happening is that we don't focus on the policy—we focus on the tones, the references, the culture."[55] The reality, then, is that many, if not most, Americans, might not particularly feel represented by the existing electoral structure.

Alternatives to Our Current System

Although the SMDP system is not mandated by the US Constitution, it is difficult to imagine Americans embracing PR after two centuries of selecting leaders under this system. Consequently, the two-party system is probably here to stay. And, as we will see later in the book, Americans tend to oppose the notion of quotas, so a system of racial or (as France instituted in 2000)[56] gender quotas is unlikely to attract support. There are, however, other alternatives to electoral choice that could work within the existing structure. These, too, are dramatic departures from what Americans have come to expect, but discussing them allows us to come closer to understanding the systemic barriers to racial and economic equality in the United States.

Legal scholar Lani Guinier[57] has argued that a cumulative voting system could be more advantageous to power minorities in the United States. Cumulative voting would violate the one-person, one-vote standard established by the US Supreme Court, but it is not undemocratic because each citizen retains the same voting power as every other citizen. It works like this: rather than casting a single ballot in an election, under a cumulative voting system, each voter has a number of votes equal to the number of candidates in the race and can cluster them as he or she sees fit. For instance, if the race for US Senate features seven candidates, each voter has seven votes for that contest. A voter who really liked the Republican candidate could cast all seven votes for him or her. If she likes the Republican candidate but sort of likes the Libertarian candidate, too, she can split her votes between them in a variety of ways (six for the Republican candidate and one for the Libertarian, four and three, etc.). During tabulation, the candidate with the most votes wins the seat. A voter who prefers a minor party candidate can vote for that candidate without "wasting" her vote because she can also give some of her votes to a major-party candidate. This type of system could encourage minor parties to run on platforms that focus on issues relevant to racial minorities and low-income Americans in ways that the big tent parties cannot. While those parties might not garner enough support for an outright majority, if they have enough seats to deny larger parties of a majority, they will need to be welcomed into a governing coalition, thus giving them some level of influence in policymaking.

Two other possibilities for changing electoral systems to encourage third-party involvement are Borda voting and instant runoff voting (IRV). Both of these systems ask voters to rank order their preference of candidates in a contest. A voter who liked the Republican candidate the most would place a number 1 next to that candidate's name. Unlike first-past-the-post voting, though, the voter would rank the other candidates in order of preference. The Borda system assigns weight to those preferences (e.g., four points for a first-place vote, three points for a second-place vote, etc.) and adds up all the points to determine a winner.[58] With IRV, after all first-place votes are tabulated, if no candidate receives a majority of votes cast, the candidate in last place is removed from the race, and the second-place votes for all those voters who chose that candidate are redistributed to the other candidates in a process that continues until one candidate has a majority of support.[59]

These models encourage support for minor-party candidates because a vote for them is not "wasted." Even if they have little chance of winning, support for them is registered and the voter has a hand in choosing among the major-party candidates. With a highly polarized party climate like the one in twenty-first-century America, a gain of even a handful of seats by minor parties could force the Democrats and Republicans to attend to the needs of small parties that represent minority interests. This could shift the balance of representation—perhaps significantly—away from the powerful. One can also imagine that a presidential election could be shifted with such a system.[60] Americans are generally skeptical of this type of fundamental change, though. Even if such procedures were adopted, there is no guarantee that addressing these procedural matters will lead to more substantive equity or justice. Moreover, the current system of representation should not be viewed as inherently inadequate to address the needs of those with little power. Through substantive representation by elected leaders, potentially counter-majoritarian courts, and through the work of organized interests, ordinary Americans can affect government and politics in meaningful ways.

American Pluralism

America is pluralistic in the sense that it is characterized by many types of diversity (economic, gender, age, racial, geographic, ideological, etc.). The pluralist model of democracy emerged as a response to the elitist model, which was put forth in the 1950s by sociologist C. Wright Mills.[61] The elitist perspective did not argue that America should be controlled by elites, but rather observed that it is. Mills noted that a small group of important people (and families) have access to a disproportionate amount of power and thus are responsible for much of the formal and informal decision-making in the United States. In such a system, it is difficult for individuals who are not born into the elite class to gain entrance. Consequently, members of the elite are able to maintain their power generation after generation. Pluralism,[62] on the other hand, while not denying the existence of an elite class in the United States (it would be hard to argue that such a class does not exist), paints a more optimistic picture of American democracy by noting that individuals are in fact able to influence government through interest groups. These groups put pressure on the elites and consequently affect public policymaking in ways not available to individuals. From this perspective, the power minority—who are the numerical majority (or, as US senator Bernie Sanders would put it, the 99 percent)[63]—is represented through the collective strength of voices, ballots, and pooled economic resources. In some cases, this approach has taken the form of social movements (such as the African American civil rights movement, the women's movement, the Chicano civil rights movement, the Native American civil rights movement, and the immigrant rights movement), whereas in other instances it has resulted in advocacy groups such as those we will encounter in the following chapters.

This brings us full circle to where we began this chapter. Recall that Madison warned of the potential "violence of faction" in *Federalist 10*, a concern that he certainly would have applied to the prevalence of organized interest groups in contemporary politics. The paradox, then, is how the pluralist model of democracy—which allows less powerful individuals to have their needs addressed through interest groups—can operate in a way that does not realize Madison's fears. Complicating the issue, powerful elements of American society such as wealthy individuals and corporations also (appropriately so) have the ability to form interest groups to pressure leaders to make decisions that will benefit them.[64] This marketplace of competition results in a similarly skewed power balance because wealthier individuals and groups gain disproportionate access and exert disproportionate influence in a political system where money (by way of organized lobbying and campaign contributions) matters. As we will see in the following chapter, this reality has resulted in a gap between those who have and those who do not have or who "have too little."[65] This gap has existed for generations but has grown very rapidly over the past couple of decades.

Conclusion

James Madison was among the elite in his day, and his concern to protect minority interests stemmed, at least in part, from a desire to protect the powerful few from the passions and preferences of the masses. But America has made great strides in opening the political system to more and more citizens in the past 200 years, and the Framers' ideas and words have often grounded those struggles. Yet as Patricia Ireland, former president of the National Organization for Women, astutely notes, "progress is not equality."[66] It would be difficult for a reasonable person to argue that America is not a more equal place than it was even a generation ago; it would be just as difficult for a reasonable person to argue that America's promise of equality has been fulfilled. Capitalism assumes a certain amount of inequality with respect to wealth, but democracy promises each citizen some degree of control over his or her life. As we will see in the next chapter, it will be uncomfortable to hold onto the myth that Americans start off more or less on equal footing and that those who play by the rules and work hardest succeed.

Further, it is impossible to deny that poverty in America is primarily white, but it is disproportionately African American and Hispanic. We need to examine the root of that reality and ask why, nearly 50 years after the passage of landmark civil rights legislation and more than 150 years after the end of the Civil War, such a racial gap continues to exist. We also need to examine the ways that gender is related to both racial and economic inequality. Activists and public officials from across the ideological spectrum and from both parties have recognized systemic inadequacies that give tremendous advantages to some Americans while deeply disadvantaging others. This book offers insight into the nature of those problems and highlights just a few of the individuals who have worked hard to solve them.

Ultimately, we need to address the paradox of compromise as a guiding principle of American democracy. We generally celebrate the willingness of officials to work together to get things done, but incremental changes have not led to meaningful improvements in the lives of the poorest Americans. We must consider the importance of holding firm to such values as justice and equality, as well. As we move through this volume, we must repeatedly ask when it is appropriate to be unyielding in our desire to move toward increased social and economic justice and when it is important to work with those who seek to solidify or otherwise preserve the current structures that have led to and perpetuate injustice.

Discussion Questions

1. Consider Madison's dilemma. Can you think of specific contemporary policy issues where majority will have thwarted minority rights? What about the other way around? Are there times when the numerical minority seems to dominate the majority?

2. Donald Trump twice ran for (and was once elected) president on a platform that emphasized the plight of the worker, even though he is, and has always been, very wealthy. What would the Framers (such as James Madison) say in regard to the wealth gap between the political leaders and the majority of citizens? Is it consistent with their ideal of democracy? If not, would you attribute the disconnect to a design error in the system, an implementation error, or something else?

3. How do you feel about the way David Yassky's candidacy was received by members of the CBC (see Box 1.2)? Can you understand Yassky's position? Can you understand the CBC's position? What does this case teach us about the differences between symbolic and substantive representation?

4. Discuss how the judicial system has intervened with respect to issues of representation at various times throughout American history. Do these cases serve to enhance or detract from broad democratic principles, such as liberty, freedom, and justice? How so?

5. Do you generally prefer the delegate model of representation or the trustee model? Does the salience of the issue affect your preference?

6. Do you think that the SMDP model of elections is appropriate for American democracy? How does it compare to the PR system? Discuss the benefits and drawbacks of each. How would Americans react to the adoption (or even the proposal) of a proportional model? What about an alternative voting system, such as IRV?

2

· ·

Income and Wealth

ST. JOHN'S UNIVERSITY EDUCATION PROFESSOR ALLAN ORNSTEIN argues that "no country has taken the idea of equality more seriously than the United States," though he notes that "we are witnessing the rise of a new aristocratic class, based on wealth and power, far worse than the European model our Founding Fathers sought to curtail."[1] Americans largely accept the notion that capitalism will produce unequal outcomes with respect to income and wealth, but we prefer a more equal distribution than currently exists. In 2011, a nationally representative sample of Americans was asked to (1) estimate the actual level of wealth inequality in the United States and (2) indicate preferences for ideal distribution of wealth. The researchers found that:

> Respondents vastly underestimated the actual level of wealth inequality in the United States, believing that the wealthiest quintile[2] held about 59% of the wealth when the actual number is closer to 84%. More interesting, respondents constructed ideal wealth distributions that were far more equitable than even their erroneously low estimates of actual distributions, reporting a desire for the top quintile to own just 32% of the wealth.[3]

The researchers also found that this preference existed across demographic groups (including participants' expressed presidential vote choice from 2004): "All groups—even the wealthiest respondents—desired a more equal distribution of wealth than what they estimated the current United States level to be, and all groups also desired some inequality— even the poorest respondents."[4] Finally, and perhaps most interesting, all groups agreed that the way to move toward this ideal is through redistributing wealth from the top to the bottom three quintiles.

DOI: 10.4324/9781003043041-3

The disconnect between what Americans of all ideological backgrounds desire and the reality of inequality is striking and calls into question the effectiveness of our representative system. So, why is this happening? One answer could be that our elected officials wish to make changes to bring the wealth gap more in line with what Americans want but are constrained by systemic forces that make such meaningful change possible. Another answer is that our elected officials, most of whom (at the federal level at least) are wealthier than the average American, are trying to protect themselves and their elite friends and family members. More likely, though, as the researchers suggest, we generally are not aware that the gap is so large; we are optimistic about our chances of getting into higher quintiles; we are not clear about the causes of inequality; and we often do not make a connection between these beliefs and our public policy preferences.[5] In this chapter, we explore the statistical realities of income and wealth inequality, as well as the relationship between that inequality and race. We will focus on the various elements in American society that perpetuate economic inequality in an attempt to understand how the current gap has not only persisted but also has been greatly expanded over the past generation or so.

Income

Economic inequality is customarily discussed in terms of two distinct but related concepts: income and wealth. Wealth is a person's (or household's) total worth (assets minus debt), whereas income is simply the amount of money a person (or household) earns in a year. We will explore wealth disparities later on, but in this section we consider the differences in annual household income and the ability to provide for oneself or one's family as a result.

Income and Employment

For most Americans, income is tied to employment; we only get paid when we work. Of course, there are exceptions. Disabled and retired individuals can collect Social Security from the federal government. Unemployed workers can receive benefits for a limited period after losing a job. Some wealthy individuals have invested money and earn from dividends and interest. For the most part, though, income is related to work.

Work is correlated with a number of factors that we will consider in more detail in the chapters that follow (specifically, education opportunities, immigration status, and incarceration rates). Most recently, though, attention has been focused on the sluggish economy and the degree to which it has affected Americans in the workforce. With respect to recessions, it has been said that when America catches a cold, African Americans get the flu. That sentiment was clearly reflected in the recession that began with the housing crisis in 2008. As Figure 2.1 reveals, there has been a persistent racial gap in unemployment for decades.

As a result of the Great Recession, which began in December of 2007, white unemployment among the college educated rose from 1.8 percent in 2007 to 3.9 percent in 2011, while black unemployment among the college educated spiked from 2.7 percent in 2007 to 7.0 percent in 2011.[6] By 2015, the overall numbers were much improved, but not much had changed in relation to the gap, with white, college-educated unemployment at 2.4 percent and African American, college-educated unemployment hovering at 4.1 percent—still higher than its white counterpart during the recession.[7] A second major recession of the twenty-first century, brought on by the emergence of the Covid-19 pandemic, resulted in higher levels of unemployment over a prolonged period of time.[8] The overall rate peaked

FIGURE 2.1. Unemployment Rate by Race, 2000–2020

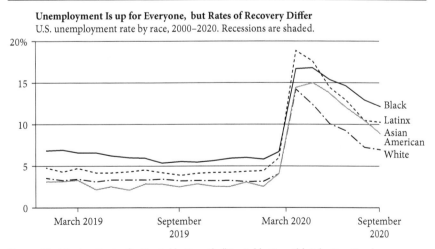

Unemployment Is up for Everyone, but Rates of Recovery Differ
U.S. unemployment rate by race, 2000–2020. Recessions are shaded.

Source: Washington Center for Equitable Growth, "Equitable Growth's Jobs Day Graphs: September 2020 Report Edition," October 2, 2020, https://equitablegrowth.org/equitable-growths-jobs-day-graphs-september-2020-report-edition/.

somewhere between 14 percent and 16 percent.[9] Unemployment rates for January 2021 indicated a nationwide level of 3.5 percent, but a closer look reveals that the rate for whites (3.0 percent) was lower than for Hispanics (4.3 percent) or African Americans (6.1 percent, or more than twice the rate for whites).[10]

Unemployment naturally has an effect on earnings. Data from 2019 demonstrate a notable income gap between white, black, and Hispanic families. In that year, the real median household income for non-Hispanic whites was $76,057, while the real median income for African Americans was $45,438, and for Hispanics, $56,113.[11] Those numbers reflect a fairly stable gap over the past five decades (see Figure 2.2). The emergence of the Covid-19 pandemic in early 2020 brought about another significant recession that disproportionately affected African American and Hispanic workers and households. As we will explore in more detail in Chapter 7, frontline health and hospitality workers are disproportionately Black and

FIGURE 2.2. Real Median Household Income by Race and Hispanic Origin, 1967–2019

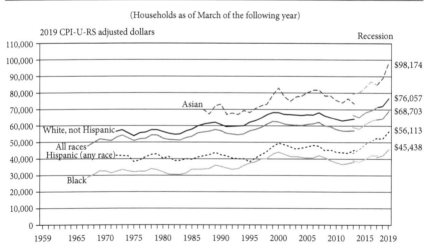

Notes: The data for 2017 and beyond reflect the implementation of an updated processing system. The data for 2013 and beyond reflect the implementation of the redesigned income questions. See Table A-2 for historical race footnotes. The data points are placed at the midpoints of the respective years. Median household income data are not available prior to 1967. For more information on the CPI-U-RS dollar adjustment and recessions, see Appendix A. For information on confidentiality protection, sampling error, nonsampling error, and definitions, see <https://www2.census.gov/programs-surveys/cps/techdocs/cpsmar20.pdf>.

Source: US Census Bureau, "Income and Poverty in the United States, 2019," September 15, 2020, https://www.census.gov/library/publications/2020/demo/p60-270.html.

Brown, which means that in the earliest days of the pandemic, those individuals and their families were more likely to be unable to shelter in place to avoid exposure to the virus. As spring turned to summer, however, many jobs that were temporarily or permanently eliminated as a result of the virus were also those held by African American and Hispanic workers, such that the economic impact of the virus disproportionately hit those communities and served to exacerbate the income gap.[12]

The income gap is most pronounced among Hispanics and African Americans, but its growth is notable among all segments of the population. In 2019, the highest quintile (20 percent) of earners collected nearly 52 percent of the mean total income in the United States. Put another way, households in the top quintile of income earned more than those in the bottom four quintiles combined. The bottom three quintiles combined brought in just over 25 percent of the total income that year.[13] The quintiles do not tell the entire story about income concentration at the top, however. The upper 5 percent of income earners in 2019 accounted for 23 percent of the income earned that year.[14] There has been a steady increase in this trend over the past 50 years, such that the top 5 percent of earners in 1970 accounted for just over 16.6 percent of the total income. That number rose steadily to 18.5 percent in 1990 and to 21.3 percent in 2010.[15]

Gender is also related to income disparity. Much attention has been given to the wage gap in recent years, which stands today at about 18 percent. Put another way, women make an average of 82 cents for every dollar a man makes in the United States.[16] This figure has been creeping toward equality for some time; the Institute for Women's Policy Research currently predicts that the gap will not close completely until 2059.[17] The gap is largest for Hispanic women (56 percent compared to white men; 85 percent compared to Hispanic men) and smallest for Asian American women (89 percent compared to white men; 77 percent compared to Asian men). The gap for African American women is 63 percent compared to white men and 92 percent compared to black men.[18] This wage gap holds at every level of educational attainment and, in fact, is slightly larger for women who hold college degrees.[19] It should be noted that while the figure has fluctuated from year to year, based on differing indicators, some commentators have argued that the gap is most attributable to choices that women make compared to men.[20] As we will explore in Chapter 8, however, we must be careful in evaluating individual-level choices in a system where gender norms serve as a constraint.

On the opposite end of the spectrum, evidence of racial disparity is illustrated by an examination of the board members of America's top corporations. In 2018, Whites comprised 84 percent of the board seats at Fortune 500 companies in the United States. African Americans held 8.6 percent, Hispanics held 3.8 percent, and Asian/Pacific Islanders held 3.7 percent. More specifically, 75 percent of those seats were held by white men; 25 percent of seats were held by women of any racial/ethnic category.[21] This is a marked improvement over the same analysis just six years previous, when white men comprised 86.7 percent of the seats, African Americans held 7.4 percent, Hispanics held just 3.3 percent, and Asian/Pacific Islanders accounted for 2.3 percent.[22] It was not until 1999 that an African American became CEO of a Fortune 500 company,[23] and there have been only 18 more since;[24] in January 2021, there were only four African American CEOs in such positions.[25] A record 38 women-headed Fortune 500 companies in August 2020,[26] which accounts for just 7.6 percent of top positions for women, who comprise more than half the nation's population.

It might not seem important to look toward the composition of these 500 seats, but the lack of diversity there compounds another reality: the tremendous shift in the ratio of Fortune 500 CEO pay to the income of an average worker. Although the ratios found on bumper stickers and pro-union literature vary (from as much as 500 to 1 to as low as 253 to 1),[27] the reality is complicated by the various types of compensation (besides monetary income) that CEOs receive. In 2019, according to the Economic Policy Institute, "the ratio of CEO-to-typical-worker compensation was 320-to-1 under the realized measure of CEO pay; that is up from 293-to-1 in 2018 and a big increase from 21-to-1 in 1965 and 61-to-1 in 1989."[28] The average CEO in the top 350 US firms brought home $21.3 million 2019.[29] The monetary portion of these figures relates to gross income (before taxes). Since the United States has a progressive income tax structure (higher annual incomes relate to higher tax brackets), some of this income inequality will ostensibly be resolved once taxes are collected. As we see in the next section, though, it is not that simple.

Taxes

There is no denying that the US income tax code is tremendously complicated. It is full of complex rules and regulations that are designed to add fairness to the system. But "fair" is in the eye of the beholder and open to interpretation by Americans with differing ideological leanings. Those who earn a lot often complain that the so-called progressive tax structure punishes (and, more important, de-incentivizes) financial success, while those who earn less sometimes wish that a higher percentage of the nation's revenue would be paid by those who can most afford it. In sum, our tax code is a collection of deals and compromises between representatives who have different preferences—and who represent constituencies that have different preferences (see Box 2.1).

On the surface, the United States income tax system is progressive in that it appears to tax those who earn more at a higher rate than those who earn less. In 2020, the rate began with a base of 10 percent, with a married couple earning more than $19,750 paying an increasingly higher rate on the money they make over the first 10 percent—from 12 percent to 37 percent (for those couples earning more than $622,050).[30] The effective tax rates (which includes all forms of income tax, not just taxes on wages, divided by income) for the highest earners have been reduced over the past 40 years, from 66.4 percent after World War II to 47.7 percent in 1982 to 36.4 percent in the 1990s. The George W. Bush tax cuts further reduced the top bracket to 32.4 percent.[31] In 2018, it was 23 percent, which is a percentage lower than the effective rate paid by the bottom 50 percent of US earners that year.[32] This represents a continuation of a trend that began in the 1980s, when the effective tax rate for the highest earning Americans was 47 percent, up from 56 percent in the 1960s.[33]

Before the seemingly progressive tax rate is applied, the taxable income amount can be reduced by a host of deductions that are disproportionately available to higher earners. A recent study found that more than half of all tax benefits went to the wealthiest 5 percent of taxpayers and that "the top 1 percent of taxpayers, those making more than $1 million, received an average $95,000 in assistance.... By contrast, the poorest taxpayers, including families making $50,000, received less than $500 in benefits."[34] The most widespread of these policies is the mortgage interest deduction, which allows for a reduction in taxable income related to money paid toward interest on a home mortgage. The more expensive the home, the larger the deduction. There are also deductions for contributions to retirement plans, and a flat tax rate (either 15 percent or 20 percent depending on the amount) on income made from the sale of capital assets held for more than a year.[35] Mitt Romney, the 2012 Republican presidential candidate, revealed that he

Box 2.1. *Representing*: Steve Forbes and the Flat Tax

The publisher of *Forbes* magazine, Steve Forbes, championed a flat tax in his bids for president of the United States in 1996 and 2000, as well as in a 2005 book called *Flat Tax Revolution: Using a Postcard to Abolish the IRS*.[41] While some progressives worry that a program touted almost exclusively by wealthy conservatives will not ultimately benefit the neediest Americans, the underlying premise addresses one of the more egregious inequalities about the current tax structure: those who are able to hire tax professionals benefit most because of the complicated nature of the process.

For individuals, the proposed tax form has just 12 lines and can literally fit on a piece of paper the size of a postcard. After reporting wages and salary earned, a taxpayer deducts for adults ($13,200 each) and children ($4,000 each) in the household, calculates 17 percent of the remaining amount, and then earns an additional $1,000 deduction for each child under age 16. The Earned Income Tax Credit (EITC) could also be claimed by those who qualify.[42]

While conservatives call the plan "simple, fair, and good for growth,"[43] progressives call it "a game of three-card monte that deliberately confuses the issues of simplicity, fairness, and the total tax burden on society."[44] Nonetheless, it is an idea that has some intrinsic appeal to anyone who has filed a federal tax return. Because most of the wealthiest individuals pay others to compute their taxes, Forbes's proposal would likely generate significant mass appeal if elected officials ever took it seriously. Whether the result would be an increase in economic equality is unclear, but some scholars[45] have argued that it ought to be adopted to eliminate the complicated (often nearly invisible) benefits that the current system provides to those who need it least.

In 2016, after his party's candidate won the presidency for the first time since 2004, Forbes repeated his call for a simplified tax system. Although he did not call for President-elect Trump to adopt a flat tax, he offered a plan with only two tax brackets, in addition to reduction in capital gains taxes and taxes on corporations.[46]

paid 14 percent of his income in federal taxes in 2010 and 2011 (the only years for which he released returns during the campaign), even though he earned $13.7 million and $21.7 million in those years, respectively, because most of the income was from investments.[36] Multibillionaire Warren Buffett has famously quipped that his secretary pays a higher percentage of her annual income than he does as a result of these complicated regulations.[37] Donald Trump famously refused to provide his tax returns during the 2016 campaign, but a leak obtained by the *New York Times* suggested that despite his estimated $3.7 billion estimated wealth,[38] he may have paid no federal income taxes for nearly 20 years.[39] Subsequent analysis of other leaked documents revealed that he paid $750 in federal taxes in 2016 and the same amount in 2017.[40] Clearly, the income tax structure can disproportionately benefit those with the most income.

At the same time, other taxes that disproportionately affect those who are not wealthy have increased. These are called regressive taxes. For example, Social Security is funded by a flat payroll tax (12.4 percent in 2021, with half paid by the employee and the other half by the employer). Individuals pay only on the first $142,800 earned.[47] Those who earn more make no further contributions. That means that higher earners pay a smaller percentage of their overall income to help fund the program than do lower earners. Sales taxes are applied by state and local governments to products and services. Everyone needs to buy food and necessities, so everyone, rich and poor, is subject to these taxes. But a 3 percent tax on milk or an 18 percent excise tax on gasoline (in addition to local gas taxes) will have a more significant impact on a working family's budget than on a millionaire's. In this manner, increases in regressive taxes to make up for revenue lost from providing income tax breaks to the wealthy can cause a significant burden for those who are already economically vulnerable.

On the other hand, a number of provisions in the US tax code provide tax breaks that benefit low earners disproportionately (such as the deductions for children, tuition, and government-backed low-interest student loans) or solely (such as the low-income housing tax credit and credit for rent paid). One such program, the EITC, was expanded between 1984 and 1996 to provide an incentive for single mothers to work.[48] The EITC benefits working families (particularly those with children) by providing a reduction in taxable earnings for families earning less than $57,414 (in 2021, married with three children or more).[49] The mortgage interest deduction program also benefits Americans in a variety of income ranges. So, while it is not the case that the high earners are the sole beneficiaries of

US tax policy, they benefit disproportionately, even though they represent a distinct numerical minority of citizens.

Minimum Wage and the Poverty Line

In 1938, Congress set a federal minimum wage (at 25 cents per hour),[50] but it was not indexed to increase with inflation. As a result, there have been significant lags in the buying power of the dollar for minimum wage workers. The current federal minimum wage, set in 2009, is $7.25 per hour, though the highest level (in real dollars) was in 1968 ($10.04 in 2010 dollars).[51] Twenty-nine states and the District of Columbia have minimum wages higher than the federal level.[52] Individuals in occupations where tips are expected are not protected by minimum wage laws.

A full-time worker at the federal minimum wage will fall below the poverty line for a family of four. In 1968, a full-time minimum wage worker earned about 90 percent of the poverty level, but from the mid-1980s until Congress raised the minimum wage in 2006, full-time minimum wage workers with a family of four only earned between 50 percent and 60 percent of the federal poverty level.[53]

The poverty line (technically "poverty threshold") is not without its critics (those who think it is too low and those who think it is too high). The poverty threshold was developed in the 1960s and is based on the cost of food, under the assumption that a family of three or more spends about one-third of its income on food.[54] In 2021, the poverty threshold for an individual was $12,880; the threshold for a family of four was $26,500.[55] In 2010, the poverty rate in the United States was the highest since 1993, with 15.1 percent of individuals living in poverty. That rate has declined rather dramatically since 2014; the 10.5 percent rate in 2019 (before Covid-19) was the lowest in 60 years.[56] That overall good news masks the racial and ethnic disparities. While the poverty rate for non-Hispanic white Americans and Asian Americans was 7.3 percent, it was more than double that for African Americans (18.8 percent) and Hispanics of any race (15.7 percent).[57]

Once again, gender matters, and its effect is intersectional. Fifty-six percent of individuals living in poverty in the United States in 2018 were women. Across each racial and ethnic category, there are more women than men living in poverty.[58] Yet the poverty rate for white women

(9.0 percent), while higher than that for white men (7.1 percent), is still lower than for men or women in any other racial category.

If we hold our analysis at the household level, a similar pattern emerges: female-headed households have higher poverty rates than male-headed households. First, people living with relatives are less likely to be living in poverty than those living alone; the overall poverty rate for families in 2018 was 9 percent. Only 4.7 percent of households with a married couple were in poverty, compared to 12.7 percent of families with a male head of household and 24.9 percent for families with a female head of household.[59]

Poverty rates are even higher for women of color who are the head of a household. For example, the poverty rate for black families with a single, female head of household in 2019 was 27.3 percent, a full ten points higher than for white families with a single, female head of household that year.[60] That gap has been narrowing and, in fact, the 2019 figure for both black and white women-led families is the lowest since 2019, but this historically low level for black women is still higher than the highest level for white women in the past 30 years (25 percent in 1993).[61]

Children are also disproportionately affected by poverty. Nearly 11 million children (14.4 percent) were living in poverty in 2019, which is approximately one in seven children.[62] As is the case with the poverty rate for women, race matters. More than one in four Black children (26.5 percent) and one in five (20.9 percent) Hispanic children were living in poverty that year.[63] American Indian and Alaska Native children were at similar levels to Hispanic children; Asian children (7.7 percent) and white children (8.3 percent) experienced poverty at far lower rates.[64] These statistics give life to the notion of proportionality that is a central component to the statistics in this chapter: even though black children comprise only 14 percent of all the children in the United States, they account for more than a quarter of the children who are living in poverty.[65]

As is always the case with statistics and classifications, there is disagreement about how to appropriately operationalize poverty. Those who argue that the existing formula sets the level too low point to the fact that income from federal programs (often referred to as welfare; see below) is not counted in this calculation.[66] Those who argue that the level is too high note that while the rationale for calculating based on food as one-third of a family budget might have been appropriate a half-century ago, housing prices in particular (not to mention transportation and utility costs) have increased at a rate disproportionate to food.[67]

Similarly, there are competing ideas about whether raising the minimum wage would help relieve income inequality. By one calculation, if the minimum wage had risen proportionately with worker productivity, it would be at about $24 per hour, which would allow a full-time worker to earn $48,000 per year.[68] If it had risen at the pace of Wall Street bonuses, it would be more than $33 per hour.[69] The wisdom of raising the minimum wage can be considered in terms of our shared American values (*should* the minimum wage rise at the same rate as CEO compensation?), as well as in terms of more practical considerations.

Amid the flurry of voices calling for an increase in recent years is a persistent argument about equity—if this wage was established to help keep people out of poverty, and the value is far short of what it was at that time, it is not fulfilling its function. Some states have adopted laws that will move their minimum wage to $15 incrementally, and some early analysis of big-box retail stores that have raised the minimum wage resulted in an increase of jobs in the local economy[70] by putting more disposable income in the hands of consumers and reducing family debt burdens. In his 2014 State of the Union Address, President Obama called on Congress to raise the federal minimum wage to $10.10 per hour,[71] and both Bernie Sanders and Donald Trump[72] supported a minimum wage increase in their respective 2016 presidential election campaigns. None of those initiatives were implemented, and by 2020, President Trump opposed an increase in the minimum wage.[73] In 2021, President Biden tried to include a hike to $15 per hour into his Covid-19 relief package, but as the date of this writing, it faced an uncertain future.[74]

Those who oppose raising the minimum wage argue that doing so would harm job creation, force layoffs, or lead to hours being cut back for those earning the minimum wage.[75] They note, for instance, that many minimum wage workers are not trying to support families—they have a second earner, have supplemental income (such as Social Security retirement for seniors working part-time), or are students. In combination with other government programs, advocates of this position feel as if there is enough of a safety net in place to protect low-wage workers and that the government should not meddle with the invisible hand of the economy. In 2021, the non-partisan Congressional Budget Office issued results of their analysis of the $15 minimum wage proposal, concluding that the initiative would drive up prices on goods and services and increase the national debt by increasing government spending as a result of job loss.[76]

Welfare

Many advanced democracies have expansive welfare states that are designed to provide a safety net so that no citizen falls into economic despair. Such societies are generally characterized by high tax rates and active central governments that are involved in many segments of the economy.[77] The United States has sponsored a number of programs over the years that are designed to provide such protections, but the scope and duration of those programs was dramatically reduced in the 1990s.

Welfare is a catchall term for government-funded and -operated programs that provide different forms of financial assistance to those who need it. While various levels of assistance have been in place since colonial times, New Deal programs established during the Great Depression were more expansive than their predecessors. Many of these programs, such as unemployment compensation, Aid to Families with Dependent Children, and the program that we now know as Social Security are still in place.[78] Although not income per se, health care programs, such as Medicare (for senior citizens) and Medicaid (for needy persons who are not seniors), provide additional assistance to offset costs associated with taking care of oneself and one's family.

There has been significant debate in the United States about how much assistance should be provided to the needy and under what circumstances. These debates involve conflict of several core values to which Americans subscribe.[79] While Americans have a commitment to equality in a broad sense, they also have a commitment to individualism that has roots deep into US history. Further, the language used to discuss welfare in the 1980s was highly racialized, causing persistent inaccuracies in perceptions about whom these programs benefit and how much money is spent in this area.

Ronald Reagan's reference to a "welfare queen" in Chicago with "80 names, 30 addresses, 12 Social Security cards and is collecting veterans' benefits on four non-existing deceased husbands" to the tune of $150,000 per year[80] created an enduring image of poverty in America that is characterized by undeserving African Americans who are cheating the system to get rich on the backs of hardworking (white) taxpayers. The story he told on the campaign trail in 1976 about Linda Taylor was likely an exaggeration,[81] but the retelling of the story suggested that she was typical of welfare recipients. As a result, the welfare queen script came to dominate the imagination of white Americans who were asked to consider reforms to the welfare system in the following decade.[82] As political scientist Martin Gilens notes:

> The connection between "poor" and "black" exists simply because African Americans account for a disproportionate number of poor people in the United States. Only one in ten white Americans falls below the official government poverty line, but three out of ten blacks are poor. Still, blacks are a small segment of the American population, and even though they are disproportionately poor, they comprise only a minority (currently about 27 percent) of all poor people.[83]

Gilens's study reveals that white respondents who viewed blacks as hardworking were much less willing to decrease welfare spending than those who viewed blacks as lazy.[84] In this way, it is very difficult to disentangle Americans' views of the poor generally with their perceptions of poor persons of color. Deservedness lies at the heart of welfare policy debates. In a political culture that values individualism and has a history that is deeply rooted in racial animosity toward African Americans in particular (and more recently Latinos), support for benefits to veterans, retired persons, and the physically disabled is more plentiful than support for the working poor, the homeless, or the mentally ill. Further, we must consider that Reagan chose to focus on a welfare queen, not a welfare king. The public disdain for the poor that is reflected in Gilens's study and that led to reforms in the 1990s is rooted in patriarchal views of personhood that marginalize women's voices and delegitimize their lived experiences.[85] In other words, Reagan's simplistic and atypical story resonated with Americans because of pre-existing sexist and racist narratives that Americans hold in our subconscious.

Public attitudes about welfare drove significant reforms in the mid-1990s. Congress now provides grants to states to distribute to needy citizens. This procedural change, along with federal guidelines, has resulted in a dramatic decrease in the number of Americans who receive cash assistance to offset their poverty. In 2018, only 22 percent of poor families received cash assistance,[86] compared to 82 percent in 1980. It was 60 percent in 1996.[87] Twenty-five years after the reforms, there is mixed evidence about the results: "The new program did work for millions of families, but not all. Many of the most disadvantaged people have been unable to get or keep jobs, and they're worse off than they were before, in part because there's now a five-year lifetime limit on welfare benefits—and in some states, it's lower."[88]

The reality, of course, is much more complicated. Government "handouts" do not only go to the needy. So-called corporate welfare refers to tax incentives and subsidies for businesses.[89] Most Americans may not be aware of these policies, and even if they are, such programs as these are generally not lumped into the category of "welfare." Although subsidies and tax breaks to corporations (even if they are profitable) are not income in the individual sense of the word, they help to make businesses successful, which sometimes translates into job creation (and thus income for workers) and often results in increases in wealth for top executives and major stockholders.

Wealth

Whereas income is the amount of money a person or household earns in a year, wealth is the value of that person or household overall. Wealth is calculated by subtracting debt from assets, and in many ways, it is a more accurate window into economic and racial inequality in America. Although it is important to understand income gaps as part of the cycle of disadvantage (and advantage) in the United States, wealth signifies the command over financial resources that a family has accumulated over its lifetime along with resources that have been inherited across generations. Such resources, when combined with income, can create the opportunity to secure the "good life" in whatever form is needed—education, business, training, justice, health, comfort, and so on.[90]

Some Americans (both rich and poor) earn no income on an annual basis. In that respect, they are equal in terms of income even though their opportunities may be quite different. Further, wealth and income are not highly correlated, and there is great variation in wealth within income categories.[91] In this section, we will briefly consider some markers of wealth inequality before turning our attention to the systemic factors that reflect and perpetuate the growing gap between the wealthy and the poor in the United States.

Wealth Gap

While the income gap is large (and growing), the wealth gap is even more dramatic.[92] Median household wealth in the United States grew from $79,100 in 1989 to $126,400 in 2007 before falling dramatically to $77,300 in 2010.[93] In 2016, the median household wealth rebounded to $101,800 (in 2018 dollars), which is still less than what it was in 1998.[94] According to the Pew Research Center:

> The wealth gap between upper-income and lower- and middle-income families has grown wider this century. Upper-income families were the only income tier able to build on their wealth from 2001 to 2016, adding 33% at the median. On the other hand, middle-income families saw their median net worth shrink by 20% and lower-income families experienced a loss of 45%. As of 2016, upper-income families had 7.4 times as much wealth as middle-income families and 75 times as much wealth as lower-income families. These ratios are up from 3.4 and 28 in 1983, respectively.[95]

As the authors of this report note, this trend persists because most middle-income families have assets mostly related to home ownership, so the housing bubble burst has had a disproportionate effect on their wealth.

Rather than accumulating wealth throughout a lifetime, a sizable percentage of Americans struggle through their senior years, living primarily on Social Security income. Nearly half of Americans die with less than $10,000 in assets.[96] Research over the past decade has demonstrated that the gap between the rich and poor in America has been increasing over the past 30 years and that it is more exaggerated when race is factored in.[97]

Specifically, the top 10 percent of US households now control 70 percent of the nation's total wealth (up from 49 percent in 2005).[98] That increase, however, somewhat masks the reality that is faced by persons of color. In 2016, the net median worth of a white family in the United States was

$171,000, compared to $17,150 for a black family.[99] While the amounts tend to fluctuate together over time, the gaps are persistent.[100] The disparities hold across all income levels except the lowest, with the highest-earning black families' median wealth ($343,160) is far smaller than their white counterparts ($1,789,300).[101]

As the authors of one report noted,

> [I]f the past 30 years were to repeat, the next three decades would see the average wealth of White households increase by over $18,000 per year, while Latino and Black Households would see their respective wealth increase by about $2,250 and $750 per year.... If average Black family wealth continues to grow at the same pace it has over the past three decades, it would take Black families 228 years to amass the same amount of wealth White families have today.[102]

At this point, it should come as no surprise that gender is also relevant with respect to wealth, though it is much more difficult to measure since wealth is most often reported at the household, rather than individual, level. The data that are available center on nonmarried households and tend to show that women are less likely than men to own almost every type of asset. The median value of assets held by women is almost always lower than that of their male counterparts. A smaller percentage of women own stocks, bonds, and other financial assets compared to men. Women are also less likely to hold retirement accounts, and a woman's pension is typically smaller than a man's.[103] A recent analysis revealed that women own 32 cents for every dollar a man owns.[104]

When married couples divorce or when a spouse dies, women often face a disproportionate financial burden. If they were not in the labor force during marriage, they are disadvantaged when competing for positions with more experienced candidates. Children most often live with their mother after a separation or divorce, and men are not always willing or able to pay child support.[105] Women are also more likely than men to lose health insurance after a divorce,[106] which, as we will see later, can result in significant, even debilitating, financial strain. A woman whose husband dies tends to own only 59 cents for every dollar of wealth that men have when a wife dies.[107] As we saw with income, because women of color are more likely to be heads of households, there is an interactive effect between race and gender, as well.

Gifts and Inheritance

Some individuals get a head start on the road to financial security by having parents or other relatives with money. Whether gifts are made early in one's adult life or assets are left after a relative dies, being able to count on money that one has not personally earned can be a tremendous help. While many people who are wealthy have parents who were not as wealthy, the majority of poorer Americans come from poor families and thus do not have the opportunity to get a head start in this way.

The racial gap with respect to inheritance is significant. While slavery and legal racial segregation seem to be in the distant past, when we consider the passing of wealth through generations, it becomes clear that African Americans who are alive today and who trace their heritage to enslaved persons have been systemically disadvantaged because accumulation of wealth was illegal or nearly impossible given the conditions in which their ancestors lived. Researchers Gittelman and Wolff conclude that "African Americans would have gained significant ground relative to whites [between 1984 and 1994] if they had inherited similar amounts."[108] Similarly, Menchik and Jianakoplos estimate that white households are at least twice as likely to receive an inheritance and that "racial differences in inheritances can explain between 10 percent and 20 percent of the average racial difference in household wealth (in 1989)."[109] A windfall inheritance—even if it is modest—can help to offset existing debt, be invested in a major purchase (such as a home), or be put aside for an emergency or to plan for retirement. Because whites are, on average, able to count on inheritance or financial help from family members more than persons of color, their starting line is closer to the finish line (economic security). This should not obscure the reality, however, that millions of whites have also not been able to rely on significant family support or inheritance and, as well, have lived for generations in poverty, at least partly due to the rapid decrease in manufacturing jobs.[110]

Savings and Investments

Children are often encouraged to save their money for a rainy day. As adults, we have historically been expected to have some sort of reserve in the event of a job loss, an illness, or some other unforeseen event that affects our earning (see Box 2.2). But savings and investment can only

---

Box 2.2. *What Can I Do?*: Community Education

Understanding personal finance is difficult for everyone, irrespective of educational background. Even those of us with advanced degrees have trouble making sense of tax forms, understanding the difference between an IRA and a 401(k), knowing what mutual fund to consider, and choosing a savings account or certificate of deposit. If you have a good grasp of these matters, you can be helpful to people in your local community. See whether your college (or another local college) has a community program related to finance, or check with the library to see whether it has programs designed to educate the public (often these pop up around tax time in March and April).

There are also a number of not-for-profit groups that offer this sort of assistance. Foundation Communities (www.foundcom.org) in the Austin, Texas, area, for instance, sponsors a program, Community Tax Centers, that provides free income tax preparation help to low-income families in the area. Participants work with volunteers who have a detailed understanding of tax law and who, in turn, educate additional volunteers to give hands-on assistance. The Community Financial Education Foundation (CFEF) is a nationwide group whose mission is "to educate the American public and reach underserved communities by teaching meaningful financial life skills, encouraging positive financial behaviors, and providing access to outcome-based, educational resources over the long-term" (www.communityfef.org). It works with volunteers and community partners to provide these services in a number of communities, as well as through online educational tools.

---

occur after basic needs (housing, food, utilities, school supplies, etc.) are satisfied. The Personal Savings Rate (PSR) is the ratio of savings to disposable income,[111] which is a somewhat confusing term that refers to money available after taxes (but before other necessities are met). The PSR tended to hover around 6.5 percent to 7.5 percent in the United States over the past decade, but it increased dramatically as the Covid-19 pandemic essentially forced savings for middle-income Americans because travel and other recreational opportunities were unavailable. The rate shot up to 16.1 percent in 2020.[112] For families directly affected financially by the pandemic, those savings would quickly evaporate as they struggled to ensure their basic needs were met. The reality, of course, is that most Americans have little-to-no money saved: a recent survey revealed that 60 percent of Americans have less than $1,000 in savings.[113]

In total, black Americans held about $6 in assets for every $100 owned by whites.[114] Whites held four times as much in real estate alone than African Americans had in all types of investments (and nearly six times as much as Hispanic Americans).[115] While these raw numbers are to be expected given the uneven proportion of the population, the overall picture is powerful on its face, in addition to being disproportionate. Whites' real estate assets are generally worth more than non-whites' (which is a function of housing values in each neighborhood, as will be discussed further in Chapter 3).[116] This is significant because for most Americans, a home is their most significant asset. As of March 2020, nearly 74 percent of non-Hispanic white Americans owned homes, compared to 44 percent of African Americans and 56 percent of Hispanic Americans.[117]

The stock market is another potential place for investment that can lead to income and financial security, not to mention wealth accumulation, but here again, there is a significant racial gap. In 2019, about 61 percent of white households owned stocks, compared to just over 33 percent of black households.[118] As the stock market indices soared between 2009 and 2020, those who held stocks stood to benefit in terms of their wealth (so long as this increase in assets was not accompanied by a proportionate increase in debt). With white Americans investing at higher rates, they benefitted disproportionately, thus increasing the racial wealth gap.

Credit and Debt

The ability to get credit—borrow money—both reflects wealth and determines one's ability to accumulate it. Automobile commercials frequently promise low (or no) finance charges for "well-qualified" buyers—those whose high credit score and income are deemed sufficient by the lender. Of course, those who fit that categorization will certainly *appreciate* a better deal on the car, but they probably do not *need* the better deal nearly as much as those who are not "well qualified" by those criteria. The person with less income or worse credit thus pays more for the car, which only contributes to unsteady economic circumstances. Banks often charge fees on checking accounts that fail to maintain a minimum balance throughout the billing cycle, give stiff fines for overdrafts, and place restrictions on savings account withdrawals if there is not a minimum balance. While all of these practices can be justified from the perspective of the banks in terms of their ability to conduct business, there is a potential for exponentially adverse effects on those with limited funds in their accounts.

Missing a payment or making a late payment can trigger a higher interest rate, which only exacerbates the problem for borrowers with financial uncertainty. (As detailed in Chapter 3, adjustable-rate mortgages can leave families in financial trouble even if bills are paid on time.) Missing payments or paying late, with the accumulation of late fees and interest, can harm credit scores or lead to bankruptcy.

Calculations of creditworthiness are complicated (sometimes including up to 100 variables),[119] but are essentially based on factors such as income, available existing credit, and history of repayment. Other factors such as zip code, marital status, and length of time at the present address may also be considered.[120] It is not difficult to understand how poorer Americans—those who live in less desirable zip codes, rent their home, earn relatively low income, and so on—are disadvantaged by a system that is used by middle-class folks to increase their wealth. Credit scores do not affect only consumer financing or credit card applications. They are often used in determining whether a person is granted a lease for an apartment, rates for automobile and homeowner's insurance, and sometimes for evaluating candidates for employment.

Ability to secure conventional loans or access to credit, like other measures of economic inequality, is not unrelated to race. Because African Americans and Latinos are poorer on average than whites, there is a disproportionate tendency for persons of color to be victimized by predatory lending with respect to all aspects of consumerism.[121] Those who cannot secure traditional forms of credit often turn to riskier (and more costly) alternatives to stay afloat.[122]

Predatory Practices and Gambling

While gambling (betting on sporting events, at a casino, or through state-sanctioned lotteries) is available to and enjoyed by Americans from all social and ethnic groups, there is a tendency for those who are the most needy to turn to these potentially quick sources of revenue. Problem gambling can be so debilitating because the more desperate people are, the more likely they are to gamble.

Type of gambling is related to income. For instance, while only 6 percent of individuals with a household income under $30,000 per year gamble on sports, 17 percent of those with a household income between $30,000 and $75,000 do.[123] In general, gambling is much more common among higher-income than lower-income Americans.[124] However, individuals who play the lottery and have a household income of under $10,000 per year bet nearly four times as much on lotteries annually as do those with a household income over $75,000 per year.[125]

More systematic than gaming, however, is the existence and persistence of predatory loan businesses that are disproportionately located in communities that are most likely to use them (i.e., poorer communities). Payday loan shops offer quick access to cash in exchange for a commitment to have the amount (and an interest fee) deducted from the customer's next pay check. There is no credit check or lengthy application. One must generally produce a valid form of identification and proof of employment (with wages and pay date). Payday loans are mostly for small amounts (less than $300), but the fees range from $15 to $30 for each $100 borrowed,[126] an interest rate that exceeds that of most credit cards. Researcher Michael A. Stegman describes the market for such services:

> The core demand for payday loans originates from households with a poor credit history, but who also have checking accounts, steady employment, and an annual income under $50,000.... A 2001 survey of low-income families in Charlotte [North Carolina] ... estimated that African Americans were about twice as likely to have borrowed from a payday lender in a two-year period as whites ..., and that, after controlling for a wide range of socioeconomic characteristics, blacks were five times more likely than whites to take out multiple payday loans.[127]

In 2016, the United States Consumer Financial Protection Bureau (CFPB) imposed new regulations on payday loan establishments,[128] at which time it was expected that the industry would respond to these guidelines with creative options that are no less predatory.[129] As it turns out, they did not need to, as the Trump Administration sought to delay the compliance date to the new regulations, ultimately revoking key protections of the guidelines in 2020.[130] A number of lawsuits were being pursued as of winter 2021, when President Biden nominated a new director of the CFPB who is expected to reinstate those protections[131] and address systemic racism from that agency's perspective.[132]

Americans who lack access to traditional forms of credit may also turn to rent-to-own (RTO) establishments to furnish their homes and buy appliances or such items as televisions. RTO programs allow customers to pay a small amount on a regular basis (rent) and then have a chance to buy (own) the item at the end of the contract. More than two-thirds of RTO customers earn less than $36,000 per year,[133] and those customers understand that they are going to end up paying more for the item than they would if they were able to pay cash outright.[134] *Consumer Reports* explains that customers are generally unaware, however, that they are paying what amounts to a 250 percent annual interest rate on some RTO transactions.[135] Further, a recent study showed that inflation was rising at higher rates on goods that are disproportionately consumed by poorer Americans, placing those Americans with less wealth at an even greater disadvantage as a result of market forces.[136]

Not everyone sees such systemic disadvantage as victimizing the poor, however. Historian Thomas Woods Jr. asks why poor Americans are not more responsible with money.[137] He suggests that Americans who cannot afford such luxuries as television sets should not purchase them or should save money so that they can purchase them later. He argues that consumers who pay RTO prices have "character flaws" that cause them to spend irresponsibly. Woods raises a valid point in terms of the wisdom of such purchases, but he is inattentive to the tremendous psychological pressure placed on all consumers—not just those who are economically disadvantaged—to appear to be in the middle class by, well, *consuming*. Each of us should practice frugality, spend wisely, and not live beyond our financial means. Those who have significant amounts of disposable income, however, can be financially irresponsible without life-altering consequences; those who do not, cannot. If we all had the same income, it would be difficult to argue with such commentators as Woods, who make ostensibly reasonable points without considering the inherently unreasonable nature of the circumstances.

Such a position fits neatly within the myth of American meritocracy explained in the previous chapter: those who are able to access traditional methods of credit (and secure reasonable interest rates to borrow) are considered to be in such a position because of their wisdom, hard work, and perhaps some good luck. In exchange, they deserve to have beneficial terms for borrowing and spending, whereas poorer Americans do not, ostensibly because they have contributed to their own poverty. This individualistic view of inequality is convenient for those who have privilege because it removes any concerns about either the legitimacy of their own financial comfort or the responsibility to take action against a system that is flawed. As this chapter demonstrates, however, the convenient response is too simplistic to capture the reality of contemporary economic and racial inequality in the United States.

Further, as jarring as the statistics presented in here might be, it is important to keep in mind that as of the writing of this edition, the full effect of the recession that followed from the Covid-19 pandemic was not completely known. It is expected that there will be long-term consequences of these financial challenges (not to mention disproportionate health challenges, as we explore in Chapter 7) that unfold over a number of years. Far from reducing economic inequality in the United States, we very well might have an acceleration of these trends in the months and years to come.[138]

Some have argued that the dramatic expansion of the wealth gap, combined with the reasons for it and the increased public need that has emerged as a result of the Covid-19 crisis, warrant consideration of a "wealth tax." Separate from the income taxes (which are nominally progressive but effectively not) and sales taxes (which are regressive), a wealth tax would be an annual tax on the wealth someone holds—not just the income they earn. Competing proposals abound, but some US Senators (and former presidential candidates) like Bernie Sanders and Elizabeth Warren have proposed that individuals with a net worth of $32 million or $50 million, respectively, should be affected.[139] Others argue that taxing "success" is a manifestation of resentment that is punitive toward the wealthy and would serve to de-incentivize the entrepreneurial spirit.[140] Similar to Woods's argument, this line of thinking inherently accepts the validity of extreme wealth as being a function of hard work and, perhaps, good fortune.

Representing the Poor

Thomas Woods's beliefs are nearest to those of most Americans: empathy for the poor does not run particularly high. In the abstract, most Americans believe that poverty is an important problem that is facing government,[141] but studies have also found that Americans believe there are multiple determinants of poverty but that individualistic or "internal" causes (e.g., lack of effort, being lazy, low in intelligence, being on drugs) tend to be more important than societal or "external" ones (e.g., being a victim of discrimination, low wages, being forced to attend bad schools).[142]

Further, polls have shown that an overwhelming majority of those who are doing well financially claim responsibility for their success, whereas less than half of those who believe they are doing poorly economically take responsibility for that condition.[143] Consider, then, the position of elected officials, who are responsible for responding to public opinion on policy issues as they seek to represent their constituents. If most Americans do not think that the system needs to be adjusted, then there will be little pressure on policymakers to make adjustments. Consequently, the belief that poorer Americans are largely responsible for their own financial condition has led to an unwillingness to address systemic barriers to greater equality. After all, if we do not believe it is broken, we will not try to fix it.

Race's relationship to wealth and poverty is a central theme of this book. Because of the way hegemonic power systems operate, the word *race* generally invokes images of persons of color in the mind of white Americans. When most people speak of "poverty and race," they assume that the conversation is about racial minorities. But poverty is widespread in the United States, and while it disproportionately affects communities of color, millions of poor whites, primarily living in rural areas, are disadvantaged by systemic forces. Because our system of representation in the United States is primarily based on geography, and because housing patterns are influenced by economic circumstances, there are some dramatic differences in the constituencies of some representatives as opposed to others. While many elected officials represent diverse economic areas (US senators, for example, represent entire states, most of which have both rich and poor families, and big-city mayors often have very economically diverse constituencies), many others represent areas that are overwhelmingly wealthy or overwhelmingly poor. In the strictest sense, these representatives are responsible for giving voice to the poorest Americans in national and state legislatures, even (and especially) if other elected officials fail to do so. In attempting to understand the relationship between representation and inequality, we will consider the demographics of some

FIGURE 2.3. Poverty Rates by Region and Metro/Nonmetro Status, 2014–2018

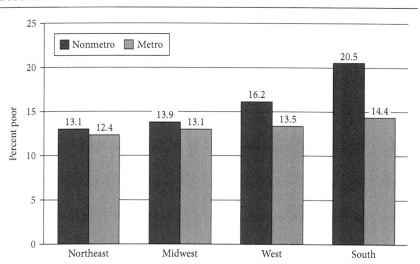

Source: US Department of Agriculture, "Rural Poverty & Well-Being," December 17, 2020, https://www.ers.usda.gov/topics/rural-economy-population/rural-poverty-well-being/#geography.

of the poorest areas in the United States and the officials who are charged with representing them.

As reflected in Figure 2.3, the highest percentage of poverty occurs in non-metropolitan areas of southern states.

The poorest congressional district in the contiguous United States[144] is New York's Fifteenth, with an annual median household income of $31,061.[145] Thirty-five percent of its residents (and 45 percent of children) live below the poverty line.[146] José Serrano, who is a Democrat, represented this district from 2013 until his retirement in 2021.[147] It is now represented by Ritchie Torres, one of the first two openly gay black men elected to Congress.[148] Kentucky's Fifth District, represented by Harold "Hal" Rogers, who is a Republican, is also among the most impoverished congressional districts in the nation with an annual median household income of $35,636.[149] Twenty-five percent of its residents (and 32 percent of children) live below the poverty line. Torres's district is distinctly urban (covering the South Bronx); Rogers's is rural. Torres's district is 64 percent Hispanic and 30 percent African American[150] Rogers's district is 95 percent white.[151] Of the ten poorest congressional districts,[152] only Rogers's and Louisiana's 5th are majority non-Hispanic white.[153] Two are majority Hispanic (New York 15 and Texas 34), and six are majority black (Alabama 7, Georgia 2, Michigan 13, Mississippi 2, Ohio 11, and South Carolina 6).[154] Eight of the districts are represented by Democrats.[155] Two of the representatives of America's poorest congressional districts are Hispanic,[156] five are non-Hispanic African American, one is Palestinian American, and one is non-Hispanic white.[157] Six of the representatives are men.

Leaving aside questions about voting behavior of constituents,[161] it is important to consider what this means at a policy level. All ten of these

Box 2.3. *Representing:* Alexandria Ocasio-Cortez

The 2018 midterm elections brought in the most diverse classes of first-year members of Congress in the nation's history. One hundred non-incumbents won seats, with an average age of 49—the youngest class in three election cycles.[158] Among those elected that year was Alexandria Ocasio-Cortez from New York's 14th congressional district, encompassing parts of the Bronx and Queens.

Ocasio-Cortez's story caught the attention of the press nationwide, and she has remained one of the most visible members of what is often referred to as the progressive wing of the Democratic Party. At age 29, she was able to command attention from younger citizens by effectively leveraging social media platforms (she livestreamed herself making food or putting together Ikea furniture while answering questions and talking about her political, social, and economic policy preferences).[159] A self-described democratic socialist, Ocasio-Cortez has pressured those in her party, as well as Republicans, to consider large, systemic issues and the ways they affect America's most vulnerable citizens. From her Green New Deal plan, which seeks to acknowledge and ultimately stem climate change while providing jobs in a reimagined economy to abolishing the Immigration and Customs Enforcement (ICE) agency,[160] Ocasio-Cortez has captured the excitement and imagination of a significant section of the population with the rare combination of an accessible nature and lofty, sophisticated approach to politics.

House members have constituents who are very poor but differ from one another in many ways. How might these representatives work together to consider policies that could help their citizens? Should they? If inequality is a result of individual shortcomings and behavioral elements, it is difficult to argue that there should be any governmental solutions to alleviate it. If, however, systemic factors contribute to and perpetuate economic and racial inequality, then it would seem that these officials, as well as others who represent large numbers of poor families, would have their sights set on advocating for meaningful change that will result in more opportunities for Americans who are suffering the most.

Conclusion

It is tempting to think of income as fluid (relating to securing a job, losing a job, getting a raise or a promotion, etc.) while wealth is more or less stable, growing over time (where possible). This characterization is inappropriate, though, as losses in income or an unexpected rise in expenses (due to an illness, a death in the family, etc.) can lead to a sudden and dramatic drop in wealth. According to sociologist Dalton Conley, "a significant proportion of individuals in the U.S. experience at least one drop in wealth."[162] Whites and African Americans have approximately the same number of drops (on average), but African Americans are more likely to have a greater drop.[163]

Researchers Shapiro, Meschede, and Sullivan argue that while America's racist past is certainly a driving factor behind the existence of the racial wealth gap, the fourfold increase in such a short time reflects policies, such as tax cuts on investment income and inheritances, which benefit the wealthiest, and redistribute wealth and opportunities. Tax deductions for home mortgages, retirement accounts, and college savings all disproportionately benefit higher income families. At the same time, evidence from multiple sources demonstrates the powerful role of persistent discrimination in housing, credit, and labor markets.

They note that persons of color pay more to access credit and are particularly susceptible to predatory lending in the mortgage industry. In short, while there may be overt, individualized bigotry involved in shaping income and wealth inequality, such incidents cannot come close to explaining these larger trends. First, while income and wealth inequality are pronounced between whites and persons of color, there is a tremendous

FIGURE 2.4. Cycle of Advantage and Disadvantage

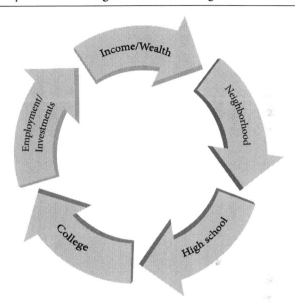

gap between the highest earning whites and all other whites, as well. Second, the policies that perpetuate and exacerbate these trends are ostensibly colorblind. That is, they are not infused with explicit advantages for whites or disadvantages for persons of color.

Taking a colorblind approach to policy within a racist systemic context cannot lead to increased equality. As Figure 2.4 indicates, there is a cycle of advantage and disadvantage that centers on three major elements of American life: jobs, education, and housing. To earn access to the middle class in the twenty-first century, a college degree is increasingly necessary. Gaining admission into and succeeding in college is more difficult if one does not have a rigorous education in high school (which begins in elementary school). Because most areas fund the local public school districts disproportionately through property tax revenues, the neighborhood in which one lives is strongly related to the quality of education that is available. Of course, most people live in the neighborhood they can afford, so having money in the first place is important. This can be thought of as a cycle of disadvantage, but it is also a cycle of advantage. That is, if one is disadvantaged, it is quite difficult to break the cycle and gain access to economic security (let alone prosperity). Conversely, those who are privileged to be in an advantageous position have numerous opportunities to avoid falling into economic despair.

The cycle is not a guarantee of success or failure. There are many Americans who started in poverty and became financially comfortable and even wealthy, and there are wealthy individuals who fall on hard times and are unable to recover. The idea, however, is that the starting line is not the same for everyone, and that far from simply being behind (as the foot race metaphor suggests), there are systemic obstacles that are difficult to overcome. Many ideas and programs have been designed to interrupt this cycle at various points. As will become clear in the following chapters, the reasons for its persistence are complicated and affected by other related elements (such as disparities in health and in the criminal justice system). Solutions are multifaceted and present opportunities and challenges for ordinary Americans to become involved and make a difference.

Discussion Questions

1. St. John's University professor Allan Ornstein claims that the United States is witnessing the rise of an aristocratic class. Do you agree or disagree with this observation? What evidence can you offer to support your position? In what ways might the rise of an aristocratic class hinder or improve American democracy?

2. Does the existence (and persistence) of wealth and income gaps in the United States lend support for substantive representation or symbolic representation? Why?

3. In the welfare section of this chapter, we encounter some negative stereotypes about poverty and wealth. To what extent have you heard these claims? By whom? In what ways can average Americans work to dispel these myths and stereotypes? What can be done at the elite level? Does the government have a role to play in helping citizens to think beyond stereotypes like these?

4. Discuss Thomas Woods's argument regarding the source of poverty. Is his opinion likely to resonate with Americans? Is it consistent with American values? If so, which? Does it contradict any

core American values? If so, which? Discuss how these core values affect the discussion of poverty in the United States.

5. Consider the heterogeneity of America's impoverished regions. Do you perceive this to be a barrier to combating poverty? Why or why not? If you believe that it is an issue, what could possibly be done to help overcome it?

6. Discuss each element of the cycle of advantage and disadvantage (Figure 2.4). Provide examples of salient policy issues that are relevant to the various elements.

3

....

Housing

PERHAPS WE SHOULD BEGIN OUR EXPLORATION OF HOUSING IN equality with some normative questions that can serve as a baseline. After all, we are interested in not only the *difference* in housing that exists in America, but also the degree to which there is access to *sufficient* housing. Are Americans entitled to any housing at all? If so, what sort? Basic shelter (i.e., protection from the weather)? Security from harm? Is access to electricity a right? Plumbing? Internet? If so, is it enough to make sure that Americans are not denied these services? Should they be provided to those who cannot afford them? Does everyone have a right to live in a mansion? Does anyone? What about owning two mansions? Or ten? Should some Americans have two or three homes when others do not have even one? If not, would it be fair to prohibit wealthy individuals from buying additional homes? What if they rent them to those who cannot afford to buy? Should there be a limit on how much rent they can charge or how much they can raise it from lease to lease? Where do we draw the lines in the proverbial sand? What is reasonable to expect from a wealthy nation such as the United States, and how much should be left to the free market? It is hard to argue against the notion that access to shelter is a basic human right, but how is "shelter" defined, and to what lengths are we willing to go to protect all citizens' housing rights? Answers to these questions form the basis for guidelines to which policymakers must be attentive in a representative democracy. Simply considering them is the first step to providing a blueprint for how we want our leaders to act.

The Roots of Disadvantage

For most Americans, their home is their largest asset, though many Americans are unable to achieve home ownership at all, and many own a home in an area (rural or urban alike) that is substandard by a number

DOI: 10.4324/9781003043041-4

of criteria. It has been estimated that "upwards of 100 million people in the United States live in housing that is physically inadequate, in unsafe neighborhoods, over-crowded or way beyond what they can reasonably afford."[1] In addition, discriminatory redlining (see below) policies during much of the twentieth century resulted in greatly segregated housing patterns that feature wealthy suburbs and poorer inner-city neighborhoods and rural areas.

As indicated in Figure 2.4 (page 71), one of the elements of systemic inequality is housing.[2] The route to economic security runs through our neighborhoods for three reasons: (1) our system of representation is based on geography; (2) access to quality education is related to place of residence; and (3) access to jobs—especially for those who do not have reliable transportation—relies on affordable housing near employment centers. After emancipation, and especially since the Great Migration, African Americans became concentrated in America's largest urban centers while continuing to live in rural areas of former slaveholding states. In recent years, however, African Americans in particular have been leaving urban centers, in what some have called, "a reverse Great Migration."[3] Latinos, who are now the second largest ethnic group in the United States (19 percent of the population),[4] live in every state but most prominently in rural areas in the South, suburban and urban areas in the Midwest and Northeast, and, most heavily, in the Southwest (particularly Southern California, New Mexico, Arizona, and Texas) and southern Florida.[5]

These broad geographical guidelines are helpful in terms of understanding issues of representation, as state legislators often take racial and ethnic housing patterns into account when drawing legislative district lines (see Chapter 1). With respect to systemic advantages and disadvantages, however, smaller units of analysis are relevant. School districts are organized mostly around neighborhoods in densely populated areas, and access to schools, healthful food, and jobs is often more limited in low-income areas (both urban and rural). And homelessness has adverse consequences that extend beyond lack of shelter. In this chapter, we will explore historic and current patterns of housing inequality in order to understand the relationship between housing and opportunities for equality in education, employment, and health.

Opportunities for Home Ownership

Owning a home is a core component of the American Dream, but on any given night, more than half a million Americans not only do not own a home, but are also sleeping outside, in an emergency shelter, or participating in a transitional housing program.[6] Many others are staying with friends or relatives on a temporary basis. Figure 3.1 shows the percentage of homeless individuals by the type of shelter they had (or did not have). Nearly one-third of the homeless population includes families with children, which is difficult to measure accurately. The US government reports just over 100,000 individuals under the age of 18 were homeless in 2019,[7] but that "does not count precariously housed or doubled-up families, only those living on the street or in shelters."[8] While most homeless persons are white (47.7 percent), they are disproportionately African American (39.8 percent) and Latino (22 percent).[9] On the whole, the number of homeless individuals has dipped in recent years, though that overall trend masks some significant increases in major cities

FIGURE 3.1. **Percent of Homeless Persons by Household Type and Sheltered Status, 2019**

Source: Meghan Henry, Rian Watt, Anna Mahathey, Jillian Ouellette, and Aubrey Sitler, "The 2019 Annual Homeless Assessment Report to Congress," US Department of Housing and Urban Development, January 2020, https://www.huduser.gov/portal/sites/default/files/pdf/2019-AHAR-Part-1.pdf.

like Los Angeles and New York.[10] Although the vast majority of homeless persons are not chronically homeless,[11] being without shelter for even a couple of days presents challenges that can quickly accumulate and prove to be debilitating.

People are homeless for a number of reasons, including (but not limited to) job loss, domestic abuse, medical or other emergency in the family, mental disorders, and addiction. About one-fifth of homeless adults struggle with mental illness, substance abuse, or health challenges,[12] though advocates point out that these conditions are often a result of homelessness rather than a cause.[13] Most homeless persons have worked within the past month.[14] These facts, however, deeply cut against most Americans' image of the homeless as being on the street as a result of being insane, addicted, and/or lazy. Such stereotypes undermine empathy for homeless Americans, which in turn makes it difficult for policymakers to place the issue atop the list of those to be addressed. After all, if individuals are homeless because of bad choices they made (assuming they had a reasonable start in life), few Americans would support using governmental resources to help them. If there are systemic reasons for homelessness that put individuals at a distinct disadvantage from a very early age or because of situations beyond their control (e.g., returning home from military service or an illness), then it is more likely that we would turn to our elected officials for help.

In addition to various state initiatives, the federal government has been involved in helping Americans to find affordable housing since the Great Depression. In 1934, Congress created the Federal Housing Administration (FHA) to encourage banks to offer home loans to individuals and families. That program has resulted in some 46 million home loan mortgages.[15] The Housing Act of 1937 established the United States Housing Authority (USHA) to subsidize the building of low-rent public housing. In 1938 and 1970, Fannie Mae and Freddie Mac were created, respectively, to increase the amount of home ownership money available in the lending market.[16] In 1965, the Department of Housing and Urban Development (HUD) was created as a cabinet-level agency.[17] These efforts were largely successful for decades, but when the housing bubble burst in 2008, ushering in the Great Recession, millions of Americans found themselves either in foreclosure or in a home that was worth less than the amount owed on it.[18] This means that many homeowners—particularly those who had not been in their home for very long—owed more than their home is worth, which made refinancing more difficult or impossible, contributing to the debt cycle for these families and individuals. Homeownership continued to decline since 2006, reaching a historic low in the summer of 2016.[19] The rate steadily climbed throughout the Trump Administration until it saw a sharp decline in the summer of 2020 (during the Covid-19 pandemic).[20]

The 2008 housing crisis was created by risky lending practices and complex financial arrangements among lenders and traders that greatly overvalued the properties they were backing.[21] While that created a housing boom for a period of time, which resulted in a record

Box 3.1. *Representing*: Mike Lee

While government entities are largely responsible for and involved in helping to set and execute housing policy, there is a strong role for the private sector, as well. After all, developers build units with the goal of making a profit, and landlords with rental property are similarly not primarily focused on charitable gestures. So what is the role of the private sector in solving the affordable housing crisis?

US Senator Mike Lee, Republican of Utah, has weighed in on this issue directly and through surrogates in the last few years. Situating the issue within a wider concern about erosion of the traditional family unit, Lee notes that "if we care about the strength of the American family, then we should also care about high housing prices."[23] At a public forum, Senator Lee's legislative correspondent, Heath Hansen, identified a "false choice" between government and private solutions. He believes that families, neighborhoods, churches, and businesses can play an important role alongside government initiatives.[24]

Senator Lee points to innovative initiatives, such as Modal Living's "accessory dwelling units," which are "pre-fab" dwellings that can be placed on existing properties at low costs and with high levels of mobility,[25] as just one example of how creative energy in the entrepreneurial sphere can move toward greater levels of housing security and quality for Americans.[26]

number of Americans owning a home in the early part of the twenty-first century (largely as a result of low-interest rates), many of the loans had adjustable interest rates. When the initial offering rate expired, home owners faced monthly payments that they could not afford. Complicating this was an increasing demand for packages of securities backed by these mortgages. Several large investment firms fell apart, and a domino effect was instigated.[22] Even though mortgage rates remained low through the Great Recession, the housing market stagnated because investors were hesitant to lend, especially to borrowers with less than stellar credit ratings, and existing home owners had trouble selling their home to buy another.

In some areas, renting is a safe and affordable option, but it is not optimal for a number of reasons. First, although renters do not need to have the same credit rating or income as home buyers, they may find it difficult to produce the up-front money necessary to rent a desirable unit. Often a lump sum equal to two months' rent and an additional month's rent in security deposit is required before occupancy. This forces many to rent more costly (and often less desirable) motel rooms by the week or by the month. Similar to the rent-to-own and payday loan practices described in Chapter 2, these arrangements have short-term utility, but they are costly over the long term. For the money spent, more stable accommodations in a traditional rental unit might have been purchased, but saving enough for the deposit can be impossible. Second, not all landlords maintain their property well (including cities responsible for maintaining public housing). Living quarters can deteriorate without regular maintenance. Renters are not responsible for repairs and often cannot afford to make them or are prevented by the lease from doing so. Whereas home owners receive a deduction on their federal income taxes for the interest they pay on their mortgage, renters are not similarly rewarded. Finally, although renting may be initially affordable, rent prices can increase from year to year, and moving is often expensive as well. As a result, Americans with few resources to begin with can be stuck in a costly cycle of disadvantage that home owners can avoid. More than that, renting produces no equity to draw on for the future, and there are adverse effects on property values when a high percentage of units are rentals. Further, many believe that there is an increased sense of community when individuals have long-term investments in homes, so becoming a "nation of renters" has effects beyond the immediate, individual-level inability to access the American Dream.

The USHA continues to work with local housing authorities to provide low-rent options for America's poorest citizens. Through the Section 8 program,[27] landlords can secure low-interest loans to rehabilitate a property in exchange for their promise to rent a percentage of the units to low-income residents. Individuals and families who qualify for Section 8 assistance can rent apartments in designated properties (or, through the Housing Choice Voucher Program, any available unit) at a rate below market value. The local housing authority, by way of grants from USHA, pays the difference in value directly to the landlord.[28]

In 1977, Congress passed the Community Reinvestment Act (CRA), which requires lenders to consider the rate of lending in low-income rural and urban communities when it seeks federal government approval for opening new branches, acquiring other banks, or mergers. There were scattered rumblings that the 2008 housing crash was a result of banks being forced to lend to poorer Americans in these communities, but a bipartisan congressional commission's investigation into the crash found that the CRA "was not a significant factor in subprime lending or the crisis."[29] While direct accusations that people of color were responsible for the crisis were limited to the blogosphere, it was not surprising to many to detect undertones of racism as lawmakers, economists, and pundits searched for answers.[30]

Racial Inequality and Housing

The homeownership gap between whites and African Americans is as large as it has been in 50 years (30 percent).[31] Education level positively correlates with homeownership for both whites and African Americans, but once income is considered, there is no relationship. Put another way, the economic reality of the racial wage gap is more consequential than the positive effect of having a college degree, such that black households with a college degree or higher are less likely to own a home than white households without a high school diploma.[32] When black and Hispanic Americans do own a home, the median value is far less than that of white

Americans.[33] The reasons for disproportionately low home ownership among African Americans and Hispanics are several:

> Because blacks, Mexicans, and other Hispanics face distinct demographic, economic, and educational disadvantages in the housing market they may be less able to afford a home. Because these minority groups are younger on average and, in the case of blacks, less likely to be married, the life-cycle situation may also contribute to a lower demand for owned housing.[34]

People of color comprise a disproportionate share of the rental market as well.[35] We are in the midst of a decade-long boom in demand for rental units, largely fueled by the sharp and persistent decrease in home ownership following the 2008 crisis and the resulting Great Recession.[36] But the increases in demand have resulted in an uptick in average rental prices, which has not been matched by an increase in the salary of renters.[37] As a result the percentage of families that are "rent burdened" (defined as spending 30 percent or more of their pretax income on rent) is climbing.[38] The percentage of rent-burdened families grew from 19 percent in 2001 to 38 percent in 2015; there is a 12 percent gap between white and black renters. Further, as noted in Chapter 2, homeownership can provide an opportunity to build wealth, while renting cannot. According to a 2019 Census Bureau study, "[h]omeowners' median net worth is 80 times renters' median net worth."[39]

Irrespective of the reasons, inequality in housing opportunities has implications beyond wealth calculations. In the epilogue to the tenth anniversary edition of *Black Wealth/White Wealth*, Melvin Oliver and Thomas Shapiro argue that residential segregation is the lynchpin of race relations in America.... [Residential] segregation structures the "segregation tax" producing far less housing wealth in African American communities and the way in which substandard, inferior schools are located predominantly in neighborhoods where minorities and low-income families are concentrated.[46]

Racial inequality, like income and wealth inequality, is widespread and complex. With respect to economics, the housing crisis that began in 2007 and 2008 led to record numbers of foreclosures, so by that measure, we can identify a parallel with the increasing income and wealth inequality addressed in the previous chapter. On the other hand, neighborhoods are integrating with respect to race in a number of areas, though that story too is a bit complicated.[47]

Box 3.2. *Representing*: ACORN

Before it disbanded in December 2010, the Association of Community Organizers for Reform Now (ACORN) was the "largest grassroots community organization of low- and moderate-income people."[40] With some 1,200 local organizations in 75 cities (in 40 states), the interest group, created in 1970, advocated for housing opportunities and civil rights broadly in urban areas.

In 2010, a series of videos that were secretly filmed and edited by two conservative activists were posted on the Internet and covered by major news organizations. In the videos, ACORN workers were seen providing fraudulent tax advice to the activists, who presented themselves as a pimp and a prostitute. Conservative groups argued that the tapes were evidence of widespread misbehavior by the group, which had been in trouble previously for questionable practices relating to voter registration, as well as financial problems.[41] The videos put strong pressure on the group, as well as on Barack Obama, whom the group supported in his 2008 presidential bid.[42]

ACORN assisted America's poorest families—officials claim that the group helped more than 150,000 low-income families prepare tax returns and receive some $190 million in refunds between 2004 and 2009—but few organizations could withstand such accusations. Ultimately, most of the videotaped allegations were demonstrated to be the result of creative editing and partial information,[43] but the damage was done. Suggestions that a group that largely represented poor black and Latino families was engaged in illegal activity were easy for many whites to accept, as it fit preexisting stereotypes about persons of color being prone to criminality, looking out for one another, and being dishonest. A decentralized organization can be greatly harmed when its chapters or individual members behave inappropriately. The "bad apple" narrative often attributed to inappropriate behavior in corporate America is rarely applied to the poor or to minorities.[44] The important question is not whether ACORN's fate was deserved but rather what group will fill the role that ACORN served for two generations advocating for urban communities. To date, none has, though its legacy has been helpful to those who seek to make voting more challenging: an August 2016 poll found that 40 percent of Donald Trump's supporters in North Carolina believed that ACORN would steal the election for Hillary Clinton.[45]

Racial segregation in housing has existed since the end of the Civil War, but the stories of segregation in the North and South are quite different. There were high levels of integration in the South before the turn of the twentieth century because prior to emancipation, free blacks were intentionally scattered so that they would not be able to organize or form strong communities.[48] Between the end of Reconstruction and the 1960s[49]—an era commonly referred to as Jim Crow—the racial separation of neighborhoods in the South was officially written into local and state law.[50] Jim Crow affected every element of public life—buses, railroads, restaurants, bathrooms—including housing.

In contrast, most prejudice and discrimination in the North at the end of the nineteenth century affected employment, not housing: "the typical black resident of a nineteenth-century northern city lived in a neighborhood that was upward of 90 percent white."[51] In the early twentieth century, black migration to rapidly industrializing urban centers led to housing segregation in the North. European immigrants were also ushered into their own areas, but intermarriage and entrance into the middle class resulted in more notable integration patterns for those Americans.[52] In contrast, white reaction to the Great Migration was more rigid:

Northern whites viewed this rising tide of black migration with increasing hostility and considerable alarm. Middle-class whites were repelled by what they saw as uncouth manners, unclean habits, slothful appearance, and illicit behavior of poorly educated, poverty-stricken migrants who had only recently been sharecroppers, and a resurgence of white racist ideology during the 1920s provided a theoretical, "scientific" justification for these feelings (Zuberi 2003). Working-class whites, for their part, feared economic competition from the newcomers; as first- or second-generation immigrants who were themselves scorned by native whites, they reaffirmed their own whiteness by oppressing a people that was even lower in the racial hierarchy (Ignatiev 1996).[53]

These attitudinal and behavioral components became manifested in structural elements that began as legal guidelines and informal practices and persist to the present. In 1933, a federal agency created maps that indicated creditworthiness based, in part, on the race of residents. The FHA adopted the maps, resulting in a policy that became known as "redlining,"[54] which reinforced segregated neighborhoods.[55] African

Americans were also kept out of white neighborhoods by violence (including bombings) and threats[56] and by the formation of "neighborhood improvement organizations" that influenced local policymakers, boycotted real estate agents who did not respect their preferences, and bribed black residents to leave.[57] The most prominent aspect of the neighborhood association was the restrictive covenant, a legally enforceable contract among white home owners who promised not to sell or lease to African Americans and members of other racial and ethnic minority groups such as Asians and Jews.[58]

Where legal documents were not in place or were ineffective, whites responded by fleeing urban centers. Even the presence of a single middle-class black family could set off panic selling by whites, often resulting in a white neighborhood turning black. White property owners dug in deliberately in their new neighborhood firmly establishing lines that created what are often referred to as ghettos.[59] After World War II, segregation in housing remained, but white flight, aided by public transportation systems and highways that provided access to employment, continued away from inner cities, forming the beginnings of the suburbs.[60] Such trends exemplify the difference between *de jure* (by law) and *de facto* (by fact) segregation. While the former was rendered illegal by federal legislation and Supreme Court decisions in the middle of the twentieth century, the latter has persisted as a result of Americans' attitudes and behaviors, as well as the economic realities of disproportionate poverty in communities of color.

Today, our cities are highly segregated on the basis of race, but there are trends toward integration, particularly in urban centers, as whites seek to live in the inner cities to take advantage of cultural opportunities and affordable housing.[61] This, however, creates a new set of dilemmas that must be resolved.

For example, the Cabrini-Green public housing center in Chicago was dismantled in 2010, replaced with mixed-income town homes and zoned for retail development. The housing project (as public housing clusters are often called) was more than 50 years old when it was demolished, housing up to 15,000 residents.[62] The high-rises were not properly maintained by the Chicago Housing Authority, became dilapidated, and were grounds for gang activity and other crime. While the units provided shelter for Chicagoans who might otherwise have been homeless, the conditions were sometimes horrifying. Individuals can disagree about whether graffiti is art or is used by violent gangs to mark territory (or both), but inoperable elevators inarguably make life difficult for senior citizens living on a high floor. Persistent problems with rats and cockroaches further compromised living standards and residents' health.[63] Still, people resisted eviction when the orders came to close the complex, noting that the community was tight-knit in some ways and was the only home many residents had ever known. Further, residents learned important organizing and advocacy skills as part of a community organization.[64] While some of the residents would be invited back to live in publicly subsidized apartments (next door to units whose owners paid market value), many others were forced to move to different areas of the city or the state.[65] The shift in focus—from clustering poor families together to dispersing them among middle-income families—presents new issues for public officials to consider. The hope was that the higher property values would maintain, largely because of the desirability of urban housing, with opportunities for better education and jobs to follow.

During the reconstruction, low-income residents were displaced, with a promise of "right of return." Columnist Eugene Robinson has referred to them as "the Abandoned."[66] A few years into the new developments, and just months after approximately 60 percent of Cabrini-Green's displaced residents moved back, there are mixed reports about how well the economic integration is working.[67]

To make matters even more complicated, employment opportunities have increasingly moved from inner cities to the suburbs, further disadvantaging low-income city residents,[68] unable to chase the jobs that they (or their ancestors) moved to the city to be near. Higher-income individuals are increasingly making reverse commutes from their urban homes to their suburban jobs on the very highways and public transportation systems designed to facilitate the opposite commute over the past half-century.

Poverty and Housing in Rural America

It is sometimes tempting to think about substandard housing as a function of inner-city life. While inner-city public housing projects often form the public face of housing inequality in the United States, millions of Americans living in rural areas are burdened with conditions that rival Third World countries (see Box 3.3).[69]

Box 3.3. *Representing*: Justin Maxson

With generations-deep Kentucky roots, Justin Maxson might be perceived as a natural voice for rural Americans living in poverty. His lifelong commitment to bringing attention and finding solutions to economic challenges in rural areas is anything but typical. For over a decade, Maxson served as director of the Mountain Association for Community Economic Development (MACED), an organization that works to reduce poverty in Kentucky and Central Appalachia through programs related to energy and conservation.[70] Although common wisdom would lead us to believe that citizens in these areas would be averse to energy suggestions that could be seen as competitors to coal, Maxson's projects have focused on "creating a new sense of what is possible [by creating] tangible examples on the ground of sustainable development at work."[71] These efforts, however, run counter to the direct representation of Kentucky's powerful voices at the national level—Senate majority leader Mitch McConnell, Congressman Hal Rogers, and US senator Rand Paul—all Republicans who tend to oppose environmental regulation and efforts to shift the energy conversation to include renewable sources.[72]

In 2015, Maxson left his position at MACED to serve as executive director at the Mary Reynolds Babcock Foundation in North Carolina.[73] In this position, he was a vocal advocate for private and public funding for programs that will disproportionately benefit rural Americans. A recent study[74] found that rural communities received only 6–7 percent of private foundation grants between 2005 and 2010, even though nearly one-fifth of the US population lives in rural areas.[75] Maxson notes that because of the vast expanse and lack of population density in rural communities, it is common for big-city foundations to believe that their funds cannot have a significant effect on economic growth. However, he points out that there is evidence that, by working with local leaders and slowing down enough to learn, then meaningful progress can be made.[76] In January 2021, Maxson was named Deputy Undersecretary for Rural Development at the US Department of Agriculture.[77]

The US Census Bureau and the US Department of Agriculture report that the nonmetropolitan poverty rate since 1967 has been consistently higher than poverty rates in cities and suburbs[78] (and recall Figure 2.3 on page 68). The poverty rate in rural areas between 2012 and 2016 was 2.2 percent higher than the national average and 1.6 percent lower than the rate in urban areas. In contrast, the poverty rate in suburban areas is 3.3 percent lower than the national average. In addition, according to the US Department of Agriculture,[79] the welfare reform policies discussed in Chapter 2 have posed disproportionate challenges for individuals and families in rural communities.

Especially since the 2016 and 2020 presidential elections, where national commentators tended to use the word "rural" as a synonym for "white" and "urban" to refer to persons of color, it is important for us to keep in mind the racial and ethnic diversity in America's small cities and towns.[80] To be certain, non-Hispanic whites comprise 80 percent of the rural population of the United States, but the 8 percent of African Americans is not nearly as small compared to their presence in the population overall (just over 13 percent) as many would assume.[81]

In rural America, as is the case nationwide, there are more whites in poverty than persons of color, but poverty in those areas is also disproportionately black and Hispanic.[82] According to the US Department of Agriculture, black Americans comprise 15 percent of the poor population in rural areas, holding the highest poverty rate of any racial or ethnic group (32 percent) in 2017. Native Americans' poverty rate was 31 percent, followed by Hispanics at 24.5 percent and whites at 13.5 percent.[83]

Even though the challenges faced by impoverished rural Americans are similar in many ways to those faced by poor Americans in metropolitan areas, they are less visible because major media outlets are farther from them and tend to cover them less frequently. Because of the structure of government at the federal level, there are fewer members of the representatives with rural constituents; US senators—all of whom have rural families in their states—are responsible for representing a much broader spectrum of citizen concerns than their counterparts in the House. As a result, poverty often feels urban in the United States, although in reality it is more widespread and reflective of American diversity than stereotypes allow.

Box 3.4. *What Can I Do?*: **Graduate Degrees in Public Policy and Urban Planning**

Postgraduate degrees are proliferating in the twenty-first century. As the perceived value of a bachelor's degree diminishes and colleges and universities struggle with budgets in poor economic contexts, graduate programs are increasing.[84] Hundreds of colleges and universities offer graduate programs or certificates in areas related to housing and socioeconomic/political issues. Finding the one that is right for you could open the door to a rewarding career advocating for increased equality of opportunity in urban and rural settings.

The programs vary in terms of focus, requirements, outcomes, and even names (do a search of the terms "urban planning," "urban affairs," "urban politics," "rural development," or "rural studies"). Some programs can lead to a doctoral degree in sociology, political science, or a related field, but also offer a gateway into public- or private-sector jobs centered on improving the lives of people in rural or urban areas. Further, there are a number of master's level degrees available. For example, Morgan State University (Maryland) offers a master of city and regional planning (MCRP) degree; the University of California, Davis offers a master of science (MS) degree in community development; the University of Akron (Ohio) offers a master of arts (MA) degree in geography, planning and geographical information science; and Oregon State University offers a master of public policy (MPP) degree with a rural policy concentration. Most doctoral programs are in traditional fields with concentrations in urban or rural studies, but others are more specific, such as the PhD in agricultural history and rural studies at Iowa State University and the PhD in urban studies at Temple University.

Conclusion

Our examination of inequality in America centers on disparities in wealth and, to a lesser extent, income, but central to those components is availability of housing and the benefits that availability provides (as well as the disadvantages that accompany a lack of access). Although home ownership is considered to be an important component of the American Dream, many policymakers and commentators do not believe that every American should be able to own a home because everyone cannot afford it. In fact, there have been a number of claims that the government's desire to help low-income families own a home was a primary cause of the Great Recession.[85] Such criticisms return us to the normative questions that opened this chapter. What should be expected with respect to housing in America? What is deserved by all? What is reserved for some? And, most important for political scientists, what measures (if any) should be taken to help low-income Americans gain security, invest in their futures, and take part in middle-class American life?

Even if we agree that all adults do not deserve to achieve middle-class comfort (presumably because of poor choices they made at some time in their lives), it is difficult to reconcile core American values of opportunity with the notion of punishing children who live in substandard conditions and, as we explore in the next chapter, start out at a further disadvantage because of the way the United States structures and funds its elementary and secondary educational institutions. With a college degree being more important than ever in a post-industrial society, housing patterns and in-equality—and the resultant effect on educational opportunities—will continue to serve as the linchpin to our ability to achieve social justice for all.

Discussion Questions

1. Consider the list of normative questions from the beginning of this chapter. To what extent do you agree or disagree with each idea presented?

2. Use examples from this chapter to explain how housing inequality intersects with other elements of inequality discussed in previous chapters. Then project forward to estimate how housing inequality interacts with education, employment, criminal justice, immigration, and health to perpetuate the cycle of advantage and disadvantage (see Figure 2.4).

3. Discuss the case of the Cabrini-Green housing complex as compared to public housing in your city or town. What are the

similarities and differences with respect to living conditions and public perception? What specific public policy complexities does public housing highlight? How should we, as a community, approach public housing today and in the future? Does government have any role at all in helping Americans to find and afford housing? If so, what are the minimal standards that should be expected for residents with respect to both quality of accommodations and their role as tenants or owners?

4. Compare and contrast urban and rural poverty while trying to avoid stereotypical thinking. Do the differences and similarities simplify or complicate public policy questions that center on housing inequality?

5. The boxes in this chapter present different approaches to addressing housing inequality: top-down (HUD) and grassroots (ACORN and the Babcock Foundation). Discuss the pros and cons of each approach and offer your opinion of which can be most effective.

4

· ·

Education

EDUCATION HAS BEEN CALLED THE GREAT EQUALIZER, AND THERE is little doubt that it can be (and often is). Particularly in a post-industrial age, most Americans who achieve economic and social success after being born into poverty do so as a result of their educational achievements. Reasonable people can disagree about whether equality in educational *outcomes* is a fundamental human right, but there is near consensus—at least in theory—that access to educational *opportunity* is. Even so, American schools remain segregated on the basis of income and race, and educational opportunities are quite unequal.

In this chapter, we explore the roots and persistence of education ine-quality in the United States. To that end, we start with a set of norma-tive questions. To what quality of education are Americans entitled? Does everyone deserve to earn an advanced degree? A four-year college degree? Advanced vocational training beyond high school? If all Americans are not guaranteed such outcomes, are they at least promised access to pro-grams that lead to those degrees? Or does the circumstance of each child's parent appropriately determine the quality of education he or she receives? If many of our schools really are failing, who is to blame? Teachers (some, most, or all)? Parents? Government agencies that fund schools and set standards? The mass public (for not putting appropriate pressure on poli-cymakers to improve educational opportunities)?

Recall Figure 2.4 (page 71). Educational opportunities are determined in a significant way by housing patterns, and educational opportunities, in turn, help to determine one's ability to succeed in higher education and secure a well-paying job. Accordingly, we will focus most of our attention on elementary and secondary education, but will conclude the chapter with an examination of disparities in college performance,

DOI: 10.4324/9781003043041-5   **93** as well. Along the way, we will see evidence of systemic disadvantage perpetuated by and within the American institution (education) that is designed to interrupt it.

The Roots of Inequality in Education

As we discovered in the previous chapter with housing inequality, disadvantages in educational opportunities are similarly concentrated in rural and inner-city areas, whereas suburban schools, by and large, show the strongest performance by a number of indicators. Also consistent with our exploration to this point is the fact that limited educational opportunities disproportionately affect African Americans and Hispanics. Before we move to a discussion of funding inequality, we consider the purely racial nature of school segregation that traces to the arrival of the first slave ships in the seventeenth century.

The idea of public responsibility for education has roots that run deep in the United States. Thomas Jefferson strongly believed in the importance of education and advocated for it during his lifetime. Compulsory education for all children (not just children of wealthy parents) was in place in Massachusetts in the middle of the nineteenth century, and by 1918 mandatory attendance through elementary school was in place in every state.[1]

Slaveholders largely prohibited education of any type. After all, if enslaved persons learned to read, write, and think critically,[2] it would be difficult to consider them property (and thus, inhuman). And educated enslaved persons would have a much greater chance of organizing to demand rights or freedom.[3] At the time of the Emancipation Proclamation, black literacy rates were estimated at 5 percent.[4] The transition from slavery to freedom was quite slow, so it is not surprising that beliefs about the proper role of education for African Americans were similarly slow to evolve to the point where no reasonable person in a position of power believes (or at least expresses) that a child's race or ethnicity should determine his or her educational opportunities.

Such acceptance of educational opportunities was ushered in at the turn of the twentieth century by such African American leaders as Booker T. Washington and W. E. B. Du Bois (see Box 4.1). By 1910, literacy among African Americans was 70 percent,[5] but there was disagreement about schooling beyond the elementary level. Washington focused on vocational

Box 4.1. *Representing*: Booker T. Washington and W. E. B. Du Bois

At the turn of the twentieth century, when women were still largely excluded from public and intellectual life, Booker T. Washington and W. E. B. Du Bois disagreed publicly about the proper route to political and economic justice for black Americans. Washington, who was born enslaved on a plantation in Virginia, attended school after emancipation and went on to found Tuskegee Normal and Industrial Institute in Alabama. Although he believed wholeheartedly in the deserved freedom of African Americans, his approach was at times conciliatory and tentative, particularly in comparison to his contemporary, Du Bois.

In his most famous address, Washington discussed the state of race relations and the possibilities of mutual progress among black and white Americans at the Cotton States Exposition in 1895. He explained that southern whites should not look to newly arriving European immigrants for labor but to African Americans to help pull the South out of its postwar economic troubles. He similarly told his fellow African Americans that they could find prosperity in the South, just as many of them were considering moving north to escape harsh treatment and to find opportunity. The most notable passage in the address has come to be known as the Atlanta Compromise: "In all things that are purely social we can be as separate as the fingers, yet one as the hand in all things essential to mutual progress."[12] He continued the speech by noting that the "wisest" blacks of his time understood that equality would not come from force or demands but rather from earned respect, and that vocational training for African Americans was preferred over liberal arts education.

Du Bois, while indicating his respect for Washington's work on behalf of African Americans, was unsettled by these suggestions. Du Bois was born free in Massachusetts, but faced his share of racist intimidation and harassment. After being educated at Fiske College in Nashville and later at Harvard, he studied in Germany, where he gained a global perspective on racial oppression and inequality. He completed a doctorate at Harvard. For Du Bois, suggestions that African Americans had to earn rights that were assumed to be granted "by our creator" to whites in America's founding documents reaffirmed the racist notion that blacks were not morally equal to whites. In response to Washington's philosophy, Du Bois wrote, "Mr. Washington represents in Negro thought the old attitude of adjustment and submission."[13] Responding to Washington's accepting attitude toward Jim Crow policies, such as literacy tests and poll taxes, Du Bois wrote:

> The way for a people to gain their reasonable rights is not by voluntarily throwing them away and insisting that they do not want them; ... the way for people to gain respect is not by continually belittling and ridiculing themselves; ... on the contrary, Negroes must insist continually ... that voting is necessary to modern manhood, that color discrimination is barbarism, and that black boys need education as well as white boys.[14]

Du Bois argued that the most gifted African Americans—whom he called the "Talented Tenth"—could, with proper education, lead black Americans through the transition from slavery to full participation.

While some contemporary scholars and activists regard Washington as overly submissive (and read through twenty-first-century eyes, he certainly was), most note that his pragmatism was driven by the reality of race relations of his day, and that he was being strategic in his attempts to gain full citizenship for African Americans. Du Bois continues to be a tremendous influence to scholars and activists who value education of the whole person and an approach to racial justice that considers fundamental psychological and structural barriers to equality.[15]

training for black men, but Du Bois argued for a more broad-based education that included such liberal arts staples as science, mathematics, and literature.[6] This disagreement on specifics did not prevent a push toward full citizenship facilitated by education and training.

The US Supreme Court's 1896 decision in *Plessy v. Ferguson*[7] established a legal precedent for having "separate but equal" public facilities—including schools—for white and black citizens. For more than 50 years, elementary and secondary schools were segregated throughout the southern states, and institutions of higher education (both private and public) openly denied admission to African American students. Even in the North, opportunities for free black citizens to attend college were rare, so during Reconstruction, a number of black colleges (what are now referred to as historically black colleges and universities, or HBCUs) opened their doors.[8]

In 1950, the Supreme Court heard the case of an African American applicant to the University of Texas Law School who was denied admission because he was black.[9] Heman Sweatt asked a state district court to compel university officials to admit him because his qualifications were sufficient. In view of the fact that the Texas state constitution prohibited integration of educational facilities, the court continued the case for six months so that the state could build a new law school for African Americans. When Sweatt refused to attend the new school, he appealed, and the US Supreme Court heard the case. The Court ruled that Sweatt must be admitted to the University of Texas Law School, and in the opinion, Justice Frederick Vinson set the stage for the more famous case (*Brown v. Board of Education*)[10] that came four years later. Rather than simply note that the newly created school violated the separate-but-equal doctrine based on tangible inequalities (which clearly existed and were enough to lead to Sweatt's victory in the case), Justice Vinson explained that more harm comes from racial segregation than disadvantage based on unequal facilities:

> In terms of number of the faculty, variety of courses and opportunity for specialization, size of the student body, scope of the library, availability of law review and similar activities, the University of Texas Law School is superior. *What is more important, the University of Texas Law School possesses to a far greater degree those qualities which are incapable of objective measurement* but which make for greatness in a law school. Such qualities, to name but a few, include reputation of the faculty, experience of the administration, position and influence of the alumni, standing in the community, traditions and prestige. It is difficult to believe that one who had a free choice between these law schools would consider the question close.... The law school to which Texas is willing to admit petitioner excludes from its student body members of the racial groups which number 85 percent of the population of the State and include most of the lawyers, witnesses, jurors, judges and other officials with whom petitioner will inevitably be dealing when he becomes a member of the Texas Bar. With such a substantial and significant segment of society excluded, we cannot conclude that the education offered petitioner is substantially equal to that which he would receive if admitted to the University of Texas Law School.[11]

It is this additional attention to the intangible inequalities that result from racially segregated education that Chief Justice Earl Warren (see Box 4.2) relied on in the Court's unanimous decision in *Brown*, as he concluded that "in the field of public education, the doctrine of 'separate

Box 4.2. *Representing:* Chief Justice Earl Warren

People often are surprised to hear that presidents used to appoint US senators, governors, and even a former president (William Howard Taft) to the US Supreme Court. Today, most appointments come from lower courts, which helps perpetuate the myth that members of the Court are above politics. When President Eisenhower nominated Earl Warren, the governor of California, to become chief justice of the Court in 1953, however, it was no secret that politics was at work, as Warren had supported Eisenhower in his presidential bid in 1952.

While neither Eisenhower nor Warren was considered particularly conservative, it would have been difficult to predict that Warren would preside over a Court that, just a year after his appointment, would make one of the most controversial decisions in history. Warren convinced all eight of his colleagues to support the decision in *Brown v. the Board of Education*, and the Chief Justice himself wrote the opinion.

There was widespread dissatisfaction and noncompliance throughout the South. One of the most notable instances was when Governor Orval Faubus ordered the Arkansas National Guard to block nine black students from entering Little Rock Central High School in 1957. Days of protest ensued and angry white parents gathered outside the school, shouting racist epithets at the black students. In response Eisenhower issued an executive order that sent members of the army's 101st Airborne Division to make sure that the students entered the school safely. The protests continued for weeks, and the students faced harassment inside the school as well.

Earl Warren was persistently criticized. Calls for his impeachment appeared on billboards and bumper stickers throughout the South. Eisenhower would call Warren "the biggest damned-fool mistake" he ever made, but most people now regard his actions as not only brave but also morally justified. Despite continuing racial inequality, few Americans believe that forcing African American children into separate schools was an appropriate policy. The Supreme Court, operating with full awareness of, but mostly immune from, public pressure made a decision that would have been politically impossible for elected officials to make. Earl Warren's actions represented the part of Madison's dilemma that is so often overlooked: minority rights must be respected, even if they conflict with majority will.[17]

but equal' has no place. Separate educational facilities are *inherently* unequal."[16] This statement—indicating that there is no remedy that maintains
segregation—was revolutionary and set the legal tone for the civil rights
movement that was to begin, rooted in the moral principles outlined by
African American thinkers dating back to before emancipation.

Much as *de jure* segregation in housing ended as a result of legislation and
subsequent attitude shifts in the latter part of the twentieth century, legally
mandated racial segregation in public schools ended in the decades following the *Brown* decision. And just as *de facto* segregation has continued in
housing, it continues in K-12 education.[18] The number of children attending
school with children of other races has risen dramatically since 1995 (from
5.9 million to 10.8 million), largely as a function of the diversification of the
American public.[19] Measured another way, the number of school districts
considered to be "diverse"[20] doubled, from 20 percent to 40 percent in that
time period.[21] At the school level, though, the picture is less clear. In larger
cities, a recent analysis revealed, very little progress had been made toward
meaningful school integration.[22] In short, the diversifying population in
smaller towns and suburbs results in more students attending school with
students of different races and ethnicities, but city schools remain largely
segregated. This is understandable given the housing segregation described
in Chapter 3, as most students attend school near where they live.

By some measures, then, America's elementary and secondary schools
are more racially segregated today than they were in the 1960s.[23] If facilities at majority-white schools were equal to those at majority-minority
schools, the rationale in *Sweatt* and *Brown* would still hold that children
of color are being denied their Fourteenth Amendment right to equal protection as a result of the segregation. As will become clear in the following
sections, however, intangible inequality is only part of the disadvantage
that African American and Hispanic students face in school.

Inequality in Funding

In his comprehensive treatment of educational inequality in the United
States, researcher Richard Rothstein notes that the overly simplistic common sense approach to addressing so-called failing schools (i.e., placing
the blame and burden on teachers) is inadequate because it ignores how
social class characteristics in a stratified society like ours may actually
influence learning in school. Low income and skin color themselves do

not influence academic achievement, but the collection of characteristics that define social class differences inevitably influences that achievement.[24] As Rothstein and others have noted, the amount of money flowing into schools is not the only concern. While it poses a significant challenge for educators, it is also a reflection of deeper socioeconomic hardship, which, as will become clear, also affects student learning.

The problem of vastly disproportionate funding in education stems from relying on local property taxes as the primary source of revenue for most public schools. The proportions in each state vary, but the federal government provides only 10 percent of the funding for K-12 public schools in the United States. The rest is composed of a combination of statewide distributions and funding from local taxes. As a result, there are tremendous per-pupil spending disparities between states,[25] as well as within states.[26]

The issue of education funding is fundamental to broad American principles in a number of ways. First, there is the obvious interest in having an informed and intelligent citizenry as a necessary condition for a participatory democracy. If citizens are unaware of how government works, unsure of their role in it, and confused about the issues of the day, those who have such knowledge (and skills to process it) are at a distinct advantage in terms of controlling public policy. Second, there is an element of federalism that complicates the first principle. If we believe that all Americans deserve to have access to quality education, who should pay for it? If some states think it is important to spend tax revenue on education and others prioritize infrastructure or services, should the federal government intervene? Finally, beyond the state-national division, there is the popular philosophy that the government closest to the people governs most effectively. Even if taxpayers within a state have a commitment to education, they must reconcile that preference with the idea that people can choose to live where they want—which is often at least partially determined by the quality of the school district—and that local areas will have vastly different levels of resources that must be distributed among the various budget items (police, social services, road maintenance and snow removal, etc.) that are important to a community.

The result, of course, is that even if the percentage of revenue is equal in different neighborhoods, the amount of funding available can differ substantially because of the amount of money in the community. Further, as state revenues were affected by the Great Recession and then the Covid-19-related recession, and state and local tax revenues have declined, there are increased challenges for funding public schools at all income levels.

Inequality in Outcomes

Much of the public discourse about education policy over the past decade has focused on outcomes and accountability, two concepts that are difficult to oppose in principle. The outcomes portion is clear: there are achievement gaps that can be measured in a variety of ways. Beginning with the *A Nation at Risk* report[27] in 1983, policymakers and the public have been concerned about how the nation is slipping with respect to student learning. There is a gap in achievement between the United States and other nations, as well as increasing evidence of educational attainment disparities between white students and students of color.[28] Data from 2013 were examined as part of an *Education Next* series commemorating the fiftieth anniversary of James S. Coleman's landmark study "Equality of Educational Opportunity." The findings are sobering:

> In both math and reading, the national test-score gap in 1965 was 1.1 standard deviations, implying that the average black 12th grader placed at the 13th percentile of the score distribution for white students. In other words, 87 percent of white 12th graders scored ahead of the average black 12th grader. What does it look like 50 years later? In math, the size of the gap has fallen nationally by 0.2 standard deviations, but that still leaves the average black 12th-grade student at only the 19th percentile of the white distribution. In reading, the achievement gap has improved slightly more than in math (0.3 standard deviations), but after a half century, the average black student scores at just the 22nd percentile of the white distribution.[29]

That gap has continued to narrow very slowly since the report was published, but it still remains.[30] In short, as with the racial wealth disparity that we discussed in Chapter 2, the gap is narrowing, but at a very slow rate.

The accountability portion of the argument is very controversial, as citizens and public officials look to identify the source of unsatisfactory outcomes so that remedies can be devised and implemented. The manifestation of this dilemma has been high-stakes testing[31]—standardized testing where the results are not only made public but also tied to funding decisions in a variety of ways. This approach has intuitive appeal but has received persistent criticism from educators and educational researchers. The most notable of the policies to emerge from this philosophy is the federal No Child Left Behind (NCLB) law ushered in by President George W. Bush in 2001.[32] NCLB was designed to provide stronger accountability, more local freedom, and choices for parents by way of proven methods.[33] But no reduction in achievement gaps was documented,[34] and Congress replaced it with a new law—Every Student Succeeds Act (ESSA)—in 2015. Unlike NCLB, the new law does not contain top-heavy incentives from the federal government based on standardized test scores. Rather, local districts and schools are empowered to craft interventions to improve student learning, and there are particular provisions in place to support schools with traditionally underserved students.[35]

For many scholars, the move away from standardized testing as a benchmark tied to funding is welcome. There was a sense that teachers were encouraged to "teach to the test" so as to secure (or not lose) funding under NCLB. To further complicate matters, it is not clear that the standardized assessments of student learning are accurate and unbiased. While seemingly objective test scores would appear to be a fair marker to determine how much students are learning (and how well teachers are teaching), there are several disadvantages to this approach.[36] Both race[37] and economic circumstances[38] have been found to affect test scores, but not directly. Children from economically disadvantaged families often go to school hungry, which can affect their performance.[39] Students who have a stressful home life—whether because they live in a dangerous neighborhood or because adults in their life face high levels of stress and may be abusive—have more difficulty with academic performance.[40] To the extent that America is characterized by racially segregated housing and a racial wealth and income gap (as well as nutrition and health disparities, which we explore in Chapter 7), we must acknowledge the interrelationship between these factors and academic performance. Further, as we consider the way that representation matters with respect to such policies, it is interesting to note that many of the strongest voices for charter schools, vouchers, and high-stakes testing in public schools were actually educated in elite private schools.[41] Even if they did attend public school, few grew up or currently live in areas with inadequate school funding.

If we reject standardized testing because it is problematic, however, we must replace it with another form of assessment because we must have some way to compare students against one another. In particular, institutions of higher education need to find ways to choose applicants for admission. Grade point average (GPA) is not necessarily an appropriate indicator. Consider a scenario in which one student, among the brightest in her high school, earns mostly A's, many of them in advanced placement courses. This results in her earning five grade points (rather than the standard 4) for each A, so she can graduate with a GPA greater than 4.0, even if she earns a B or two. Another student at a different school, who is similarly gifted, may not be able to take advanced placement courses because her high school does not offer them. Therefore, even if she earns all A's and scores as well as the first student on her board exams (ACT or SAT), her application may not look as attractive to colleges, even though both students took full advantage of their natural abilities and opportunities.

In fact, data from a number of studies reveal significant socioeconomic and racial disparities in students' access to and success in higher education settings. Finishing high school (which is a precursor to being admitted to college, absent completion the General Educational Development test, or GED) is largely dependent on socioeconomics and family history. Consider, for instance, that the high school dropout rate for whites (4.2 percent) is persistently lower than for black students (6.4 percent), Hispanic students (8.0 percent), Pacific Islanders (8.1 percent), and American Indian/Alaska Native students (9.5 percent)[42] and that there continues to be a gap in college-entrance exams (SAT) for both gender (males have a 15-point advantage) and race/ethnicity (whites have a 177-point advantage over African Americans and a 133-point advantage over Hispanics).[43] General Social Survey data reveal that children whose parents did not graduate from high school are eight times more likely to not graduate.[44] This is, of course, all connected with economic status.

As Figure 4.1 shows, college enrollment for traditional-age students increased overall between 2000 and 2010 and leveled off by 2018. Those increases held across racial and ethnic groups, as well as for women. Racial and ethnic gaps remain, though they are considerably smaller than they were two decades ago: in 2018, white enrollment was 39 percent, black enrollment was 37 percent, and Hispanic enrollment was 36 percent.

Moreover, the discrepancies are not magically removed for students who gain entrance into college. Figure 4.2 reveals the gaps in college degree attainment by racial and ethnic group: Asian Americans and non-Hispanic whites graduate at or above the national average for four-year completion, while all other races and ethnicities take longer or do not graduate within six years.

Students who drop out of college before earning a degree are characterized by disproportionate poverty: about one-third of poor students finish college, compared to two-thirds of students from wealthier families.[45] Recently, graduation rates at many historically black colleges and

FIGURE 4.1. College Enrollment Rates of 18- to 24-Year-Olds, by Race/ Ethnicity: 2000, 2010, and 2018

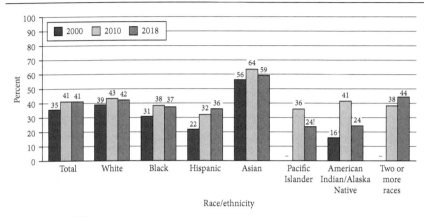

Race/ethnicity

Note: – Not available.

! Interpret data with caution. The coefficient of variation (CV) for this estimate is between 30 and 50 percent.

Data are based on sample surveys of the civilian noninstitutionalized population. Separate data for 18- to 24-year-olds who were Pacific Islander and of Two or more races were not available in 2000. In 2000, respondents of Two or more races were required to select a single race category. Prior to 2003, data for Asian 18- to 24-year-olds include Pacific Islander 18- to 24-year-olds. Race categories exclude persons of Hispanic ethnicity. Although rounded numbers are displayed, the figures are based on unrounded data.

Source: National Center for Education Statistics. "College Enrollment Rates," US Department of Education, n.d., [URL], based on data from the Census Bureau's Current Population Survey (CPS), October Supplement, 2000, 2010, and 2018. See Digest of Education Statistics, 2019, Table 302.60.

universities have risen,[46] though they are still low compared to predominately white institutions (PWIs).[47]

Besides the fact that poorly funded high schools may not prepare students for college as well as some better funded public schools in wealthy neighborhoods (let alone expensive private schools), poor students of color may face additional hurdles that white students who attended underfunded schools might not. For example, one study revealed that African American students who experienced stereotype threat, which is "a disruptive apprehension about the possibility that one might inadvertently confirm a negative stereotype about one's group," performed far worse on a language test than African American students who did not experience it.[48] In other words, simply being African American or Latinx in America—all other things being equal (and they rarely are)—can serve as a disadvantage:

The stark inequities manifest in inner-city and some rural schools help to explain the low achievement rates of large numbers of poor children, a

FIGURE 4.2. **Graduation Rates from First Institution Attended for First-Time, Full-Time Bachelor's Degree-Seeking Students at 4-Year Postsecondary Institutions, by Race/Ethnicity and Time to Completion: Cohort Entry Year 2010**

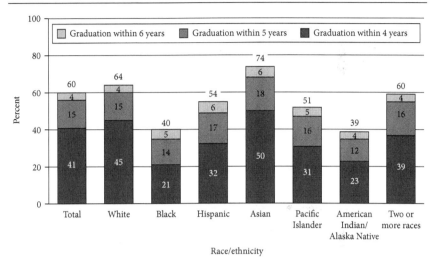

Note: Data are for 4-year degree-granting postsecondary institutions participating in Title IV federal financial aid programs. Graduation rates refer to students receiving bachelor's degrees from their initial institutions of attendance only. The total includes data for persons whose race/ethnicity was not reported. Race categories exclude persons of Hispanic ethnicity. Although rounded numbers are displayed, the figures are based on unrounded data.

Source: National Center for Education Statistics. "College Enrollment Rates," US Department of Education, n.d., [URL], based on data from the Census Bureau's Current Population Survey (CPS), October Supplement, 2000, 2010, and 2018. See Digest of Education Statistics, 2019, Table 302.60.

disproportionate number of whom are African American and Latino. Left unexplained is the lagging performance of middle class and poor African American and Latino children who have access to better schools.[49]

This is an example of the systemic meeting the psychological (Box 4.3). Even though middle-class minority children may escape the systemic disadvantage of underfunded schools, they may face other barriers to achievement. For instance, dramatic racial imbalances with respect to discipline have been well documented.[50] Many scholarly efforts have been put forth to explain the disparity, and most conclude that differential treatment of students of color as compared to white students is a significant factor.[51]

Box 4.3. *Representing:* Jonathan Kozol

Jonathan Kozol has conducted gripping research on inequality in America's schools. Having worked as a public school teacher, Kozol provides heart-wrenching depictions of America's most underfunded inner-city schools. In *Savage Inequalities*,[52] we meet children, teachers, and administrators at poorly funded, dilapidated schools in six cities. In addition, we learn about standing raw sewage in neighborhoods and rat-infested apartment complexes. In *Amazing Grace*,[53] we read more stories of crumbling schools and residences, as well as about the violence that awaits so many inner-city kids after the final bell.

Kozol's *The Shame of the Nation* (2005)[54] is his most pointed criticism of K-12 educational inequality. The book's provocative subtitle, *The Restoration of Apartheid Schooling in America*, primes the reader to think more deeply about our national priorities by using a word that is not commonly associated with the United States. Kozol explains that most inner-city black and Latino students attend schools with few or no whites. These students are "tracked" into curriculums that anticipate their failure and prepare them to overcome mistakes in their lives (such as committing a felony) in a way that predominantly white suburban schools would never consider. Corporations fund school-to-work programs that do not even suggest college, but rather put students squarely on a path to low-skill employment and, optimistically, management. Federally mandated testing with financial penalties tied to failure and the resulting test-based lessons exacerbate the trend. This, Kozol argues, leads to a race-based economy where whites are trained for advanced degrees and higher paying jobs (with access to power) while racial minorities by and large are not.

In contrast to a public discourse that often blames teachers and administrators for school failure, Kozol portrays teachers who love their job, love their students, and set high expectations, but are hampered by low investments (in the schools and the communities broadly) that result in few examples of success that can be used to motivate students to high academic achievement.

Through his writing, Kozol strives to make the families and school officials visible to those of us who do not have personal experience with such conditions. By educating America about the state of education in America, Jonathan Kozol is representing those whose voices too often go unheard.[55]

Box 4.4. *What Can I Do?:* Teach for America

In her senior thesis at Princeton University in 1989, Wendy Kopp suggested training outstanding college graduates to spend at least two years teaching in America's poorest schools. Today, Teach for America[58] has an annual budget of over $200 million and a staff of 1,400. Each year, nearly 20,000 applicants compete for 2,500 positions.

Some of the best teachers have not only earned degrees in education but have also spent years developing classroom skills, which calls into question the potential effectiveness of teachers who majored in other areas, received limited training (just five weeks), and will likely stay in the classroom for only a couple of years. The point of Teach for America is for participants to make a difference in the lives of children for a few years in the classroom and then go on to other professions and leadership positions, effecting broader change when the opportunity to do so arises. In other words, people who have spent two years in struggling schools will be less likely to make decisions that perpetuate inequality in education.

Donna Foote, who followed four Teach for America participants in her book *Relentless Pursuit*,[59] believes that while these teachers face obstacles (including resentment from experienced teachers), the lesson of the program is clear: do not "dismiss these children or relegate them to the ghetto. If you teach them, they will learn. They have something to offer, and we have an obligation to give it to them. This is a national disgrace—we should be ashamed that 20 minutes from my comfortable home, there are children that have no future."[60]

Still, Teach for America has received criticism over the years, for example, that it is little more than a résumé booster for privileged white students[61] and that the teachers do not do a good job in the classroom. While such criticisms were valid in the earliest days of the program, today nearly a third of Teach for America teachers are persons of color, and many come from state schools rather than Ivy League private colleges.

As large as the organization has become, it is only a small part of a larger national effort by teachers and administrators to provide the best education possible to all students, irrespective of their working conditions. Teach for America demonstrates how not-for-profit entities can fill gaps in social and political institutions and that attitudinal shifts, particularly among those who will be in positions of power, can lead to more thoughtful and sophisticated consideration of the reasons for inequality.[62]

Researchers Pedro Noguera and Antwi Akom report that a desire for peer acceptance, combined with "racial images rooted in stereotypes … diminish the importance of intellectual pursuits" among young minority students.[56] This internalized racism works as a self-fulfilling prophecy. It is a powerful but often misunderstood aspect of systemic oppression.

Because college degree attainment is associated with higher levels of income (see Chapter 2), the cycle we explored in Figure 2.4 continues. Worse, students who begin college but do not graduate often carry a burden of student loans, which are harder to repay without the income bump related to having earned a degree.[57]

Covid-19

The Covid-19 pandemic affected education dramatically, and we will not know for some time the full effects of any exacerbation of racial and economic disparities. In March 2020, students were suddenly forced to stop attending school, and teachers and administrators had to quickly pivot their instructional approaches to deliver in a remote format. For students who had a safe home learning environment,[63] enough food,[64] and access to high-speed Internet and computers,[65] the challenges were significant; for those who lacked any or all of those elements, continuing to learn at the same level as before the pandemic was almost impossible.

As we encountered in Chapter 2, the pandemic forced many people from their jobs altogether, which put additional economic strains on the most vulnerable. If it was not possible to buy students a computer (let alone several, if there were a number of students in school) prior to the pandemic, the loss of income put such a purchase further out of reach. For other low-income families, while jobs were not lost, their status as "essential employees" working in supermarkets or hospitals, for example, left them vulnerable to contracting the highly contagious virus,[66] as well as unable to supervise children who were trying to learn from home. Fortunate parents who were not laid off and, indeed, were expected to work from home, also had to struggle—particularly with very young children—to balance the students' needs with the demands of their jobs (in addition to the demand for electronic devices and Internet bandwidth for the entire family).[67]

Students who relied on school meals, the warmth of a school building, and the safety of having teachers and others nearby during the school day quickly found themselves without those necessities,[68] which added psychological stress to their pursuit of an education.[69] For older students, the inability to have in-person help preparing for college admission,[70] and the cancelation of sports seasons where many would normally compete for scholarships[71] added yet more barriers to access.

Colleges, too, moved learning to remote-only for the second half of the spring 2020 semester, and many continued to offer mostly online instruction throughout the 2020–21 academic year. Some high school graduates delayed attending college,[72] but this was no traditional "gap year," as both prospects for employment or travel (for those who otherwise could afford it) were slim. Students who were enrolled in college struggled to meet the new reality; many performed well, but others experienced heightened anxiety and levels of stress.[73]

Some small colleges that had struggled with enrolment prior to the pandemic were unable to withstand the loss in tuition revenue,[74] as fewer students came and those who did come needed more financial aid than previously. Further, many colleges rely on the revenue from dormitories and cafeterias, which were closed for several months and then opened at reduced capacities after that. With the additional loss of revenue from community-facing programming such as camps and fine arts programming, some schools found it impossible to keep the doors open, even with help from the federal government.

Disparities in learning for students of all ages will not be evident for some time, but it is expected that they will be significant and consistent with the patterns that we have explored in this chapter.[75] Policies and practices to rectify those longer-term casualties of the pandemic will need to be creative and aggressive or many of the gains that have been made over the past two decades will be erased or worse.

Conclusion

As is true with most important political issues, finding consensus on how to rectify the situation is difficult. First, some believe that inequality in education is appropriate, as it reflects inequality in other segments of American life, which is part and parcel of capitalism. In other words, if the adults in a family are economically successful and move to a neighborhood where the schools are strong, that is part of the American way. Without these sorts of consequences, the theory goes, individuals would not be motivated to work hard, take risks, and be productive. Most Americans, though, believe in equality of opportunity for all, even if one's parents have not been financially successful (for whatever reason).

A recent survey reveals that there is an appetite among the general public—at least in the abstract—to rectify the educational opportunity and achievement gaps. Nearly two-thirds of American adults agreed that it is "essential or a high priority" to close the gap between wealthy and poor students (though only about half that many agreed that it is a priority to close the racial gap).[76] In fact, empathy for black and Hispanic students was low among these respondents; nearly half said that the gap could not be explained by discrimination or injustice.[77] Still, whether the desire is driven by economic or racial considerations, there seems to be some level of public support for more educational equality.

This desire for equality of opportunity, however, leads to a second difficulty in finding consensus: we cannot agree about who or what deserves the blame for failing schools. For some, it is mostly about funding; if we can just make per-pupil funding more equal, each student will have a chance to succeed. Others, however, feel that "throwing money at the problem" is not an effective solution.[78] For these folks, teachers (usually teachers' unions) are often blamed for protecting bad teachers who are not using the resources they do have effectively. Third, if there is agreement that there needs to be more equality in terms of funding, how should that be achieved? Should the federal Department of Education provide supplemental resources? Should it come from the state (which is essentially a redistribution of tax money from wealthier neighborhoods to poorer ones)? Should we discontinue the practice of using property taxes to fund schools?

Among the more dramatic solutions proposed are voucher programs that would provide a certain amount of money to families to offset the cost of private school education. Those who support vouchers argue that they are effective because they force schools to compete for students or risk closing, which should increase the quality of education at schools or eliminate schools that cannot attract students. Opponents argue that putting vouchers in the hands of parents drains resources from schools that might be struggling precisely because they are underfunded.[79] Additionally, the voucher amount is rarely enough to cover the entire cost of school tuition, so only families who have enough resources to cover the difference can escape a failing school.

In January 2011, Kelley Williams-Bolar spent nine days in jail after being convicted of lying about her address so that her daughters could attend better schools near Akron, Ohio.[80] The case caught national attention because it vividly illustrated the desperation so many parents feel as they try to provide the best educational opportunities for their children.[81] Charter schools have become increasingly popular, allowing parents to group together to form quasi-public schools on their own with the endorsement (and funding) of the state. However, many states limit the number of charter schools that can form, which leads to over-enrollment that is often rectified by a lottery system. As dramatized in the documentary film *Waiting for Superman*,[82] there is a cruel irony to hoping for a random number to be called to be able to secure a good education in a country with so much wealth and an avowed dedication to providing (and mandating) education for all of its children. In fact, in 2016, the National Association for the Advancement of Colored People (NAACP) and a collective of groups organized by Black Lives Matter called for a moratorium on charter schools, arguing that they have "exacerbated segregation, especially in the way they select and discipline students."[83]

The case for school choice (whether through private school vouchers or charter schools) does not cut neatly across ideological lines. Conservatives champion the competitive nature of the process, forcing schools to produce measurable outcomes or close their doors if they (and their teachers) cannot attract students. Progressives who advocate for the poor note that the wealthy in America already have school choice—it is only the poor who do not.[84] Any program that does not relegate students to underfunded, deteriorating, and physically unsafe (both in terms of health concerns and the risk of violent crime) schools is a welcome shift in policy for poorer Americans who want better for their children. Progressives who oppose such programs highlight larger systemic issues in school funding, unfairness in testing, and dedication of teachers even in the poorest schools. They believe that every school should be well funded and provide quality education. Put another way, no child should be left behind. Because those left behind are not just left behind at the schoolhouse door; they are left behind at the college admissions desk and in the employment line as well. Some may resort to illegal activities to earn money and the respect of peers, further complicating prospects for employment, which could otherwise be an escape route from the cycle of disadvantage depicted in Figure 2.4 (see page 71). Kelley Williams-Bolar was studying to be a teacher when she was convicted of altering her address so that her daughters could go to a better school. As a convicted felon, she has to search for another career, which, as we will see in the next chapter, is no easy task for a convicted felon.[85]

Discussion Questions

1. Discuss the concept of education as a great equalizer. How do educational opportunities and educational outcomes play into this concept? Do our public officials have a responsibility to help secure either (or both)?

2. Does the federal government have a role in determining how states prioritize their funding? What about in extreme circumstances (such as when states spend significantly less than the nationwide average)? How does educational funding demonstrate an intersection between liberal and conservative ideological values?

3. What are some ways that capitalist principles rub against access to education? For example, while we value and seek to reward both hard work and success, in what ways are children vicariously rewarded and punished by the status of their parents? Discuss ways that we might address this friction if we wish to have more equal access to quality education for American children.

4. Consider the inequalities surrounding K-12 education and higher education separately. How are the challenges in addressing these inequalities different from one another? How are they similar? Does government have a role to play in attempting to rectify inequalities in either or both contexts?

5. Reflect on the ways that Booker T. Washington and W. E. B. Du Bois fought for the rights of African Americans. Does one approach seem more appropriate to you? Which seems more productive in today's political context? Consider how your own social standing and learned values inform your opinion about these different perspectives. Do modern leaders appear to be closer to Washington's approach or Du Bois's? Give specific examples.

5

∙∙

Crime and Criminal Justice

NOW THAT WE HAVE EXPLORED THE INTERRELATIONSHIP BETWEEN the wealth gap and housing, as well as the relationship between housing and education, we will examine how the criminal justice system is related to poverty and racism. Certain types of crime are associated with poverty, and as we have established, poverty in the United States disproportionately affects citizens of color. Felony convictions make securing employment much more difficult. We need to ask very pointed and complex questions about the way the criminal justice system operates in the United States. Of course, we collectively believe that persons guilty of committing crimes should be punished while those who are not are never falsely accused or convicted. If that ultimate goal is impossible (and it is), how should the system be structured to minimize the number of false convictions and maximize the number of offenders who are punished? Further, what should be considered a crime, and what are appropriate punishments for conviction? As we have seen with the legalization of marijuana, an activity that was once considered criminal (where convictions disrupted or ruined lives of perpetrators and their families) can later be deemed acceptable, with no restitution paid to those previously convicted. Irrespective of these answers, we most likely agree that race and ethnicity should have no bearing. To the extent that there are disproportionate arrests, convictions, or deviations in sentencing between whites and persons of color, we must consider the reasons for such disparities and the relationship to employment opportunities.

Social contract theorists have considered for centuries how to explain the way that societies are organized. Our Framers borrowed most heavily

DOI: 10.4324/9781003043041-6

from John Locke, who viewed the arrangement as an implicit contract between the people and government. This arrangement is necessary because absent formal rules (a "state of nature"), individuals retain the rights they have by virtue of being human ("natural rights"), but do not have protection from those who might seek to infringe upon them. Channeling Locke, the Framers wrote in the Declaration of Independence that "all men are created equal [and] they are endowed by their Creator with certain inalienable Rights, that among them are Life, Liberty and the pursuit of Happiness." While that sounds reasonable enough, if my pursuit of happiness involves killing someone who is bothering me, that infringes on that person's fundamental right (life), which is problematic. The Framers recognized this and followed the aforementioned phrase with another reference to Locke: "That to secure these rights, Governments are instituted among Men, deriving their just powers from the consent of the governed...." Collectively, we enter into an arrangement with government—not members of government, but the very notion of government. Like all contracts, there is a *quid pro quo*, which means that each side both gives and receives something of value. In this case, citizens receive protection of their natural rights from government, and government receives a voluntary relinquishing of some liberty (i.e., agreeing to follow the rules). If citizens break their end of the contract, it—to the extent that it applies to that individual—is void (at least for a period of time), and the government can impose punishment. If government breaks its end of the agreement, the citizens can overthrow the government. This delicate balance manifests in many varied ways, and as we will see, unequally.

James Madison famously wrote in *Federalist 51*, "If men were angels, no government would be necessary."[1] Since we are not, societies must have rules, and members of society should be incentivized to abide by those rules. The normative questions we face as we embark on this chapter, then, center on how we should punish those who do not follow the rules. How should we decide if someone has broken the law? Who should decide? Do context or extenuating circumstances matter? Who decides that? What is an appropriate punishment? Death? Disfigurement? Public humiliation? Seizing of personal assets? If removing one's liberties (i.e., imprisonment) is an essential element of punishment, we need to decide what that looks like. For how long? In what conditions? With what provisions for release? Should prisoners have available programs that might help them avoid committing crimes when they are released (see Box 5.1)? Or do we believe

---

Box 5.1. *What Can I Do?:* Veterans Healing Veterans from the Inside Out

Volunteering for organizations dedicated to addressing elements of inequality can be rewarding. Some, such as Goodwill (www.goodwill.org) or the Salvation Army (http://www.salvationarmyusa.org), are widely known and work to address economic inequality broadly, but others have unique missions that address specific aspects of the cycle of disadvantage.

Veterans Healing Veterans from the Inside Out (http://www.veteranshealingveterans.com/) emerged in 2012 at San Quentin State Prison in California. Ron Self, a former Marine who was serving time for attempted murder at the prison,[2] was working on understanding the complexities of the effects of the trauma he faced as a combat veteran. Moved by the high rate of veteran suicides,[3] he was motivated to develop a way for incarcerated veterans to work together.[4] In meetings rooted in narration therapy, participants respond to writing prompts and share personal stories to instigate insight into their struggles. Combined with yoga and meditation, the aim is to help incarcerated veterans "foster ... self-awareness and behavioral change that allow veterans ... to make successful transitions back into society."[5]

---

that individuals are fundamentally either good or bad, and no amount of work can keep a bad person out of trouble? Answers to these questions are no simpler than those posed in previous chapters, and they are important to consider as we seek to better understand inequality in the criminal justice system.

Due Process v. Crime Control Models

We are confronted with a stark reality that presents a fundamental dilemma: How do we know whether someone has broken a law? A seemingly obvious way would be for the person to confess to the crime. In June 2015, a young white man joined a prayer group at a predominantly African American church in Charleston, South Carolina. Partway through the meeting he rose, declared his hatred of African Americans, and opened fire, killing nine people.[6] The man confessed to the crime after he was arrested, and his attorneys did not argue for his innocence during the trial.[7]

However, not everyone who commits a crime confesses, of course, and not everyone who confesses has committed a crime. A notable case of wrongful conviction based on a false confession is that of the so-called Central Park Five, a group of black and Hispanic teenagers who were convicted of raping and brutally beating a young white woman as she was jogging in New York City in 1989. The boys (aged 15–18 at the time) confessed and served between 6 and 13 years in prison before DNA evidence (unavailable at the time of their trial) exonerated all of them in 2002.[8] The case garnered renewed interest during the 2016 presidential election because Donald Trump had taken out a full-page ad in the *New York Times* after the attack, arguing that the death penalty be reinstated in New York. He has never apologized for the mistake and, indeed, when asked about it during the campaign, said that he still believed that the boys were guilty because they confessed.[9] Yet false confessions have been involved in about a quarter of convictions that have been reversed by DNA evidence.[10] Most of us cannot imagine ever confessing to a crime that we did not commit, so why would anyone do so?

The way we empower law enforcement officials to do their work is at the heart of the fundamental dilemma captured by the due process and crime control models of criminal justice. If we assume that (1) society has an obligation to punish those who break the law; and (2) there will not always be a clear way to know when someone has broken the law, then we need to agree on a set of guidelines that strive to punish everyone who commits a crime yet avoids punishing anyone who has not. While this goal is impossible in a practical sense, we can consider a continuum with these perfect scenarios at the poles. Our task as a society, then, is to decide where on that continuum we should position ourselves. If we move too far to one side, too many criminals will remain on the street, unpunished; if we move too far the other way, we might capture most of those who commit crimes, but we also risk punishing innocent people. The former approach is known as the *due process* model.[11] Here, the most important thing is for government to follow its own rules, even if that means some guilty people are never punished. In this model, law enforcement officials have very strict guidelines for what they may and may not do, and deviation from those guidelines results in important sanctions. The other approach is the *crime control* model, whereby priority is given to punishing those who commit crimes,[12] even if that means that innocent people are sometimes wrongly convicted. Here, law enforcement personnel have wider latitude in terms of their own procedures in an attempt to not disadvantage them as they work to apprehend those who have committed crimes.

At this point, a wise reader will be thinking, "That's a false dichotomy; we can both limit government power and apprehend criminals." In theory, that is accurate, but in practice, it is much more difficult. The Founders were very interested in having a safe society, but they also desired to make sure that government (which includes law enforcement) would not abuse its power over citizens. Rights of the criminally accused (or suspected) are codified in many portions of the Bill of Rights: protection against illegal search and seizure (Fourth Amendment); the right to not have to incriminate oneself (Fifth Amendment); the right to counsel, speedy trial by jury of one's peers, ability to confront witnesses (Sixth Amendment); and protection against excessive bail and cruel and unusual punishment (Eighth Amendment). The axiom that individuals are innocent until proven guilty is relevant for the judicial branch (the courts), but would be impossible to implement for the executive branch (in this case, the police or other law enforcement agents). The notion that officers would not be permitted to arrest anyone until they were proven to be guilty is preposterous. On the contrary, law enforcement officials must decide whom they believe is guilty and then, within the rules we have established, work to capture them and attempt to bring them to justice.

The most powerful restraint on police officers has been the *exclusionary rule*, which holds that officers are required to observe the rights of those suspected of crimes while collecting evidence to be used against the suspected at trial. If any evidence is collected in a way that does not protect the rights of the suspected, that evidence cannot be used at trial. While it all seems rather neat here in these pages, in practical application, it is quite a murky area.[13]

One notable case highlights the dilemma between the crime control and due process models. After a ten-year-old girl went missing from a YMCA (where she was watching her brother participate in a wrestling match) in Des Moines Iowa on Christmas Eve 1968, a man who was living at the YMCA was arrested in connection with her murder. The arrest was made in Davenport, Iowa, some 160 miles from Des Moines, and the suspect, Robert Williams, contacted attorneys in both Davenport and Des Moines. When the police who arranged Williams's return to Des Moines refused to let an attorney accompany them on the car ride, the lawyer asked them not to talk to him about the case during the trip. Knowing that Williams was deeply religious, one of the detectives began a conversation about religion during the trip, and ultimately told Williams that he wanted him to "think about" the snowy conditions and that the little girl's family would be able to provide a Christian burial for her if only they could locate her body. Williams subsequently led the detectives to where the body was buried in the woods, and that fact was used in his conviction.

Box 5.2. *Representing*: Bryan Stevenson

As founder and executive director of the Equal Justice Initiative (EJI, http://eji.org), attorney Bryan Stevenson has dedicated his life and talents to providing legal representation to the most economically vulnerable. The EJI has been responsible for reversing convictions for over 100 wrongfully convicted prisoners on death row.[14]

Stevenson's grandfather was murdered in a Philadelphia housing project when Stevenson was a teenager growing up in Delaware. When he graduated from Harvard Law School, he began representing poor clients in Georgia, and later in Alabama.[15] Since then, his work has attracted international attention; South Africa's Archbishop Desmond Tutu called him "America's Nelson Mandela," referring to the icon who worked to bring an end to the brutal system of apartheid in that nation.[16] Stevenson is hopeful that his work will lead to a broader examination of systemic inequality, not merely a focus on individual miscarriages of justice. Recently, he has been involved in local efforts in southern cities to erect markers recognizing the role of slavery, so as to provide a fuller picture of the history of those cities and towns.[17]

Stevenson has been recognized many times for his work, including with the MacArthur "Genius" Award in 1995 and the Olaf Palme Prize for international human rights in 2004.[18] In 2016, he was featured on an episode of the acclaimed podcast *Criminal*,[19] his TED Talk has been viewed millions of times,[20] and in 2019, his early work was dramatized in the major Hollywood film, *Just Mercy,* based on Stevenson's bestselling book by the same name.

Brewer v. Williams[21] is a challenging case because while it appears that Williams's rights were, in fact, infringed upon (he was questioned outside the presence of counsel), we know that he is guilty (at least at some level) because he was able to take police to the body. Further, though Williams was informed of his rights to counsel and to remain silent, he chose to take the officers to the body (that is, to effectively confess). The Supreme Court ruled, in a 5–4 decision, that the speech by the officer outside the presence of counsel constituted a form of subtle interrogation and, therefore, should have been excluded from trial. (On retrial without the confession included, Williams was convicted anyway.)

These blurred lines present challenges for law enforcement officials, citizens, and defense attorneys alike. While some rules are well established, others remain in flux. Moreover, officers are routinely put in a position to make split-second decisions while pursuing suspects or investigating crimes, and those decisions form the basis of what will be the outcome of a case. To the extent that procedures are administered equally across subgroups of Americans, there is much to be debated; however, far too often data reveal that suspects who are poor and those who are black or Hispanic are treated disproportionately more harshly than their wealthy or white counterparts, and that leads us to another area of concern.

Police Brutality and Black Lives Matter

The most significant popular attention with respect to race and criminal justice in recent years has been focused on police brutality.[22] Anecdotes of officers harassing and brutalizing African American men have abounded for decades—immortalized in popular music recordings such as NWA's "Fuck tha Police," Body Count's "Cop Killer," Rage Against the Machine's "Killing in the Name," and System of a Down's "Deer Dance." But it was the extrajudicial killing of 18-year-old Michael Brown, who was African American, by a police officer in Ferguson, Missouri, on August 9, 2014 that propelled Black Lives Matter (BLM) to prominence. BLM was cofounded by Alicia Garza, Opal Tometi, and Patrisse Cullors in the wake of the shooting death of 17-year-old Trayvon Martin by George Zimmerman (and Zimmerman's subsequent acquittal).[23] BLM seeks to call attention to inequality in the criminal justice system, as well as dismantle structures that have perpetuated the unequal treatment of African Americans in all areas of society. That infrastructure would be useful when, in the summer of

2020, more high-profile killings of unarmed African Americans occurred, and weeks of energetic protests erupted in the streets—not only in the United States, but worldwide.

On August 9, 2014, Michael Brown, a black man living in Ferguson, was suspected of shoplifting from a convenience store in the north St. Louis community and was walking on the street when Officer Darren Wilson, who was notified of the theft, encountered Brown and his friend and confronted them, believing they matched the description of the suspects. A struggle ensued with Wilson inside his police car, and Brown outside, at the window. Wilson's weapon fired during the struggle. When Brown and his friend fled, Wilson gave chase, and when Brown turned around, Wilson fired a dozen shots, hitting him with six and killing him. Brown was not armed.[24] His body remained on the street for four hours after his death.[25]

In the days that followed, a number of protests—most peaceful, but some violent—erupted in Ferguson, in nearby St. Louis, and then all over the country. A month before Brown was killed, another black man, Eric Garner, was strangled to death by police officers on the street in New York City. The protests and national uproar that followed their deaths caused the hashtag #BlackLivesMatter, first used by Garza after Zimmerman's acquittal, to trend on several social media platforms. A powerful indictment of systemic racism, the phrase has come to symbolize not only the struggle against police brutality but also broader struggles for racial justice.[26]

Unpacking the phrase, we can note that it appears to state an obvious fact. This feature provides much of its poetic power. It ought to be intuitive that every life "matters," so the need to state that black lives do, in fact, matter, is jarring. In fact, an empathetic onlooker would affirm that all lives (should and do) matter, and indeed, that was the refrain from those who embrace a post-racial approach to American political and social life.[27] Social justice advocates quickly pointed out the inherent racism and privilege in such a response, however, noting that "all lives matter" is a theoretical and hopeful statement, but it does not square with the reality of many black Americans' lives. Worse, some argued that BLM—as a movement, as well as a phrase—was racist itself, as it suggests that the only lives that matter are those of African Americans. This sentiment was heightened as a number of police officers were killed by African American men, prompting the additional slogan Blue Lives Matter.[28] That, of course, brings the topic full circle in a cruel, ironic way, since the original phrase originated in the wake of police killings of unarmed black men. Activists and scholars have argued that the disproportionate number of exonerations of (or refusals to even indict) police officers in these conflicts is further evidence that black lives do not matter.[29]

When four police responded to a 911 call on May 25, 2020, where a suspect was accused of using fake money to purchase cigarettes in Minneapolis, Minnesota, George Floyd informed them that he was claustrophobic, was having trouble breathing, and did not want to enter the squad car. Handcuffed, Floyd dropped to the ground, while one officer, Derek Chauvin, placed his knee against Floyd's head and neck and kept it there for almost nine minutes, whereupon Floyd lost consciousness after calling for his mother (who died two years before the incident) and saying repeatedly that he could not breathe. An onlooker recorded video of the incident, which spread across the Internet quickly.[30]

This video evidence surfaced just over two months after police in Louisville, Kentucky, issuing a so-called "no knock" warrant for suspected drug activity, shot 26-year-old Emergency Medical Technician Breonna Taylor eight times as she lay in her bed. She died, as did Ahmaud Arbery in Brunswick, Georgia, when he was confronted by three white men (who, like in the Trayvon Martin case, were not police officers) chased him down, finding him suspicious as he was jogging, and shot him multiple times.[31] As with George Floyd, there was video evidence, which heightened the effect of the news. There was no video when other unarmed black men (and boys) were killed in recent years: Tamir Rice, Walter Scott, Alton Sterling, Philando Castile, and Stephon Clark, to name just a few.[32] Cumulatively, these killings, and the video evidence that sometimes accompanied them, have awaked a nation that for years turned a blind eye to such atrocities.

Beyond protests and slogans, there have been real effects of this increased attention. A recent survey of nearly 8,000 officers found that 86 percent believed that their jobs are harder as a result of these killings (and the subsequent media attention); 93 percent think that officers worry more about their personal safety than they had previously.[33] More striking, however, is the discrepancy in the ways that white and black police officers view race relations. That same survey found that 92 percent of white officers agreed that African Americans have equal rights in the United States; only 29 percent of black officers concurred; and "[w]hile 60 percent of white and Hispanic officers said that police relations with blacks were either excellent or good, only 32 percent of black officers agreed."[34] The degree to which officers' attitudes about race and African Americans in particular leads to increased killings is yet to be fully examined. "Shooter bias" studies are designed to examine implicit biases and the relationship between these beliefs and behavior. Simulating the life-or-death context of a real-world situation in the laboratory, of course, is challenging, and a recent overview of shooter bias studies found that the results are too inconclusive or contradictory to rely upon.[35]

Compounding the pain for members of the black community in particular is the reality that very few officers are charged and even fewer convicted of these killings.[36] Derek Chauvin was charged with and ultimately convicted of the death of George Floyd, which millions of people all over the world watched on video, but a recent analysis shows that even since Michael Brown was killed and more attention is focused on police killings, the number of charges and convictions has remained stagnant.[37] Families of victims have been more successful winning civil suits against police departments and cities because the burden of proof in those cases is lower (and many municipalities are eager to enter into settlements).[38]

BLM[39] is more than a slogan or a social media hashtag; it is a multi-national organization that seeks to foster systemic change with an eye toward justice. As a result, many whites—even those who claim to be racially progressive—have sought to distance themselves from a movement that they consider to be too radical.[40] The etymology of the word "radical," however is "at the root."[41] Because BLM is centered on significant, structural change aimed at dismantling white supremacy, not simply speaking out against prejudice or dramatic moments of injustice, their focus is very much toward the root of the problems we are addressing here. In that way, the organization is leveraging attention from injustices in the criminal justice system to eradicate the inequities that permeate each chapter of this book.

Since BLM emerged, there has been increased media focus on extra-judicial killings (either by police officers or others acting as vigilantes). At the moment, this is the most visible relationship between race and the criminal justice system, but it is not the only connection. Systemic disadvantage and implicit bias within the system is at once reflective of and a perpetuation of both racism and economic disadvantage.

A Case in Contrast: The Siege at the US Capitol

Throughout Donald Trump's presidency, he often relied on a number of racially powerful images and phrases to connect with his core base of supporters. From noting that there were "very fine people" on both sides of the deadly white supremacist rally in Charlottesville, Virginia in 2017[42] to asking the white nationalist group Proud Boys to "stand back and stand by" during a presidential debate in 2020,[43] President Trump trafficked in racist language[44] and well-tilled fields of racial animosity.[45] A consistent refrain that he invoked during the social unrest in the summer of 2020 was that we need to be a nation of "law and order." This phrase, which he aimed at rioters who looted stores and destroyed property (often hours after the organized rallies were over), has a long history in American political discourse that space does not permit us to explore fully.[46] It is relevant, however, to setting up the events that occurred on January 6, 2021, when an angry group of mostly white Americans stormed the US Capitol, entered the building illegally, and tried to interfere with the constitutional process of counting electoral votes, which rendered Joe Biden the winner of the presidential election over Donald Trump.[47]

The connection to law and order messages is multi-faceted. First, the force with which Trump condemned the multi-racial protests in the summer of 2020 is at great odds with both the silence and then timid requests for peace that characterized his communication on the day of the siege.[48] In fact, he was impeached by the House of Representatives (the second impeachment of his presidency) for encouraging the attempted insurrection that day.[49] Second, the storming of the Capitol was rooted in a falsehood that the 2020 presidential election was stolen from Donald Trump, a lie[50] that the President, as well as his supporters in Congress[51] and in the mass public continued to spread as winter turned to spring in 2021.[52] While there was no evidence of any level of voter fraud that would have come close to overturning the Electoral College majority for Joe Biden, the accusations were rooted in cheating in large, urban areas in four competitive states that Biden won (Georgia, Pennsylvania, Michigan, and Wisconsin).[53] The accusations are powerful in part because of long-standing stereotypes of African Americans being untrustworthy and prone to criminality.[54] It is no coincidence that the onus was placed here for a charge that the President leveled well before any voting took place: he told his supporters that the only way he could lose the election was if there was widespread cheating, so they were predisposed to believing that, when he lost, it was because of fraud.[55]

That frustration boiled for weeks as the Trump campaign lost legal challenges (more than 60 in all) in courts all across the country,[56] with many thrown out by judges appointed by President Trump.[57] When the destruction was over, five people were dead[58] from activities related to the riot, and a nation was left wondering how something of this magnitude could have happened in one of the largest and oldest democracies in the world. The explanation, however, is found within the pages of this book. Long-standing inequities and unearned privilege led to hostilities and frustrations, and the result was a powerful set of symbolic images, with Confederate flags flying inside the US Capitol building[59] that was overrun with white people demonstrating various symbols of white supremacy, from Proud Boys to Nazi iconography.[60]

There is a striking contrast between millions of people from all races taking to the streets night after night for weeks demanding an end to centuries of unequal treatment[61] and thousands of white people violently taking over the Capitol because they believed a lie rooted in a racist premise. Several commentators remarked that the events that day were "unprecedented" and difficult to believe.[62] While the Capitol itself had not been invaded since 1814[63] (and then, by a foreign power, not American citizens), the day can also be seen as a natural extension of a white supremacist ideology that has permeated the country since before its founding—despite the millions of well-meaning Americans who were shocked and offended by the culmination they witnessed that winter day.

Our last section of this chapter explores the inequities built into the criminal justice system—an important element of the cycle of advantage and disadvantage illustrated in Figure 2.4, even though it is not found directly on the graphic. Those injustices permeate because they affect income and wealth, as well as education, in meaningful ways.

Criminal Justice and the Perpetuation of Inequality

America imprisons more citizens per capita than any other nation,[64] and convicted felons are not proportionally distributed across racial and ethnic groups. Approximately 1.4 million Americans were incarcerated[65] and another 4.4 million were on parole or on probation[66] in December 2018. The incarcerated figure represents a 9 percent decrease from 2009,[67] and a 17 percent drop since 2006.[68] The probation and parole number reflects a 13.6 percent drop since 2008.[69] These numbers have been declining for more than a decade, though the racial gaps—which are also shrinking—persist: in 2018, African Americans comprised 33 percent of the US prison population (and 12 percent of the overall adult population), Hispanics comprised 23 percent of the prison population (and 16 percent of the overall adult population), and whites comprised 30 percent of the prison population (and 63 percent of the overall adult population).[70] Approximately 92 percent of incarcerated persons are men.[71]

Disparities in convictions are most dramatic with respect to drug violations. Before Chicago decriminalized small amounts of marijuana in the summer of 2012, 78 percent of marijuana possession arrests in the city were African Americans. Eight-nine percent of convictions and 92 percent of those jailed for small amounts of marijuana possession were black.[72] According to one *Washington Post* article:

> In 2003, black men were nearly 12 times more likely to be sent to prison for a drug offense than white men. Yet national household surveys show that whites and African Americans use and sell drugs at roughly the same rates. African Americans, who are 12 percent of the population and about 14 percent of drug users, make up 34 percent of those arrested for drug offenses and 45 percent of those serving time for such offenses in state prisons.[73]

In addition to the difficulty they experience in seeking employment after release, convicted felons in many states lose their voting rights.[74] While reasonable people can disagree as to whether such a policy is appropriate, it is important for this discussion because the disproportionate rate of African American incarceration subsequently affects the numbers of potential voters in the electorate, which can have significant electoral consequences that in turn can affect substantive and symbolic representation for black Americans.[75]

Apart from convictions,[76] arrests are also disproportionate in black and Hispanic communities. In 2019, 26.4 percent of all arrests were of African American suspects,[77] which is more than double the proportion of African Americans in the population. This disproportionate rate of arrests and convictions—even stops and detainments[78] that do not result in arrest—for racial minorities is facilitated by stereotypes that link African Americans and Hispanics with criminality.[79] The statistics in turn perpetuate those stereotypes.[80] Further, media portrayals of violent crime exaggerate these numbers, which results in a distorted view of the relationship of minorities to crime among the mass public.[81]

White Americans tend to overestimate black criminality,[82] and race of the victim is relevant. For all the fear of interracial crime, most black victims are killed by black assailants, and the same is true for whites.[83] In the midst of the national outcry over police killings of black men, several observers have noted that more African Americans are killed by other African Americans than are killed by whites, let alone by white police officers.[84] This claim, while statistically accurate, is problematic for at least two reasons. First, violent crime is proximate; because America is racially segregated, it is more likely for a victim of a violent crime to be the same race as his or her attacker. Second, the argument serves to shift focus away from unarmed black men being killed at the hands of armed government officials and places emphasis back on persistent problems in neighborhoods that are characterized by high levels of poverty. Similar to the claim that "all lives matter," urging a renewed focus on "black-on-black" crime rings hollow when it comes from individuals, groups, or news agencies who were not focused on relieving such suffering until they were asked to consider police abuse.

This complicated relationship between facts and perception must be considered in context. The numbers cannot be detached from the broader racial and socioeconomic factors that both affect and are affected by the presentation by the media and absorption by the public. Such fears and resentments undergird public opinion, which has an effect on public policy such as police tactics and procedures. For example, even before our focus turned to killings by police officers, racial profiling and stop-and-frisk policies had been under increased scrutiny for at least a decade. Defense of these policies is often justified by such cyclical logic.[85]

These trends have a striking effect on the ability of convicted felons to secure employment after release. Former inmates are "one-half to one-third as likely to receive initial consideration from employers as equivalent applicants without criminal records."[86] Here, as in every other area we have examined, race matters. Whites with no criminal record receive job interview callbacks about 34 percent of the time compared to blacks, who receive callbacks about 14 percent of the time. Whites with criminal records receive callbacks about 17 percent of the time (still higher than blacks with no criminal record), but African Americans with a criminal record receive callbacks only 5 percent of the time.[87]

There are a number of government-sponsored programs designed to help convicted felons to (re)enter the workforce. The Work Opportunity Tax Credit[88] is a federal program that provides tax incentives to businesses for hiring individuals from groups who have historically faced challenges in gaining employment.[89] The federal bonding program "guarantees honesty for 'at-risk' hard-to-place job seekers" in the form of a six-month bond with no cost to the applicant or employer.[90] The federal Workforce Investment Act[91] funds education programs and the development of regional workforce investment boards, which are designed to be collaborations of businesses, labor unions, and policymakers focused on economic development.[92] While these programs are not specific to convicted felons, the holistic approach they take can be a positive influence on the job prospects for individuals with criminal records. Finally, there are a number of state-specific programs—both governmental and not-for-profit—that are designed to help bridge the gap between job seekers and employers (see Box 5.3).

Activists, however, are addressing this problem from various angles. In recent years, criminal justice reform initiatives have been underway in many states, and President Trump heralded a number, as well.[93] Initiatives such as sentencing reform and decriminalization (and legalization) of

---

Box 5.3. *What Can I Do?*: Together We Bake

Founded in 2010 by two women with training in mental health and a desire for social justice, Together We Bake (new.togetherwebake.org/) seeks to "provide a comprehensive workforce training and professional development program to help women gain self-confidence, transferable workforce skills, and invaluable hands-on experience" to help them transition to the workforce and become self-sufficient.[98]

Previously incarcerated women are invited to participate in the training programs and work at the bakery, which is located in Alexandria, Virginia. Together We Bake is not only a training ground but a successful business operation that makes products sold in local restaurants, cafés, and grocery stores.[99] Graduates of the program sometimes return to lead groups and provide training to others, establishing a scaffold-type model that serves to encourage and inspire. Eighty-nine percent of women who have been through the program pass the exam for the ServSafe Food Protection Manager's Certification Course from the National Restaurant Association's Educational Foundation.[100] Holding this credential affords opportunities for supervisory positions in the industry.

marijuana are likely to lead to a continuation of the decline in the prison population overall, and perhaps to the racial disparities that have characterized it. Additional reforms such as expansion of voting rights after a felony conviction and eroding the practice of trying juveniles as adults are underway in various states.[94]

Conclusion

As of this printing, 15 states and the District of Columbia permit marijuana to be used recreationally;[95] 36 states and the District of Columbia permit marijuana to be used for medicinal purposes.[96] There is disagreement about the effect of the war on drugs on the spike in incarcerations,[97] so estimating how decriminalization and legalization of marijuana will affect arrests and convictions is difficult. This trend, however, raises important questions about our core thoughts concerning what is permissible and, conversely, what behaviors are appropriate to punish. It is important to remember that laws are written and enforced by people, and in a democracy, people can change laws and the policies for enforcing them.

It is tempting to think about racial disparities in the criminal justice system as being purely a function of blacks and Hispanics committing more crimes and, appropriately, being disproportionately punished. Such a view legitimizes our system as fair and race-neutral. As we continue to explore the intersection of race and economic opportunity with other aspects of social life, however, it becomes increasingly difficult to explain away the multitude of statistical evidence as being rooted in individual choice or behavior or in cultural norms. As we turn our attention to employment and immigration status, we should keep in mind the effect that being involved in the criminal justice system has on one's ability to interrupt the cycle of disadvantage.

Discussion Questions

1. What do you make of the phrase "black lives matter"? Given the context in which it emerged, are you supportive of its use in attempting to bring attention to and ultimately reduce systemic inequality? Has it outlived its utility? Have responses such as "all lives matter" and "blue lives matter" served to erode or strengthen its effectiveness?

2. Are you more likely to favor a crime-control model of criminal justice, or a due process model? Given that a perfect combination is desirable but impossible, on which side should we err? What sorts of policies should be put in place to reflect your decision?

3. What do you think about the fact that some states revoke voting rights for citizens if they have been convicted of a felony? What core American values come into play with these policies? To what extent do individuals convicted of felonies deserve to have a voice in the way they are represented when they are incarcerated? What about after they have served their time?

4. How and to what extent do the media influence inequality related to crime? Do the media have the ability to help reduce inequality in the criminal justice system? Do they have the responsibility to do so? Why or why not?

5. The United States is one of the only industrialized democracies to use the death penalty (it is legal in 32 states). What are your thoughts as to its appropriateness? If you are supportive, do you believe that it is likely to serve as a deterrent (to prevent crime) or an appropriate punishment for the most heinous crimes? If you are opposed to the death penalty, on what grounds do you find it problematic? Is the emergence of DNA evidence relevant to this discussion?

6

. . . .

Immigration and Employment

NOW THAT WE HAVE EXPLORED THE INTERRELATIONSHIP BETWEEN the wealth gap and housing, the relationship between housing and education, and the importance of the criminal justice system, we turn our attention to the ways that inequality in employment opportunities and immigration status intersects with those challenges. Whereas some very wealthy individuals can rely on investments to provide a revenue stream, the vast majority of Americans rely on work—either their own or that of a family member—to be able to afford everything from basic needs to luxury items. The ability to find and keep a job is at the core of democracy's promise.

The normative questions relevant to this chapter are even more complicated than in the previous chapters. While it is difficult to deny that each American has a right to a quality education, a safe place to live, or protection against improper punishment, guarantees of employment are thorny. First, in a capitalist economic system, it is expected that there will be some level of unemployment, underemployment, and discrepancy in compensation based on experience, training, performance, and so on. While an honest consideration of the employment dynamic in any system would lead to an appreciation of each and every component, we might agree that jobs requiring certain skills or that can be performed by a relatively small group of people should earn more than jobs that most people could be trained to do. That is, even though surgery could not be performed without the surgical assistants, the electricians who wired the room for lighting, the plumbers who installed the pipes, the contractors who built the

DOI: 10.4324/9781003043041-7

hospital, and the custodians who clean and sterilize the operating room, surgeons will be paid more because they have abilities that comparatively few others possess.

Thus, we need to focus on more fundamental questions: does each American deserve a job? If so, should a basic standard of living be expected with the compensation from that job? Should all Americans simply have a fair chance to have the job they would like to have? Beyond the basic standard of living, how should wages be determined? As we wrestle with these questions, we keep in mind Figure 2.4 (page 71) and the previous chapters so that we are mindful that all Americans do not begin with the same opportunities.

Discrimination in Hiring

In Chapter 4, we considered the role of education in Americans' quest for financial security. Education is one—and increasingly the most important—form of training that situates candidates for employment in comparison to one another. In theory, the person most qualified for a job opening will get the position. Neither race nor ethnicity, nor any other characteristic unrelated to the position, will be taken into account.

Reality, of course, does not match this abstract goal. In January 2009, at the beginning of the Great Recession, the unemployment rate for white Americans (7.8 percent) was lower than for Latino Americans (11 percent) or African Americans (13.4 percent).[1] By July 2010, unemployment grew overall, with black unemployment at 15.8 percent—nearly double that of whites (8.1 percent).[2] (This disparity is related in part to cuts to federal, state, and local budgets that occurred at the start of the Great Recession. Black Americans are 30 percent more likely to work in government jobs than are members of other racial/ethnic groups.[3]) As noted in Chapter 2, unemployment rates for African Americans hold to nearly double that of non-Hispanic whites, with Hispanic unemployment falling somewhere in the middle. This discrepancy is not a function of the Great Recession or the Covid-19 pandemic, however; the gap between white and black Americans has been shown to be persistent and impervious to the narrowing gap in educational attainment.[4] Further, black men, who have the most difficult time with respect to employment discrimination, tend to experience higher rates of long-term unemployment as compared to their white counterparts.[5]

White women and persons of color face discrimination in employment and promotion. Although there are documented examples of blatant discrimination in employment,[6] the US Constitution has been interpreted as prohibiting the government from discriminating against citizens without due process and requiring equal protection of citizens, and overt discrimination in the private sector has been addressed by a series of laws and court rulings. The most notable is Title VII of the Civil Rights Act of 1964, which makes it unlawful for employers to discriminate based on race, color, religion, sex, and national origin. A number of court cases and pieces of legislation (such as the Lilly Ledbetter Fair Pay Act of 2009) have reinforced these principles and provided remedies for victims of such discrimination. As sociologist Devah Pager notes, while overt forms of discrimination are shocking, they have become relatively rare; however, "contemporary forms of discrimination may be simply more subtle and covert, leading to less frequent detection and awareness by the general public."[7] The most widespread incidents relate to these hidden biases. Absent "gotcha" cases where there is evidence of explicit prejudice at work in hiring or promotion, it is therefore important to reflect on the ways that subconscious processes can affect employment decisions.

As noted in the Introduction to this book, implicit prejudice can be equally damaging (if not more so, since it is often somewhat invisible).[8] To demonstrate this dynamic with respect to hiring, let us consider a series of innovative studies[9] that involve sending fictitious résumés and cover letters to potential employers, using traditionally "white-sounding names" on some and "African American–sounding names" on others, keeping the qualifications the same. The authors of one of these studies report a 50 percent gap in callbacks such that "a white name yields as many more callbacks as an additional eight years of experience" on a résumé.[10] A separate study found that the race of hiring managers affected the racial composition of new hires,[11] but that does not necessarily mean that the discrimination was intentional, explicit, or conscious. Although it is tempting to believe that such results are attributable to overtly bigoted individuals responsible for the hiring at these companies, we must consider the effects that hidden or unconscious racism has on such decisions.

Additionally, there are systemic elements of the racial wage gap as it relates to employment. African Americans (both men and women), for instance, are largely segregated in job markets in a way that leads to inequality, particularly in geographical areas where there are heavy concentrations of African Americans.[12] One study found that "blacks are systematically segregated into jobs with disproportionate black representation" and that "jobs with more black workers ... tend to pay less than other jobs, even with stringent controls."[13] While there is certainly an attitudinal component to these patterns,[14] such that whites living in areas with high concentrations of African Americans have been found to perceive a greater racial threat, these dynamics work at the macro level as well. For instance, when a job is perceived to be "black" (or "women's work"), the perceived value of the work decreases.[15] If the difference in pay is related to that market-based perceived value, as opposed to being directly related to the race or ethnicity of the person in the position, it is much harder to demonstrate that there is *discrimination* (even though there is clearly *segregation*), as it does not fit our colloquial understanding of racism.

Finally, there is the problem identified in Chapter 3—jobs moving to the suburbs while persons of color primarily live in urban areas (particularly in the North).[16] Such a reverse commute would require access to reliable transportation; that is, individuals living in areas that lack extensive public transportation systems would need a car even to submit an application or get to an interview, as well as to get to work on a regular basis.[17]

One proposed solution to these interrelated problems is the creation of enterprise zones and empowerment zones.[18] Championed by former professional football player and congressman Jack Kemp (see Box 6.1), enterprise zones are designed to provide tax incentives to businesses to open (and thus create jobs) in urban and rural centers. When an area is identified as economically depressed, it can be designated as an enterprise zone, which means that businesses operating there qualify for lower taxes and possibly less government regulation.[19]

There is mixed evidence regarding the effectiveness of enterprise zones to create employment opportunities; even when opportunities do exist, white males tend to have an advantage in learning about them.[20] Further, even controlling for other relevant factors, African Americans are employed less frequently in areas that have high proportions of racial segregation.[21] Possessing a college degree does not mitigate employment disparities related to race. Indeed, early in the Great Recession, having a degree was observed to exaggerate racial disparities—during that time, the employment rate for African Americans with a college degree was consistently nearly twice the rate of that of whites.[22]

Box 6.1. *Representing:* Jack Kemp

Born in Los Angeles during the Great Depression, John French "Jack" Kemp Jr. was a public servant who had deep concerns about racial and economic inequality in the United States. A Republican, he wished for his party to work harder to reach out to racial minorities, and he sought tax reform and market-based incentive programs to encourage economic development in majority-minority communities.

Kemp was a strong advocate for supply-side economics, which is the theory that keeping taxes low on those who supply goods (businesses and investors) will stimulate economic growth by encouraging reinvestment and job creation. As a member of Congress from Buffalo, New York (where he played professional football for the Buffalo Bills), he advocated for tax reform and passed his ideas along to Ronald Reagan during Reagan's 1980 bid for the White House.

As founder and president of the American Football League Players Association, Kemp supported black players boycotting New Orleans as a site for an all-star game because nightclubs and cabs in that city had been refusing to serve them. Kemp said on a number of occasions that his participation in professional football helped to raise his consciousness about civil rights issues in the 1960s: "I can't help but care about the rights of the people I used to shower with." But Kemp understood that racism is not simply an issue of interpersonal relations. After an unsuccessful attempt at securing the Republican presidential nomination in 1988, Kemp was appointed by President George H. W. Bush to be secretary of Housing and Urban Development (HUD). In his four years of service at HUD, he argued for destruction of failed housing projects and for tax incentives called enterprise zones to offer tax incentives for business to invest in economically depressed areas.

In 1996 Kemp ran for vice president (with US Senator Bob Dole of Kansas) and oversaw one of his organizations, Empower America, until it merged with another organization in 2004 to become FreedomWorks. He worked as a consultant and lobbyist in the early years of the twenty-first century. Kemp died from cancer complications on May 2, 2009, leaving behind a legacy of activism and advocacy for underserved Americans through fiscally conservative, innovative ideas that bridged ideological and partisan divides.[26]

Education and Training Opportunities

The reasons for employment disparities among college-educated minorities are similar to those who do not have college degrees (movement of jobs away from urban centers, subconscious bias, etc.),[23] and it would be foolish to suggest that young African Americans and Latinos should forgo college to increase their employment chances over the long term. National labor projections demonstrate that most of the jobs expected to be plentiful in the coming decades are service producing, many of which require schooling beyond high school.[24] But a four-year college is not an option for every American, because of either inadequate preparation in K-12 schooling, lack of interest or aptitude, or cost. In this section, we consider alternate forms of job training and preparation.[25]

Community colleges offer affordable alternatives to four-year institutions. Many students attend community colleges expecting to transfer to a four-year college after two years,[35] but others attend for skills that can lead directly to employment. Miami Dade College in Florida is the largest brick-and-mortar college in the nation, with an enrollment of 125,000, 90 percent of whom are racial minorities.[36] The college has an open admissions policy and graduates more Hispanic students than any other institution in the nation.[37] The former president, Dr. Eduardo J. Padrón, was explicit about how the school is working to combat systemic disadvantage: "If we say, 'You are not prepared. We won't admit you,' thousands and thousands would not be able to come to college. The cycle of poverty would continue."[38]

Trade schools—sometimes referred to as vocational schools or technical schools—are another alternative to four-year colleges. Rather than preparing students to transfer to a four-year institution, these schools focus solely on the skills and knowledge related to a particular area of employment. While traditional programs such as carpentry, electronics, and auto mechanics are still offered, emerging programs in computer engineering, culinary fields, and graphic arts have become increasingly popular. Business and health-care fields have dominated the occupational training landscape over the past three decades.[39] Training for skills that will help candidates compete for jobs is also available through many public libraries and faith-based organizations. All of these are related to government in one way or another. For instance, community colleges and four-year state institutions are heavily subsidized by public funds, and

Box 6.2. *What Can I Do?:* Helping Others Find Employment

During difficult economic times, there are numerous opportunities for community involvement through volunteer activities. Some positions are organized on a national level,[27] but most are local. A growing number of these opportunities are related to helping others acquire skills to improve their chances of securing (and keeping) a good job. This box provides a few possibilities, but a well-worded Google search that includes a local geographical area can quickly lead to options that fit multiple skill levels and availability.

An estimated 24 million people are functionally illiterate, which means that they do not have basic competencies in reading, writing, and mathematics. Illiteracy affects up to 50 percent of people who are chronically unemployed—defined as unemployment resulting from "deficiencies in labor demands above and beyond cyclical fluctuations."[28] The Literacy Information and Communication System (LINCS)[29] provides numerous programs designed to reduce illiteracy, many through regional resource centers that are funded by the US Department of Education's Office of Vocational and Adult Education. Although there are no opportunities to volunteer through LINCS directly, it provides a gateway resource to connect individuals seeking services, as well as volunteers, with local opportunities. The not-for-profit advocacy group ProLiteracy[30] maintains a database with user-friendly searchable features to find local programs. Simply choose "Find a U.S. Program" and type in your zip code for a list of programs (most with websites) in your area.

Other organizations are dedicated to skills training (often in addition to literacy work). The San Francisco–based Idealist[31] offers classes on basic computer skills, for instance, run by volunteers. Literacy Chicago[32] helps connect volunteers to community members who wish to learn such skills as bookkeeping, filing, or data entry. Also in Chicago, Growing Home[33] "provides transitional employment and training for individuals facing multiple barriers to securing permanent and unsubsidized employment through a social enterprise business based on organic agriculture." The organization works with volunteers to offer job training in a variety of areas on both long-term and short-term bases.

It is important to remember that the pluralist model of democracy features group involvement to solve common problems. Sometimes

that involvement comes in the form of lobbying policymakers or contributing to campaigns, but often it involves public education and direct
advocacy in the community. Being a part of a volunteer group that
works to make one's community more vibrant, safe, and engaged can
be a rewarding experience that does not require financial resources
or even a burdensome time commitment. The key is to connect those
who have skills and those who seek to gain them.[34]

even private schools benefit from government support through grants and
financial aid awarded to students who attend. Public libraries are funded
by local municipalities and government grants, and faith-based organizations operate tax-free, which can be considered to be a type of government
subsidy.

Immigrants and Employment

The demographic makeup of the United States has always shifted along
with trends in immigration. From the earliest settlers who displaced
Native Americans, to waves of eager migrants from Europe at the turn of
the twentieth century, to our current wave of newcomers from Asia and
Central and South America, the United States has always been a destina-
tion for those seeking to better their opportunities. At each stage, however,
resistance to immigration has come on a number of fronts, not the least of
which is the perceived increased competition for employment. In this section, we turn our attention to the recent issues surrounding immigration
and employment as a way to more fully understand the challenges that
face citizens, immigrants who are in the country legally, and those who
are here without papers.

America has been and still is widely known as a "nation of immigrants,"
though immigration policies were always considered based on the nation's
economic needs as much as its good will.[45] Racism and xenophobia have
been persistent drivers of immigration policy, as well.[46] According to the
Pew Research Service:

Today, more than 40 million people living in the U.S. were born in another
country, accounting for about one-fifth of the world's migrants. The population of immigrants is also very diverse, with just about every country in

Box 6.3. *Representing:* Isa Noyola

Isa Noyola, a self-identified translatina activist, exemplifies the importance of intersectional approaches to social justice issues. As director of programs (and later Deputy Director) at the Transgender Law Center (https://transgenderlawcenter.org), Noyola was charged with "raising awareness of the conditions affecting transgender people detained in immigration facilities."[40] Her efforts to call attention to the unique struggles of transgender immigrants effectively pull together activists from a number of causes. Most immigration-rights workers tend to ignore the ways that gender identity might complicate the issue, and Lesbian, Gay, Bisexual, Transgender, and Queer (LGBTQ) activists are not always focused on the unique challenges faced by transgender individuals who are in the country without documentation.

There are an estimated quarter-million undocumented transgender immigrants in the United States, but Noyola is quick to note that the numbers are challenging because of the ways that the Immigration and Customs Enforcement Department collects information.[41] Transgender women are often placed with cisgender men in detention centers, which constitutes a danger to their physical safety, not to mention their emotional well-being.[42] Many of these immigrants are fleeing persecution due to their gender identity in their home country,[43] which renders their mistreatment in the United States all the more tragic.

Noyola is currently serving as Deputy Director of Mijente and Mijente Support Committee.[44]

the world represented among U.S. immigrants.... The U.S. foreign-born population reached a record 44.8 million in 2018. Since 1965, when U.S. immigration law replaced a national quota system, the number of immigrants living in the U.S. has more than quadrupled. Immigrants today account for 14.7% of the U.S. population, nearly triple the share (4.8%) in 1970. However, today's immigrant share remains below the record 14.8% share in 1890, when 9.2 million immigrants lived in the U.S.[47]

Changes in immigration law have been accompanied with changes in the documentation status of the immigrant population.[48]

The past three decades have seen an increase in the number of individuals entering the United States without proper authorization. The number has decreased over the past decade, but there are still an estimated 10.5 million persons in the United States without documentation,[49] compared to 8.4 million in 2000.[50] Those who favor policies that would imprison or deport undocumented people refer to them as "illegal aliens" or simply "illegals," while those who favor policies rooted in amnesty and paths to citizenship usually refer to them as "undocumented workers" or "undocumented immigrants," noting that a person's *actions* might be illegal but that a person cannot be "illegal." The difference in language choice echoes the interaction between race and criminal justice that we explored in the previous chapter.

While space does not permit a thorough treatment of how illegal immigration affects job prospects for black and Latino Americans, it is important to consider both the rhetoric of the contemporary immigration debate as well as the effects illegal immigration has on job prospects for American citizens. This issue is racialized today because the focus is on immigration from Mexico and other parts of South and Central America. Migrant workers from this region form an important part of several sectors of the US economy, and dire economic conditions tend to highlight competition for jobs among new arrivals and persons who have been in the United States for generations.

Whether or not a person enters the United States legally, the presence of additional potential competitors for scarce jobs can be seen as threatening. In the early years of the twentieth century, immigrants from eastern and southern Europe came in great waves looking for economic prosperity. Although they faced many obstacles such as unfamiliarity with the language and culture as well as overt bigotry, their European background allowed them to eventually assimilate into American culture and simply become classified as white.[51] In contrast, Latinos and Latinas[52] face persistent stereotypes and discrimination to a degree that their very presence reflects illegality or criminality to many.[53] They are not incarcerated at the same rate as African Americans but at higher rates than whites, and they are burdened by a stereotype of untrustworthiness and dishonesty.[54]

It is often argued that illegal immigrants from Central and South America take jobs that other Americans do not want.[55] While there may be some truth to the claim that second-, third-, or fourth-generation Americans would balk at working for substandard wages in jobs that are dangerous and or require grueling physical labor (such as housekeeping or working in agriculture fields), such sentiment has the potential to perpetuate race-based assumptions about Latinx persons generally. In contrast to the assumption that African Americans are lazy and seek public assistance (recall the welfare queen stereotype discussed in Chapter 2), Latinx individuals are often perceived to be hard workers but undeserving of their jobs because they are presumed to be in the country illegally. As the Great Recession wore on, there was increased sentiment that US citizens would in fact perform some of the jobs that were then regularly performed by undocumented workers.[56] Some of the most vocal advocates of this position were African Americans,[57] who, as noted in the beginning of this chapter, face unemployment rates that are twice as high as whites. Yet as the economic recover entered full swing, those attitudes shifted.[58] It remains to be seen how Americans will feel as America recovers from the Covid-19 recession.

Attitudes toward children of undocumented immigrants are particularly complicated. It is impossible to argue that they (as opposed to their parents) did anything wrong (to the extent one believes that, given the context, entering the country without authorization is wrong at all). On the other hand, those who oppose leniency in such circumstances argue that a policy that provides a path to citizenship for immigrants who entered the country illegally at a young age would serve as an incentive to unauthorized entrance for parents who wish to help their children become US citizens. In 2011, California—one of the states with the highest number of undocumented immigrants—passed the Development, Relief, and Education for Alien Minors Act (DREAM Act), a state version of a federal proposition that creates a path to citizenship for children who entered the country illegally but are attending college or serving in the US military. The California bill allows undocumented college students to secure private funding to attend school.[59] By the summer of 2012, Congress had refused to pass a federal version of the DREAM Act, so President Obama signed an executive order halting deportations of approximately 800,000 students who would be covered under the measure.[60] In 2017, President Trump's Administration rescinded the 2012 directive and announced that there would be a "wind down" of the Deferred Action for Childhood Arrivals (DACA) program.[61] In 2020, the United States Supreme Court ruled (in a 5–4 decision) that the reversal was unconstitutional, effectively restoring the program to its pre-2017 status.[62] President Joe Biden issued an order to fortify the DACA program on his first day in office,[63] and he has signaled that he would like to put so-called "Dreamers" on a path to citizenship.[64]

Such efforts reflect the widely held proposition (discussed in Chapter 4) that education is the most important equalizing element in American culture. Even some policymakers who are perceived to be tough on illegal immigration support the notion that those who are here ought to be educated and have a chance to contribute meaningfully to their community. Consider the case of Asian Americans. While they face numerous difficulties resulting from stereotypes and hostility (some of which can be traced back to World War II)[65], the presence of immigrants and US-born South and Southeast Asians in high-skill fields that require advanced education (e.g., medicine, engineering) illustrates the power of education to help clear barriers of prejudice and systemic discrimination. However, significant numbers of Asians in the United States work at low-wage jobs without access to education, as well; the proportion of Asians in manual service jobs is generally higher than that of whites but lower than African Americans and significantly lower (with the exception of those hailing from the Pacific Islands or Vietnam) than Latinos.[66] Further, the tendency for many Americans to not differentiate between South Asian and Middle Eastern individuals, as well as the problematic conflation of those regional origins with Islam (not to mention the association of Muslims with acts of terror), leads to an often-challenging daily life for many individuals from these backgrounds.

Conclusion

Conscious or subconscious perceptions of criminality, untrustworthiness, and laziness among employers and the mass public interact with systemic barriers to employment in ways that make it difficult for lawmakers to support meaningful reform without facing electoral consequences. If Americans generally believe that the economic system in the United States is fundamentally fair, then disparities in unemployment will be viewed as resulting from individual behavioral flaws that do not merit government-based solutions. Only a minority of Americans believe that the economic system is fair,[67] yet the unresponsiveness of elected leaders to the perceived injustice reflects the lack of saliency of the issue. While 60 percent of Americans indicated in August 2011 that the economy was the "most important problem facing America,"[68] that broad category is usually interpreted by policymakers to refer to rates of unemployment or the performance of the stock market, rather than fundamental flaws with capitalism.[69] Responses to Gallup's open-ended question about the most important problem facing America between July 2020 and January 2021 fluctuated between 9 percent and 14 percent of individuals mentioning anything at all related to the economy.[70] Such beliefs are not surprising, as polls asking Americans how they feel about increasing government regulation in the free market vary greatly depending on the timing or the ideology of the polling organization.[71] And while polls show more young Americans embracing the label (and ideas) of democratic socialism,[72] the term continues to have a net negative impression by Americans overall.[73] Consequently the status quo persists, and generation after generation of poorer Americans, particularly persons of color, have difficulty overcoming systemic barriers to advancement.

Besides the obvious disadvantages that have been addressed to this point (inability to save money for the future or investment, difficulty in securing desirable housing, and inability to provide educational opportunities for their children), poorer Americans face unique health challenges that affect each of these other elements. In the next chapter, we turn to a consideration of those factors and the ways that they are rooted in systemic racism.

Discussion Questions

1. Is such legislation as the Civil Rights Act and the Lilly Ledbetter Fair Pay Act useful and/or necessary in contemporary America? Why or why not? Does such legislation have an effect on explicit or implicit prejudices?

2. How does the issue of immigration complicate employment-related inequality? How is immigration different from other issues presented in this chapter? In particular, consider how the issue contributes to political discourse about employment.

3. What do you make of the idea that capitalism itself is responsible for some of the inequality that exists with respect to employment? How does such consideration differ from most discussions of employment that you have experienced? What is your impression of "socialism" as you understand it?

7

···

Health

IT IS COMMONLY UNDERSTOOD THAT POOR HEALTH IS OFTEN A SYMPTOM of economic inequality. However, nutrition, access to preventative health care, and environmental factors also play a role in perpetuating inequality. The connection not only centers on the ability to afford healthful food and health-care services, but also includes awareness and education about the importance of such care. In this chapter, we consider an aspect of inequality that, like involvement in the criminal justice system and immigration status, is not a distinct part of the cycle of advantage and disadvantage (recall Figure 2.4 on page 71) but is related to a number of elements within that cycle.

We start once again with some broad normative questions about the importance and value of health in a wealthy democratic society. In the 1940s, psychologist Abraham Maslow proposed a theory of human motivation that is often depicted as a pyramid[1]; we must satisfy the lower levels before addressing the higher ones. At the base of the pyramid are immediate physiological needs, such as food and water that we need to physically survive. Until we have satisfied those needs, we will not be able to move forward to the next level, which is safety. When we feel safe (so long as we remain nourished), we can consider satisfying other desires—one at a time—such as love and affection, esteem, and finally self-actualization.[2] To what is every individual entitled? Most of us would agree that a person bleeding profusely on a hospital sidewalk should be taken inside and treated, irrespective of ability to pay. But should that person receive follow-up treatment after the life-saving surgery? Should an obese person be provided access to nutritional consulting to regain a healthy weight and avoid illnesses (such as diabetes) that can result from excess weight? Does it matter how the person became overweight in the first place? What about

DOI: 10.4324/9781003043041-8

someone who smoked for 50 years and developed lung cancer but has no insurance? To what extent should that person be treated? Who should pay for it? Should all people have the opportunity to purchase fresh produce and healthful foods, no matter where they live? If parents cannot afford such food, should it be provided to children?

Much of the debate about health in the United States over the past two generations has focused on health care—how individuals and health-care providers are connected to one another and who pays the bills. A host of private, for-profit insurance companies offer health insurance that individuals can purchase directly or receive as compensation through their employer. As the costs of these plans have increased, health-care providers have complained about increasing restrictions, consumers have complained about being denied treatment, and public officials have argued over how to resolve the problems while continuing to encourage innovation in the medical field and provide a high quality of care. Yet evidence shows that having access to preventative care is directly related to overall health.[3]

There have been two major efforts for meaningful (if not fundamental) reform of the health-care system in the modern era. The first, in 1993, failed; the second, in 2010, resulted in the Patient Protection and Affordable Care Act (sometimes called "Obamacare"), a bill that President Obama believed would usher in meaningful reform but progressives dismissed as too timid and conservatives criticized as a "hostile government takeover" of the health-care system.[4] Between 2010 (when the law was passed) and 2016, an estimated 20 million more Americans obtained health insurance[5] (that number remained stable through 2019).[6] Still, the program was an issue in the 2012, 2016, and, to a lesser extent, 2020 presidential elections.[7] Donald Trump vowed in 2016 to dismantle it early in his presidency,[8] and he tried in a number of ways. The major provisions of the program, however, sustained attacks from both lawmakers[9] and through the courts.[10] America still has a large number of people who, for one reason or another, are without health insurance.[11]

In most industrialized democracies, access to preventative health care is considered a basic human right and thus is provided at no charge to citizens, either by the government or by private providers who are paid by the government. In the United States, we have considered access to health care (with the exception of emergency care) to be a privilege, which means that social inequality is strongly related to disparities in not just health care but also in health. Those inequalities, as we will see, have

a powerful effect on the ability of individuals and families t
cycle of disadvantage.

Access to Health Care

The number of Americans who lack health insurance at any given time
fluctuates and is the subject of some debate[12] but it hovered around the
40–50 million mark prior to the full implementation of the aforementioned Patient Protection and Affordable Care Act (hereafter, ACA), a law
sometimes referred to as Obamacare.[13] This means that, with the exception of emergency care, about one in six Americans went without regular
medical consultation and treatment. In recent years, the number has hovered around 30 million non-elderly uninsured Americans.[14] Unlike most
of the examples that we have considered to this point, however, it is not
generally the poorest Americans who were uninsured.

American citizens who participate in governmental cash assistance
programs, such as Social Security Supplemental Income or those who
have limited income, may be eligible for Medicaid.[15] Senior citizens
(citizens over the age of 65) and others with certain disabilities are eligible
for Medicare, which can cover hospitalization, outpatient treatment, and
prescriptions.[16] Those without insurance were often middle-class working
people whose employers did not provide it as a benefit and who did not
make enough money to purchase it independently.

About 15.6 percent of Americans between the ages of 19 and 34 were without health insurance in 2019, compared to 11.3 percent of those in the next
largest uninsured group (ages 35–64).[17] Uninsured rates overall are higher
for American Indian/Alaska Natives (21.7 percent), African Americans
(11.4 percent), and Hispanics (20.0 percent) than for Asians (7.4 percent)
and whites (7.8 percent).[18] Some young people choose not to buy insurance,
using their disposable income for other things because they do not get sick
very often. This, however, creates some problems for attempts at reform.

One of the most controversial provisions of the ACA is the requirement
that individuals purchase insurance from private health insurance companies. Some policymakers and pundits argued that the requirement is an
unconstitutional mandate by the federal government, but the US Supreme
Court upheld it in 2012.[19] Most agree that it is ethically and even morally
questionable for health insurance companies to deny individuals the right
to purchase coverage if they have a pre-existing health condition. Yet it was

argued that it would be financially unsustainable for the insurers if people were allowed to wait until they got sick to purchase coverage. In 2017, Congress stripped the penalty for not having health care from the program,[20] but this move did not result in a decline in coverage in the first year it was in effect (2019), presumably because so many people had already enrolled.[21]

One of the least controversial provisions of the ACA mandates that parents can keep their children on their health insurance plan until the age of 26. This provision, which went into effect before some of the other provisions, resulted in 2.3 million young people gaining coverage prior to full implementation of the act. Nearly 4 million other young Americans gained coverage between 2013 and 2016, which resulted in a nearly 50 percent drop in the rate of uninsured within that age group.[22]

Further, most medical professionals acknowledge that preventative care is essential not only for promotion of long-term health but also for saving money on costly procedures that result from a lack of health maintenance. This is particularly true with respect to prenatal care.[23] As we turn our attention to health disparities, we begin with prenatal care because of the normative questions that have structured our discussion to this point. If every American deserves an equal chance at achieving the American Dream, a focus on the opportunities of children from the earliest stages of development—from education to safety to health—is appropriate. Here, as in the previous chapters, we see that all children do not begin life with an equal chance for growth and prosperity.

Disparities in Health-Care Access

The evidence for the effectiveness of prenatal care in preventing birth defects, developmental problems, and infant mortality is consistent. There are expected disparities in prenatal treatment for low-income women,[24] and there is ample evidence of racial disparities, as well. For instance, a recent study found that Asian and white mothers were more likely to take prenatal vitamins in the month prior to delivery than are African American, American Indian, or Hispanic women. In addition, scholarly research has shown historically that:

- African American women are more likely to report not receiving advice about the importance of quitting smoking and avoiding alcohol during pregnancy.[25]

- African American infants are born with a low or very low birth weight at twice the rate of whites.[26]

- African American and Hispanic expectant mothers experienced a higher rate of such conditions as intrauterine growth restriction, preeclampsia, preterm premature rupture of membranes, gestational diabetes, placenta previa, preterm or very preterm birth, cesarean delivery, and vaginal bleeding compared to white expectant mothers.[27]

While at least one study found racial disparities slightly reduced at the turn of the twenty-first century,[28] their persistence[29] reflects the types of systemic disadvantages discussed in previous chapters.

Although health disparities begin before birth, they certainly do not end there. For example, the infant mortality rate has dropped in recent years, yet disparities remain. The national rate in 2017 was 5.79 per 1,000 live births (a historic low in the United States), but for African American infants it was 10.8.[30] Moreover, black newborns are more likely to die if they are cared for by a white doctor than by a black doctor.[31] African American infants are nearly twice as likely to die from sudden infant death syndrome (SIDS) or unintentional injuries as are whites, and American Indian/Alaska Native infants have sudden unexpected death rates that are even higher (see Figure 7.1).[32]

FIGURE 7.1. **Sudden Unexpected Infant Death by Race/Ethnicity, 2014–2018**

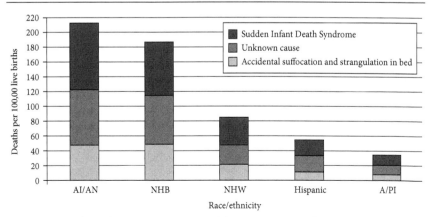

AI/AN = American Indian/Alaska Native; NHB = Non-Hispanic Black; NHW = Non-Hispanic White; A/PI = Asian/Pacific Islander

Source: "Sudden Unexpected Infant Death and Sudden Infant Death Syndrome," Centers for Disease Control and Prevention, November 10, 2020, https://www.cdc.gov/sids/data.htm#:~:text=Deaths%20 due%20to%20SIDS%20accounted,Hispanic%20White%20infants%20(43%25)

On a host of indicators—including levels of lead in the blood, incidence of asthma, obesity, and hunger, as well as treatments (such as receiving cranial CT scans)[33]—children of color are at a distinct disadvantage when compared to whites.[34] Not surprisingly, disparities based on income[35] and race and ethnicity[36] persist into adulthood. For example, even though breast cancer is more prevalent among white women,[37] African American women have the disease diagnosed later, so the size and stage at which a tumor is detected puts black women at greater risk for not receiving potentially life-saving treatment.[38] White women between the ages of 50 and 74 are slightly less likely than African American women (but more likely than Hispanic women) to have received a mammogram in the past two years and a Pap smear in the past three years.[39] Black women and Hispanic women with breast cancer have a higher mortality rate than white women, though they have a lower rate of contracting the disease. In fact, black women are more likely to die from breast cancer, heart disease, and cervical cancer than are white women.[40] Even adjusting for socioeconomic status and a number of other factors (such as body mass index), older African Americans have significantly higher levels of cardiovascular disease than do older whites.[41] There are also racial disparities with respect to kidney disease,[42] HIV/AIDS,[43] rate and severity of strokes,[44] diabetes,[45] and prostate cancer,[46] as well as high blood pressure, high cholesterol, and even car crashes.[47]

Some disparities are rooted in behavioral differences, although in ways that are clearly related to systemic disadvantages. For example, children who grow up in poverty are more likely to be obese and to have diabetes, and are "less likely to graduate high school and more likely to engage in risky sexual behavior as teens."[48] Although eating too much (or eating unhealthy food), not studying, and engaging in risky sexual acts are behavioral, they are related to external pressures that center on economic factors (such as access to healthful food). Research demonstrates that brain development is significantly impacted by the stress related to poverty during formative years, which can affect behavior.[49]

Ostensibly behavior-related health disparities can be racial as well as economic. Although whites smoke more cigarettes than African Americans, the latter are more susceptible to health consequences related to smoking.[50] While the rates of alcohol consumption vary by age, as well as race and ethnicity,[51] African Americans and Hispanics are less likely to complete treatment programs than are whites.[52] A similar pattern exists with respect to illicit drugs.[53] Although low-income Americans are generally more likely to rate their oral health as poor, the discrepancy is greater among African Americans.[54]

In addition to access to health providers, affordability, and levels of education in poorer communities, there is some evidence that a distrust of whites and medical institutions may also contribute to racial disparities.[55] Such attitudes may or may not be conscious, but they nonetheless interfere with a person's ability to have access to care.

As we saw in Chapter 3, housing has a lot to do with perpetuating disadvantage. In addition to the issues already noted, there are health-related concerns with substandard housing. The term *environmental racism*[56] refers to institutional factors and public policy outputs that result in people of color being disproportionately at risk for illness as a result of proximity to pollution and other types of environmental irresponsibility.[57] This aspect of inequality in America is traceable directly to the nation's representative system of government. Hazardous waste facilities tend to be placed in neighborhoods where people are poor, have less education, and have little political power; wealthier and politically savvy citizens are able to pressure public officials to keep such facilities away from them and their children. People of color (over 5 million) compose the majority of those who live within 1.8 miles of a hazardous waste facility.[58] One study revealed that African Americans are more than twice as likely to live in areas where air pollution poses the greatest health threat in 19 states,[59] while another showed that individuals who lived in neighborhoods that were more than 60 percent white were significantly less likely to be exposed to air pollution than those in neighborhoods that were less than 25 percent white.[60]

In 2016, President Obama and Governor Rick Snyder declared a state of emergency in Genesee County, Michigan, because of the unusually high levels of lead found in the drinking water.[61] This crisis began when officials in Flint (a town that is majority African American and in which 40 percent of residents live in poverty), looking for a cost-saving measure, shifted residents' water supply from the Detroit Water and Sewage Department to the Flint River. The result: Flint residents were provided with water that, because of pollution in the river, improper treatment of the water, and resulting corrosion to the pipes delivering the water, contained nearly three times the level of lead considered to be hazardous.[62] A switch was made back to the Detroit provider, but the long-term consequences to residents, particularly to children, who drank the water will not be known for some time.

Box 7.1. *Representing:* Lupus Foundation of America

Lupus is an autoimmune, chronic disease that can cause inflamma-tion and pain in any part of the body.[63] Lupus is estimated to affect 1.5 million Americans and 5 million people worldwide.[64] Approximately 90 percent of people with Lupus are women, and persons of color are at a greater risk than non-Hispanic whites.[65]

Beyond the specific focus of Lupus, however, the Lupus Foundation of America (LFA) has taken a broader view of health disparities, creat-ing a resource page to help individuals navigate the health-care sys-tem, educate about inequities in health care, and advocate for a more equitable approach to health care in America.[66] This portal combines up-to-date information about health disparities and offers many links to resources, such as organizations that can help Americans gain access to services and additional information. At the peak of the Covid-19 pan-demic, LFA sought to inform the public about how the novel coronavirus was exacerbating health disparities, including for people with Lupus. They offered a resource page that linked to governmental reports and provided a summary of those reports in a digestible format.[67]

In these ways, the LFA has demonstrated a commitment to tran-scend the narrow focus of one debilitating disease in order to realize their broader mission.

Because of their developmental physiology, children are particularly susceptible to the effects of contaminants in the environment.[68] Schools with lower levels of funding are less able to safely remove asbestos from facilities, appropriately remove lead paint, or replace lead pipes that carry water to cafeterias and water fountains. These conditions are also linked to learning disabilities,[69] which in turn interfere with the potential of educational opportunities to break the cycle of disadvantage, as students with learning disabilities in underfunded schools are less likely to receive additional resources to overcome their challenges.[70] This is further com-plicated by the fact that students of color are also more likely to be labeled as having a learning disability, which may be related to cultural misunder-standings or lack of trained professionals in underfunded schools.[71]

Adults also face disparities with respect to mental health.[72] Racial and ethnic minorities have less access to mental health services than do white Americans, are disproportionately more likely to perceive shame or stigma in relation to mental health disorders, and consequently shoulder a disproportionately high burden from unmet mental health needs.[73] Environmental factors have been attributed to this aspect of inequality as well. For example, a connection between proximity to industrial centers and mental health has been documented.[74]

It is difficult to firmly establish links between health problems and environmental factors on such a wide scale, particularly given the geographic variability in the United States. Part of the problem for researchers is trying to figure out the interrelated factors of race and socioeconomic status,[75] but varying levels of environmental racial inequality have been found in the nation's largest metropolitan areas,[76] which renders insignificant simplistic answers to questions of representation and advocacy.[77]

Disparities in Nutrition and Access to Healthy Foods

Preventing health problems requires maintaining a healthy body weight (by eating healthy food and exercising) and getting enough rest. There are disparities with respect to both factors.

A recent study found that whites sleep longer (average of 7.4 hours per day compared to 6.9 hours for African Americans and 6.8 hours for Hispanics) and more soundly than persons of color.[78] The interrelationship between sleep and exercise,[79] as well as findings that sleep enhances athletic and academic performance and overall health, are well documented.[80] In 2019, 31.4 percent of American adults were considered to be obese[81] (defined by a Body Mass Index of 30 or higher). Rates of adult obesity and overweight among African Americans (40.7 percent), American Indian/Alaska Natives (37.9 percent), and Hispanics (34.5 percent) are significantly higher than for non-Hispanic whites (30.4 percent). While adult obesity more than doubled (from 15 percent to 34 percent) between 1980 and 2008, childhood obesity rates more than tripled (from 5 percent to 17 percent) in that time period.[82] Today, 18.5 percent of children are obese.[83] Obesity rates are inversely related to income and education, which means that higher levels of each generally correspond to lower levels of obesity.[84]

It may seem counterintuitive that those who have the least money tend to weigh the most, but nutrition is as much about the quality of food as the quantity. It is true, of course, that millions of Americans are hungry. The US Department of Agriculture separates food insecurity into two broad categories: low food security, which is defined as "reduced quality, variety, or desirability of diet" with little or no indication of reduced food intake, and very low food security, which includes "multiple indications of disrupted eating patterns and reduced food intake."[85] In 2019, approximately 25 million Americans adults and 10 million American children struggled with food insecurity.[86] During the Covid-19 pandemic, the number was estimated to be around 50 million people, including 17 million children.[87] Some 30 million schoolchildren participate in the federal government's National School Lunch and School Breakfast programs[88] that provide free or reduced-price meals; in some cases, that is the only meal participants are certain to receive. Subsequently, children go hungry or eat unhealthily on weekends and during the summer months. Adults are typically not eligible for school meals[89] and often rely on food banks or soup kitchens for sustenance (see Box 7.2).

As anyone who has gone grocery shopping can confirm, eating healthfully is often more expensive than eating processed, pre-packaged foods. This reality helps to explain the paradox of poorer Americans being more overweight. Consider, for instance, the "dollar menu" or "value menu" in fast-food chain restaurants. Such menus have become popular over the past decade, with most major chains featuring a number of items at very low prices. For about five dollars, a consumer can get one or even two double hamburgers, a medium order of french fries, and a large soda. That is a bargain, and it will stave off hunger for a while, but it is quite unhealthy in terms of the number of calories and the type of nutrition it provides.[93] It is often advised that shopping around the perimeter of the grocery store will lead to more healthy choices than shopping in the aisles, but fresh produce is expensive (even if it is not organic), as are fresh meats and fish.

To add yet another layer of complexity, millions of Americans live in "food deserts," where they do not have access to fresh produce even if they can afford it. The United States Department of Agriculture (USDA) has determined, based on 2010 census data, that approximately 10 percent of the United States' population lives in a food desert.[94] While over 10,000 new supermarkets were opened by America's 75 top food retailers in recent years, only about 250 of those were in food deserts.[95] In urban areas, food deserts usually force residents to buy processed food to prepare at home or

---

Box 7.2. *What Can I Do?:* Food Banks, Soup Kitchens, and Community Work

Food banks (sometimes called food pantries) and soup kitchens are among the most popular, visible, and accessible volunteer opportunities in the United States. Food banks generally collect and redistribute unprepared food, whereas soup kitchens serve prepared meals. Food banks and soup kitchens are often run by faith-based organizations, such as churches, mosques, and synagogues.

Pressure on food banks and pantries hit record levels in 2020 and 2021, during the Covid-19 pandemic and related recession.[90] Between drops in donations (as individuals had fewer resources, businesses closed or paused operations, and restaurants shuttered) and the dramatic increase in demand, programs across the country found it impossible to keep up with the needs in their community.

Although many people volunteer at food banks and soup kitchens over the holidays—particularly Thanksgiving—large numbers of families and individuals count on these organizations on a weekly or daily basis for sustenance. Volunteers need not travel far to find a soup kitchen or food bank. Feeding America (previously known as Second Harvest), a network of some 200 food banks and 60,000 food pantries and meal programs, provides help to nearly 50 million Americans each year.[91] Many other local organizations run food banks and soup kitchens independently, and they are always grateful for additional help and contributions.[92]

---

encourage them to eat at inexpensive fast-food restaurants. In rural areas, the "solution" is no more appealing:

> Rural residents pay up to 30 percent more for their food from local merchants who cannot offer the prices found in most major supermarkets. Pride and physical isolation coupled with lack of public transportation keep many people from applying for food stamps. In a ten-county area in southwestern Virginia, 90,197 families qualified for food stamps in February 1992; however only 51,649 received food stamp assistance.[96]

The discrepancy between those eligible for assistance and those who request and receive it is rooted in some fundamental American values.

Irrespective of our position on the ideological spectrum or our political party identification, part of the American ethos involves individualism and the belief that hard work will eventually pull us out of despair. We do not like to ask for help (especially from the government, which we want to be involved in our lives as little as possible), and our pride is hurt when we are forced to do so. The result is another paradox: many Americans who qualify for assistance are not getting it, yet a majority of Americans believe that government is providing too many services.[97]

Schools are the place where government has been most active in trying to provide healthful food and instill eating habits that lead to a healthy lifestyle. In 2010, the federal National School Lunch Program requirements were rewritten; more funding was allocated to the program so that school chefs are able to make more health-conscious choices for ingredients and recipes. At the same time, public interest groups, such as the Food Research and Action Center, have been trying to force vending machine suppliers to stock more healthful products in school vending machines.[98]

Covid-19

The first novel coronavirus case was detected in the United States on January 21, 2020.[99] While many public health experts warned of the potential for a global pandemic the likes of which we had not witnessed in a century, others, including President Trump, downplayed the disease, assuring the American public that it would be contained and that we could continue to live our lives normally.[100] Fearing the economic collapse that would come from widespread sheltering-in-place, President Trump acted slowly and, particularly in hindsight, with recklessness by minimizing the threat and not being forthcoming with the public about its potential disastrous effects.[101]

As it turned out, the virus not only killed a half-million Americans in its first year and caused yet-unknown long-term effects of those who survived it, but it also triggered a global economic recession that, as could be predicted by readers of this book, had disproportionate effects on the poor and in communities of color. While the economic impacts are not fully known (and have been discussed in previous chapters), it is worth considering the specific health disparities revealed and exacerbated by Covid-19.

The US Centers for Disease Control and Prevention issued a series of reports in December 2020 that detailed the multiple ways that racial and ethnic minorities were more susceptible to the disease. To that point in the pandemic, among those who were tested for Covid-19, positivity rates were as follows: 13.8 percent for African Americans, 13.5 percent for "other race," 11.9 percent for Hispanics/Latinos, 7.2 percent for Asians, and 7.0 percent for non-Hispanic whites.[102] African Americans, Hispanics, and American Indians/Alaska Natives were also more likely to be hospitalized than others who contracted the disease[103] and were more likely to die from the disease.[104] A report from the Kaiser Family Foundation succinctly summarizes the reasons for these disparities:

> [T]he higher infection rate among people of color likely reflects their increased risk of exposure to coronavirus due to their work, living, and transportation situations. They are more likely to be working in low-income jobs that cannot be done from home, to be living in larger households in densely populated areas, and to utilize public or shared modes of transportation. Despite being at increased risk of exposure to the virus, people of color did not have markedly higher testing rates compared to White patients and were more likely to be positive when tested and to require a higher level of care at the time they tested positive for COVID-19. These findings suggest that people of color may face increased barriers to testing that contribute to delays in them obtaining testing until they are in more serious condition.[105]

In short, a similar pattern emerges from these data as we have observed in other contexts: the cycle of advantage and disadvantage worked to the detriment of those who are most vulnerable, and the results in such a dire public health emergency were dramatic.

Conclusion

At the intersection of nutrition and lack of access to health care reside tremendous health disparities for America's poor and racial and ethnic minority communities. One study about the effect of social factors in the United States resulted in the following estimates about the indirect effects of racism and poverty:

> Approximately 245,000 deaths in the United States were attributable to low education, 176,000 to racial segregation, 162,000 to low social support, 133,000 to individual-level poverty, 119,000 to income inequality, and

39,000 to area-level poverty. These mortality estimates are comparable to deaths from the leading pathophysiological causes [such as] acute myocardial infarction ... a subset of heart disease that was the leading cause of death in the United States in 2000[,] cerebrovascular disease ... the third leading cause of death in 2000 ... and lung cancer.[106]

Individual government programs can mitigate the effects of this systemic disadvantage, but at least so far, they have been unable to eliminate it. For example, the food stamp program, now known as the Supplemental Nutrition Assistance Program (SNAP), has been in place since the Great Depression. To qualify for the program, an individual's gross monthly income cannot exceed $1,383 ($16,596 per year).[107] The persistently high unemployment rate combined with escalating food prices created a greater demand for the program during the Great Recession; in August 2012, the number of participants rose to a record level, with 47.1 million individuals—15 percent of the population—relying on SNAP for food.[108] In 2019, 38 million Americans were participating in the program.[109]

One perspective would be that it is fortunate that such a program is in place at a time when so many Americans would be hungry or malnourished without it. But in an era of increased partisanship and heightened concern about federal spending, not everyone saw it that way. In the spring of 2011, Republican presidential hopeful and former House speaker Newt Gingrich referred to President Barack Obama as a "food stamp president,"[110] a charge that several progressive bloggers, as well as *Meet the Press*'s David Gregory, believed contained racial undertones.[111] Seemingly Gingrich was trying to argue that Obama had been ineffective as a job-creating president, but the racialized reference to what many Americans consider to be welfare in connection with the first African American president was insensitive at best and racially nefarious at worst.[112] Criticism of publicly funded programs to help the needy is consistent with conservative philosophy in many ways, however, as Republicans have argued for charitable, rather than governmental, solutions to poverty and suffering.

Ultimately, it will be the interaction of government, the private sector, not-for-profit groups, and individual attitudes and behaviors that will close the health gap in the United States. As we have seen in other aspects of economic and racial disparity, individuals act within the parameters of systemic constraints, yet at the same time, in a democracy, individuals— usually working together in groups—can put pressure on those parameters to move the boundaries and make meaningful change. In the next chapter, we will examine how gender interacts with other demographic categories and social pressures to further complicate the portrait of inequality in America.

Discussion Questions

1. Consider the normative questions at the beginning of this chapter. To what extent do you agree or disagree with the ideas presented?

2. How do core American values intersect with health disparities? To what extent do these values coincide or contrast with the issues raised in this chapter? In what ways are these issues similar to or different than the topics raised in the previous chapters?

3. Do you agree with the idea that the language used to discuss inequality is important? Or is this an example of a professor simply making much ado about nothing?

4. Recall the cycle of advantage and disadvantage in Figure 2.4 on page 71. Health inequality was not part of the dynamic presented. Where does it fit, if at all?

5. If there are behavioral elements to health that also need to be considered, does health need to be thought of as a political issue at all? Discuss your thoughts using evidence from your own experience, as well as statistics from this chapter to support your position.

6. There is evidence that some individuals abuse government-sponsored food and nutrition programs by filing fraudulent claims, finding ways to convert funds designed for food allocation for other uses, etc. These cases get great media attention, which causes fraud to be perceived as much more rampant than it is. What, if any, responsibility do media outlets have to report on examples of fraud and/or contextualize them to offer an accurate picture of the efficacy of such programs?

8

. . . .

Gender

WHILE OUR PRIMARY FOCUS IS THE SYSTEMICALLY ROOTED INTERSECTION of poverty and race, it is essential to understand the powerful interactive effect of gender in this dynamic. Much more than other forms of demographic categorization beyond race and ethnicity (e.g., sexual orientation, religious affiliation), gender has had a disproportionate impact on poverty in the United States. How it intersects with economics, race, and ethnicity is important to consider.

We Just Don't Get It

During the second presidential debate in 2012, a citizen asked the candidates what new proposals they had to "rectify the inequalities in the workplace, specifically regarding females making only 72 percent of what their male counterparts earn." President Obama responded first and talked about his upbringing (being raised by a single mother), his signing of the Lilly Ledbetter Act,[1] and his advocacy for access to Pell Grants for college. When it was Governor Mitt Romney's turn to answer, he provided fodder for weeks of ridicule, as well as an excellent starting point for our exploration of gender inequality:

> Thank you. An important topic, and one which I learned a great deal about, particularly as I was serving as governor of my state, because I had the chance to pull together a cabinet and all the applicants seemed to be men.
>
> And I—and I went to my staff, and I said, "How come all the people for these jobs are—are all men." They said, "Well, these are the people that have the qualifications." And I said, "Well, gosh, can't we—can't we find some—some women that are also qualified?"
>
> And—and so we—we took a concerted effort to go out and find women who had backgrounds that could be qualified to become members of

DOI: 10.4324/9781003043041-9

our cabinet. I went to a number of women's groups and said, "Can you help us find folks," and they brought us whole binders full of women. I was proud of the fact that after I staffed my cabinet and my senior staff, that the University of New York in Albany did a survey of all 50 states, and concluded that mine had more women in senior leadership positions than any other state in America. Now one of the reasons I was able to get so many good women to be part of that team was because of our recruiting effort. But number two, because I recognized that if you're going to have women in the workforce that sometimes you need to be more flexible. My chief of staff, for instance, had two kids that were still in school. She said, I can't be here until 7 or 8 o'clock at night. I need to be able to get home at 5 o'clock so I can be there for making dinner for my kids and being with them when they get home from school. So we said fine. Let's have a flexible schedule so you can have hours that work for you.

We're going to have to have employers in the new economy, in the economy I'm going to bring to play, that are going to be so anxious to get good workers they're going to be anxious to hire women. In the—in the last [*sic*] women have lost 580,000 jobs. That's the net of what's happened in the last four years. We're still down 580,000 jobs. I mentioned 3½ million women, more now in poverty than four years ago.

What we can do to help young women and women of all ages is to have a strong economy, so strong that employers that are looking to find good employees and bringing them into their workforce and adapting to a flexible work schedule that gives women opportunities that they would otherwise not be able to afford.

This is what I have done. It's what I look forward to doing and I know what it takes to make an economy work, and I know what a working economy looks like. And an economy with 7.8 percent unemployment is not a real strong economy. An economy that has 23 million people looking for work is not a strong economy.[2]

The revealing aspect of this answer is not the "binders full of women" comment, which was ridiculed for sounding silly[3] (Romney meant binders full of women's résumés, not binders with actual women in them). It is illuminating because it was seen as a Freudian slip that revealed how Governor (now US Senator) Romney, as well as most Americans, views the issue of sexism. He invoked the common "add women and stir" approach that treats sexism with quota-like solutions (something, ironically, that conservatives have long opposed in the legal realm, as we will explore in Chapter 9). What would seem to the casual observer to be a perfectly logical answer actually reveals many limitations of individual-level treatment of structural disadvantage.

We can start with Governor Romney's immediate instinct to answer a question about systemic disadvantage with a personal story about his experience with women in the workforce. He suggests that he recognized sexism when he was presented with a list of candidates who were all men,[4] and most of his answer was about creating an economy with a lot of jobs so that women (and presumably men) have opportunities for employment. But that was not the question. The question was about the pay gap (discussed in more detail later in this chapter) among people who are already employed.

Governor Romney's multiple references to women needing flexible schedules so that they can get home to make dinner for their families are equally illustrative of his seeming inability to understand systemic sexism. In the twenty-first century, both men and women have assumed a more equal (but as yet not equitable)[5] share of household duties,[6] as an increasing percentage of couples are characterized by both adults working outside of the home.[7] Further, women are the primary breadwinners in an increasing number of households with both an adult man and an adult woman.[8] While Governor Romney's statements might have resonated with middle-aged voters, many young voters would find such an assumption curious at best and offensive at worst. Men would also benefit from a flexible work schedule so that they can get home to make dinner for the family and, if they have children, be available to pick them up from school, get them to after-school activities, and so on (and if they had it, they might be more likely to assume a greater share of childcare responsibilities, which are still falling disproportionately on women).[9] Such an antiquated view of gender roles reflects not only the degree of progress that needs to be made to eliminate sexism, but also the overly simplistic nature of our collective understanding of the problems that remain.

Getting Our Language Straight

Our approach to the definitional elements of this discussion should parallel our treatment of the words *racism, bigotry,* and *prejudice* in the Introduction. That is, being precise with our language is the first step toward a more sophisticated understanding of how gender works in the United States.

Sex and Gender

Many researchers hold that the term *sex* refers to anatomical and physiological differences, whereas *gender* refers to the social construct that differentiates men from women. For instance, the fact that only women can become pregnant is a function of sex; the fact that women are disproportionately expected to be child-care providers is a function of gender. Beyond breastfeeding, there is nothing inherent about a man's biology that makes him less capable of caring for infants or children than a woman, but there are significant social constraints about parental responsibilities that center on gender.[10]

Sexism and Misogyny

As with racism, the important element that is often neglected in discussions of sexism is power. False equivalency claims are common: real or perceived disadvantages for men are presented as evidence that sexism "goes both ways." As with racism, the word *sexism* is most accurately reserved for the notion that men are inherently superior to women. This systemic hierarchy, known as patriarchy, involves largely unspoken and powerful assumptions and expectations that privilege men in our society.

The dynamic is reflected in the language that we have available for communication. For instance, prior to 2019, we had no gender-neutral singular pronoun—we only had *he or she*, and *him or her*—so we were forced to consider gender, even when it should not matter. Now, however, most of the major style guides recommend using "they" or "them" even in the singular to avoid this problematic dynamic.[11] This is important with respect to occupations, too (e.g., fireman, policeman, mailman). Even though political scientists and most journalists use the more acceptable term *member of Congress* or the clumsier *congressperson* to refer to representatives in the US Congress, most Americans continue to refer to them as "congressmen." This matters for more than symbolic reasons (though they are also important). First, it does not accurately reflect the idea that it is designed to capture (i.e., there are women who are members of Congress) and, second, it perpetuates gender inequality by setting up an abstract ideal with which women must compete (in addition to competing with their opponents) when they run for election. Because men can more easily present themselves as closer to the ideal, they are advantaged by having the vague term presented as a gendered construct.

This is an example of *sexism*. It is systemic and often subconscious. *Misogyny*, on the other hand, while it can also be subconscious, most accurately refers to individual-level resentment or even outright hatred for women. There is no question that misogyny is rooted in sexism, but it is important, as with racism, to separate the systemic from the individual so that we can adequately address both without conflating the concepts.[12] At the individual level, women can harbor resentment toward men. We might refer to that as prejudice or bigotry, but calling it sexist undermines the historic reality of male privilege in the same way that using the term *racist* to refer to animosity toward whites by persons of color does.[13]

The 2016 presidential election provided fertile ground for discussion about these constructs. As the first female candidate nominated for president by a major political party, Hillary Clinton sought to leverage her place in history through her slogans ("I'm with her.") and campaign imagery (shattering the glass ceiling). In contrast, Donald Trump was accused of both sexism[14] and misogyny[15] as a result of his behavior and statements during the campaign, as well as information that surfaced from his past.[16] Most egregious was the recording that surfaced from an appearance on the *Access Hollywood* entertainment program wherein Trump, seemingly not knowing he was being recorded, boasted about instigating unwanted sexual contact and sexually assaulting women ("I just start kissing them … I don't even wait") without punishment because "when you're a star, they let you do it."[17] Those comments, along with his reference to Hillary Clinton as a "nasty woman" during a debate,[18] solidified persistent concerns from some commentators that his sexism and misogyny were issues to be considered on Election Day.

Indeed, 2016 featured the largest gender gap recorded since 1976,[19] with Hillary Clinton having a 13-percentage point advantage with women and Donald Trump having an 11-percentage point advantage among men.[20] More women voted than men (53 percent),[21] which partially accounted for Secretary Clinton's popular vote victory.[22] It is important to note, however, that a gender gap in this context reflects more than just the simple fact that one candidate was male and the other was female. Donald Trump embodied a gendered persona that was an important thread throughout his first campaign (as well as his presidency):

> This was an election in which the grievances of white men—their economic upheaval, their cultural displacement—exploded. The fallout included toxic paroxysms of racism, Islamophobia, anti-Semitism and sexism. Misogyny,

it appears, thrives in the corners of the United States. Donald J. Trump's hyper-masculinity—the sexual swagger, the belittling of his opponents, his need to dominate—appealed to some men who believed he could restore them to their rightful place.[23]

However, the overall gender gap in 2016 masks a powerful truth related to intersectionality: black women and Latinas supported Hillary Clinton by 90 points and 44 points, respectively, while the majority of white women (52 percent) supported Donald Trump, reflecting a gap of nine points. The gaps for women of color are greater than the gaps for men of color—black men favored Clinton by 69 points; Latinos favored her by 31 points. None of these trends is a function of two candidates during one campaign, however; the campaign and the candidates operate as part of a larger, longer narrative that is rooted in our deeply held beliefs and expectations about how members of each gender should behave.

In 2020, Donald Trump faced another woman on the ballot—this time as a Vice Presidential candidate, US Senator Kamala Harris of California.[24] Harris identifies as both African American and South Asian (Indian), and as such, her candidacy and eventual victory are historic. The gender gap was prevalent in the 2020 election, as well, as Joe Biden had a 13-point lead with women and Trump had a 8-point lead with men.[25] Again, though, it was the strength of black women in particular, 91 percent of whom voted for Biden and Harris, which solidified that gap and, indeed, their victory.[26] This reminds us that we cannot and should not assume that women will vote for women (Biden's share of the women's vote was greater than Hillary Clinton's in 2016) and that all women—anymore than all members of a racial or ethnic group—vote for the same reasons. Much of the vote choice, like all of our attitudes and behaviors, are shaped by explicit and implicit signals we receive throughout our lives.

Socialization

The process by which we acquire beliefs, attitudes, and behaviors from previous generations is referred to as socialization. It is certainly clear by now that we absorb racist ideas throughout our lives; sexist beliefs are acquired in much the same way. There is ample anecdotal evidence to support the notion that we are socialized into accepting gender roles even earlier and more deliberately than we are with respect to racial categorizations. For gender, the work begins in utero. With ultrasound technology,

Box 8.1. *Representing*: Jessica Valenti

Jessica Valenti is co-founder and former managing editor of the now-shuttered Feministing.com, "an online community for feminists and their allies." She was named one of the top 100 inspiring women in the world by the *Guardian* in 2011,[28] and she is the author or co-author of seven books: *Full Frontal Feminism: A Young Woman's Guide to Why Feminism Matters; Yes Means Yes: Visions of Female Sexual Power and a World Without Rape; He's a Stud, She's a Slut, and 49 Other Double Standards Every Woman Should Know; The Purity Myth: How America's Obsession with Virginity Is Hurting Young Women; Why Have Kids? A New Mom Explores the Truth about Parenting and Happiness; Sex Object: A Memoir;* and *Believe Me: How Trusting Women Can Change the World.* She wrote for the *Guardian* and currently is a contributing columnist for *Medium.*[29]

Valenti started Feministing because she felt that young women's voices were not being heard. Although feminists are often considered to be politically liberal, for Valenti reaching conservatives is an important goal. She sought to make feminism accessible and said that "more people are feminists than they realize … they hear the word, and they don't want to identify as feminists, but they believe in feminist values [such as] equal pay for equal work, [eliminating violence against women, and] reproductive justice." Feministing was characterized by humor and insight that were consciously designed to be accessible.[30] Valenti recognizes that white, middle-class women are still disproportionately at the helm of feminist institutions; she is consistently reflecting on her own privilege and advocating for more voices to be heard.[31]

Feministing, like other online efforts, struggled with economic viability. Feministing had advertising, but some users prefer not to see ads. Valenti notes, however, that revenue is important to sustain the site that profits are distributed equitably among staffers, and that contributors are compensated.[32] In this way, she has sought to model the justice that she so vocally demands.

it is common for parents to learn the sex of their unborn as early as the 20th week of pregnancy, at least partially driven by a desire to buy clothes and decorate a nursery in colors that are considered appropriate.[27] As soon as a baby is delivered, the first question future parents receive is "What is it?"

Advertisements, catalogs, and websites for toy companies are clearly delineated in blue and pink tones, and stories (both in print and on film) that are directed to toddlers contain powerful messages relating to gender norms and expectations.

Fairy tales and Disney princess movies are prime carriers of sexist (and heteronormative) messages about the proper roles for men and women in society. Cinderella sings as she cleans and dreams of attending a grand ball to be chosen by the prince, and Ariel from *The Little Mermaid* gives up her voice so that she can be with a man, for that is how women are taught that they will find happiness.[33] Messages about standards of beauty are also prevalent in these stories, as are stereotypes about appropriate appearance, attitudes, and behavior for men and boys.[34]

Feminism

Sometimes referred to as the "f-word" by feminists,[35] the word *feminism* has been attacked for decades and saddled with much pejorative baggage. Most Americans assume that feminists are women, though many men criticize patriarchy and advocate for increasing equality between men and women.[36] Many Americans believe that feminists hate men and wish to see a world where women are superior. Feminists, however, come from many perspectives,[37] and the zero-sum mentality mirrors concerns that whites harbor with respect to increasing racial equality.

It is mostly agreed that feminism can be conceptualized historically into three waves.[38] The first wave dealt primarily with women's suffrage (late nineteenth and early twentieth centuries); the second wave (1960s through 1980s) centered on consciousness raising, equal rights more broadly, and (at least toward the end), expanding consideration of nonwhite women's voices; the third wave began in the 1990s and is concerned with a sophisticated critique of the conceptualization and construction of gender.[39]

One particularly compelling perspective emerged from the second wave and persisted into the third: the notion of the male gaze. In the 1970s, Laura Mulvey[40] put forward a critique of film that invoked the notion that there is a tendency for the world to be seen (and filmed) from the perspective of men. This notion has come to serve as a theoretical lens through which all aspects of culture can be viewed. Central to this perspective is the notion of women as objects (rather than subjects).[41] Some third-wave theorizing and activism has involved women reclaiming their sexuality in ways that make some second-wave feminists uncomfortable.[42] Beyond content, however, third-wave feminists are using modern technology and cultural trends to engage with one another and with the world in ways that would have been impossible for their predecessors. Blogs and social networking have afforded these writers the opportunity to express themselves without filters or editors, but they face pressures that are inherent in this type of communication, as well (see Box 8.2).

Box 8.2. *What Can I Do?:* Blogs and Podcasts

Reading feminist blogs and websites and listening to feminist podcasts is a useful (and enjoyable) way to stay apprised of the way contemporary culture can be viewed through feminist lenses. Below is a list of some prominent feminist blogs, websites, and podcasts, but it is important to stay alert because new outlets are being created all the time. Since blogging avoids gatekeepers, writing one's own analysis of current events, popular culture, or other interesting aspects of life can be a meaningful form of expression with a potential to reach a very wide audience. Make sure that your blog or podcast is integrated with your other social networking sites, such as Twitter, Instagram, and Facebook, and do not be shy about tagging more established bloggers and columnists to try to get them to read what you are writing. A well-placed re-tweet or share from someone with many followers can garner attention and give you a chance to interact in a meaningful and fulfilling way with others:

Bitch Media: https://bitchmedia.org
Black Girl Dangerous: https://bgdblog.org
Call Your Girlfriend (podcast)
Feminist Frequency: https://feministfrequency.com
Jezebel: http://jezebel.com
Makers (Yahoo!): https://www.yahoo.com/lifestyle/makers/
Popaganda (podcast)
TransGriot: http://transgriot.blogspot.com
Therapy for Black Girls (podcast)
Unladylike (podcast)
Viva La Feminista: http://www.vivalafeminista.com/

Third-wavers have been more intentional about recognizing their own privileges (when and where they exist) with respect to social class, sexual orientation, able-bodiedness, and race, as well as being inclusive of voices that previous generations of feminists have been accused of neglecting.[43] One might speculate that the more democratic nature of our communication has converged with theoretical and empirical work by scholars to create an ideology that is better positioned to consider the ways that various hegemonic forces intersect to provide advantages and disadvantages, privileges and challenges.

Intersectionality

As noted in the Introduction, we cannot simply assume that privilege (or disadvantage) is additive, as if being white has privilege and being male has privilege, then being white and male carries twice as much privilege. Sometimes that is the case,[44] but interactions among demographic elements are complex and sometimes counterintuitive. As we consider the degree to which gender intersects with economic inequality in the United States, we must also consider how race forms an interaction that will complicate our work.

Gender Inequality and Poverty

Much has been written about how patriarchy operates in the United States and globally, but here we will focus on ways that these systemic and attitudinal factors relate to economic inequality. Like each topic we have explored, this one is complicated, though it is rarely presented that way in public discourse.

Income and Wealth

The most visible element of gender inequality in the United States is the wage gap. As noted in Chapter 2, it is well documented that women earn less pay for comparable work. This gap has been relatively consistent for decades—at least since women began to enter the paid workforce in high numbers.[45] One reason for such inequity could be interpersonal—women are not valued as much as men, so they are paid less. However disturbing this reason may be, it is also too simple and far too convenient. If the problem of pay equity were limited to men in power not valuing women they hire, then the solution would be to punish those who are making inequitable decisions or wait until they retire and then replace them with Americans socialized in later eras who tend to have more explicitly egalitarian views. Unfortunately, the reality is not so straightforward.

The share of women in the labor market had increased steadily since the 1980s, peaked in 1999 (at 60 percent), and has been decreasing since.[46] In 2019, women comprised 47 percent of the US labor force; 57.4 percent of women were in the labor force, compared to 69.2 percent of men. Women have not yet achieved pay equity in most occupations. Women are disadvantaged for a number of reasons relating to deeply held beliefs about their proper place (in the home versus in the workplace), their abilities and intelligence, and their biology. With respect to the latter, it is important to understand the notion of the mommy track,[47] which is a result of women taking time away from workplace participation as a result of childbirth and sometimes child rearing. While biology necessitates rest and healing after childbirth, cultural pressures dictate that women function as the primary caretaker of children,[48] which results in longer periods of time away from their career. When a woman returns to the office or worksite, a man who was hired at the same time and performed comparably will have advanced, while she returns to the position that she had before her leave. A heterosexual couple with both adults working outside the home may choose to have multiple children, and with each child the woman's career may be suspended, leading to disparities in pay and rank.[49]

Further, there are deeply held beliefs in our culture about what types of jobs are appropriate for men and for women. Such occupational segregation is partially responsible for the persistent wage gap. Women are hired disproportionately into occupations that have lower pay. These so-called pink-collar occupations (most often service-oriented positions, such as cashiers, food servers, and caretakers for the sick, elderly, and children)[50] are disproportionately populated by women and pay less than those that are populated primarily by men. Women comprise 62.8 percent of minimum wage workers (compared to 37.2 percent for men).[51] Besides being paid less for the same job, women also tend to dominate occupations with the lowest pay.[52] As we have seen in other contexts, race matters here, too, with women of color faring even worse than their white female counterparts in terms of the effect of occupational segregation on earnings.[53]

A 2016 report attributed the persistence of the wage gap in part to an emerging trend in labor compensation overall:

> Hourly pay has risen more than twice as fast over the past three decades for men working long hours, as employers increasingly reward employees willing to work extra hours with raises or promotions.... Men make up a bit more than half the full-time workforce, but they account for more than 70 percent of those working 50 hours a week or more. So as wage gains have gone disproportionately to people working long hours, they have also gone disproportionately to men, widening the earnings divide between men and women overall.... [This] trend contributes to the wage gap because men are so much more likely than women to work those long hours. That, in turn, is the result of a confluence of factors that are deeply embedded in the American economy and society: Women, on average, spend much more time than men on housework, while men ... are expected to work as much as possible. And of course, most importantly, mothers are still far more likely than fathers to be the primary caregiver for their children.[54]

It is clear that women face systemic challenges to equality that are much more complicated than our colloquial understanding of sexism as individual-level preferences for men over women with respect to workforce participation.

All of this contributes to what has been termed the feminization of poverty.[55] In 2018, 21.4 million women lived in poverty (56 percent of all those living in poverty); nearly half of the women who were living in poverty lived in extreme poverty (with income at or below 50 percent of the federal poverty level),[56] and adult women compose 36 percent of Medicaid recipients.[57] Across all races and ethnicities, women have higher rates of poverty than men. American Indian/Alaska Native women have the highest rates of poverty (24.6 percent), followed by African American women (22.5 percent), Hispanic women (19.4 percent), and Asian/Pacific Islander women (10 percent). White women's poverty rate is 9 percent.[58]

As noted in Chapter 2, however, poverty has at least as much to do with wealth as it does with income. While it is often difficult to measure wealth from the perspective of gender because wealth is measured as a function of household rather than individuals, we can gain an appreciation for the relationship between gender and poverty if we consider the case of single women. Households led by women that do not have other adult earners in the home constitute the highest levels of poverty, particularly when there are children in the home. It will be no surprise to readers at this point that race factors into these numbers in predictable ways: in 2018, 38 percent of black single mothers, 38 percent of Hispanic single mothers, and 43 percent of Native American single mothers were living in poverty, as compared to 28 percent of white single mothers.[59] The poverty rate for married couples with children (all races) was 4.7 percent.[60]

Women who are divorced are likely to have custody of children, and if they were not working outside the home while they were married, they find themselves at a competitive disadvantage for gainful employment (not to mention struggles with finding affordable child care if the children are not in school) after separation.[61] Senior women face similar challenges: in 2017, married women aged 65 or older had a poverty rate of 4.3 percent, compared to 13.9 percent of widows, 15.8 percent of divorced women, and 21.5 percent of women who were never married.[62] Although women account for more than half of all Social Security beneficiaries, their benefits are smaller because their earnings, on average, were lower. In 2017, the average retired woman earned $14,353 per year in Social Security benefits compared to $18,041 for men.[63] African American men received, on average, $16,265 per year in Social Security in 2017, compared to African American women, who received $13,574.[64] Widows are more likely to be impoverished than widowers, and because women tend to live longer than men, widows have a longer period of time to live without their partner than widowers do. In fact, "two-thirds of women who are married at retirement will outlive their husbands by an average of 8.5 years."[65] Two-fifths of women experience poverty within five years of the death of their husband.[66]

Social Class

While poverty is the focus of this discussion, women in high-status occupations also face relative disadvantages that parallel the experiences of poor women. As referenced in Chapter 2, there is a stigma attached to receiving some forms of public assistance in the United States, and the correlation with racialization of the assistance is great. While few harbor animosity toward those who receive veterans' benefits, Social Security, Medicare, or even unemployment compensation, many resent Americans who participate in assistance programs, such as Temporary Assistance for Needy Families (TANF); the Women, Infants and Children (WIC) program; and the Supplemental Nutrition Assistance Program (SNAP; formerly food stamps).[67] Ronald Reagan was successful in invoking the term "welfare queen" not only because Linda Taylor was African American, but also because she was a woman.[68]

However, the notion of women being less valuable to society is a recurring narrative that stretches from the welfare line to the boardroom. Studies of women in executive positions shed additional light on gender inequality among the highest ranked positions in corporate America. As noted in Chapter 2, women headed 38 Fortune 500 companies in 2020.[69] While some inequity is surely a result of issues that we have already discussed, a body of research demonstrates that socialized gender norms may be a contributing factor.[70] Further, the pattern exists in work outside of business; there is gender imbalance at the highest levels in academia, particularly in science, technology, engineering, and mathematics (STEM), because, as will be discussed in a later section, girls are not encouraged to pursue those subjects in school, and young women are discouraged from pursuing advanced degrees in those fields.[71]

Poverty, Reproductive Health, and the Struggle for Control of a Woman's Body

Mommy track norms are connected to overt attempts to exert reproductive control over a woman's body, particularly those of poor women and women of color. From decades of eugenics policies in the United States at the beginning of the twentieth century[72] (some states continued the practice of forced sterilization into the 1970s)[73] to assumptions about poor women and women of color and promiscuity, the tendency has been to ignore or remove agency from women, especially as it relates to reproductive health.

Popular assumptions hold that poverty is at least partly a result of poor individuals reproducing when they cannot afford to raise children. Because child rearing in our culture is largely presumed to be the province of women, our collective fingers are often pointed squarely at poor teens and women for not being more responsible. Ignoring for a moment that the same folks who make those accusations are often those who work to deny access to birth control or abortion (and the fact that boys and men are equally responsible for a pregnancy in consensual situations), it is important to consider the direction of the causal arrow. In other words, it is also logical to consider that poverty leads to unplanned or even unwanted pregnancy rather than the other way around. Recent research has found that to be the case with respect to teen pregnancies,[74] and our exploration here suggests that the interrelationships among such factors as education, health, and economic opportunities likely serve as constraints on the choices that poor young women make with respect to reproduction.

But the link between reproductive health and sexism is also not limited to women who experience poverty. The provision in the Patient Protection and Affordable Care Act that requires employers to provide free birth control as part of their insurance coverage for employees has been extensively debated. Wheaton College, an evangelical institution in Illinois, and Catholic University in Washington, DC, both sued the Obama administration over the provision,[75] arguing that the mandate would force them to violate core elements of their faith.[76] Debate about religious institutions and patriarchy dates back much farther than these recent policy squabbles, and reasonable people can disagree about the appropriateness of termination of pregnancies at various stages of gestation. Irrespective of one's position on those issues, however, it must be noted that women (and women's bodies) are often discussed as though they are primarily or even wholly designed to be vessels for fetal development.[77]

Sexual Harassment

Women's struggle for control of their own bodies extends beyond reproductive health. As long as women and girls have been studying and working outside the home, they have been subject to harassment related to their gender. The term "sexual harassment" dates to the mid-1970s, but prior to that, organizers worked to bring attention to sexual violence in various contexts.[78] As women began to enter the workforce in greater numbers, though, they were subjected to "unwelcome sexual advances, requests for sexual favors, and other verbal or physical harassment of a sexual nature."[79] When US Supreme Court Justice Clarence Thomas (see Box 9.1) was seeking confirmation to the bench, a former associate, Professor Anita Hill, came forward to accuse him of having sexually harassed her when they worked together. Those hearings brought the concept to even greater levels of awareness, which resulted in challenges to judicial interpretation and administrative enforcement of existing laws, including Title IX, providing protection in educational settings, and Title IV, which covers employment.[80]

In 2017, actor Alyssa Milano tweeted about the harassment she faced at the hands of movie producer Harvey Weinstein, using the hashtag #MeToo, a phrase originally coined by Tarana Burke more than a decade earlier.[81] Soon came a website[82] and heightened use of the phrase on social media as a way to alert men about the pain and damage harassment causes, as well as assure women that they are not alone in enduring such treatment. Time's Up[83] followed shortly thereafter, advocating not only for awareness but also for change leading to safety and equity in the workplace.[84] When President Trump nominated Brett Kavanaugh to the US Supreme Court in 2018, history from the Thomas hearings seemed to be repeating, as multiple women came forward with claims that he sexually assaulted (not harassed) them while in college.[85] As with Clarence Thomas, Kavanaugh was confirmed.

In addition to the psychological trauma of experiencing sexual harassment and violence, there is evidence that there is an economic cost, as well. In 2018, those costs were estimated to be more than $3 billion in productivity and other costs, and an additional $250 million in lost well-being.[86]

Gender and Housing Access

As is the case with wealth, it is difficult to discuss housing inequality with respect to gender because men and women cohabitate at far greater rates than do members of different racial and ethnic groups. As was the case with wealth, statistical analysis is largely limited to women who are heads of household, whether or not they are raising children.

In a broader sense, the notion of home has been intricately linked with women throughout the nation's history. In the nineteenth century a haven model of domestic life emerged that "emphasized the importance of sequestering women in private homes, and focused on making the home a relaxing respite from the competition of capitalist society for the husband/father and a nurturing environment for the children, maintained by the wife/mother."[87] This separate-spheres approach maintained public space as the dominion of men and reserved the private sphere for women. Government policies designed to encourage home ownership in the early part of the twentieth century often included explicit policies that disadvantaged women.[88] As divorce rates climbed or children were born out of wedlock, women were in a position to find safe, affordable housing for their family. Many of the resulting issues in this area converge with our broader discussion of housing in Chapter 3 (public housing, Section 8, etc.), but we should keep in mind that women and men often experienced these challenges differently.

Gender Inequality and Education

The existence of gender inequality in education is well documented. Data collected over the past few decades do not present a clear picture of inequity (e.g., some of the differences in achievement shift when considered at different ages, and socioeconomic status is a relevant consideration), but girls tend to have lower achievement in science and mathematics and higher scores in reading, particularly at younger ages.[89] Research demonstrates that the gender gap with respect to quantitative reasoning tends to widen during K-12 schooling and that biology interacts with environmental factors to produce such divergence.[90]

In the United States girls tend to finish high school at higher rates than boys, a trend that persists across racial and ethnic groups.[91] In the past two decades, men have been slightly less likely than women to enroll in college directly after high school,[92] which correlates positively with college enrollment (delaying enrollment tends to result in lower eventual attendance rates).[93] Boys have consistently outperformed girls on the Scholastic Aptitude Test (SAT),[94] particularly on the mathematics section, with the 2018 results revealing a 20-point gap (542 to 522).[95] The science and mathematics gap persists into college[96] and is reflected in the workforce: the pay gap for women in their first year out of college is consistent with the overall gender wage gap.[97]

However, women are attending college and graduating at higher rates than their male counterparts. Within the past few years, the narrowing gender gap of the portion of the US population holding a bachelor's degree resulted in women surpassing men, though men still comprise a slight majority of degree holders in the labor force.[98] This is the result of decades of women earning more bachelor's degrees than men. This pattern holds across racial groups: since the mid-1990s, white, black, and Hispanic women were all more likely than their male counterparts to hold a bachelor's degree; by 2010, the same was true for Asian women.[99]

Women tend to drop out of college at lower rates, finish their degree more quickly, and are now more likely than men to attend graduate school and earn graduate degrees. In 2019, women earned 58.5 percent of master's degrees, and 52.9 percent of doctoral degrees.[100] These awards were not distributed evenly across fields of study, showing notable gaps in some

STEM fields.[101] Even so, the wage gap persists, which reflects the complexity of how advantage and disadvantage work in the United States.

Gender and Criminal Justice

Women are incarcerated much less frequently than men. Data for 2018 from the US Bureau of Justice Statistics reveal that 38 percent of women in state prison have been convicted of violent crimes (compared to 58 percent of men); most other inmates are serving sentences for property (24 percent) and drug (26 percent) offenses.[102] Racial minorities constitute a disproportionate number of women in prisons or jails, with non-Hispanic whites comprising 53 percent, African American women accounting for 29 percent, and Hispanic women representing 14 percent of the incarcerated population.[103] In addition to the 230,000 women and girls who were incarcerated in prisons or jails in 2019, another one million were on probation or parole.[104] In 2019, men were in state or federal prison at a rate of 789 per 100,000 adults, while women's incarceration rate was 61 per 100,000 adults.[105] These figures represented a decrease for men and an increase for women over the previous year, a steady decline for women since 2009 (when they comprised 67 per 100,000 adults), and a rapid decline for men over that same period (when they were 972 per 100,000 adults).[106] Despite the recent trends, there was a dramatic increase in the number of women incarcerated in state and federal prisons, as well as jail over the past four decades—from 1980 to 2019, the number grew from 26,378 to 222,455.[107] One out of every 12 children in the United States (5.7 million children) have experienced a parent being sent away to prison.[108] Again, there is a racial component: black (13 percent), American Indian (26 percent), and Hispanic (7 percent) children are more likely than white children (6 percent) to have had an incarcerated parent.[109]

Noting the historic level of incarceration for African American women, one legal scholar argues that:

> African American women face challenges in re-entry and reintegration that other populations do not have to face. Incarcerated African American women are mothers, care givers and heads of household before they become offenders. Once they become offenders, their children become displaced and income that is desperately needed by their families is lost. African American children languish in foster care, awaiting their parents['] release from prison or alternately become permanently severed from their families.[110]

Women of all races face these unique circumstances when they are sent to prison (and when they are released), but the disproportionate number of women of color who are incarcerated warrants increased focus on these women in particular as we seek to understand the interrelationship of crime and poverty.

Our collective narrative in this realm is familiar, as well. As is the case with public assistance (e.g., the "welfare queen" trope), there has been a tendency to blame single women (particularly women of color) for violent crime. In the early 1990s, Health and Human Services secretary Louis W. Sullivan attributed homicide figures, in part, to "the collapse of the American family," particularly in the black community.[111] Over a 40-year period, the numbers do not support such a narrative[112] (and even if they did, we would be wise to consider not only the arrow of causality but moderating and mediating factors[113] as well), but the sentiment is no less powerful for this lack of evidence. Answering a question about gun violence in the second presidential debate in 2012, Governor Mitt Romney spent time arguing for the importance of a two-parent family as a way to "make changes in the way our culture works to help bring people away from violence and give them opportunity, and bring them in the American system."[114] As we have already seen, there is certainly a correlation between crime and poverty, as well as a correlation between poverty and single-parent families. However, a sophisticated analysis is warranted; suggesting a direct relationship between single-parent households and violence provides a convenient but unfortunate opportunity for those who are less versed in the nuance of inequality to attribute the violence to poor choices made by persons of color in particular rather than larger, systemic explanations.

Gender, Reproductive Rights, and Health

While space does not permit a thorough discussion of gender disparities related to health,[115] we will look at the most politicized of women's health issues: reproductive rights. Strong moral and ethical issues are intertwined with the question of whether terminating a fetus is appropriate (including the philosophical question of whether life begins at conception, at some stage during gestation, or at birth), but few women have been part of the decision-making process. Most elected officials at all levels of government, as will be discussed in greater detail in a later section, are and have been men, as are most judges, including US Supreme Court justices, who have the last word on many aspects of this debate. In 1973, an all-male Court declared that terminating a pregnancy in the first two trimesters was a constitutionally protected right,[116] lending support for the substantive representation model of governance.

In recent years, a number of states have attempted to pass so-called personhood amendments to state constitutions, as well as the US Constitution. Such provisions would designate a fertilized human egg as a legal person, thus protecting it from termination.[117] Pro-choice advocates view such positioning as pitting the rights of a fetus against the rights of a woman.[118]

These issues are connected to broader elements of women's reproductive health and sexual violence. Georgetown University law student Sandra Fluke achieved a tremendous amount of attention[119] in 2012 when she was called a "slut" and a "prostitute" by a talk radio host for demanding that her birth control pills be covered by the Catholic institution's health-care policy. The attacks on Fluke went beyond reasonable disagreement about religious freedom or reproductive rights; she became a symbol of the collective view of women held by many Americans. Later that year, a number of candidates for public office found themselves heavily criticized for their comments about rape (as it relates to exceptions for abortion), with Missouri's Todd Akin opining that pregnancy as a result of rape is rare because if a woman is the victim of a "legitimate rape, the female body has ways to try to shut that whole thing down"[120] and Indiana's Richard Mourdock noting that if a woman does become pregnant as a result of a rape, the pregnancy (though presumably not the assault) is a "gift from God."[121] Both candidates lost their respective races.

The symbolic importance of men making statements that are factually inaccurate (Akin) and woefully insensitive (both candidates) cannot be ignored. If we revisit our consideration of symbolic and substantive representation from Chapter 1, we will be in a stronger position to examine the degree to which having more women in office might affect decisions relating not only to reproductive rights and women's health but also to core policy issues discussed throughout this chapter and book including housing, education, and crime.

Beyond reproductive rights, related issues highlight health disparities with respect to childbearing. For example, a recent study found that depression caused by discrimination leads to low birth weight in babies. Babies born to white women and Latinas are at half the risk of low birth weight as are those born to black women. The study showed, however, that even holding race constant (as well as age and type of discrimination), women who reported discrimination had higher levels of depression and babies who weighed less than those who did not report facing discrimination.[122]

Intersectional explanations for mortality and morbidity (being unhealthy) disparities over the past three decades are available as well, and this trend is not completely driven by level of education or socioeconomics; African American women with a college degree report worse health conditions than do African American men with a high school education.[123] As highlighted in the previous chapter, women of color face a variety of health disparities compared to white women. These challenges can result from disproportionate poverty and contribute to economic challenges.

Women in Office

As noted in Chapter 1, the 117th Congress (2021–2023) includes a record number of women (130—nearly 30 percent of members).[124] For half a decade now, over 100 women have occupied Capitol Hill offices, participating in committee work and debate and ultimately voting on national policy. Recall that from the perspective of symbolic (or "descriptive") representation, members of minority groups in particular benefit from having folks who have lived similar experiences in positions of power. The positive elements range from being visible role models for youngsters to serving as mentors to helping usher in a greater number of policy decisions that are perceived as beneficial. On the other hand, it could be argued that so long as the interests of white women and persons of color are meaningfully considered and their voices are heard in the process, substantive benefits can be expected. At least one set of researchers, however, do not expect that the record number of women will result in more meaningful representation of issues that are of disproportionate interest to women. Their research reveals that until a deliberative body reaches at least 60 percent women, they tend to speak less frequently than do their male counterparts, and they avoid raising issues about the most vulnerable Americans.[125]

Patricia Scott Schroeder relates a story about her first term in Congress in 1973:

> I recall thinking "Wow! Women are on the move. This is going to be wonderful, we are going to have women everywhere; I am going to have colleagues coming soon." ... And with that freshman exuberance, I asked the

Library of Congress research staff how long they thought it would be before half the House of Representatives would be female. And their answer was, "At this rate of change, four hundred years." I was totally outraged! I was ready to call out airstrikes on the Library of Congress, but I am now beginning to think they were right.[126]

Representative Schroeder wrote those words nearly two decades ago, and although the number of women in the Congress has increased, the pace has not picked up enough to undermine the quip of the research staff member. And we still have not yet elected our first female president. Why does this matter? Because the substantive representation argument is undermined by the reality that men's disproportionate access to power has resulted in persistent gender inequality throughout American history. While electoral progress is a symbolic victory for those who wish to see gender equality, the most important results will not be realized until gender disparities are reduced or eliminated.

Conclusion

All of this calls into question Americans' commitment to women's rights broadly. If we limit our discussion to narrow issues such as closing the pay gap, reducing health disparities, or being attentive to the achievement gap in education, we miss an opportunity to critique patriarchy as a powerful systemic force that undergirds these public policy issues. The Nineteenth Amendment became law in 1920, solidifying the status of women as full participants in the formal democratic process. But the bulk of the work of dismantling the systemic roots of gender inequality has taken place in the past century, with much more work to be done.

Three years after the adoption of the Nineteenth Amendment, women's rights activist Alice Paul wrote another amendment espousing equality between men and women. The ERA states that "equality of rights under the law shall not be denied or abridged by the United States or by any state on account of sex," and it gives Congress the ability to enforce the amendment through legislation.[136] A bill was introduced in every Congress until 1972, when it was finally passed and sent to the states for ratification. As of 2020, 38 states have ratified it, which is the number needed for it to become an amendment.[137] Yet the Act's future is uncertain, as some deadlines Congress attached to it in 1972 have

Box 8.3. *Representing:* Phyllis Schlafly

One of the most vocal and visible opponents of the proposed Equal Rights Amendment (ERA) to the US Constitution was Phyllis Schlafly, a veteran conservative writer and activist who continued her work until her passing in 2016. Schlafly, who was born in 1925 and died in 2016, was the author of 20 books, including *The Power of the Positive Woman* and *Feminist Fantasies*.[127] She authored *The Phyllis Schlafly Report* for nearly 50 years, she wrote a syndicated column that appeared in 100 newspapers, and she provided daily radio commentary that was broadcast on over 600 radio stations and online.[128]

Schlafly's opposition to the ERA was centered partly on her concern about courts having too much power in the political system. She (and others) feared that a failure to narrowly define *sex* and *equality* would lead to judges, rather than elected officials, deciding how those words should be interpreted.[129] Part of that concern was rooted in opposition to Lesbian, Gay, Bisexual, Transgender, and Queer (LGBTQ) rights. Even though she had a gay son (who worked with her at her foundation, the Eagle Forum), she (and he) did not believe in same-sex marriage, and she believed that the courts would have legalized it years ago if the ERA had passed in the 1970s.[130]

Although Schlafly was a nemesis for feminists, she believed that she, not feminists, stood for equality. She believed that feminists "adopt [a] victimology notion" and that a "litmus test for feminists is to agree with abortion."[131] In many ways, though, Schlafly embodied feminist ideals. She graduated Phi Beta Kappa from Washington University (where she also earned a law degree in political science from Harvard University);[132] she had six children and worked consistently throughout her life.[133] By her own admission, she "had it all."[134]

Into her ninth decade, she spoke out about public issues. For example, when Missouri Senate candidate Todd Akin made his controversial remarks about "legitimate rape" in 2012, Schlafly came to his defense, arguing that Republican Party leaders were "making a big thing about an unfortunate remark."[135] While she did not fit neatly into any particular ideological framework that is generally characterized as feminist, she was a vocal, strong female voice and a role model to millions.

expired, and five states have since rescinded approval that they voted on years ago.[138] In February 2021, however, President Biden signaled his support for the Equality Act, which amends the Civil Rights Act of 1964 to include Americans from discrimination on the basis of sexual orientation or gender identity, not just in employment, housing, and government services, but in private industry, as well.[139] While short of symbolism of enshrining those rights explicitly in the Constitution, the Act could ensure them legally and powerfully.

As complicated as our treatment of these issues has been to this point, the thorniest part is still ahead. Acknowledging the history and persistence of inequality is challenging enough, but finding consensus about how to rectify the situation to reduce (and eventually eliminate) disparities in these areas is far more controversial. The most comprehensive attempt to do so is referred to collectively as affirmative action, which is where we turn our attention next.

Discussion Questions

1. In your own words, define *sexism* and *misogyny*. Which term does the "binders full of women" excerpt from Mitt Romney's response to the question in the presidential debate exemplify? Why? What about Donald Trump's boast about kissing women without their permission?

2. How is the issue of gender different from the other sources of inequality discussed in previous chapters? In what ways is it similar?

3. Discuss the concept of feminism. What are the three waves of feminism? How do they differ from one another? How does this complicate issues of public policymaking, particularly when individuals who were socialized during each of the last two waves must work together to arrive at policy solutions?

4. Consider the socialization of gender roles, particularly during the formative years, and explain what role this has in perpetuating gender inequality. Can you identify an experience from your childhood that is relevant to this discussion?

5. Recall the concepts of delegate and trustee models of representation from Chapter 1. Do the political representatives mentioned
   in this chapter appear to embrace one method or the other? Does
   this seem ideal for a democratic society? Use specific examples in
   your response.

6. Evidence in this chapter, as well as throughout the book, suggests
   that gender inequality is all the more pronounced as it intersects
   with economics and race/ethnicity. How would you explain this
   concept to someone who has not read this book? Imagine that
   you raise the issue at a holiday gathering. How would your parents respond? Your grandparents? Would their gender matter?
   Their race? Their economic situation?

9

....

Affirmative Action

IN THE PRECEDING CHAPTERS, WE EXPLORED THE DEPTH, PERSISTENCE, and complexity of racial and economic inequality in the United States, as well as ways that government officials within the context of a representative democracy are able and willing to address it. The cycle of advantage and disadvantage that appears in Figure 2.4 (page 71) is at once simple and complex. It is simple in the sense that it involves three major elements: housing, education (both K-12 and postsecondary), and employment. It is complex because of the interrelationship among these elements, as well as additional considerations that affect those relationships (such as the criminal justice system and health disparities, as well as the way gender operates with race, ethnicity, and a host of other identities in an intersectional way to affect one's life experiences and opportunities). Along the way, we have wrestled with some difficult normative questions. This chapter is no different. In some respect, the most difficult questions reside here because rather than merely describing inequality, we are now forced to think about ways to reduce inequality and eliminate injustice. As noted in the Introduction, there is an assumption that inequality in America needs to be addressed. Otherwise, this chapter would be irrelevant. Those who believe that inequality is not problematic or that any existing inequality is the result of individuals making poor choices (as opposed to being systemic) need not wrestle with the issues that we consider here.

In this chapter, we explore steps that have been taken to address inequality in the twenty-first century, tracing the successes and failures over the past 55 years. While there has been a spattering of *ad hoc* attempts at progress, the most persistent and systematic programs fall under the umbrella term *affirmative action*.[1] The term has been heavily stigmatized, however, largely because it is frequently misrepresented as a quota system

DOI: 10.4324/9781003043041-10

that offers awards (jobs, admission to college and professional schools, etc.) to racial minorities at the expense of whites. Although quota programs have existed in the past, they are illegal in most respects today. Still, there are legitimate concerns over how affirmative action affects both whites and members of racial minority groups, so it is important to explore a brief history of these programs, their current practice, and the extent to which programs operating with this philosophical undercurrent are the remedy for systemic inequality in the United States.

Although affirmative action programs have been codified in legislation, the most important movement on this issue has come from the courts. The US Supreme Court has issued a number of decisions that give guidance (and constraint) to institutions that wish to take race into consideration for the purposes of increasing diversity or acknowledging that historical injustices place additional burdens on persons of color. Consequently, we will give disproportionate attention to the judicial branch of the US government in this chapter and focus on the potential for it to serve as a counter-majoritarian force in a representative democracy. Recall James Madison's concerns about majority tyranny and the fact that non-elected judges who serve life terms are uniquely positioned to represent those to whom the majority of citizens might deny rights. As we will see, members of racial minority groups have needed protection at times; at other times, it is whites who have claimed to be disadvantaged and have sought protection from infringement of their rights.

History of Affirmative Action in America

The legal rights of persons of color—specifically those of African descent— to avoid discrimination emanate from the Fourteenth Amendment to the US Constitution. Passed as one of the three Civil War amendments, it includes a constitutional provision that guarantees the rights of all persons to be upheld and protected by the state governments, as well as the federal government. This amendment is at the center of many legal and theoretical conflicts relating to civil rights and civil liberties in the United States. Whereas the first ten amendments to the Constitution (the Bill of Rights) were believed to apply only to the federal government for much of our nation's history, a gradual incorporation of those constitutional provisions by the courts to apply to the states through the Fourteenth Amendment has resulted in more widespread protections for citizens. With respect to racial non-discrimination, a series of Supreme Court cases has helped to clarify these protections, including the *Brown v. Board of Education* case that halted legally mandated racial segregation of public schools. Recall from Chapter 4, however, that the Court's decision in *Brown* pivoted on the psychological harm that was done to students of color as a result of being segregated from whites. It left open the question of what rights whites had with respect to actions by government and private institutions to increase diversity and/or account for historical injustice when making decisions that involved the selection of individuals for various opportunities.

A series of executive and legislative measures have also been enacted, beginning with New Deal–era requirements for avoidance of racial discrimination by employers and in public works programs[2] in the early part of the twentieth century. The most meaningful and sweeping antidiscrimination legislation has been the Civil Rights Act of 1964. Title VI of that law prohibits discrimination on the basis of race, color, or national origin by any entity that receives federal financial assistance; Title VII has clear language indicating that employment discrimination on the basis of sex is similarly prohibited.[3]

It is important to keep in mind the substantive difference between having a policy of non-discrimination, which can only be enforced through legal proceedings in which someone complains of and proves that discrimination occurred, and policies of preferential treatment, which are designed to proactively address systemic inequality. The latter category of policies falls under the umbrella of affirmative action. In the 1960s, during the height of the Civil Rights Movement, President Lyndon Johnson instigated an affirmative action policy through an executive order to force federal agencies to be attentive to their practices in hiring and awarding contracts with an eye toward avoiding discrimination.[4] Similar policies were adopted at the state level, and institutions of higher education began to use a variety of mechanisms to diversify the student body and to recognize that color-blind merit admission policies were by their nature disadvantageous to students who faced barriers to achieving those ostensibly objective markers (e.g., grade point average, board exam scores, ability to write a strong essay) that other applicants did not face (see Chapter 4).[5]

The friction generated by affirmative action policies stems from the reality that positions, whether in colleges or for employment, often reflect a zero-sum game—there are a set number of openings, with more applicants than opportunities. Traditional notions of meritocracy that are key aspects of American cultural identity suggest that individuals should compete based on their abilities and hard work and that factors that lie beyond the individual's control should never be taken into consideration.[6] The assumption of meritocracy, however, requires a relatively level playing field (or equal starting line, depending on the metaphor applied), which does not reflect the reality of American racial history. As the cartoon in Figure 9.1 suggests, whites were willing to deny access and opportunity to African Americans for centuries, and though now all Americans generally agree that racial discrimination (let alone slavery) is inappropriate, we are not nearly as willing to consider the consequences of persistent disadvantage that have followed from those centuries of exclusion.

It is not difficult to understand why there is resistance. One limitation of the cartoon, of course, is that the same two characters appear in each of the six panes. Although the cartoonist needed to use this technique to be concise and convey a powerful message, he is unable to capture

FIGURE 9.1. **A Concise History of Black-White Relations in the United States**

Source: Barry Deutsch, *Ampersand* via leftycartoons.com. Reprinted with permission.

the important temporal dynamic that arises from current generations of whites claiming that they "never owned a slave." In the cartoon, the white person in the first four panes is the same as the person who recognizes in the last two that racial prejudice and discrimination are wrong. Because the character equates racism (which is systemic) and prejudice (which is interpersonal), however, he refuses to take actions that would help to rectify past wrongs. He also feels that doing so would be equally improper because it relies on considerations of race. The notion that any consideration of race is racist has helped to perpetuate systems of disadvantage. Whites, who still overwhelmingly control the levers of power in the United States, have been led to believe that the real racists are those who advocate a sophisticated consideration of systemic racism in public policymaking and public discourse.

On the other hand, affirmative action programs should not be viewed as the solution to America's racist past. Various forms of affirmative action policies have been in place for half a century, and as we have discovered, the United States is far from having a society where all races and ethnicities have the same opportunities for success. However, America has made great progress in that time on a number of fronts, and while it would be improper to assume that affirmative action policies were solely responsible for that, dismissing them out of hand is also unwise. Instead, so as to appreciate the nuance and complexities of this controversial issue, let us consider three Supreme Court cases that have given shape to affirmative action policy in the United States.

From Davis to Ann Arbor to Austin

The first meaningful test of affirmative action policy in the United States came when Allan Bakke, who is white, complained about being denied admission to the University of California, Davis medical school in 1973 and again in 1974. He claimed that the program was unconstitutional because it denied him the opportunity to compete for all of the available seats in the incoming class. Each year, the school admitted 100 applicants but had two separate admission programs. One program, which had 84 seats, was open to applicants of any race, ethnicity, or educational background. The other program was reserved for applicants who identified themselves as "economically and/or educationally disadvantaged" or members of a racial minority group. The benefit of being considered under

Box 9.1. *Representing:* Justice Clarence Thomas

Only the second African American to be appointed to the US Supreme Court, Clarence Thomas has opposed racial preferences and affirmative action throughout his career. While critics argue that he benefited from affirmative action policies, Thomas has consistently claimed that he was harmed by the policy because he felt that it placed a stigma on him when after he graduated from Yale Law School.

Thomas was born in rural Georgia in 1948 and grew up in the sort of abject poverty described in Chapter 3. There was no sewage system or paved roads. Thomas's mother worked as a housekeeper and accepted church charity to make ends meet. He learned to value education from his grandfather, with whom he lived during his formative years. Thomas was not insulated from racism; he dropped out of seminary in Missouri and supported the work of the Black Panthers while an undergraduate at Holy Cross. President Reagan appointed Thomas to a position in the Department of Education and later at the Equal Employment Opportunity Commission. After serving on the US Court of Appeals for a year, he was appointed by President George H. W. Bush to replace Justice Thurgood Marshall, who successfully argued the *Brown v. Board of Education* school desegregation case before the Supreme Court as a lawyer and who was the first African American to serve on the Court.

While Thomas clearly benefited from racial preferences on a number of occasions throughout his career, the humiliation he felt when he applied for jobs after graduating from Yale Law School stuck with him. That experience affected his attitudes about affirmative action generally, as well as his ruling on racial preferences cases, such as *Grutter v. Bollinger* and *Gratz v. Bollinger*. Besides the stigmatization argument, Thomas believes that affirmative action programs in education are not effective because they do not guarantee assistance for minority students who may not be prepared to compete. Further, he agrees with those who argue that racial integration may not necessarily be beneficial to students of color. In fact, he has noted that forced integration suggests an underlying racism that "anything that is predominantly black must be inferior."

Opponents of racial preferences celebrate Thomas as a champion with credibility on the subject, while proponents dismiss him as a hypocrite and an opportunist. What is clear, however, is that Thomas's ideas about affirmative action have been shaped by his life experiences, and his justifications do not fall neatly in line with most of the people who agree with him on the issue. In many ways, Thomas embodies the complexity of an issue that has been oversimplified in American public discourse.[7]

the set-aside program was that one would not be compared to applicants in the other program and that the grade point average cutoff that applied to applicants in the other program was not in effect. Bakke's scores were higher than several of the students who were admitted under the second program, which meant that if he would have been permitted to compete for those seats, he would have been admitted. Although whites who were economically or educationally disadvantaged were eligible for consideration (Bakke was neither), none had been admitted in the four years that the program was in place. On this basis, Bakke argued that he was being denied equal protection under the Fourteenth Amendment by the state of California because of his race.

In *Regents of the University of California v. Bakke*,[8] the Supreme Court agreed with Bakke and ruled that such quota programs were unfair to whites (and unconstitutional), but the Court was clear that other types of programs that took race or other systemic disadvantage (including gender) into consideration were permissible. Specifically, the Court pointed to the plan that Harvard University used in admission, which considered racial minority status as a plus factor as part of a formula that contains a number of criteria for consideration. Justice Lewis Powell, who wrote the opinion for the Court, noted that race, as well as other characteristics, was part of the diversity that is valued in higher education. This established race as a factor that many institutions of higher education still use in admissions decisions.[9] It was precisely this type of plan that was challenged 25 years later when the Court heard the next case dealing with affirmative action in higher education.

In 2003 the Court considered two cases simultaneously, both relating to the University of Michigan. In *Gratz v. Bollinger*,[10] the Court struck down the policy that the university used for undergraduate admissions, but in *Grutter v. Bollinger*,[11] it upheld the policy being used by the law school. In essence, the Court felt that awarding 20 points to under-represented racial and ethnic groups in the undergraduate program was disproportionate[12] and that institutions should take a more holistic approach to admissions decisions with respect to diversity. In the law school case, however, the Court found that the policy invoked a narrowly tailored approach to consider race in admissions decisions in a way that was consistent with its desire to have a diverse incoming class in order to enrich the educational experience. Because the law school did not define diversity solely in terms of race or ethnicity and could award weight to an applicant's rating based on other factors that would enhance diversity, the Court, in a 5–4 decision, upheld the program. Justice Sandra Day O'Connor, who wrote the opinion, indicated that she hoped and expected that such policies would not be necessary in another 25 years (see Box 8.2). It is difficult to look into the future to determine the degree to which such policies will be necessary. Although rates of college graduation for African Americans are slowly increasing, as we discovered in Chapter 4, the gaps between white student graduation rates and those of African Americans and Latinos still exist.[13] More relevant to this issue, however, is the degree to which students of color would be granted admission to colleges if affirmative action plans were not in place.

It did not take 25 years for the Court to come back to the issue. On October 10, 2012, the Supreme Court first heard oral arguments in *Fisher v. University of Texas at Austin*.[14] Abigail Fisher, a white woman who was rejected by the University of Texas at Austin, complained that she had been denied equal treatment under the law as a result of the university's affirmative action policy. The Obama administration, as well as fourteen states, urged the Court to uphold racial preferences in college admissions.[15] At central issue in *Fisher* was whether colleges and universities had taken the Court's advice from *Grutter*, narrowing their use of racial preferences, or whether, as one scholar speculated, they have taken the *Grutter* decision "as a signal that court supervision of preferences would be lax."[16] After vacating (setting aside) the lower court's decision and ordering it to reconsider the case, the Supreme Court heard *Fisher* again in 2015, and a final decision was handed down in early 2016. The 4–3 decision[17] was authored by Justice Anthony Kennedy, who had not typically been viewed as a supporter of affirmative action programs. But Justice Kennedy invoked the *Sweatt* (and, by implication, *Brown*) case, noting that "a university is in large part defined by those intangible 'qualities which are incapable of objective measurement but which make for greatness.'" He argued that there must be considerable, though not exclusive, deference given to institutions of higher learning to define those intangible characteristics, which include the diversity of the student body.

Finally, Harvard University was pressed to defend its admission program in 2020, when a not-for-profit group, Students for Fair Admissions (see Box 9.3) brought suit, arguing that Harvard's affirmative action practices were discriminatory toward Asian applicants.[18] The US Court of Appeals for the First Circuit upheld the federal district court's ruling that Harvard did not violate the Constitution or Supreme Court precedent in the ways it takes race into consideration when considering undergraduate admission.[19] Other cases, involving Yale University and the University of North Carolina at Chapel Hill, are making their way through the court systems.[20] Opponents of affirmative action programs are hopeful that the more conservative composition of the US Supreme Court (President Trump appointed three justices) will swing some of these close decisions their way.

As a result of these decisions, however, colleges and universities are free to continue to invoke carefully crafted affirmative action programs to achieve a diverse student body. We, then, are left with two important and interrelated considerations.

First, affirmative action in college (or graduate/professional school) admissions is not a guarantee of a degree or a job. Once a student is admitted, he or she needs to do the same work as any other student to be successful. Given the tremendous disparities in K-12 education, many students of color who are admitted under affirmative action programs are not as well prepared for college as their white counterparts. In this way, such programs are not an effective interruption of the cycle of disadvantage, as they are essentially setting up those students for failure. Second, white students who attend underfunded schools are at a disadvantage if colleges do not consider economic or educational disadvantage in their admission process.[21] It has been argued that middle-class students of color who attend strong high schools also gain entrance under affirmative action programs, and while that is not the intent of such programs (because those students could compete in a color-blind system), we must be careful not to extrapolate these few cases too broadly. As we have seen, race and poverty are still closely related in the United States, and even minority students from financially secure families face subconscious prejudice in schools in the form of tracking.[22] One study estimated that admission of racial minority students to the most selective colleges would be reduced by more than half without racially conscious affirmative action programs.[23]

Affirmative Action Beyond the Classroom

Affirmative action receives the most attention as it pertains to college and graduate/professional school admission, but it is important to consider its effect on employment and housing separately. Neither of these areas presupposes that individuals have a college education, so even if affirmative action programs are effective in higher education, they do not always lead to equality in housing opportunities or employment (the other two primary elements of the cycle of disadvantage). Further, even if a person who faced systemic disadvantage early in life obtains a college degree, subconscious (if not overt) racial prejudice is still a relevant factor in housing, as well as in hiring (see Chapters 3 and 6, respectively).

Affirmative action policies in employment work a bit differently than they do in higher education. Employers do not necessarily have a battery of comparable items to judge applicants by, as college admissions officials do, nor do employers usually have a set number of openings with all applicants submitting by a deadline. Consequently, the sort of rankings and comparisons that are part of college admissions at the most competitive colleges and universities are not appropriate or possible for employers. Instead, hiring managers monitor diversity in terms of recruitment and promotion and, where necessary, develop policies to address deficiencies.[25] Most of the time such policies are voluntary, but occasionally a court orders a business to use affirmative action as a result of a lawsuit.[26] Hiring quotas based on race are illegal, yet many Americans (particularly whites) are suspicious about their use, and some are quick to offer a personal story about someone in their family who was denied employment (or perceived that he or she was denied employment) for being white.

This disconnect is partially psychological in the sense that whites often have a nagging suspicion that they are being discriminated against in favor of persons of color, but it is also warranted in the sense that many companies have aggressive targets or goals in terms of diversity that tread dangerously close to the quota line (or at least feel that way to white applicants). Title VII of the Civil Rights Act of 1964[27] was designed to prohibit discrimination against persons of color in the workforce. The bill, as well as subsequent Court decisions (such as *Griggs v. Duke Power Company* 1971),[28] is clear that it is not enough for employers not to *intend* to discriminate (which would be a difficult measure to prove); they must proactively avoid discrimination. Proactively avoiding discrimination, however,

Box 9.2. *Representing:* Justice Sandra Day O'Connor

Three years before she retired from the US Supreme Court, Sandra Day O'Connor wrote one of the most relevant opinions regarding affirmative action in a generation. A Republican state legislator from Arizona, O'Connor was the first woman in the United States to be minority leader of a state senate and the first woman to serve on the Court.

O'Connor was born to rancher parents in southeastern Arizona during the Great Depression. The ranch had no electricity or running water until she was seven years old. O'Connor was sent to boarding school so that she had a chance for a quality education. She attended Stanford for her undergraduate degree and law school. She was appointed to the Arizona Court of Appeals for two years prior to taking her seat on the Supreme Court in 1981.

In *Grutter v. Bollinger*, O'Connor wrote for a 5–4 majority that the University of Michigan's law school admissions program, which takes racial minority status into account when making decisions, was constitutional and advanced the cause of providing for a better education through a diverse student body. She added that in 25 years, hopefully, racial preferences in higher education would be unnecessary. Seven years after that ruling, O'Connor wrote an essay clarifying that her "25 years" remark was not meant to be a deadline, as many opponents of affirmative action inferred (and promised to hold the Court to that mark). What she meant was that social scientists should re-examine the educational benefits of diverse student bodies at that time.

While the Court has the opportunity to be counter-majoritarian (and thus protect minority rights), research has demonstrated that it rarely makes decisions that run contrary to public opinion on salient issues. George Washington University law professor Jeffrey Rosen notes that when the Court decided the *Bakke* case in 1978, public opinion was against affirmative action, so it was not surprising that the decision constrained efforts to increase racial minority enrollments in higher education. By 2003, however, when the University of Michigan cases were decided, the public was much more divided on the issue, which is consistent with the 5–4 decision in *Grutter*, as well as the decision in the companion case, *Gratz*, that limited affirmative action programs. We may never know the degree to which O'Connor or the other justices took public opinion into consideration as they reviewed the cases (and they may not know themselves), but such nuance in decisions reminds us that judges and justices, though they are not directly accountable to the people, are important aspects of representation in the United States.[24]

is not the same as affirmative action. That standard merely represents a call for equal opportunity that is intentionally protected. Affirmative action programs, such as that which was at issue in the Court's 2009 *Ricci v. DeStefano*[29] decision, go farther by instituting procedures that actively seek racial and ethnic (or gender) diversity.[30]

With respect to housing, there are few formal affirmative action policies.[31] Most of the effort in housing has been to ensure that persons of color are not discriminated against, but with respect to sales and rentals, there is no clear governmental mandate or widespread practice of ensuring diversity in neighborhoods. As noted in Chapter 3, there were efforts to increase homeownership among African Americans and Latinos through the mortgage agencies Fannie Mae and Freddie Mac (these nicknames refer to the Federal National Mortgage Association and the Federal Home Loan Mortgage Corporation, respectively), but the 2008 housing crisis hit low-income families and neighborhoods particularly hard, and many have yet to recover more than a decade later.[32]

Affirmative Action Ballot Initiatives and Referendums

Measuring public opinion about affirmative action can be difficult, as is capturing public sentiment on any issue relating to race. Americans are sensitive to accusations of being racially prejudiced, and white Americans in particular tend to be concerned with being accused of being racist when they are not conscious of harboring any racial animosity. As late as 2018, 61 percent of Americans favored affirmative action programs when asked directly and in the abstract (up about ten points from the turn of the twenty-first century), but when asked about specific policies that would reduce racial inequities, three-quarters of respondents were opposed to taking race into account, "even if it results in less diversity in the workplace."[33] When asked specifically about taking race into account for college admission, 73 percent of respondents (78 percent of whites, 62 percent of African Americans, 65 percent of Hispanics, and 59 percent of Asian Americans) offered that it should be "not a factor."[34] This opposition is slightly higher than polls that were conducted right after *Fisher* was decided in 2016, when 65 percent of Americans disagreed with the decision to allow highly selective colleges to continue to consider race in admission decisions. At that time, 76 percent of whites believed that college applicants should be admitted solely on the basis of merit (compared to 50 percent of African Americans and 61 percent of Hispanics), and 67 percent of whites indicated that race should not be taken into consideration at all (with 29 percent indicating it could be a minor factor).[35] Other research has found that support for women receiving preferential treatment for affirmative action is greater than that for racial and ethnic minorities[36] and that white women have benefited most from affirmative action programs.[37] As reflected in the post-*Fisher* data, there is sometimes an interest effect such that women[38] and racial minorities[39] are more likely than men and whites, respectively, to prefer affirmative action programs. Further, whites who oppose affirmative action with respect to racial minorities often support it when it is alternately framed as a benefit to women. As might be expected, attitudes toward both types of affirmative action are related to prejudices toward women and racial minorities.[40]

When voters have had the opportunity to weigh in on affirmative action through ballot initiative or referendum, they have mostly supported bans on race-conscious policies in hiring and school admission. The first state to adopt such a ban was California, which won approval of Proposition 209 in 1996. Prop 209, as it is known, is an amendment to Article I of the California constitution and reads as follows: "The state shall not discriminate against, or grant preferential treatment to, any individual or group on the basis of race, sex, color, ethnicity, or national origin in the operation of public employment, public education, or public contracting."[41] On its face, of course, the language is entirely race neutral and protects persons of all races and ethnicities from discrimination. The measure, though, was explicitly a response to California's affirmative action policies, and it ignores historical, systemic disadvantage for women and persons of color, assuming that each Californian starts at roughly the same point and therefore can be assured fair, unbiased competition for open positions.[42]

As expected, Prop 209 started a trend. In 1997, Washington State passed Initiative 200; in 2006, the Michigan Civil Rights Initiative passed;

in 2008, Nebraska voters passed Initiative 424; and in 2010, the Arizona Civil Rights Initiative was approved by voters. All of these measures were pushed and supported by California businessman Ward Connerly, who is multiracial. While three of his anti-affirmative action initiatives failed to be approved for ballots in 2008, the only one to fail that year was in Colorado (in an extremely close vote).[43]

To more clearly understand the dynamic of increased support for affirmative action programs that benefit women versus those that benefit persons of color, it is useful to consider some of the difference between legal challenges to affirmative action policies and ballot-based efforts to eliminate the practice. The plebiscite language almost always includes gender, as well as race, color, ethnicity, and national origin, but legal challenges are almost always narrowly targeted at advantages to persons of color (even though, as noted above, white women have benefited disproportionately from these programs). For example, the language for the Michigan measure in 2006 banned "affirmative action programs that give preferential treatment to groups or individuals based on their race, gender, color, ethnicity or national origin for public employment, education or contradicting purposes."[44] In the landmark University of Michigan cases that went before the US Supreme Court, though, whites brought the suits, alleging that the policies were unfairly beneficial to persons of color.[45] In cases that involve alleged discrimination, courts have different standards in determining whether a law relating to sex is constitutional as compared with a law relating to race. Sex-related issues are subjected to intermediate scrutiny, while race-related issues must pass strict scrutiny. This means that government policies that result in preferences or discrimination based on race are very difficult to sustain because the government must demonstrate that it has a compelling interest in having a law that on its face (i.e., without taking historical factors into consideration) discriminates and that the policy in place is narrowly tailored to achieve that interest. With respect to sex, however, government must only show that the law "further[s] an important government interest by means that are substantially related to that interest."[46] Accordingly, affirmative action policies that benefit women specifically are more likely to withstand legal scrutiny than those that specifically aim to address racial discrimination.[47]

Perhaps this is not surprising. Americans want to live in a race-neutral meritocracy and believe that they do. Many of us have friends (or at least friendly acquaintances) of different races and ethnicities. Most of us do not recognize racial resentment in ourselves, we celebrate Martin Luther King Day, and we do not use racial epithets, even when we are angry. Absent a purposeful recognition and consideration of the complexities described in this book, the language of these ballot proposals fits neatly with our core values and beliefs about what America *should* be.

The primary difference between proponents of bans on affirmative action policies and supporters of affirmative action is the degree to which they are willing to acknowledge the systemic effects of historical discrimination and prejudice. Neither Ward Connerly, nor Ed Blum (see Box 9.3), nor Jesse Jackson[48] hates America or is trying to leverage personal gain from the policies they champion. These men may disagree about the degree to which discrimination persists, the potential stigmatizing effect on minorities as a result of the programs, the value of racial diversity in

---

Box 9.3. *Representing:* Ed Blum

A former stockbroker is responsible for shepherding many of the recent affirmative action cases through the legal system toward the United States Supreme Court. Edward Blum (pronounced "bloom") has, since he founded it in 2005, led the Project on Fair Representation,[49] which seeks to "facilitate *pro bono* legal representation to political subdivisions and individuals that wish to challenge government distinctions and preferences made on the basis of race and ethnicity."[50] Blum has been successful in getting the Court to hear a number of high-profile cases relating to issues from voting rights (*Shelby County v. Holder*) to race-based gerrymandering (*Bush v. Vera*) to, perhaps most famously, affirmative action (*Fisher v. Texas*).[51]

Mr. Blum does not have a law degree, but his experience running for office and his deep desire to see America abandon racial classifications, combined with his appreciation that such issues often are resolved through the judicial branch, have compelled him to work tirelessly and in many cases, effectively, to realize his goals. Although the *Fisher* and *Harvard College* cases were not decided in his favor, he was victorious in overturning the racially drawn congressional districts in Texas in *Bush v. Vera*, and the decision in *Shelby* invalidated a portion of the Civil Rights Act of 1964 that he perceived to be reinforcing racial distinctions.

the workplace and schools, and the degree to which whites are harmed by racially conscious policies, but it would be difficult to argue that they do not all have the best interest of the country at heart.

Reasonable people can (and do) disagree about the ability of affirmative action programs to appropriately rectify systemic disadvantages or lead to more racial equality. To be considered to be reasonable, however, each of us must seriously and honestly reflect on the various ways that we may be advantaged or disadvantaged by a system that is rooted in fundamental inequality. Many Americans would argue that a color-blind—or at least color-neutral—society would be preferable, but we are unable to wish away the realities of the lingering racism that continues to characterize American society.

Conclusion

Legal rights aside, most Americans (not just whites) do not really understand how affirmative action programs are designed, what they are intended to do, or whether they are effective. An honest, holistic appraisal reveals that the evidence of the effectiveness of such programs is inconclusive. Anecdotally, we can point to individuals who were provided opportunities (and were able to capitalize on them). It is more difficult to measure the long-term psychological effects on whites, many of whom feel as if they are at a disadvantage for college admission and employment, and minorities, some of whom might interpret acceptance under these programs as a tacit indicator of their unworthiness[52] (consider Clarence Thomas's perspective from Box 9.1, for example). Under these circumstances, we need to decide whether affirmative action programs do more harm than good or, put another way, whether America would be a more just and equitable nation if we did not have them.

Ultimately, affirmative action programs serve more as a bandage than a cure, with most proponents believing that removing such programs would exacerbate the inequality that still exists.[53] Others believe that affirmative action programs will lead to a color-blind, gender-neutral society,[54] or, alternatively, a dynamic multiracial and socially just society. Opponents, however, believe that the bandage is keeping the wound from healing properly. From any perspective, it is clear that a permanent solution to America's persistent racial and economic inequality must be found elsewhere.

Discussion Questions

1. Is your opinion about affirmative action the same now as before you read this chapter? What about before you began reading this book? If you changed your mind, what caused the shift?

2. Have you heard stories about white Americans being passed over for a job or promotion because of affirmative action programs? Can you recall the context in which the story was told? How do such anecdotes work to reinforce or challenge existing ideas about affirmative action in the United States?

3. Does your college or university have an affirmative action program? Do you know how it works? How diverse is your campus with respect to race and ethnicity? What about socioeconomic status? How does the diversity on your campus (or lack thereof) affect the learning environment? Identify specific instances, if you can, where the issue of diversity on campus has been discussed.

4. What do you think about the suggestion of switching from race-based affirmative action to programs based on socioeconomic status? If you favor such a shift, what should be the criteria? Income? If so, how many years' worth of tax returns should be considered? Wealth? If so, how would that be measured? What about the idea of using zip code as a surrogate for socioeconomic status? Do your preferences change depending on the type of program (e.g., college admission, employment)? What potential benefits and drawbacks might be associated with each approach?

5. If you support affirmative action, how do you answer the critics who charge that it is unfair to both whites and persons of color? If you oppose affirmative action, how do you propose to address issues of inequality in America?

Conclusion: The Space Between Power and Powerlessness

In August 2016, San Francisco 49ers quarterback Colin Kaepernick refused to stand for the national anthem during a preseason National Football League (NFL) game. He did not hold a sign, gesture, or even turn his back. Rather, he lowered himself to one knee and waited silently until the song had ended. After the game, he told a reporter:

> I am not going to stand up to show pride in a flag for a country that oppresses black people and people of color. To me, this is bigger than football and it would be selfish on my part to look the other way. There are bodies in the street and people getting paid leave and getting away with murder.[1]

Reaction to his protest was predictably mixed. Over the next few weeks, dozens of NFL players followed suit, some simply kneeling, others raising fists in the air to replicate the black power salute that was common at the height of the Civil Rights Movement.[2] Other athletes also chose to kneel during the anthem, bringing increased attention to Kaepernick's actions.[3] Many fans (and others) were furious.[4] As with the controversy over flag burning, some could not understand how refusing to acknowledge what is widely perceived to be a unifying national symbol helped advance a cause. Even some noted progressives criticized the move: US Supreme Court Justice Ruth Bader Ginsburg said that while she did not believe his actions were criminal, she found them to be "dumb and disrespectful."[5]

Kaepernick expressed his disappointment, and Ginsburg walked back the remark a few days later, noting that she was "inappropriately dismissive and harsh" in her response,[6] but her initial reaction spoke volumes about how viscerally affected Americans are by such symbols of patriotism. From a very early age, Americans—like citizens of all nations—are taught to love their country and have deep faith in its goodness. From the childhood expectation onward that they will pledge allegiance to the flag, learn patriotic songs, and celebrate historically significant holidays, to their being taught primarily (or solely) positive information about the nation's history, it is no wonder that college students are often disturbed and frustrated to learn the complex truth of Americans' struggle for equality.

We may feel powerless to right the great wrongs that we observe around us, particularly with respect to recognizing power differences. After all, these problems are centuries old, and millions of people just like us have worked very hard for many years—some dedicating their entire lives to the cause—to dismantle systems of inequality. It is also easy to feel frustrated, as a small but vocal group of political figures (officials and pundits) seek to confuse the issues with platitudes about meritocracy, anecdotes used to disprove systematically collected data, and emotional appeals (often rooted in core values such as patriotism) that make us feel like traitors if we are critical of the system. These folks ignore systems altogether so that each success and failure is solely the responsibility of the individual. If someone is wealthy, it was the result of hard work, natural ability, and persistence that led to the success; if someone is poor, there must have been bad choices, failure to take advantage of opportunities (however limited), or simply a choice to be poor out of laziness.

It is difficult to argue against these positions because explaining systems is complicated and takes time. There is no way to explain the concept of hegemony in a sound bite. As cognitive scientists explain, appeals to reason are easily supplanted with contrasting appeals to emotion.[7] Such issues as abortion, Lesbian, Gay, Bisexual, Transgender, and Queer (LGBTQ) rights, and sex education in schools are considered to be values issues in the United States, but racial inequality and poverty are generally not.[8] So, if we care about these issues, how do we make a difference?

The theoretical roots of representation date back before the nation's founding, with James Madison, drawing from seventeenth-century philosophers, famously warning about the "violence of faction" in *Federalist 10*. Madison understood that a representative democratic system would be endangered by groups that had power (whether they constituted the numerical majority or not) to run over the wishes of those who did not. Pluralist models of democracy predict that ordinary individuals will have power over elites through the pressure exerted by organized interests. But the powerful also organize. Political scientist Dara Strolovitch concludes:

> interest group politics reinforce as much as they rectify the bias against marginalized groups.... the relative power of organizations that speak for marginalized groups remains far less than that of the multitude of other organizations that represent more advantaged constituencies.[9]

It is daunting indeed to consider what can be done when the mechanisms of democracy seem stacked against the realization of its ultimate promise.

One important improvement would be the use of sharper conceptual and rhetorical tools to adequately discuss these complex issues. For example, a recent study of attitudes about poverty in the United Kingdom found that most respondents thought about global poverty in terms of providing charity, which reinforces a power dynamic where wealthy nations are in a position to give, and poor nations are in a position to take (and to be grateful for the assistance). The study's authors argue that such a disempowering rhetorical and cognitive model is problematic and that one solution is for antipoverty actors and groups to address the roots of global poverty so that there is a creation story. An appreciation of what caused poverty, the authors argue, will be more effective in helping individuals to have a more sophisticated understanding of the issue, which will likely translate into more support for solutions.[10]

Conversations designed to improve inequality often stall when the language used in the discussion becomes muddled. For some, *racism* refers to the systemic advantages that whites have over persons of color (as the term is used in this book), while for others, it means a personal distaste or resentment for someone of a race other than one's own. For some, *equality* means that all citizens have similar opportunities to achieve financial success and political power, while for others, it means that the discrepancy of income and/or wealth between those who have the most and those who have the least should be drastically reduced.

As ordinary individuals, we are not in a position to control the way language is used in mainstream public discourse. We can, however, choose to

Box C.1. *What Can I Do?:* Own Your Privilege

Privilege is a confusing term. Often it is used as an absolute: "Jeff Bezos is privileged." However, privilege is a relative construct. While it is difficult to identify ways in which Jeff Bezos does not have privilege, most of us have characteristics that, in our cultural context, confer privilege on us, as well as others that do not. If we embrace the absolute construction, we lose the ability to understand privilege as a meaningful concept—if there is always someone who is more privileged in one way or another, privilege does not mean anything at all.

Whites, on the whole, have privilege compared to persons of color, all other things being equal. Of course, all other things are rarely equal, so white women may have some advantages over women of color, but are relatively disadvantaged compared to white men. Heterosexual and cisgender folks are privileged compared to those who are LGBTQ, but a heterosexual, cisgender Latina can hardly be considered privileged in any absolute sense. Accordingly, it is useful for us to be mindful of the ways in which we are privileged and the ways we may be disadvantaged. Owning our privilege is one way of coming to terms with the complicated realities of living in a pluralistic society with a history of discrimination based on a number of characteristics. That puts us in a much better position to evaluate policy options or select candidates who will represent our interests with respect to our views on diversity and equality.

Are you able-bodied? If so, you have privilege with respect to physical ability. Even if disabled persons are not overtly discriminated against due to conscious hostility, fear, or discomfort, the world is designed and mostly inhabited by able-bodied persons. This leads to a host of disadvantages that most able-bodied people do not even notice. Are you handsome or pretty (by some commonly accepted standards, however problematic they may be)? While there are some disadvantages to being perceived as conventionally attractive (particularly for women, as our sexist culture often reduces women to their appearance), being conventionally attractive often comes with some privilege. Are you right-handed? Of average height and weight? Do you have full vision and hearing? What other privileges can you identify? Take a day or even a couple of hours and, as you move about, try to be attentive to the ways that these characteristics give you an advantage over someone who does not possess them.

> Far from being a count-your-blessings exercise, the point of reflecting on and owning privilege is to become aware of how advantages and disadvantages are perpetuated on a daily basis. It reminds us that if we limit our critique of inequality to the intent of persons or groups of persons who are racist, sexist, homophobic, and so on, we are overlooking most of the inequality and disadvantage that exists.

be more precise in the ways we think about and subsequently talk about issues relating to inequality in all of its forms. If we are talking about individual-level prejudice, we should avoid using the term *racism*. If we are talking about systemic disadvantages for those who are not heterosexual (heterosexism), we should not call it homophobia. If we are talking about systemic disadvantages for women, we should call it sexism, but if we are talking about individuals who harbor resentment toward others on the basis of sex or gender, we should call it prejudice or bigotry. The idea is not to control what others say, but to ensure that what we say is reflective of our understanding of the complexities of these issues so that we model a more sophisticated approach to dealing with issues that are far more complex than colloquial, blunt language reflects.

We need to remember too that progress, while worthy of celebration, is not the same as equality. Those who wish to preserve the status quo with respect to inequality often point to the fact that things were worse in previous times. Such a position is inarguable, of course, but satisfaction with our current state of racial and economic progress is not a necessary component to appreciating that some of our worst abuses are in the past. When Booker T. Washington and W. E. B. Du Bois were advocating for racial equality at the turn of the twentieth century, many wondered why they were so interested in pushing for it—after all, things were much worse for African Americans during times of slavery. During the Civil Rights Movement of the 1950s, opponents of racial progress had difficulty understanding why blacks and others sympathetic to the cause were so upset—things were worse 50 years earlier. During the summer of racial reckoning in 2020, those who agitated and advocated for racial and economic justice were confronted with similar criticisms—things were so much worse during Jim Crow. It is imperative that we consider what future generations will be saying about us. How will we be evaluated?

There was a time when the smartest people believed that the world was flat, that the sun revolved around the earth, and that people of African descent were not human (and, thus, could be owned as property). In those times, it would have been very difficult to convince people that they were wrong. Only a few generations ago, most Americans found it perfectly acceptable that children—particularly poor children—worked in harsh and sometimes dangerous conditions. Child labor laws are not controversial today, but they were when they were first proposed and passed. Factory owners argued that business would be hurt by such legislation (they would lose a valuable and inexpensive part of their labor force),[11] much as businesses argue today that a rise in the minimum wage or requirements to provide health insurance would force them to close their doors. The point here is not to advocate for one policy position over another, but to point out that there is a certain amount of inertia at work in American political culture. Every social movement in history has faced resistance. Success came because of constant agitation by individuals and groups. Margaret Mead is credited with reminding us to "never doubt that a small group of thoughtful, committed citizens can change the world. Indeed, it is the only thing that ever has." There is no consensus on the answers to many of the normative questions we have considered in this book, but each reader should work toward becoming comfortable with their own positions and the degree to which those positions correspond with their core values and beliefs, as well as being open to adjusting those beliefs when new evidence is presented. It can be an uncomfortable process, but it is ultimately rewarding and absolutely necessary if the next generation will move us closer to the goal of a truly equitable and just society.

Notes

Introduction: The Politics of Inequality

1. The speech can be viewed at http://youtu.be/pWe7wTVbLUU.

2. Tavis Smiley and Cornel West, *The Rich and the Rest of Us: A Poverty Manifesto* (New York: Smiley Books, 2012).

3. Ibid., 173–175.

4. For a thoughtful treatment of the notion of meritocracy, see Kenneth Arrow, Samuel Bowles, and Steven Durlauf, eds., *Meritocracy and Economic Inequality* (Princeton: Princeton University Press, 2000).

5. Meghan McCain, "Who You Calling a Blue Blood, Sarah?" *The Daily Beast*, November 30, 2010, http://www.thedailybeast.com/articles/2010/11/30/meghan-mccain-sarah-palins-blue-blood-comment.html.

6. Mitt Romney similarly invoked this formulation during his 2012 presidential campaign. He framed the Obama administration's desire to allow tax reductions for the wealthiest Americans to expire as "punishing success," which suggests that the wealthy have worked harder and out-competed others.

7. In his farewell remarks, President Donald Trump gestured toward his three eldest children, who grew up with tremendous financial privilege, and said, "People have no idea how hard this family work, and they worked for you" (Impelli, Matthew. 2021. "Read the Full Text of Donald Trump's Final Farewell Speech at Joint Base Andrews." *Newsweek*, January 20, https://www.newsweek.com/read-full-text-donald-trumps-final-farewell-speech-joint-base-andrews-1563052.)

8. Joseph P. Williams, "Penthouse Populist: Why the Rural Poor Love Donald Trump," *U.S. News and World Report*, September 22, 2016, http://www.usnews.com/news/articles/2016-09-22/penthouse-populist-why-the-rural-poor-love-donald-trump.

9. See Ruby K. Payne, *A Framework for Understanding Poverty: A Cognitive Approach* (5th ed.). Highlands, TX: aha! Process, Inc. (2013). For a brief table summarizing Payne's theory, see http://kathyescobar.com/wp-content/uploads/2013/12/Hidden-Rules-Among-Classes.pdf.

10. Donald Trump earned 57 percent of the white vote in the 2016 election (compared to Hillary Clinton's 37 percent). He was particularly successful with white men: his 62 percent win in that demographic was double his opponent's. However, he also won amongst white women (52 percent to 43 percent). He captured the rural vote 61 percent to 34 percent. "Exit Polls," http://CNN.com, November 23, 2016, http://www.cnn.com/election/results/exit-polls.

11. For a discussion of the state of the class system in Great Britain, see Caroline Gammell, "Britain's Class System 'Alive and Well' Claims Research," *Telegraph*, April 17, 2009, http://www.telegraph.co.uk/news/uknews/5165594/Britains-class-system-alive-and-well-claims-research.html.

12. For a brief overview of the Indian caste system, see Allison Elliott, "Caste and *The God of Small Things*," 1997, http://english.emory.edu/Bahri/caste.html.

13. In her bestselling book *Caste*, Isabelle Wilkerson makes a compelling case against this assertion, arguing that America does, indeed, have a caste system that is on par with the Indian experience, as well as the ideology that undergirded the Nazi Party's rise and rule in Germany during the first half of the 20th century.

14. Alexander Chancellor, "The Class Menagerie," *Guardian*, March 9, 2005, http://www.guardian.co.uk/uk/2002/mar/09/britishidentity.comment.

15. In 2007, a CBS News poll found that only 2 percent of Americans indicated that they were "upper class," and 1 percent said that they were "lower class." Lori Robertson, "Defining the 'Middle Class,'" http://Factcheck.org, January 24, 2008, http://factcheck.org/2008/01/defining-the-middle-class.

16. "2016 Delegate Count and Primary Results." *New York Times*, July 5, 2016, http://www.nytimes.com/interactive/2016/us/elections/primary-calendar-and-results.html.

17. The terms "Hispanic" and "Latinx" are distinct. The former refers to a category of individuals characterized by a common language root, while the latter refers to individuals whose nation of origin is Latin America (which includes languages other than Spanish). "Latinx" has come to replace the previously more common "Latino," which is gendered and therefore ought not be used to refer to both men and women (Latinas). Where there is a clear distinction, these terms will be used purposefully in this book. At other times, they are used somewhat interchangeably.

18. There is ongoing debate about whether the words *white* and *black* should be capitalized when referring to race. Because Westview Press follows the *Chicago Manual of Style*, which recommends lowercase, I have followed that convention in this book. For a more detailed discussion of this issue, see the following blog entry that I coauthored: http://raceproject.org/?p=613.

19. The 2010 census revealed that white babies (under the age of two) are already a numerical minority. Dara Sharif, "White Babies Now a Minority in the U.S.," http://TheRoot.com, June 24, 2011, http://www.theroot.com/articles/culture/2011/06/census_black_and_brown_babies_outnumber_white_babies/.

20. See, for instance, Ta-Nehisi Coates, "Fear of a Black President," *Atlantic*, September 2012, http://www.theatlantic.com/magazine/archive/2012/09/fear-of-a-black-president/309064/; Ron Rosenbaum, "Is the Republican Party Racist?," *Slate*, October 8, 2012, http://www.slate.com/articles/news_and_politics/the_spectator/2012/10/is_the_republican_party_racist_how_the_racial_attitudes_of_southern_voters_bolster_its_chances_.html; "A Map of Racist Tweets About President Obama's Re-election," *AlterNet*, November 9, 2012, http://www.alternet.org/election-2012/map-racist-tweets-about-president-obamas-re-election-mississippi-alabama-lead-pack.

21. Sara Sidner, "The Rise of Black Lives Matter: Trying to Break the Cycle of Violence and Silence," *CNN*, December 28, 2015, http://www.cnn.com/2015/12/28/us/black-lives-matter-evolution/.

22. Donald Nieman, "Donald Trump's Campaign Is an Echo of Reconstruction-Era Racism," *New Republic*, October 12, 2016, https://newrepublic.com/article/137741/donald-trumps-campaign-echo-reconstruction-era-racism.

23. This phrase was made famous in recent history by Democratic US senator and 2004 presidential candidate John Edwards. Chuck Raasch, "Edwards Brings 'Two Americas' to Center Stage," *USA Today*, July 28, 2004, http://www.usatoday.com/news/opinion/columnist/raasch/2004-07-28-raasch_x.htm.

24. The first slave ships arrived in North America roughly 400 years ago, though the earliest settlers perpetuated injustices on Native Americans for more than a century prior to the arrival of Africans. Lisa Rein, "Mystery of Va.'s First Slaves Is Unlocked 400 Years Later," *Washington Post*, September 3, 2006, http://www.washingtonpost.com/wp-dyn/content/article/2006/09/02/AR2006090201097.html.

25. A recent poll revealed that 88 percent of Americans identify themselves with the term *middle class*. Peter Moore, "Poll Results: Middle Class," *YouGov*, May 28, 2015, https://today.yougov.com/news/2015/05/28/poll-results-middle-class/.

26. In 2014, 14.8 percent of Americans lived in poverty, as defined by the US Bureau of the Census. National Poverty Center, "Poverty in the United States: Frequently Asked Questions," 2016, http://www.npc.umich.edu/poverty/.

27. *Bigotry* is actually a broader term referring to resentment toward others who are different from the person who is exhibiting bigoted attitudes and behaviors. Besides race-based bigotry, bigotry may be related to gender, sexual orientation, age, religion, able-bodiedness, and so on.

28. Paul Haggis's film *Crash,* which won the Academy Award for Best Picture in 2005, depicts this dynamic artistically.

29. A number of studies have employed designs where stereotypical white, Hispanic, and African American names were used to determine levels of racial bias. These studies have shown, for example, that Latinos are less likely than whites to receive a response from an election official about a voting-related question. Julie K. Faller, Noah L. Nathan, and Ariel R. White, "What Do I Need to Vote? Bias in Information Provision by Local Election Officials," manuscript, July 11, 2014, http://scholar.harvard.edu/files/arwhite/files/fallernathanwhite_voteridexp_july2014_0.pdf. African Americans are significantly less likely to receive calls for jobs than whites with identical credentials. Marianne Bertrand and Sendhil Mullainathan, "Are Emily and Greg More Employable Than Lakisha and Jamal? A Field Experiment on Labor Market Discrimination," *American Economic Review* 94, no. 4 (2004): 991–1013. African American elected officials are more likely to respond to African Americans who write with questions, even if the person writing is not a constituent. David E. Broockman, "Black Politicians Are More Intrinsically Motivated to Advance Blacks' Interests: A Field Experiment Manipulating Political Incentives," *American Journal of Political Science* 57, no. 3 (2013): 521–536.

30. See, for instance, Anthony G. Greenwald, Debbie E. McGhee, and Jordan L. K. Schwartz, "Measuring Individual Differences in Implicit Cognition: The Implicit Association Test," *Journal of Personality and Social Psychology* 74, no. 6 (1998): 1464–1480; Allen R. McConnell and Jill M. Leibold, "Relations Among the Implicit Association Test, Descriminatory Behavior, and Explicit Measures of Racial Attitudes," *Journal of Experimental Social Psychology* 37, no. 5 (2001): 435–442; Andrew Karpinski and James L. Hilton, "Attitudes and the Implicit Association Test," *Journal of Personality and Social Psychology* 81, no. 5 (2001): 774–788; Bertram Gawronski, "What Does the Implicit Association Test Measure? A Test of the Convergent and Discriminant Validity of Prejudice-Related IATs," *Experimental Psychology* 49, no. 3 (2002): 171–180.

31. See, for instance, P. J. Henry and David O. Sears, "The Symbolic Racism 2000 Scale," *Political Psychology* 23, no. 2 (2002): 253–283; David O. Sears and P. J. Henry, "Over Thirty Years Later: A Contemporary Look at Symbolic Racism," *Advances in Experimental Psychology* 37 (2005): 95–150; Christopher Tarman and David O. Sears, "The Conceptualization and Measurement of Symbolic Racism," *Journal of Politics* 67, no. 3 (2005): 731–761; Brad T. Gomez and J. Matthew Wilson, "Rethinking Symbolic Racism: Evidence of Attribution Bias," *Journal of Politics* 68, no. 3 (2006): 611–625; Joshua L. Rabinowitz et al., "Why Do White Americans Oppose Race-Targeted Policies? Clarifying the Impact of Symbolic Racism," *Political Psychology* 30, no. 5 (2009): 805–828; Anthony G. Greenwald et al., "Implicit Race Attitudes Predicted Vote in the 2008 U.S. Presidential Election," *Analyses of Social Issues and Public Policy* 9, no. 1 (2009): 241–253.

32. https://implicit.harvard.edu.

33. One recent study suggests that implicit bias may not be as closely related to electoral outcomes as explicit prejudice. Nathan P. Kalmoe and Spencer Piston, "Is Implicit Prejudice Against Blacks Politically Consequential?" *Public Opinion Quarterly* 77, no. 1 (2013): 305–322.

34. Jeremy Hogeveen, Michael Inzlicht, and Sukhvinder S. Obhi, "Power Changes How the Brain Responds to Others," *Journal of Experimental Psychology: General*, 2013; Susanne Quadflieg et al., "Exploring the Neural Correlates of Social Stereotyping," *Journal of Cognitive Neuroscience* 21, no. 8 (2008): 1560–1570; Jennifer A. Richeson et al., "An fMRI Investigation of the Impact of Interracial Contact on Executive Function," *Nature Neuroscience* 6, no. 2 (2003): 1323–1328; David M. Amodio et al., "Alternate Mechanisms for Regulating Racial Responses According to Internal vs External Cues," *SCAN* 1 (2006): 26–36; David M. Amodio et al., "Neural Signals for the Detection of Unintentional Race Bias," *Psychological Science* 15, no. 2 (2004): 88–93; David M. Amodio, "Can Neuroscience Advance Social Psychological Theory? Social Neuroscience for the Behavioral Social Psychologist," *Social Cognition* 28, no. 6 (2010): 695–716.

35. US Constitution, Article I, Section 2, paragraph 3.

36. See, for instance, Patricia Hill Collins, *Fighting Words: Black Women and the Search for Justice* (Minneapolis: University of Minnesota Press, 1998); Patricia Hill Collins, *Black Feminist Thought: Knowledge, Consciousness, and the Politics of Empowerment* (New York: Routledge, 2000); Kimberlé Crenshaw, "Demarginalizing the Intersection of Race and Sex: A Black Feminist Critique of Antidiscrimination Doctrine, Feminist Theory, and Antiracist Politics," *University of Chicago Legal Forum*, 1989, 139–167; Kimberlé Crenshaw, "Intersectionality, Identity Politics, and Violence Against Women of Color," *Stanford Law Review* 43 (1991): 1241–1299; bell hooks, *Ain't I a Woman: Black Women and Feminism* (Cambridge: South End Press, 1981); bell hooks, *Feminism Is for Everybody: Passionate Politics* (Cambridge: South End Press, 2000); Audre Lorde, *Sister Outsider: Essays and Speeches* (Berkeley, CA: Crossing Press, 1984).

37. C. Wright Mills, *The Power Elite* (New York: Oxford University Press, 2000).

38. For a summary of the Charlottesville tragedy, see Debbie Lord, "What Happened at Charlottesville: Looking Back at the Rally that Ended in Death," *Atlanta Journal Constitution*, August 13, 2019, https://www.ajc.com/news/national/what-happened-charlottesville-looking-back-the-anniversary-the-deadly-rally/fPpnLrbAtbxSwNI9BEy93K/; for information about the insurrection at the Capitol, see the Associated Press's page entitled "Capitol Siege," https://apnews.com/hub/capitol-siege.

Chapter 1: Representation and the Roots of Inequality

1. See, for instance, Arnaud Lefranc, Nicholas Pistolesi, and Alain Trannoy, "Equality of Opportunities vs. Inequality of Outcomes: Are Western Societies All Alike?" *Review of Income and Wealth* 54, no. 4 (2008): 513–546.

2. Anne Phillips, "Defending Equality of Outcome," *Journal of Political Philosophy* 12, no. 1 (2004): 1–19.

3. For further discussion of these concepts, including the root of the words, see Miriam-Webster, "'Equity' and 'Equality': How They Differ and Overlap." https://www.merriam-webster.com/words-at-play/equality-vs-equity-difference.

4. James Madison [Publius], "The Federalist 10: The Utility of the Union as a Safeguard AGAINST Domestic Faction and Insurrection (continued)," *(New York) Daily Advertiser*, November 22, 1787, http://constitution.org/fed/federa10.htm.

5. "The Enslaved Community," James Madison's Montpellier, http://www.montpelier.org/visit/plan-your-visit/enslaved-community; "James Madison," http://American-Presidents.com, 2011, http://www.american-presidents.com/james-madison;

"James Madison: Life before the Presidency," Miller Center at the University of Virginia, 2011, http://millercenter.org/president/madison/.

6. Donald J. McCrone and James H. Kuklinski, "The Delegate Theory of Representation," *American Journal of Political Science* 23 (1979): 278–300.

7. George Sadowsky, Raul Zambrano, and Pierre Dandjinou, "Internet Governance: A Discussion Document" (paper presented to the United Nations ICT Task Force, 2004), https://www.internetsociety.org/sites/default/files/Internet%20Governance%20A%20Discussion%20Document%20%28George%20Sadowsky%29.pdf.

8. Herbert Asher, *Polling and the Public: What Every Citizen Should Know*, 8th ed. (Washington, DC: CQ Press, 2010).

9. The median net worth of members of the 116th Congress (2019–2021) was just over $1 million; more than half of the 535 members were millionaires (Karl Evers-Hillstrom, "Majority of Lawmakers in 116th Congress are Millionaires," Center for Responsive Politics, April 23, 2020, https://www.opensecrets.org/news/2020/04/majority-of-lawmakers-millionaires/). Data for the 117th Congress were not available as of the writing of this edition.

10. Ninety-six percent of members of the 116th Congress held a college degree; 68 percent of House members and 77 percent of Senators held a degree beyond the bachelor's, including 214 with law degrees, 25 with doctoral degrees, and 25 with medical degrees (Congressional Research Service, "Membership of the 116th Congress: A Profile." Updated December 17, 2020, https://fas.org/sgp/crs/misc/R45583.pdf). Data for the 117th Congress were not available as of the writing of this edition.

11. Hanna Fenichel Pitkin, *The Concept of Representation* (Berkeley: University of California Press, 1972).

12. Of the eleven African Americans to serve in the US Senate, seven were elected by the people. The first two black senators were elected by the Mississippi state legislature (prior to the passage of the Seventeenth Amendment to the Constitution in 1913), and three others were appointed to fill vacancies. (One of those three, Tim Scott, Republican of South Carolina, was appointed in 2013 but subsequently won a special election in 2014 and was elected to a full term in 2016.) There are two African Americans (both men) serving in the 117th Congress (2021–2023).

13. The 117th Congress features the most women ever to serve in the US Congress. There are 118 women in the House and 24 in the Senate. (Bailey K. Sanders and Danielle M. Thomsen, "A Record Number of Women Are Serving in Congress. That's Good News for Constituents," *The Washington Post*, January 26, 2021, https://www.washingtonpost.com/politics/2021/01/26/record-number-women-are-serving-congress-thats-good-news-constituents/.)

14. For example, despite the legal gains African Americans made with respect to voting in the 1960s, only six black Americans have been elected to the US Senate and only two black governors have been elected since Reconstruction. (In addition, one African American—David Patterson of New York—was appointed to fill a vacant governorship but did not seek election for an additional term.)

15. Jackson Baker, "Cohen, Hart, and the Schools," *Memphis Flyer*, July 7, 2011, http://www.memphisflyer.com/memphis/cohen-hart-and-the-schools/Content?oid=3014581; "Congressional Black Caucus to Remain an All-Black Organization," http://EmergingMinds.org, September 8, 2006, http://emergingminds.org/Congressional-Black-Caucus-to-Remain-an-All-Black-Organization.html; Michael Cooper, "Councilwoman Wins Primary for House Seat," *New York Times*, September 13, 2006, http://www.nytimes.com/2006/09/13/nyregion/13cong.html; Jonathan P. Hicks, "Rivals in House Race Debate White Candidate's Motives," *New York Times*, August 25, 2006, http://www.nytimes.com/2006/08/25/nyregion/25brooklyn.html; Jonathan P. Hicks, "Each Candidate Claims the Advantage in a Fierce 4-Way Congressional Race in Brooklyn," *New York Times*, September 2, 2006, http://www.nytimes.com/2006/09/02/

nyregion/02brooklyn.html; Shailagh Murray, "Candidacy Fosters a Debate on Race," *Washington Post*, July 6, 2006, A1.1.

16. Alexander Hamilton [as Publius], "The Federalist 79: The Judiciary Department," [New York] *Independent Journal*, June 14, 1788, http://www.constitution.org/fed/federa78.htm.

17. This too deserves a bit of clarification. Because the Electoral College chooses the president and its members are awarded based on state allocations, five US presidents, including Donald Trump, were elected while having lost even a plurality of the popular vote.

18. The Court's decision in *Bush v. Gore* is a notable exception to this rule (531 US 98 [2000], http://www.law.cornell.edu/supct/html/00-949.ZPC.html). After the 2020 presidential elections, President Trump sought to challenge election outcomes in several states, with more than 60 suits being tossed out for lack of evidence, including one to the US Supreme Court (William Cummings, Joey Garrison, and Jim Sergent, "By the Numbers: President Donald Trump's Failed Efforts to Overturn the Election," *USA Today*, January 6, 2021, https://www.usatoday.com/in-depth/news/politics/elections/2021/01/06/trumps-failed-efforts-overturn-election-numbers/4130307001/).

19. 369 US 186 (1962), http://www.law.cornell.edu/supct/html/historics/USSC_CR_0369_0186_ZS.html.

20. 377 US 533 (1964), http://www.law.cornell.edu/supct/html/historics/USSC_CR_0377_0533_ZS.html.

21. This principle is not a universal truism. For instance, both the US Senate and the Electoral College are structural examples of the ways that the Framers devised a system that would be attentive to minority preferences. In the former example, states with small populations have the same voting power as states with large populations; and in the latter example, small states have disproportionate power in selecting the president because of the formula that is used to determine electoral votes. Both of these mechanisms are consistent with Madison's concern with majority factions, but they also violate the one person, one vote standard that characterizes most other aspects of political life in the United States.

22. D'Vera Cohn, "Imputation: Adding People to the Census," Pew Research Center, May 4, 2011, http://pewresearch.org/pubs/1981/census-imputation-missing-housing-units-people-number-type.

23. *Utah v. Evans*, 536 US 452 (2002), http://www.law.cornell.edu/supct/html/01-714.ZS.html.

24. Cohn, "Imputation."

25. Danny Vinik, "Trump's Threat to the 2020 Census." *Politico*, April 9, 2017, https://www.politico.com/agenda/story/2017/04/trumps-threat-to-the-2020-census-000404/; Tara Bahrampour and Brittany Renee Mayes, "Census Battle Ends as Trump Administration Gives Up on Excluding Undocumented from Apportionment," *The Washington Post*, January 16, 2021, https://www.politico.com/agenda/story/2017/04/trumps-threat-to-the-2020-census-000404/.

26. Michael Wines, "2020 Census Won't Have Citizenship Question as Trump Administration Drops Effort," *The New York Times*, July 2, 2019, https://www.nytimes.com/2019/07/02/us/trump-census-citizenship-question.html.

27. Joseph Ax, "Delay in U.S. Census Data Could Muddle 2022 Congressional Elections, Reuters," February 12, 2021, https://www.reuters.com/article/us-health-coronavirus-usa-census-idUSKBN2AC2G1.

28. "2020 Census: Apportionment of the U.S. House of Representatives," US Bureau of the Census, April 30, 2021, https://www.census.gov/library/visualizations/2021/dec/2020-apportionment-map.html.

29. Joshua Tucker, "Turnout Rates among the Rich and Poor," *The Monkey Cage*, July 5, 2013, http://themonkeycage.org/2013/07/05/turnout-rates-among-the-rich-and-poor/?utm_source=feedburner&utm_medium=feed&utm_campaign=Feed%3A+themonkeycagefeed+%28The+Monkey+Cage%29. Tucker cites evidence from Kimuli Kasara and Pavithra Suryanarayan, "When the Rich Vote Less Than the Poor and Why? Explaining Turnout Inequality across the World" (paper prepared for the International Society for New Institutional Economics Annual Conference, March 15, 2013), http://pavisuridotcom.files.wordpress.com/2012/08/kasarasuyanarayan_turnout 20131210.pdf.

30. Data from the 2010 census reveal that women comprise 50.9 percent of the US population. Lindsay M. Howden and Julie A. Meyer, "2010 Census Briefs: Age and Sex Composition: 2010," US Bureau of the Census, May 2011, http://www.census.gov/prod/cen2010/briefs/c2010br-03.pdf. Census Bureau estimates for 2019 put the figure at 50.8 percent (https://www.census.gov/quickfacts/fact/table/US/SEX255219#SEX255219).

31. While the election of Barack Obama to the presidency in 2008 and 2012 seems to serve as a counterfactual, a closer examination reveals otherwise. Although he garnered a plurality of votes in enough states to win Electoral College victories both years (and no state is majority-minority), he won only 43 percent of the white vote in 2008 and 39 percent in 2012. Paul Steinhauser, "Five Things We Learned on Election Night," http://CNN.com, November 8, 2012, http://www.cnn.com/2012/11/07/politics/5-things-election-night/index.html. As noted above, only seven African Americans have been elected to the US Senate, and only three African Americans have been elected governor.

32. *Shaw v. Reno*, 509 US 630 (1993), http://www.law.cornell.edu/supct/html/92-357.ZO.html. See also Linda Greenhouse, "The Supreme Court: Reapportionment; Court Questions Districts Drawn to Aid Minorities," *New York Times*, June 29, 1993, A1. A number of subsequent Court cases have also constrained the process of drawing of majority-minority districts. See, for instance, *Miller v. Johnson*, 515 US 900 (1995) and *Georgia v. Ashcroft*, 539 US 461 (2003).

33. See also Carol M. Swain, *Black Faces, Black Interests: The Representation of African Americans in Congress* (Cambridge: Harvard University Press, 1993).

34. In 2020, for instance, 87 percent of African Americans voted for Joe Biden, the winner of the election. Latinos preferred the Democratic candidate as well, but by a far slimmer margin—65 percent to 32 percent. CNN Politics, "Exit Polls," 2020, https://www.cnn.com/election/2020/exit-polls/president/national-results.   While Latinos collectively favor Republicans on a number of social issues, there are important ideological differences between Latinos in southern Florida, who tend to have a Cuban national background, and Latinos in the Southwest and in large northern and Midwestern cities, who tend to come from Central and South America, as well as Puerto Rico and the Dominican Republic. Oscar Corral, "Hispanics and Cuban Americans Varying Political Views Yield Surprises," *Havana Journal*, April 5, 2004, http://havanajournal.com/cuban_americans/entry/hispanics_and_cuban_americans_varying_political_views_yield_surprises/. There is evidence that this trend may be shifting, as in 2012 when President Obama won 60 percent of Cuban American voters who were born in the United States. Emily Deruy, "Cuban-Americans No Longer a Sure Bet for the GOP," *ABC News*, November 13, 2012, http://abcnews.go.com/ABC_Univision/Politics/cuban-voters-swinging-democratic/story?id=17700174#.ULPCI-Oe8f9. However, the Republican candidate, Donald Trump, earned at least 54 percent of the Cuban American vote in Miami-Dade County, Florida in 2016, and he earned up to 69 percent of that population's support in 2020. (Norma Gámez Torres, "'Invisible Campaign' and the Specter of Socialism: Why Cuban Americans Fell Hard for Trump," *Miami Herald*, November 19, 2020, https://www.miamiherald.com/news/politics-government/election/article247233684.html.)

35. Michael C. Dawson, *Black Visions: The Roots of Contemporary African-American Political Ideologies* (Chicago: University of Chicago, 2001); Karen M. Kaufmann, "Black and Latino Voters in Denver: Responses to Each Other's Political Leadership," *Political Science Quarterly* 118 (2003): 107–125.

36. C. Vann Woodward, *The Strange Career of Jim Crow* (1955; New York: Oxford University Press, 2001); Jerrold M. Packard, *American Nightmare: The History of Jim Crow* (New York: St. Martin's Griffin, 2003); Michael J. Klarman, *From Jim Crow to Civil Rights: The Supreme Court and the Struggle for Racial Equality* (New York: Oxford University Press, 2006).

37. The entire act is on the Department of Justice website: http://www.justice.gov/crt/about/vot/intro/intro_b.php.

38. Associated Press, "New Rules in These States Are Frustrating Voters," *Forbes*, November 7, 2016, http://fortune.com/2016/11/07/minority-voters-election/; Pete Williams, "Judge Says North Carolina Illegally Purged Voter Lists," *NBC News*, November 4, 2016, http://www.nbcnews.com/storyline/2016-election-day/judge-says-north-carolina-illegally-purged-voter-lists-n677431; "Florida's Discriminatory Voter Purge," *New York Times*, May 31, 2012, http://www.nytimes.com/2012/06/01/opinion/floridas-discriminatory-voter-purge.html.

39. Kwame Holman, "Voting Rights," *The NewsHour with Jim Lehrer*, December 15, 2000, http://www.pbs.org/newshour/bb/election/july-dec00/voting_12-15.html.

40. Mark Joseph Stern, "America Is Already in the Midst of a Voter Suppression Crisis," *Slate*, October 31, 2016, http://www.slate.com/articles/news_and_politics/jurisprudence/2016/10/republicans_are_already_suppressing_minority_votes_all_over_america.html; Erika L. Wood, "Florida: How Soon We Forget," Campaign Stops, April 5, 2012, http://campaignstops.blogs.nytimes.com/2012/04/05/florida-how-quickly-we-forget/.

41. Paula D. McClain, *"Can We All Get Along?" Racial and Ethnic Minorities in American Politics* (Boulder, CO: Westview, 2010), 191; Mark Berman, William Wan, and Sari Horwitz, "Voters Encounter Some Malfunctioning Machines, Other Headaches on Election Day," *Washington Post*, November 8, 2016, https://www.washingtonpost.com/news/post-nation/wp/2016/11/08/election-day-voters-report-long-lines-intimidation-and-confusion-in-some-parts-of-the-country/?utm_term=.4fe21f8b6fcc.

42. Jess Bravin, "Court Upends Voting Rights Act," *Wall Street Journal*, June 25, 2013, http://online.wsj.com/article/SB10001424127887323469804578521363840962032.html; Adam Liptak, "Supreme Court Invalidates Key Part of Voting Rights Act," *New York Times*, June 25, 2013, http://online.wsj.com/article/SB10001424127887323469804578521363840962032.html.

43. Jasmine C. Lee, "How States Moved toward Stricter Voter ID Laws," *New York Times*, November 3, 2016, http://www.nytimes.com/interactive/2016/11/03/us/elections/how-states-moved-toward-stricter-voter-id-laws.html. For scholarly work related to the relationship between voter identification laws and voter turnout, see R. Michael Alvarez, Delia Bailey, and Jonathan N. Katz, "The Effect of Voter Identification Laws on Turnout," Social Science Working Paper 1267, California Institute of Technology, October 2007, http://jkatz.caltech.edu/research/files/wp1267.pdf and Matt A. Barreto, Stephen A. Nuño, and Gabriel R. Sanchez, "Voter ID Requirements and the Disenfranchisements of Latino, Black and Asian Voters" (paper prepared for presentation at the 2007 meeting of the American Political Science Association), http://citeseerx.ist.psu.edu/viewdoc/download?doi=10.1.1.175.23&rep=rep1&type=pdf.

44. Morgan Chalfant, "Trump: 'The Only Way We're Going to Lose this Election is if the Election is Rigged,'" *The Hill*, August 17, 2020, https://thehill.com/homenews/administration/512424-trump-the-only-way-we-are-going-to-lose-this-election-is-if-the.

45. David Smith and Sabrina Siddiqui, "Trump Claims 'Cheating' Is Only Way He Can Lose Pennsylvania," *The Guardian*, August 13, 2016, https://www.theguardian.com/us-news/2016/aug/13/donald-trump-claims-cheating-is-only-way-he-can-lose-pennsylvania.

46. Aaron Blake, "Trump's 'Big Lie' Was Bigger than Just a Stolen Election," *The Washington Post*, February 12, 2021.

47. Cummings, Garrison, and Sergent.

48. In addition to the 2020 lawsuits and the insurrection, further evidence of the race-based nature of the concerns is the proliferation of voter suppression law proposals in states that have arisen since the November 2020 election. Turnout was historically high, in part because mail-in balloting was permitted in states where it was previously not in practice to protect the public during the Covid-19 pandemic. Democrats, who believe they benefitted by a greater turnout, have moved to solidify those practices for future elections, while Republicans, fearful that more expansive turnout will be harmful to them and, they argue, result in voter fraud, have worked to restrict access to the polls ("Voting Laws Roundup: January 2021," Brennan Center for Justice, January 26, 2021, https://www.brennancenter.org/our-work/research-reports/voting-laws-roundup-january-2021).

49. Lauren Leatherby, Arielle Ray, Anjali Singhvi, Christiaan Triebert, Derek Watkins, and Haley Willis, "How a Presidential Rally Turned Into a Capitol Rampage," *The New York Times*, January 12, 2021, https://www.nytimes.com/interactive/2021/01/12/us/capitol-mob-timeline.html.

50. "Identifying Far-Right Symbols that Appeared at the U.S. Capitol Riot," *The Washington Post*, January 15, 2021, https://www.washingtonpost.com/nation/interactive/2021/far-right-symbols-capitol-riot/.

51. David Wasserman, Sophie Andrews, Leo Saenger, Lev Cohen, Ally Flinn, and Griff Tatarsky, "National Popular Vote Tracker," *The Cook Political Report*, n.d., https://cookpolitical.com/2020-national-popular-vote-tracker.

52. The title of this section is borrowed from Raymond A. Smith, *The American Anomaly: U.S. Politics and Government in Comparative Perspective*, 4th ed. (New York: Routledge, 2019).

53. The term *single member district plurality* reflects the process of the state drawing district lines and having one person per district represent that geographical area in the legislative body (i.e., the US House of Representatives or state legislatures). Each district has a single member chosen, who must win a plurality of the votes to take office.

54. Jennifer E. Manning, "Membership of the 112th Congress: A Profile," Congressional Research Service, August 4, 2011, http://fpc.state.gov/documents/organization/170493.pdf.

55. Helena Bottemiller Evich, "Revenge of the Rural Voter," Politico, November 13, 2016, http://www.politico.com/story/2016/11/hillary-clinton-rural-voters-trump-231266.

56. French law mandates that in most elections an equal number of men and women must appear on ballots. It does not mandate gender parity in elected bodies, but the provision has led to an increase in women both seeking office and being elected. Janine Mossuz-Lavau, "Gender Parity in Politics," *France in the United States: Embassy of France in Washington*, November 30, 2007, http://ambafrance-us.org/spip.php?article612.

57. Lani Guinier, "The Representation of Minority Interests: The Question of Single-Member Districts," *Cordozo Law Review* 14 (1993): 1135–1174.

58. William G. Ludwin, "Strategic Voting and the Borda Method," *Public Choice* 38 (1978): 85–90.

59. Matt Gehring, "Information Brief: Instant Runoff Voting," Minnesota House of Representatives Research Department, February, 2007, http://www.house.leg.state.mn.us/hrd/pubs/irvoting.pdf.

60. In 2016, there were two prominent third-party candidates on the ballot in most states. If voters who selected them in states that were decided by a small margin had the chance to indicate a second choice, the outcome might have been different.

61. C. Wright Mills, *The Power Elite* (New York: Oxford University Press, 1956).

62. See, for example, Robert Dahl, *Who Governs? Democracy and Power in an American City* (New Haven: Yale University Press, 1961).

63. Toby Eckert, "Sanders Targets Highest-Income Americans with 'Extreme Wealth Tax' and 'National Tax Reigistry,'" *Politico*, September 24, 2019, https://www.politico.com/story/2019/09/24/bernie-sanders-wealth-tax-1763426.

64. The right of corporations and labor unions to participate in the electoral process was widened in 2010 with the Supreme Court's decision in *Citizens United v. the Federal Election Commission* (558 US 310). The Court ruled that the First Amendment protects such organizations from restrictions on using their treasuries (as opposed to associated political action committees) to spend money independently (i.e., not contribute directly) to influence the outcome of an election: http://www.law.cornell.edu/supct/pdf/08–205P.ZO.

65. Cornel West, *Race Matters* (New York: Vintage, 1993), 94.

66. Patricia Ireland, "Progress versus Equality," in *The Difference "Difference" Makes: Women and Leadership*, ed. Deborah L. Rhode (Stanford, CA: Stanford University Press, 2003), 193.

Chapter 2: Income and Wealth

1. Allan Ornstein, *Class Counts: Education, Inequality, and the Shrinking Middle Class* (Lanham, MD: Rowman & Littlefield, 2007), 117, 150.

2. A quintile represents 20 percent of the population. In this case, if all households in the United States were listed from the wealthiest to the poorest and then divided equally into five groups, the top quintile would be the group that includes the wealthiest 20 percent of households.

3. Michael I. Norton and Dan Ariely, "Building a Better America—One Wealth Quintile at a Time," *Perspectives on Psychological Science* 6, no. 1 (2011): 9–12.

4. Ibid., 10.

5. Norton and Ariely, 12.

6. Jesse Washington, "The Disappearing Black Middle Class," *Chicago Sun-Times*, July 10, 2011, http://www.suntimes.com/6397110-417/the-disappearing-black-middle-class.html.

7. Valerie Wilson, "Black Unemployment Is Significantly Higher Than White Unemployment Regardless of Educational Attainment," Economic Policy Institute, December 17, 2015, http://www.epi.org/publication/black-unemployment-educational-attainment/.

8. Pew Research Center, "Unemployment Rose Higher in Three Months of COVID-19 than It Did in Two Years of the Great Recession," June 11, 2020, https://www.pewresearch.org/fact-tank/2020/06/11/unemployment-rose-higher-in-three-months-of-covid-19-than-it-did-in-two-years-of-the-great-recession/.

9. Ibid.

10. US Bureau of Labor Statistics, "The Employment Situation—January 2021," February 5, 2021, p. 9, https://www.bls.gov/news.release/pdf/empsit.pdf.

11. U. S. Census Bureau, "Income and Poverty in the United States, 2019," September 15, 2020, https://www.census.gov/library/publications/2020/demo/p60-270.html.

12. Jack Stanton, "How the Pandemic Is Worsening America's Racial Gaps," *Politico*, October 16, 2020, https://www.politico.com/news/magazine/2020/10/16/coronavirus-pandemic-race-black-inequality-economics-429887.

13. U.S. Census Bureau, "Historical Income Tables: Households," September 8, 2020, http://www2.census.gov/programs-surveys/cps/tables/time-series/historical-income-households/h02ar.xls, Table H-2, "Share of Aggregate Income Received by Each Fifth and Top 5 Percent of All Households: 1967 to 2019"; see also Tax Policy Center, "Household Income Quintiles," March 24, 2020, https://www.taxpolicycenter.org/statistics/household-income-quintiles.

14. Ibid.

15. Ibid.

16. Sonam Sheth, Sayanne Gal, Madison Hoff, and Marguerite Ward, "7 Charts that Show the Glaring Gap Between Men's and Women's Salaries in the U.S.," *Business Insider*, August 26, 2020, https://www.businessinsider.com/gender-wage-pay-gap-charts-2017-3.

17. Ibid.

18. Institute for Women's Policy Research, "The Gender Wage Gap: 2019," March 2020, https://iwpr.org/wp-content/uploads/2020/07/2020-Weekly-Wage-Gap-2020-FINAL.pdf.

19. That is, while women with college degrees earn more than women without college degrees, the income gap between women with college degrees and men with college degrees is larger than the gap between women and men without college degrees. Jennifer Cheeseman Day, "College Degree Widens Gender Earnings Gap," U.S. Census Bureau, May 29, 2019, https://www.census.gov/library/stories/2019/05/college-degree-widens-gender-earnings-gap.html#:~:text=Among%20the%20Educated%2C%20Women%20Earn%2074%20Cents%20for%20Every%20Dollar%20Men%20Make&text=More%20education%20leads%20to%20higher,degree%20than%20among%20those%20without.

20. Hanna Rosin, "The Gender Wage Gap Lie," http://Slate.com, August 30, 2013, http://www.slate.com/articles/double_x/doublex/2013/08/gender_pay_gap_the_familiar_line_that_women_make_77_cents_to_every_man_s.html.

21. Carey Oven, "Missing Pieces Report: The 2018 Board Diversity Census of Women and Minorities on Fortune 500 Boards," Deloitte, n.d., https://www2.deloitte.com/us/en/pages/center-for-board-effectiveness/articles/missing-pieces-fortune-500-board-diversity-study-2018.html.

22. Alliance for Board Diversity, "Missing Pieces: Women and Minorities on Fortune 500 Boards," August 15, 2013, https://fortunedotcom.files.wordpress.com/2014/02/2012_abd_missing_pieces_final_8_15_13.pdf.

23. Gregory Wallace, "Only 5 Black CEOs at 500 Biggest Companies," *CNN Money*, January 29, 2015, http://money.cnn.com/2015/01/29/news/economy/mcdonalds-ceo-diversity/.

24. "Black Chairmen & CEOs of Fortune 500 Companies," Black Entrepreneurs & Executives, January 28, 2021, https://www.blackentrepreneurprofile.com/collections/black-fortune-500-ceos.

25. Ibid.

26. Alexis Benveniste, "The Fortune 500 Now Has a Record Number of Female CEOs: A Whopping 38," *CNN*, August 4, 2020, https://www.cnn.com/2020/08/04/business/fortune-500-women-ceos/index.html.

27. Jana Kasperkevic, "America's Top CEOs Pocket 340 Times More Than the Average Worker," *Guardian*, May 17, 2016, https://www.theguardian.com/us-news/2016/may/17/ceo-pay-ratio-average-worker-afl-cio; *CNN Money*, "GDP Growth Not Reaching Paychecks," http://CNN.com, September 5, 2007, http://money.cnn.com/2007/09/03/news/economy/epi_report/index.htm; http://MoveOn.org, "Something Big Happened to America in 1979."

28. Lawrence Mishel and Jori Kandra, "CEO Compensation Surged 14% in 2019 to $21.3 Million," Economic Policy Institute, August 18, 2020, https://www.epi.org/publication/ceo-compensation-surged-14-in-2019-to-21-3-million-ceos-now-earn-320-times-as-much-as-a-typical-worker/#:~:text=In%202019%2C%20the%20ratio%20of,in%20the%20top%200.1%25.

29. Ibid.

30. Amir El-Sibaie, "2020 Tax Brackets," *Tax Foundation*, November 14, 2019, https://taxfoundation.org/2020-tax-brackets/.

31. Dave Gilson and Carolyn Perot, "It's the Inequality, Stupid," *Mother Jones*, March–April, 2011, http://www.motherjones.com/politics/2011/02/income-inequality-in-america-chart-graph.

32. Christopher Ingraham, "For the First Time in US History, U.S. Billionaires Paid a Lower Tax Rate than the Working Class Last Year," *The Washington Post*, October 8, 2019, https://www.washingtonpost.com/business/2019/10/08/first-time-history-us-billionaires-paid-lower-tax-rate-than-working-class-last-year/.

33. Ibid.

34. Ben Rooney and Julianne Pepitone, "$400 Billion in Tax Breaks Seen Favoring Wealthy," *CNN Money*, September 22, 2010, http://money.cnn.com/2010/09/21/news/economy/wealth_building_tax_policy/index.htm. For more recent analyses consistent with these findings, see Chuck Marr, Samantha Jacoby, and Kathleen Bryant, "Substantial Income of Wealthy Households Escapes Taxation or Enjoys Special Tax Breaks," Center for Budget and Policy Priorities, November 13, 2019, https://www.cbpp.org/research/federal-tax/substantial-income-of-wealthy-households-escapes-annual-taxation-or-enjoys and Camilo Maldonado, "Trump Tax Cuts Helped Billionaires Pay Less Taxes than the Working Class in 2018," *Forbes*, October 10, 2019, https://www.forbes.com/sites/camilomaldonado/2019/10/10/trump-tax-cuts-helped-billionaires-pay-less-taxes-than-the-working-class-in-2018/?sh=64673fe43128.

35. Dan Froomkin, "The Top 10 Tax Breaks—and How They Help the Wealthy the Most," *Huffington Post*, April 18, 2011, http://www.huffingtonpost.com/2011/04/18/the-top-10-tax-breaks-_n_850534.html.

36. Michael D. Shear, "Romney Releases 2011 Tax Returns," *New York Times*, September 21, 2012, http://thecaucus.blogs.nytimes.com/2012/09/21/romney-to-release-2011-tax-returns/; Brody Mullins, Patrick O'Connor, and John McKinnon, "Romney's Taxes: $3 Million," *Wall Street Journal*, January 24, 2012, http://online.wsj.com/article/SB10001424052970204624204577179740171772850.html.

37. "Buffett Slams Dividend Tax Cut," *CNN Money*, May 20, 2003, http://money.cnn.com/2003/05/20/news/buffett_tax/; Steve Wamhoff, "How to Implement the Buffet Rule," *Citizens for Tax Justice*, October 19, 2011, http://www.ctj.org/pdf/buffettruleremedies.pdf.

38. Jennifer Wang, "Donald Trump's Fortune Falls $800 Million to $3.7 Billion," *Forbes*, September 28, 2016, http://www.forbes.com/sites/jenniferwang/2016/09/28/the-definitive-look-at-donald-trumps-wealth-new/#208b7e9b7e2d.

39. David Barstow, Susanne Craig, Russ Buettner, and Megan Twohey, "Donald Trump Tax Records Show He Could Have Avoided Taxes for Nearly Two Decades, The Times Found," *New York Times*, October 1, 2016, http://www.nytimes.com/2016/10/02/us/politics/donald-trump-taxes.html.

40. Russ Buettner, Susanne Craig, and Mike McIntire, "The President's Taxes: Long-Concealed Records Show Trump's Chronic Losses and Years of Tax Avoidance," *The New York Times*, September 27, 2020, https://www.nytimes.com/interactive/2020/09/27/us/donald-trump-taxes.html.

41. Steve Forbes, *Flat Tax Revolution: Using a Postcard to Abolish the IRS* (Washington, DC: Regnery, 2005).

42. Ibid., 73. Other versions of the plan do not include the additional deductions for children under 16 or the EITC. See Daniel Mitchell, "A Brief Guide to the Flat Tax," *Heritage Foundation*, July 7, 2005, http://www.heritage.org/research/reports/2005/07/a-brief-guide-to-the-flat-tax.

43. Mitchell, "A Brief Guide to the Flat Tax."

44. Michael Kinsley, "Steve Forbes's Flat Tire," *Washington Post*, August 7, 2005, http://www.washingtonpost.com/wp-dyn/content/article/2005/08/05/AR2005080501490.html.

45. Dorothy Brown, "Let's Kill the Progressive Tax Rate System," http://CNN.com, April 17, 2012, http://www.cnn.com/2012/04/17/opinion/brown-progressive-tax-rates/index.html.

46. Steve Forbes, "Why Trump's Tax Cuts Should Be Big and Bold," *Forbes*, December 14, 2016, http://www.forbes.com/sites/steveforbes/2016/12/14/why-trumps-tax-cuts-should-be-big-and-bold/#1f0df9186298.

47. Robert Exley, Jr. and MacKenzie Sigalos, "The Social Security Tax Cap Kicks in at This Salary Figure in 2021," *CNBC*, January 7, 2021, https://www.cnbc.com/2021/01/07/social-security-tax-cap-2021-heres-how-much-you-will-pay.html. Medicare contributions were similarly regressive until 2013, but now there is now no wage cap on the 1.45 percent tax (US Internal Revenue Service, "Topic No. 751: Social Security and Medicare Withholding Rates," February 5, 2021, https://www.irs.gov/taxtopics/tc751).

48. Bruce D. Meyer and Dan T. Rosenbaum, "Welfare, the Earned Income Tax Credit, and the Labor Supply of Single Mothers," *Quarterly Journal of Economics* 116, no. 3 (2001): 1063–1114.

49. US Internal Revenue Service, "Earned Income and Earned Income Tax Credit (EITC) Tables," February 3, 2021, https://www.irs.gov/credits-deductions/individuals/earned-income-tax-credit/earned-income-and-earned-income-tax-credit-eitc-tables.

50. Court Smith, "Minimum Wage History," 2011, http://oregonstate.edu/instruct/anth484/minwage.html.

51. Ibid.

52. National Conference of State Legislatures, "State Minimum Wages," January 8, 2021, https://www.ncsl.org/research/labor-and-employment/state-minimum-wage-chart.aspx.

53. Smith, "Minimum Wage History."

54. Jessie Willis, "How We Measure Poverty: A History and Brief Overview," Oregon Center for Public Policy, February 2000, http://www.ocpp.org/poverty/how.htm.

55. US Department of Health and Human Services, "Poverty Guidelines," January 15, 2021, https://aspe.hhs.gov/poverty-guidelines.

56. John Creamer, "Inequalities Persist Despite Decline in Poverty for All Major Race and Hispanic Origin Groups," United States Census Bureau, September 15, 2020, https://www.census.gov/library/stories/2020/09/poverty-rates-for-blacks-and-hispanics-reached-historic-lows-in-2019.html#:~:text=In%202019%2C%20the%20poverty%20rate,race%20and%20Hispanic%20origin%20groups.

57. Ibid.

58. Robin Bleiweis, Diana Boesch, and Alexandra Cawthorne Gaines, "The Basic Facts about Women in Poverty," Center for American Progress, August 3, 2020, https://www.americanprogress.org/issues/women/reports/2020/08/03/488536/basic-facts-women-poverty/.

59. Samuel Stebbins and Thomas C. Frohlich, "The Poverty Rates for Every Group in the US: From Age and Sex to Citizenship Status," *USA Today*, November 6, 2019, https://www.usatoday.com/story/money/2019/11/06/united-states-poverty-rate-for-every-group/40546247/.

60. "Percentage of White, non-Hispanic Families with a Single Mother in the U.S. Who Live Below the Poverty Level from 1990 to 2019," *Statistica*,

January 20, 2021, https://www.statista.com/statistics/205049/percentage-of-poor-white-families-with-a-female-householder-in-the-us/#:~:text=Economy-, Poverty%20rate%20of%20white%2C%20non%2DHispanic%20single,mother%20 households%20U.S.%201990%2D2019&text=In%202019%2C%2017.1%20per-cent%20of,level%20in%20the%20United%20States; "Poverty Rate of Black Families with a Single Mother in the United States 1990 to 2019," *Statistica*, January 20, 2021, https://www.statista.com/statistics/205114/percentage-of-poor-black-families-with-a-female-householder-in-the-us/.

61. Ibid.

62. Areeba Haider, "The Basic Facts about Children in Poverty," Center for American Progress, January 12, 2021, https://www.americanprogress.org/issues/poverty/reports/2021/01/12/494506/basic-facts-children-poverty/.

63. Ibid.

64. Ibid.

65. Ibid.

66. Willis, "How We Measure Poverty."

67. Ibid.

68. Dean Baker, "This is What Minimum Wage Would Be If It Kept Pace with Productivity," Center for Economic and Policy Research, January 21, 2020, https://cepr.net/this-is-what-minimum-wage-would-be-if-it-kept-pace-with-productivity/.

69. Sarah Anderson, "How Wall Street Drives Gender and Race Pay Gaps," Institute for Policy Studies, March 26, 2019, https://inequality.org/great-divide/wall-street-bonus-pool-2019/.

70. Martha C. White, "Increasing the Minimum Wage Would Help, Not Hurt, the Economy," *NBC News*, October 23, 2020, https://www.nbcnews.com/business/economy/increasing-minimum-wage-would-help-not-hurt-economy-n1244586.

71. *Washington Post*, January 28, 2014, http://www.washingtonpost.com/politics/full-text-of-obamas-2014-state-of-the-union-address/2014/01/28/e0c93358-887f-11e3-a5bd-844629433ba3_story.html.

72. Candidate Trump gave a number of conflicting and sometimes confusing responses to questions about the minimum wage, however. For a review, see Michelle Ye Hee Lee, "A Guide to All of Donald Trump's Flip-Flops on the Minimum Wage," *Washington Post*, October 3, 2016, https://www.washingtonpost.com/news/fact-checker/wp/2016/08/03/a-guide-to-all-of-donald-trumps-flip-flops-on-the-minimum-wage/.

73. Martha C. White, "Increasing the Minimum Wage Would Help, Not Hurt, the Economy."

74. Caitlin Emma and Aaron Lorenzo, "Democrats Plot Their Plan B to Save Minimum Wage Hike," *Politico*, February 22, 2021, https://www.politico.com/news/2021/02/22/democrats-minimum-wage-increase-plan-470860.

75. Marilyn Geewax, "Does a Higher Minimum Wage Kill Jobs?" *National Public Radio*, April 24, 2011, http://www.npr.org/2011/04/24/135638370/does-a-higher-minimum-wage-kill-jobs.

76. US Congressional Budget Office, "The Budgetary Effects of the Raise the Wage Act of 2021," February 8, 2021, https://www.cbo.gov/publication/56975.

77. Raymond A. Smith, *The American Anomaly: U.S. Politics and Government in Comparative Perspective* (New York: Routledge, 2011), 165–169.

78. Social Security Administration, "Historical Background and Development of Social Security," 2011, http://www.ssa.gov/history/briefhistory3.html.

79. For example, see Stanley Feldman and John Zaller, "The Political Culture of Ambivalence: Ideological Responses to the Welfare State," *American Journal of Political Science* 36, no. 1 (1992): 268–307.

80. "'Welfare Queen' Becomes Issue in Reagan Campaign," *New York Times*, February 15, 1976, http://picofarad.info/misc/welfarequeen.pdf.

81. Although prosecutors argued that the characterization of her crimes was accurate, she was only indicted for theft of $8,000 from public welfare and for perjury. Dan Miller, "The Chutzpa Queen: Favorite Reagan Target as Welfare Cheat Remains Unflappable at Trial in Chicago," *Washington Post*, March 13, 1977, A3.

82. See Frank Gilliam Jr., "The 'Welfare Queen' Experiment: How Voters React to Images of African-American Mothers on Welfare," UCLA Center for Communications and Community, 1999, http://escholarship.org/uc/item/17m7r1rq; Ange-Marie Hancock, *The Politics of Disgust: The Public Identity of the Welfare Queen* (New York: New York University Press, 2004). Reagan did not mention the woman's race explicitly. Rather, he made references to Chicago or to the South Side of Chicago or to the inner city, which served as code for "African American." Paul Krugman, "Republicans and Race," *New York Times*, November 19, 2007, http://www.nytimes.com/2007/11/19/opinion/19krugman.html. As Gilliam explains, "The implicit racial coding is readily apparent. The woman Reagan was talking about was African-American. Veiled references to African-American women, and African-Americans in general, were equally transparent. In other words, while poor women of all races get blamed for their impoverished condition, African-American women commit the most egregious violations of American values. This story line tips into stereotypes about both women (uncontrolled sexuality) and African-Americans (laziness)."

83. Martin Gilens, *Why Americans Hate Welfare: Race, Media, and the Politics of Antipoverty Policy* (Chicago: University of Chicago Press, 1999), 68.

84. Ibid., 68–69.

85. Ange-Marie Hancock, *Politics of Disgust*.

86. Laura Meyer and Ife Floyd, "Cash Assistance Should Reach Millions More Families to Lessen Hardship," Center on Budget and Policy Priorities, November 30, 2020, https://www.cbpp.org/research/family-income-support/cash-assistance-should-reach-millions-more-families-to-lessen.

87. Marketplace, "Your State on Welfare," American Public Media, n.d., http://linkis.com/marketplace.org/EaI13.

88. Pam Fessler, "20 Years Since Welfare's Overhaul, Results Are Mixed," *National Public Radio*, August 22, 2016, http://www.npr.org/2016/08/22/490245470/20-years-since-welfares-overhaul-results-are-mixed.

89. Stephen Slivinsky, "The Corporate Welfare State: How the Federal Government Subsidizes U.S. Businesses," *Policy Analysis* 592 (2007): 1–21.

90. Melvin L. Oliver and Thomas M. Shapiro, *Black Wealth/White Wealth: A New Perspective on Racial Inequality*, 10th ed. (New York: Routledge, 2006).

91. Lisa A. Keister, *Wealth in America: Trends in Wealth Inequality* (New York: Cambridge University Press, 2000), 10.

92. Ibid.; Joseph E. Stiglitz, *The Price of Inequality: How Today's Divided Society Endangers Our Future* (New York: Norton, 2012).

93. Figures are expressed in 2010 dollars (Linda Levine, "An Analysis of the Distribution of Wealth Across Households, 1989–2010," Congressional Research Service, July 17, 2012, http://www.fas.org/sgp/crs/misc/RL33433.pdf). Household wealth grew faster than median wealth over that period, suggesting concentration at the upper end of the wealth distribution. As Levine notes, while both declined by 2012, the greater decline in the median reflects that the recession "affected those in the lower half of the wealth distribution more than those higher up in the distribution" (p. 3).

94. Juliana Menasce Horowitz, Ruth Igielnik, and Rakesh Kochhar, "Trends in Income and Wealth Inequality," Pew Research Center, January 9, 2020, https://www.pewresearch.org/social-trends/2020/01/09/trends-in-income-and-wealth-inequality/.

95. Ibid., n.p.

96. Bonnie Kavoussi, "Nearly Half of Americans Die Without Money, Study Finds," *Huffington Post*, August 6, 2012, http://www.huffingtonpost.com/2012/08/06/americans-die-without-money_n_1746862.html.

97. Paul Taylor et al., "Wealth Gaps Rise to Record Highs Between Whites, Blacks and Hispanics: Twenty-to-One," Pew Research Center, July 26, 2011, http://www.pewsocialtrends.org/2011/07/26/wealth-gaps-rise-to-record-highs-between-whites-blacks-hispanics/; Dedrick Asante-Muhammad, Chuck Collins, Josh Hoxie, and Emanuel Nieves, "The Ever-Growing Gap," August, 2016, http://cfed.org/policy/federal/The_Ever_Growing_Gap-CFED_IPS-Final.pdf.

98. Michael Batty, Jesse Bricker, Joseph Briggs, Elizabeth Holmquist, Susan McIntosh, Kevin Moore, Eric Nielsen, Sarah Reber, Molly Shatto, Kamila Sommer, Tom Sweeney, and Alice Henriques Volz (2019). "Introducing the Distributional Financial Accounts of the United States," *Finance and Economics Discussion Series* 2019-017. Washington: Board of Governors of the Federal Reserve System, https://doi.org/10.17016/FEDS.2019.017, https://www.federalreserve.gov/econres/feds/files/2019017pap.pdf, as cited in Mark DeCambre, "The Richest 10% of Households Now Represent 70% of All Wealth," *MarketWatch*. May 31, 2019, https://www.marketwatch.com/story/the-richest-10-of-households-now-represent-70-of-all-us-wealth-2019-05-24.

99. Kriston McIntosh, Emily Moss, Ryan Nunn, and Jay Shambaugh, "Examining the Black-white Wealth Gap," Brookings Institution, February 27, 2020, https://www.brookings.edu/blog/up-front/2020/02/27/examining-the-black-white-wealth-gap/.

100. If we examine mean rather than median, the results hold, though they are slightly less dramatic (as they are driven by very wealthy families): white average wealth is $929,800 compared to $138,100 for African American families. Ibid.

101. Ibid.

102. Ibid.

103. Karuna Jaggar, "The Race and Gender Wealth Gap," *Race and Regionalism* 15, no. 1 (2008), http://urbanhabitat.org/node/2815.

104. Janice Traflet and Robert E. Wright, "America Doesn't Just Have a Gender Pay Gap. It Has a Gender Wealth Gap," *The Washington Post*, April 2, 2019, https://www.washingtonpost.com/outlook/2019/04/02/america-doesnt-just-have-gender-pay-gap-it-has-gender-wealth-gap/.

105. Megan Thibos, Danielle Lavin-Loucks, and Marcus Martin, "The Feminization of Poverty," *YWCA Dallas*, 2007, http://www.ywcadallas.org/PDF/womens-health/FeminizationofPoverty.pdf.

106. Bridget Lavelle and Pamela Smock, "Divorce and Women's Risk of Health Insurance Loss in the U.S.," *Population Studies Center Research Report* no. 11–734, Institute for Social Research, University of Michigan, March, 2011, http://www.psc.isr.umich.edu/pubs/pdf/rr11-734.pdf.

107. Karuna Jaggar, "Race and Gender Wealth Gap." For more information on gender and race in wealth disparity, especially with respect to homeownership, see Beverlyn Lundy Allen, "Race and Gender Inequality in Homeownership: Does Place Make a Difference?" *Rural Sociology* 67, no. 4 (2002): 603–621.

108. Maury Gittleman and Edward N. Wolff, "Racial Differences in Patterns of Wealth Accumulation," *Journal of Human Resources* 39 (2004): 193–227.

109. Paul L. Menchik and Nancy Ammon Jianakoplos, "Black-White Wealth Inequality: Is Inheritance the Reason?" *Economic Inquiry* 35 (2007): 428–442, quote 441.

110. Victor Tan Chen, "All Hollowed Out: The Lonely Poverty of America's White Working Class," *Atlantic*, January 16, 2016, http://www.theatlantic.com/business/archive/2016/01/white-working-class-poverty/424341/.

111. Federal Reserve Bank of St. Louis, "Personal Savings Rate," January 29, 2021, https://fred.stlouisfed.org/series/PSAVERT.

112. Luca Ventura, "Household Saving Rates 2021," *Global Finance*, January 25, 2021, https://www.gfmag.com/global-data/economic-data/916lqg-household-saving-rates.

113. Cameron Huddleston, "Survey: 69% of Americans Have Less than $1,000 in Savings," *Go Banking Rates*, December 16, 2019, https://www.gobankingrates.com/saving-money/savings-advice/americans-have-less-than-1000-in-savings/.

114. Alexandre Tanzi, "Five Charts that Show the Extent of the Black Wealth Gap in the U.S.," *Bloomberg*, July 18, 2020, https://www.bloomberg.com/news/articles/2020-07-18/five-charts-that-show-the-extent-of-the-black-wealth-gap-in-u-s.

115. Ibid.

116. Laura Shin, "The Racial Wealth Gap: Why a Typical White Household Has 16 Times the Wealth of a Black One," *Forbes*, March 26, 2015, http://www.forbes.com/sites/laurashin/2015/03/26/the-racial-wealth-gap-why-a-typical-white-household-has-16-times-the-wealth-of-a-black-one/#cd5e4066c5bc.

117. Alexandre Tanzi, "Five Charts that Show the Extent of the Black Wealth Gap in the U.S."

118. Stan Choe, "Stocks Are Soaring, and Most Black People Are Missing Out," *Chicago Tribune*, October 12, 2020, https://www.chicagotribune.com/featured/sns-stocks-are-soaring-and-most-black-people-are-missing-out-20201012-ozafz24mcvd mpohnlu6pg5lpwu-story.html.

119. See David J. Hand and William E. Henley, "Statistical Classification Methods in Consumer Credit Scoring: A Review," *Journal of the Royal Statistical Society* 160, no. 3 (1997): 523–541.

120. Ibid.

121. Statistical and qualitative studies of black business owners, for example, identify unique and persistent challenges in securing loans, intrusion of larger companies into traditionally black markets, and lack of experience. See Timothy Bates, *Banking on Black Enterprise: The Potential of Emerging Firms for Revitalizing Urban Economics* (Washington, DC: Joint Center for Political and Economic Studies, 1993); Michael Bonds, "Looking Beyond the Numbers: The Struggles of Black Businesses to Survive: A Qualitative Approach," *Journal of Black Studies* 37, no. 5 (1997): 581–601; Jan E. Christopher, "Minority Business Formation and Survival: Evidence on Business Performance and Visibility," *Review of Black Political Economy* 26, no. 7 (1998): 37–72; Robert W. Fairlie and Alicia M. Robb, "Why Are Black-Owned Businesses Less Successful Than White-Owned Businesses? The Role of Families, Inheritances, and Business Human Capital," University of California–Santa Cruz, 2005, http://repositories.cdlib.org/ucscecon/618; Robert Mark Silverman, "Black Business, Group Resources, and the Economic Detour: Contemporary Black Manufacturers in Chicago's Ethnic Beauty Aids Industry," *Journal of Black Studies* 30, no. 2 (1999): 232–258; Joe William Trotter Jr., *Black Milwaukee: The Making of an Industrial Proletariat, 1915–1948* (Urbana: University of Illinois Press, 1985).

122. There is a rich literature in economics regarding conditions under which individuals tend to be risk averse as opposed to risk seeking. See, for instance, Daniel Kahneman and Amos Tversky, "Choices, Values, and Frames," *American Psychologist* 39, no. 4 (1984): 341–350.

123. Jeffrey M. Jones, "One in Six Americans Gamble on Sports," *Gallup*, July 30, 2008, http://www.gallup.com/poll/104086/One-Six-Americans-Gamble-Sports.aspx.

124. Ibid.

125. Kate Gibson, "Who Buys Lottery Tickets? Those Who Can Least Afford Them," *CBS News*, September 12, 2018, https://www.cbsnews.com/news/who-buys-lottery-tickets-those-who-can-least-afford-them/; see also H. Roy Kaplan, "The Social and Economic Impact of State Lotteries," *Annals of the American Academy of Political and Social Science* 474 (1984): 91–106.

126. Michael A. Stegman, "Payday Lending," *Journal of Economic Perspectives* 21, no. 1 (2007): 169–190.

127. Michael A. Stegman and Robert Faris, *Welfare, Work, and Banking: The North Carolina Financial Services Survey* (Chapel Hill, NC: Center for Community Capitalism, 2001); Stegman and Faris, "Welfare, Work, and Banking: The Use of Consumer Credit by Current and Former TANF Recipients in Charlotte, North Carolina," *Journal of Urban Affairs* 27, no. 4 (2005): 379–402, cited in Stegman, "Payday Lending," 173–174.

128. Reuters, "New Rules Could Dramatically Alter the Payday Loan Market," *Fortune*, June 2, 2016, http://fortune.com/2016/06/02/cfpb-payday-loan-rules/.

129. Gillian B. White, "Payday Loans' Potentially Predatory Replacement," *Atlantic*, August 12, 2016, http://www.theatlantic.com/business/archive/2016/08/what-will-replace-payday-loans/495656/.

130. Katherine Kirkpatrick, Andrew Michaelson, Steven Miller, and Brian Thavarajah, "CFPB Focus on Payday Lending: A Look Around the Corner," *JD Supra*, January 15, 2021, https://www.jdsupra.com/legalnews/cfpb-focus-on-payday-lending-a-look-7629208/.

131. Ibid.

132. As of June 2021, the Senate had yet to vote on President Biden's nominee, Rohit Chopra. (Caitlin Reilly, "Congressional Democrats to Push Biden's CFPB to Confront Racism," *Roll Call*, May 4, 2021, https://www.rollcall.com/2021/05/04/congressional-democrats-push-bidens-cfpb-to-confront-racism%EF%BE%A0/).

133. Kristin Stoller, "The True Cost of Rent to Own—And Alternatives," *Forbes*, February 27, 2020, https://www.forbes.com/advisor/credit-cards/the-true-cost-of-rent-to-own-and-alternatives/.

134. Ronald Paul Hill, David L. Ramp, and Linda Silver, "The Rent-to-Own Industry and Pricing Disclosure Tactics," *Journal of Public Policy and Marketing* 17, no. 1 (1998): 3–10.

135. "Consumer Protection: Reforming the 'RTO' Rip-Off," *Consumer Reports*, August 1995, 507, cited in Hill, Ramp, and Silver, "Rent-to-Own Industry and Pricing Disclosure Tactics."

136. Shankar Vedantam, "Why High-Income Households Benefit More from Product Innovations," *National Public Radio*, August 16, 2016, http://www.npr.org/2016/08/16/490174061/why-high-income-households-benefit-more-from-product-innovations.

137. Thomas Woods Jr., "Do Rent-to-Own Stores Hurt the Poor?" Ludwig von Mises Institute, August 3, 2006, http://mises.org/daily/2261.

138. Brea L. Perry, Brian Aronson, and Bernice A. Pescosolido, "Pandemic Precarity: COVID-19 is Exposing and Exacerbating Inequalities in the American Heartland," *Proceedings of the National Academy of Sciences of the United States of America*, February 23, 2021, https://www.pnas.org/content/118/8/e2020685118; Patricia Buckley and Akrur Barua, "COVID-19's Impact on US Income Inequality: It's Going to Get Worse Before It Gets Better," *Deloitte Insights*, July 2020, https://www2.deloitte.com/us/en/insights/economy/issues-by-the-numbers/covid-19-impact-on-income-inequality.html; Aaron van Dorn, Rebecca E. Cooney, and Miriam L. Sabin, "COVID-19 Exacerbating Inequalities in the US," *The Lancet*, April 18, 2020, https://www.thelancet.com/journals/lancet/article/PIIS0140-6736(20)30893-X/fulltext.

139. Danielle Kurtzleben, "How Would a Wealth Tax Work?" *National Public Radio*, December 5, 2019, https://www.npr.org/2019/12/05/782135614/how-would-a-wealth-tax-work.

140. Jessica Bursztynsky, "Elizabeth Warren's Wealth Tax Is 'Pretty Nuts', Says Billionaire Lifelong Democrat Ron Baron," *CNBC*, October 25, 2019, https://www.cnbc.com/2019/10/25/elizabeth-warrens-wealth-tax-is-pretty-nuts-says-ron-baron.html.

141. Elizabeth T. Powers and Emilie Bagby, "Poverty and Inequality in Illinois," Institute of Government and Public Affairs, University of Illinois, 2008, http://igpa. uillinois.edu/system/files/08-ILRept08-Pov-IneqPg49–60.pdf.

142. Catherine Cozzarelli, Anna V. Wilkinson, and Michael J. Tagler, "Attitudes Toward the Poor and Attributions for Poverty," *Journal of Social Issues* 57, no. 1 (2001): 207–227, 209.

143. Powers and Bagby, "Poverty and Inequality in Illinois"; see also Matthew O. Hunt, "Race/Ethnicity and Beliefs About Wealth and Poverty," *Social Science Quarterly* 85, no. 3 (2004): 827–853.

144. Puerto Rico is the poorest congressional district with nearly 44% of its residents living in poverty (Census Reporter, "Puerto Rico," n.d., https://censusreporter. org/profiles/04000US72-puerto-rico/). While Puerto Rico has a delegate ("resident commissioner") in the US House of Representatives, Jenniffer González, she does not vote; because Puerto Rico is not a state, it has no representation in the US Senate.

145. Census Reporter, "Congressional District 15, NY," n.d., https://censusreporter. org/profiles/50000US3615-congressional-district-15-ny/.

146. Ibid.

147. Andrew Taylor, "Rep. Jose Serrano to Retire at Term's End," Associate Press, March 25, 2019, https://apnews.com/article/415a0ea345634458b693272a218ce5a3.

148. Nicole Acevedo, "Rep. Ritchie Torres Feels 'the Weight of History' on His Shoulders," *NBC News*, January 31, 2021, https://www.nbcnews.com/news/nbcblk/ rep-ritchie-torres-feels-weight-history-his-shoulders-n1256081.

149. Census Reporter, "Congressional District 5, KY," n.d., https://censusreporter. org/profiles/50000US2105-congressional-district-5-ky/.

150. Census Reporter, "Congressional District 15, NY," n.d.

151. Census Reporter, "Congressional District 5, KY," n.d.

152. Measured by median income.

153. "Congressional District Analysis and Insights," *Proximity One*, January 2021, http://proximityone.com/cd.htm#table.

154. Ibid.

155. Ibid. One of the other two is represented by Hal Rogers and the other—Louisiana's 5th district—was vacant as of the time of this writing, as the winner of the 2020 election died of Covid-19 prior to being sworn into office (Jaclyn Diaz, "Louisiana Congressman-Elect Dies of COVID-19," *National Public Radio*, December 30, 2020, https://www.npr.org/2020/12/30/951332740/louisiana-congressman-elect-dies-after-battling-covid-19). It was most recently served by Ralph Abraham, who is white.

156. Ibid. Ritchie Torres identifies as Afro-Latino.

157. Ibid. Louisiana's fifth district was vacant at the time of this writing (see note 154).

158. Beatrice Jin, "Congress's Incoming Class is Younger, Bluer, and More Diverse than Ever," *Politico*, November 23, 2018, https://www.politico.com/interactives/2018/ interactive_116th-congress-freshman-younger-bluer-diverse/.

159. Charlotte Alter, "'Change is Closer Than We Think.' Inside Alexandria Ocasio-Cortez's Unlikely Rise," *Time*, March 21, 2019, https://time.com/longform/ alexandria-ocasio-cortez-profile/.

160. Ibid.

161. For a detailed analysis of voting behavior and representation in minority communities, see John D. Griffin and Brian Newman, *Minority Report: Evaluating Political Equality in America* (Chicago: University of Chicago Press, 2008), especially pt. 2. See also Robert M. Stein, Stacy G. Ulbig, and Stephanie Shirley Post. 2005. "Voting for Minority Candidates in Multiracial/Multiethnic Communities," *Urban Affairs Review*, 41, no. 2: 157–181.

162. Dalton Conley, *Being Black, Living in the Red: Race, Wealth, and Social Policy in America*, 10th ed. (Berkeley: University of California Press, 2010), 157.

163. Ibid.

Chapter 3: Housing

1. Rachel G. Bratt, Michael E. Stone, and Chester Hartman, "Why a Right to Housing Is Needed and Makes Sense: Editors' Introduction," in *A Right to Housing: Foundation for a New Social Agenda*, ed. Rachel G. Bratt, Michael E. Stone, and Chester Hartman (Philadelphia: Temple University Press, 2006), 1.

2. Lauren J. and Robert L. Kaufman, "Housing and Wealth Inequality: Racial-Ethnic Differences in Home Equity in the United States," *Demography* 41, no. 3 (2004): 585–605.

3. Jeremy Hobson, Chris Bentley, and Marcelle Hutchins, "Thousands of African-Americans Are Leaving Chicago Each Year. Why?" WBUR's Hear & Now, February 28, 2019, https://www.wbur.org/hereandnow/2019/02/28/chicago-african-americans-leaving.

4. Dudley L. Poston, Jr., "3 Ways That the U.S. Population Will Change Over the Next Decade," *PBS*, January 2, 2020, https://www.pbs.org/newshour/nation/3-ways-that-the-u-s-population-will-change-over-the-next-decade.

5. Pew Hispanic Center, "Latinos by Geography: Hispanic Population by County, 2009," 2011, http://pewhispanic.org/states/population/; Luis Noe-Bustamante and Antonio Flores, "Facts on Latinos in the U.S.," Pew Research Center, September 16, 2019, https://www.pewresearch.org/hispanic/fact-sheet/latinos-in-the-u-s-fact-sheet/.

6. National Alliance to End Homelessness, "State of Homelessness: 2020 Edition," https://endhomelessness.org/homelessness-in-america/homelessness-statistics/state-of-homelessness-2020/.

7. Meghan Henry, Rian Watt, Anna Mahathey, Jillian Ouellette, and Aubrey Sitler, "The 2019 Annual Homeless Assessment Report to Congress," US Department of Housing and Urban Development, January 2020, https://www.huduser.gov/portal/sites/default/files/pdf/2019-AHAR-Part-1.pdf, p. 10.

8. U.S. Department of Health and Human Services, "Child Homelessness: A Growing Crisis," Substance Abuse and Mental Health Services Administration, July 31, 2019, https://www.samhsa.gov/homelessness-programs-resources/hpr-resources/child-homelessness-growing-crisis.

9. Meghan Henry et al., "The 2019 Annual Homeless Assessment Report to Congress," p. 10.

10. Andrew Van Dam, "The Surprising Holes in Our Knowledge of America's Homeless Population," *The Washington Post*, September 17, 2019, https://www.washingtonpost.com/business/2019/09/18/surprising-holes-our-knowledge-americas-homeless-population/.

11. "Chronic homelessness" refers "to those who have been continuously homeless for a year or more, or are experiencing at least their fourth episode of homelessness in three years" (Dennis Culhane, "Five Myths About America's Homeless," *Washington Post*, July 11, 2010, http://www.washingtonpost.com/wp-dyn/content/article/2010/07/09/AR2010070902357.html).

12. Doug Smith and Benjamin Oreskes, "Are Many Homeless People in L.A. Mentally Ill? New Findings Back the Public's Perception." *Los Angeles Times*, October 7, 2019, https://www.latimes.com/california/story/2019-10-07/homeless-population-mental-illness-disability.

13. "Substance Abuse and Homelessness," National Coalition for the Homeless, July 2009, http://www.nationalhomeless.org/factsheets/addiction.pdf.

14. Dennis Culhane, "Five Myths About America's Homeless."

15. U.S. Department of Housing and Urban Development, "The Federal Housing Administration (FHA)," n.d., https://www.hud.gov/program_offices/housing/fhahistory.

16. The US government placed both of these publicly traded entities into conservatorship in 2008 as stock prices plummeted with news of the impending crisis (David Ellis, "U.S. Seizes Fannie and Freddie," *CNN Money*, September 7, 2008, http://money.cnn.com/2008/09/07/news/companies/fannie_freddie/index.htm).

17. US Department of Housing and Urban Development, "History," 2011, http://portal.hud.gov/hudportal/HUD?src=/about/hud_history.

18. Paul D. Ballew, "Housing Bubble Burst: More Than Just Foreclosures," *CNBC*, August 4, 2011, http://www.cnbc.com/id/44022473.

19. "Homeownership Rate for the United States," Federal Reserve Bank of St. Louis, February 2, 2021, https://fred.stlouisfed.org/series/RHORUSQ156N.

20. Ibid.

21. Adam Shell, Paul Davidson, and John Waggoner, "Finding Blame: Crisis in Inequality Panel Calls Recession Avoidable," *USA Today*, January 28, 2011, http://www.usatoday.com/printedition/money/20110128/crisisreport27_cv.art.htm.

22. Ibid. For an accessible yet thorough examination of the housing collapse, see *This American Life*, "The Giant Pool of Money," *WBEZ Public Radio*, May 9, 2008, http://www.thisamericanlife.org/radio-archives/episode/355/the-giant-pool-of-money.

23. Mike Lee, "Making Housing Work for Utah Families," Mike Lee U.S. Senator for Utah, June 7, 2019, https://www.lee.senate.gov/public/index.cfm/2019/6/making-housing-work-for-utah-families.

24. LaVarr Webb, "Conservative Thought Leaders Discuss Affordable Housing," *UtahPolicy.com*, June 26, 2017, https://utahpolicy.com/index.php/features/policy-buzz/13626-conservative-thought-leaders-discuss-affordable-housing.

25. See https://livemodal.com/.

26. Mike Lee, "Making Housing Work for Utah Families."

27. US Department of Housing and Urban Development, "Housing Choice Vouchers Fact Sheet," n.d., https://www.hud.gov/topics/housing_choice_voucher_program_section_8#:~:text=The%20housing%20choice%20voucher%20program,housing%20in%20the%20private%20market.&text=A%20housing%20subsidy%20is%20paid,behalf%20of%20the%20participating%20family.

28. US Department of Housing and Urban Development, Section 8 Program Background Information, 2011, http://portal.hud.gov/hudportal/HUD?src=/program_offices/housing/mfh/rfp/s8bkinfo.

29. Quoted in Kenneth J. Cooper, "Loans to Minorities Did Not Cause Housing Crisis, Study Finds," *Tribuna Connecticut*, February 16, 2011, http://www.tribunact.com/news/2011-02-16/News/Loans_to_minorities_did_not_cause_housing_crisis_s.html.

30. There is considerable evidence, however, that banks preyed on African Americans in particular in the midst of the housing boom. Wells Fargo bank, for instance, pushed African Americans who could have qualified for prime mortgage loans into subprime loans and doctored records to allow nonqualifying applicants to receive subprime loans. The bank was fined a record $85 million in the summer of 2011 as a result of these activities. Michael Powell, "Bank Accused of Pushing Mortgage Deals on Blacks," *New York Times*, June 6, 2009, http://www.nytimes.com/2009/06/07/us/07baltimore.html; Ben Rooney, "Fed Hits Wells Fargo with $85 million Fine," *CNN Money*, July 20, 2011, http://money.cnn.com/2011/07/20/news/companies/wells_fargo_fined/index.htm.

31. Jung Hyun Choi, Alanna McCargo, Michael Neal, Laurie Goodman, and Caitlin Young, "Explaining the Black-White Homeownership Gap," Urban Institute, October 2019,

https://www.urban.org/sites/default/files/publication/101160/explaining_the_black-white_homeownership_gap_a_closer_look_at_disparities_across_local_markets_0.pdf.

32. Ibid.

33. Sharmila Choudhury, "Racial and Ethnic Differences in Wealth and Asset Choices," *Social Security Bulletin* 64, no. 4 2002, http://www.ssa.gov/policy/docs/ssb/v64n4/v64n4p1.html.

34. Sanjaya DeSilva and Yuval Elmelech, "Inequality in the United States: A Decomposition Analysis of Racial and Ethnic Disparities in Homeownership," Levy Economics Institute, Working Paper no. 565 (2009), 13.

35. The Joint Center for Housing Studies of Harvard University, "America's Rental Housing: Meeting Challenges, Building on Opportunities," 2011, http://www.jchs.harvard.edu/americas-rental-housing.

36. Joint Center for Housing Studies of Harvard University, "America's Rental Housing: Expanding Options for Diverse and Growing Demand," 2015, http://www.jchs.harvard.edu/research/publications/americas-rental-housing-expanding-options-diverse-and-growing-demand.

37. Ibid., page 26.

38. "American Families Face a Growing Rent Burden," *The Pew Charitable Trusts*, April 2018, https://www.pewtrusts.org/-/media/assets/2018/04/rent-burden_report_v2.pdf.

39. Michele Lerner, "One Home, A Lifetime of Impact," *The Washington Post*, July 23, 2020, https://www.washingtonpost.com/business/2020/07/23/black-homeownership-gap/.

40. ACORN, "Who Is ACORN?" 2010, http://www.acorn.org.

41. John Fund, "More ACORN Voter Fraud Comes to Light," *Wall Street Journal*, May 9, 2009, http://online.wsj.com/article/SB124182750646102435.html; Ian Urbina, "ACORN on the Brink of Bankruptcy, Officials Say," *New York Times*, March 19, 2010, http://www.nytimes.com/2010/03/20/us/politics/20acorn.html.

42. Stanley Kurtz, "Planting Seeds of Disaster: ACORN, Barack Obama, and the Democratic Party," *National Review Online*, 2008, http://www.nationalreview.com/articles/225898/planting-seeds-disaster/stanley-kurtz#./us/politics20acorn.html.

43. Scott Shifrel, "B'klyn ACORN Cleared over Giving Illegal Advice on How to Hide Money from Prostitution," *New York Daily News*, March 1, 2010, http://www.nydailynws.com/news/crime/b-klyn-acorn-cleared-giving-illegal-advice-hide-money-prostitution-article-1.176119.

44. George Lakoff, *The Political Mind: Why You Can't Understand 21st-Century Politics with an 18th-Century Brain* (New York: Viking, 2008).

45. Public Policy Polling, "Clinton Leads in NC for First Time Since March," August 9, 2016, http://www.publicpolicypolling.com/pdf/2015/PPP_Release_NC_80916.pdf.

46. Melvin L. Oliver and Thomas M. Shapiro, *Black Wealth/White Wealth: A New Perspective on Racial Inequality*, 10th ed. (New York: Routledge, 2006), 267.

47. John Eligon and Robert Gebeloff, "Affluent and Black, and Still Trapped by Segregation," *New York Times*, August 20, 2016, http://www.nytimes.com/2016/08/21/us/milwaukee-segregation-wealthy-black-families.html.

48. Douglas S. Massey, "Origins of Economic Disparities: Historical Roles of Housing Segregation," in *Segregation: The Rising Costs for America*, ed. James H. Carr and Nandinee K. Kutty (New York: Routledge, 2008), 39–80.

49. The Fair Housing Act was passed as part of the Civil Rights Act of 1968. Administered by the Department of Housing and Urban Development, it "prohibits discrimination in the sale, rental and financing of dwellings based on race, color, religion, sex or national origin." US Department of Housing and Urban Development, "Programs Administered by [Fair Housing and Equal Opportunity]: The Fair Housing Act," 2011, http://portal.hud.gov/hudportal/HUD?src=/program_offices/fair_housing_equal_opp/progdesc/title8.

50. Nancy A. Denton, "Segregation and Discrimination in Housing," in *A Right to Housing: Foundation for a New Social Agenda*, ed. Rachel G. Bratt, Michael E. Stone, and Chester Hartman (Philadelphia: Temple University Press, 2006), 61–81; Stephen Grant Meyer, *As Long as They Don't Move Next Door: Segregation and Racial Conflict in American Neighborhoods* (Lanham, MD: Rowman & Littlefield, 2000).

51. Massey, "Origins of Economic Disparities," 44.

52. Ibid.

53. Tukufu Zuberi, *Thicker Than Blood: How Racial Statistics Lie* (Minneapolis: University of Minnesota Press, 2003); Noel Ignatiev, *How the Irish Became White* (New York: Routledge, 1996), cited in Massey, "Origins of Economic Disparities," 49.

54. The concept of redlining has been expanded to corporate behavior. So-called retail redlining refers to the practice of avoiding locating retail establishments such as restaurants and stores in middle-class communities with a significant nonwhite population as a result of preconceived notions (based primarily on anecdotal evidence) of how racial minority residents will behave. Research from the University of Illinois recently found some evidence for retail redlining practices (Emily Badger, "Retail Redlining: One of the Most Pervasive Forms of Racism Left in America?" *Atlantic*, April 17, 2013, http://www.theatlanticcities.com/neighborhoods/2013/04/retail-redlining-one-most-pervasive-forms-racism-left-america/5311).

55. Denton, "Segregation and Discrimination in Housing"; Preston H. Smith II, *Racial Democracy and the Black Metropolis* (Minneapolis: University of Minnesota Press, 2012).

56. David M. Freund, *Colored Property: State Policy and White Racial Politics in Suburban America* (Chicago: University of Chicago Press, 2007), chap. 1; Meyer, *As Long as They Don't Move Next Door.*

57. Massey, "Origins of Economic Disparities," 53–55.

58. Catherine Silva, "Racial Restrictive Covenants: Enforcing Neighborhood Segregation in Seattle," Seattle Civil Rights and Labor History Project, 2009, http://depts.washington.edu/civilr/covenants_report.htm.

59. Massey, "Origins of Economic Disparities."

60. Elizabeth Anderson and Jeffrey Jones, "Causes of Housing Segregation," The Geography of Race in the United States, University of Michigan, 2002, http://www.umich.edu/~lawrace/causes1.htm.

61. Emily Badger, "Watch These American Cities Segregate, Even as They Diversify," *Atlantic*, June 25, 2012, http://www.theatlanticcities.com/neighborhoods/2012/06/watch-these-us-cities-segregate-even-they-diversify/2346/; Ingrid Gould Ellen, *Sharing America's Neighborhoods: The Prospects for Stable Racial Integration* (Cambridge: Harvard University Press, 2000); Metropolitan Policy Program, *State of Metropolitan America: On the Front Lines of Demographic Transformation*, Brookings Institution, 2010, http://www.brookings.edu/~/media/Files/Programs/Metro/state_of_metro_america/metro_america_report.pdf, 46–49.

62. "Chicago Closes Cabrini-Green Project," *USA Today*, December 2, 2010, http://www.usatoday.com/news/nation/2010-12-01-cabrini-green_N.htm.

63. "Cabrini-Green," http://BlackHistory.com, January 23, 2008, http://www.blackhistory.com/cgi-bin/blog.cgi?blog_id=62103&cid=53.

64. Mary Schmich, "Last Residents Leave Cabrini-Green High-Rise," *Chicago Tribune*, December 1, 2010, http://articles.chicagotribune.com/2010-12-01/news/ct-met-schmich-1201-20101201_1_cabrini-green-burling-building-thousands-of-cabrini-residents.

65. Brentin Mock, "A Requiem for Chicago's Cabrini Green Housing Project," *Atlantic*: CityLab, June 17, 2016, http://www.citylab.com/housing/2016/06/a-documentary-on-cabrini-green-that-was-20-years-in-the-making/487445/; Alexandra Chachkevitch, "Door Shutting on Residents of Last Unrenoved Cabrini-Green

Row Houses," *Chicago Tribune*, February 12, 2012, http://articles.chicagotribune.com/2012-02-16/news/ct-met-cabrini-green-rowhouses-20120216_1_row-houses-cabrini-green-residents-public-housing.

66. Eugene Robinson, *Disintegration: The Splintering of Black America* (New York: Doubleday, 2010).

67. Yilun Cheng, "Former Cabrini-Green Residents Report Painful Discrimination in Redeveloped Mixed-Income Housing," *Medill Reports Chicago*, Fall 2020, https://news.medill.northwestern.edu/chicago/former-cabrini-green-residents-report-painful-discrimination-in-redeveloped-mixed-income-housing/.

68. Massey, "Origins of Economic Disparities."

69. Erik Wesley, "Poverty in Appalachia: Third World Living Conditions in America?" *USAHM-News*, August 2, 2011, https://usahitman.com/piatwlcia/.

70. MACED website, http://www.maced.org/overview.htm.

71. Quoted in Andrew Leonard, "Justin Maxson: An Appalachian Trailblazer for Sustainability," *Grist*, December 8, 2011, http://grist.org/energy-efficiency/2011-12-07-justin-maxson-an-appalachian-trailblazer-for-sustainability/.

72. Leonard, "Justin Maxson."

73. Susanna Hegner, "New Executive Director Named at Babcock," Mary Reynolds Babcock Foundation, January 14, 2015, http://mrbf.org/blog/new-executive-director-named-babcock.

74. Tim Marema, "Rural Gets Less Foundation Money," *Daily Yonder*, June 29, 2015, http://www.dailyyonder.com/rural-gets-less-foundation-money/2015/06/29/7893/, cited in Betsey Russell, "Bringing People Together: Rural Is 'Different,' Not 'Less,'" *Daily Yonder*, May 25, 2016, http://www.dailyyonder.com/bringing-people-together-rural-is-different-not-less/2016/05/25/13230/.

75. Russell, "Bringing People Together."

76. Ibid.

77. US Department of Agriculture, "Justin Maxson," n.d., https://www.rd.usda.gov/about-rd/leadership/deputy-under-secretaries/justin-maxson.

78. Housing Assistance Council, "Poverty in Rural America," October, 2011, http://www.ruralhome.org/storage/documents/info_sheets/povertyamerica.pdf; US Department of Agriculture, "Rural Poverty at a Glance," Rural Development Research Report 100, July 2004, http://www.ers.usda.gov/publications/rdrr100/rdrr100.pdf; Economic Research Service, *Geography of Poverty*, November 7, 2012, http://www.ers.usda.gov/topics/rural-economy-population/rural-poverty-well-being/geography-of-poverty.aspx.

79. US Department of Agriculture, "Rural Poverty at a Glance."

80. Hanna Love and Tracy Hadden Loh, "The 'Rural-Urban Divide' Furthers Myths About Race and Poverty—Concealing Effective Policy Solutions," Brookings Institution, December 8, 2020, https://www.brookings.edu/blog/the-avenue/2020/12/08/the-rural-urban-divide-furthers-myths-about-race-and-poverty-concealing-effective-policy-solutions/.

81. US Department of Agriculture, "Rural American at a Glance, 2018 Edition," n.d., https://www.ers.usda.gov/webdocs/publications/90556/eib-200.pdf.

82. Ibid.

83. Ibid.

84. Jon Marcus, "Universities Increasingly Turn to Graduate Programs to Balance Their Books," *The Hechinger Report*, April 23, 2019, https://hechingerreport.org/universities-increasingly-turn-to-graduate-programs-to-balance-their-books/. See also Laura Pappano, "The Master's as the New Bachelor's," *New York Times*, July 22, 2011, http://www.nytimes.com/2011/07/24/education/edlife/edl-24masters-t.html.

85. See George Will, "Burning Down the House," *Washington Post*, July 1, 2011, http://www.washingtonpost.com/opinions/burning-down-the-house/2011/06/30/

AGeRSGuH_story.html; Gretchen Morgenson and Joshua Rosner, *Reckless Endangerment: How Outsized Ambition, Greed, and Corruption Led to Economic Armageddon* (New York: Times Books, 2011). Will blames Democratic politicians, while Morgenson and Rosner describe a complex interplay between Washington insiders and Wall Street.

Chapter 4: Education

1. Deeptha Thattai, "A History of Public Education in the United States," *Journal of Literacy and Education in Developing Societies*, November, 2001, http://www.academia.edu/5177440/A_history_of_public_education_in_the_United_States.

2. Some enslaved persons defied the rules and learned to read and write. For a comprehensive overview, see Heather Andrea Williams, *Self-Taught: African American Education in Slavery and Freedom* (Chapel Hill: University of North Carolina Press, 2005).

3. PBS, *From Swastika to Jim Crow: Historically Black College and Universities*, 2011, http://www.psfp.com/fsjc.htm; Carol D. Lee, "The State of Knowledge About the Education of African Americans," in *Black Education: A Transformative Research Action Agenda for the New Century*, ed. Joyce E. King (New York: Routledge, 2005), 45–71; Ron, "Education Prohibited." U.S. Slave, March 4, 2011, http://usslave.blogspot.com/2011/03/education-prohibited.html.

4. Thattai, "A History of Public Education in the United States."

5. Ibid.

6. Booker T. Washington, *Up from Slavery: An Autobiography* (New York: Doubleday, 1901). Full text available free online at http://www.bartleby.com/1004/; W. E. B. Du Bois, *The Souls of Black Folk* (Chicago: A. C. McClurg, 1903). Full text available online at http://www.bartleby.com/114/.

7. 163 US 537 (1896), http://www.law.cornell.edu/supct/html/historics/USSC_CR_0163_0537_ZS.html.

8. PBS, *From Swastika to Jim Crow.*

9. *Sweatt v. Painter*, 339 US 629 (1950), http://www.law.cornell.edu/supct/html/historics/USSC_CR_0339_0629_ZO.html.

10. 347 US 483 (1954), http://www.law.cornell.edu/supct/html/historics/USSC_CR_0347_0483_ZS.html.

11. *Sweatt v. Painter*, 633–634 (emphasis added).

12. Washington, *Up from Slavery*, 221–222.

13. Du Bois, *The Souls of Black Folk*, 50.

14. Ibid., 54–55.

15. Ibid.; Louis R. Harlan, "Booker T. Washington, 1856–1915," Documenting the American South, 2004, http://docsouth.unc.edu/fpn/washington/bio.html; Gerald C. Hynes, "A Biographical Sketch of W. E. B. Du Bois," W. E. B. Du Bois Learning Center, http://www.duboislc.org/html/DuBoisBio.html; Washington, Up from Slavery.

16. *Brown v. Board of Education*, 495 (emphasis added).

17. "Civil Rights: The Little Rock School Integration Crisis," Dwight D. Eisenhower Presidential Library, http://www.eisenhower.archives.gov/research/online_documents/civil_rights_little_rock.html; Ed Cray, *Chief Justice: A Biography of Earl Warren* (New York: Simon & Schuster, 1997); John Fox, *Earl Warren*, PBS, 2007, http://www.pbs.org/wnet/supremecourt/democracy/robes_warren.html.

18. Half of African American Chicago public school students attend schools that are characterized by extreme segregation: 90 percent or more of the students are African American. Even though black enrollment fell by 50,000 students between 1990 and 2010, the number of schools characterized by extreme segregation increased from 276 to 287 at the same time. The number of Hispanic students in Chicago

attending racially isolated schools increased from 26 to 84 in those years. Conversely, the number of integrated schools—where no one race comprises more than 50 percent of the student body—has decreased from 106 to 66 since 1990. Linda Lutton and Becky Vevea, "Greater Segregation for Region's Black, Latino Students," *WBEZ Public Radio*, June 27, 2012, http://www.wbez.org/series/race-out-loud/greater-segregation-regions-black-latino-students-100452.

19. Laura Meckler and Kate Rabinowitz, "The Changing Face of School Integration," The Washington Post, September 12, 2019, https://www.washingtonpost.com/education/2019/09/12/more-students-are-going-school-with-children-different-races-schools-big-cities-remain-deeply-segregated/

20. Diversity is defined here as no single racial category comprising more than 75 percent of the population.

21. Ibid.

22. Ibid.

23. Gary Orfield, "Reviving the Goal of an Integrated Society: A 21st Century Challenge," Civil Rights Project at UCLA, 2009, http://civilrightsproject.ucla.edu/research/k-12-education/integration-and-diversity/reviving-the-goal-of-an-integrated-society-a-21st-century-challenge/orfield-reviving-the-goal-mlk-2009.pdf; Jacob L. Vigdor and Jens Ludwig, "Segregation and the Test Score Gap," in *Steady Gains and Stalled Progress: Inequality and the Black-White Test Score Gap*, eds. Katherine Magnuson and Jane Waldfogel (New York: Russell Sage Foundation, 2008), 181–211.

24. Richard Rothstein, *Class and Schools: Using Social, Economic, and Educational Reform to Close the Black-White Achievement Gap* (Washington, DC: Economic Policy Institute, 2004), 2.

25. For example, the average spending per student in New York in 2018 was $24,040, whereas in Utah it was $7,626. U.S. Census Bureau, "2018 Public Elementary-Secondary Education Finance Data," n.d., https://www.census.gov/data/tables/2018/econ/school-finances/secondary-education-finance.html (Summary Table 8). While this may reflect state priorities, the cost of living varies from place to place.

26. Emma Brown, "In 23 States, Richer School Districts Get More Local Funding Than Poorer Districts," *Washington Post*, March 12, 2015, https://www.washingtonpost.com/news/local/wp/2015/03/12/in-23-states-richer-school-districts-get-more-local-funding-than-poorer-districts/?utm_term=.8731d75f1367.

27. The report is available at http://www2.ed.gov/pubs/NatAtRisk/index.html.

28. George Ansalone, *Exploring Unequal Achievement in the Schools: The Social Construction of Failure* (Lanham, MD: Lexington, 2009); Katherine Magnuson and Jane Waldfogel, eds., *Steady Gains and Stalled Progress: Inequality and the Black-White Test Score Gap* (New York: Russell Sage Foundation, 2008).

29. Eric A. Hanushek, "What Matters for Student Achievement," *Education Next* 16, no. 2 (Spring 2016), http://educationnext.org/what-matters-for-student-achievement/.

30. Michael Hansen, Elizabeth Mann Levesque, Jon Valant, and Diana Quintero, "2018 Brown Center Report on American Education: Trends in NAEP Math, Reading, and Civics Scores," Brookings Institution, June 27, 2018, https://www.brookings.edu/research/2018-brown-center-report-on-american-education-trends-in-naep-math-reading-and-civics-scores/.

31. Wayne Au, *Unequal by Design: High-Stakes Testing and the Standardization of Inequality* (New York: Routledge, 2009); Ruth S. Johnson, *Using Data to Close the Achievement Gap: How to Measure Equality in Our Schools* (Thousand Oaks, CA: Corwin, 2002); Pauline Lipman, *High Stakes Education: Inequality, Globalization, and Urban School Reform* (New York: Routledge Falmer, 2004); Gary Orfield and Mindy L. Kornhaber, eds., *Raising Standards or Raising Barriers? Inequality and High-Stakes Testing in Public Education* (New York: Century Foundation Press, 2001).

32. William Hayes, *No Child Left Behind: Past, Present, and Future* (Lanham, MD: Rowman & Littlefield, 2008); Paul E. Peterson and Martin R. West, *No Child Left Behind? The Politics and Practice of School Accountability* (Washington, DC: Brookings Institution Press, 2003).

33. US Department of Education, No Child Left Behind, 2011, http://www2.ed.gov/nclb/landing.jhtml.

34. Valerie Strauss, "No Child Left Behind: What Standardized Test Scores Reveal About Its Legacy," *Washington Post*, March 10, 2015, https://www.washingtonpost.com/news/answer-sheet/wp/2015/03/10/no-child-left-behind-what-standardized-test-scores-reveal-about-its-legacy/.

35. Alliance for Excellent Education, "Everything You Need to Know About the Every Student Succeeds Act," n.d., http://all4ed.org/essa/. For an analysis of the Trump Administration's handling of ESSA, see Kenneth K. Wong. 2020. "Education Policy Trump Style: The Administrative Presidency and Deference to States in ESSA Implementation," *Publius: The Journal of Federalism* 50, no. 3: 423–445.

36. Linda Darling-Hammond, "New Standards and Old Inequalities: School Reform and the Education of African American Students," in *Black Education: A Transformative Research and Action Agenda for the New Century*, ed. Joyce E. King (New York: Routledge, 2005), 197–223.

37. "What Explains White-Black Differences in Average Test Scores?", The Educational Opportunity Project at Stanford University, 2019, https://edopportunity.org/discoveries/white-black-differences-scores/. See also Roy O. Freedle, "Correcting the SAT's Ethnic and Social-Class Bias: A Method for Reestimating SAT Scores," *Harvard Educational Review* 73, no. 1 (2003): 1–43; Christopher Jencks and Meredith Phillips, eds., *The Black-White Test Score Gap* (Washington, DC: Brookings Institution Press, 1998); Maria Veronica Santelices and Mark Wilson, "Unfair Treatment? The Case of Freedle, the SAT, and the Standardization Approach to Differential Item Functioning," *Harvard Educational Review* 80, no. 1 (2010): 106–134.

38. Christina A. Samuels, "Poverty, Not Race, Fuels the Achievement Gap," *Education Week*, October 1, 2019, https://www.edweek.org/leadership/poverty-not-race-fuels-the-achievement-gap/2019/10. See also Donald C. Orlich and Glenn Gifford, "Test Scores, Poverty, and Ethnicity: The New American Dilemma" (paper presented at the annual meeting of Phi Delta Kappa, 2006), http://www.cha.wa.gov/?q=files/Highstakestesting_poverty_ethnicity.pdf.

39. Michelle Florence, Mark Asbridge, and Paul J. Veugelers, "Diet Quality and Academic Performance," *Journal of School Health* 78, no. 4 (2008): 209–215; Diana F. Jyoti, Edward A. Frongillo, and Sonya J. Jones, "Food Insecurity Affects School Children's Academic Performance, Weight Gain, and Social Skills," *Journal of Nutrition* 135, no. 12 (2005): 2831–2839; R. E. Kleinman et al., "Diet, Breakfast, and Academic Performance in Children," *Annals of Nutrition & Metabolism* 46 suppl. 1 (2002): 24–30; Michael Murphy et al., "The Relationship of School Breakfast to Psychosocial and Academic Functioning: Cross-sectional and Longitudinal Observations in an Inner-City School Sample," *Archives of Pediatrics & Adolescent Medicine* 152, no. 9 (1998): 899–907.

40. Natasha K. Bowen and Gary L. Bowen, "Effects of Crime and Violence in Neighborhoods and Schools on the School Behavior and Performance of Adolescents," *Journal of Adolescent Research* 14, no. 3 (1999): 319–342; Camille Z. Charles, Gniesha Dinwiddle, and Douglas S. Massey, "The Continuing Consequences of Segregation: Family Stress and College Academic Performance," *Social Science Quarterly* 85, no. 5 (2004): 1353–1373; Johnnie Lassiter Dyson, "The Effect of Family Violence on Children's Academic Performance and Behavior," *Journal of the National Medical Association* 82, no. 1 (1990): 17–22; Shumow Lee, Deborah Lowe Vandell, and Jill Posner, "Risk and Resilience in the Urban Neighborhood: Predictors of Academic Performance

Among Low-Income Elementary School Children," *Merrill-Palmer Quarterly* 45, no. 2 (1999): 309–331; P. David Kurtz, John S. Wodarski, and Phyllis T. Howing, "Maltreatment and the School-Aged Child: School Performance Consequences," *Child Abuse and Neglect* 17, no. 7 (1992): 581–589.

41. Michael Winerip, "In Public School Efforts, a Common Background: Private Education," *New York Times*, April 17, 2011, http://www.nytimes.com/2011/04/18/education/18winerip.html.

42. National Center for Education Statistics, "Dropout Rates," US Department of Education, n.d., https://nces.ed.gov/fastfacts/display.asp?id=16#:~:text=The%20status%20dropout%20rate%20for,Alaska%20Native%20(9.5%20percent).

43. Possible scores on the SAT range from 400 to 1600; the average male score in 2018 was 1076, while the average white score was 1123 (National Center for Education Statistics, "SAT Scores," US Department of Education, n.d.), https://nces.ed.gov/fastfacts/display.asp?id=171.

44. Melissa S. Kearney and Phillip P. Levine, "Income Inequality and the Decision to Drop Out of High School," Federal Reserve Bank of Boston, Winter 2017, https://www.bostonfed.org/publications/communities-and-banking/2017/winter/income-inequality-and-the-decision-to-drop-out-of-high-school.aspx#ft6; Evan Soltas, "Intergenerational Inequality," *Economics and Thought*, March 21, 2013, http://esoltas.blogspot.com/2013/03/intergenerational-inequality.html, as cited in Charles Kenny, "How Did the World's Rich Get That Way? Luck," *Bloomberg Businessweek*, April 22, 2013, http://www.businessweek.com/articles/2013-04-22/how-did-the-worlds-rich-get-that-way-luck.

45. Ibid.

46. Jonathan P. Hicks, "Graduation Rates Increase at HBCUs," *BET*, April 22, 2013, http://www.bet.com/news/national/2013/04/22/graduation-rates-increase-at-hbcus.html.

47. Martel S. Sharpe, "Low Graduation Rates Continue to Plague HBCU's," *The Atlanta Voice*, February 21, 2018, https://www.theatlantavoice.com/articles/low-graduation-rates-continue-to-plague-hbcus/.

48. V. J. Taylor and G. M. Walton, "Stereotype Threat Undermines Academic Learning," *Personal and Social Psychology Bulletin* 37, no. 8 (2011): 1055–1067, at 1055.

49. Pedro A. Noguera and Antwi Akom, "The Significance of Race in the Racial Gap in Academic Achievement," In Motion, 2000, http://www.inmotionmagazine.com/pnaa.html.

50. "K-12 Education: Discipline Disparities for Black Students, Boys, and Students with Disabilities," US Government Accountability Office, March 2018, https://www.gao.gov/assets/700/690828.pdf. See also Daniel J. Losen and Jonathan Gillespie, *Opportunities Suspended: The Disparate Impact of Disciplinary Exclusion from School*, Civil Rights Project at UCLA, August 7, 2012, http://civilrightsproject.ucla.edu/resources/projects/center-for-civil-rights-remedies/school-to-prison-folder/federal-reports/upcoming-ccrr-research.

51. Maithreyi Gopalan and Ashlyn Aiko Nelson. 2019. "Understanding the Racial Discipline Gap in Schools," *AERA Open*, https://journals.sagepub.com/doi/10.1177/2332858419844613; Travis Riddle and Stacey Sinclair. 2019. "Racial Disparities in School-based Disciplinary Actions Are Associated with County-Level Rates of Racial Bias," *Proceedings of the National Academy of Sciences of the United States of America* 116, no. 17: 8255–8260; Jayanti Owens and Sara S. McLanahan. 2020. "Unpacking the Drivers of Racial Disparities in School Suspension and Expulsion," *Social Forces* 98, no 4: 1548–1577. Walter S. Gilliam, Angela N. Maupin, Chin R. Reyes, Maria Accavitti, and Frederick Shic, "Do Early Educators' Implicit Biases Regarding Sex and Race Relate to Behavior Expectations and Recommendations of Preschool

Expulsions and Suspensions?" Yale University Child Study Center, September 28, 2016, http://ziglercenter.yale.edu/publications/Preschool%20Implicit%20Bias%20Policy%20Brief_final_9_26_276766_5379.pdf.

52. Jonathan Kozol, *Savage Inequalities: Children in America's Schools* (New York: Harper Perennial, 1991).

53. Jonathan Kozol, *Amazing Grace: The Lives of Children and the Conscience of a Nation* (New York: Harper Perennial, 1996).

54. Jonathan Kozol, *The Shame of the Nation: The Restoration of Apartheid Schooling in America* (New York: Three Rivers Press, 2005).

55. American Entertainment International Speakers Bureau, Jonathan Kozol, 2009, http://www.aeispeakers.com/speakerbio.php?SpeakerID=579; Kozol, *Savage Inequalities*; Kozol, *Amazing Grace*; Kozol, *Shame of the Nation*.

56. Noguera and Akom, "The Significance of Race."

57. To compound the problem, African American, Native Americans, and Latino students were more likely than their white and Asian counterparts to attend for-profit institutions, which have higher borrowing rates than not-for-profit private or public institutions (see Morgan Taylor, Jonathan M. Turk, Hollie M. Chessman, and Lorelle L. Espinosa, "Race and Ethnicity in Higher Education: 2020 Supplement," American Council on Education, n.d.), http://1xfsu31b52d33idlp13twtos-wpengine.netdna-ssl.com/wp-content/uploads/2020/11/REHE-2020-Exec-Summary-final_web.pdf.

58. http://TeachforAmerica.org.

59. Donna Foote, *Relentless Pursuit: A Year in the Trenches with Teach for America* (New York: Knopf, 2008).

60. Quoted in Lucia Graves, "What Is Teach for America Really Like?" *U.S. News & World Report*, March 5, 2008, http://www.usnews.com/education/articles/2008/03/05/what-is-teach-for-america-really-like.

61. Mark Naison, "Why Teach for America Is Not Welcome in My Classroom," *LA Progressive*, July 18, 2011, http://www.laprogressive.com/education-reform/teach-america/.

62. Graves, "What Is Teach for America Really Like?"; Andrew J. Rotherham, "Teach for America: 5 Myths That Persist 20 Years On," *Time*, February 10, 2011, http://www.time.com/time/nation/article/0,8599,2047211,00.html.

63. "Safe to Learn During Covid-19," UNICEF, May 2020, https://www.unicef.org/sites/default/files/2020-05/STL-COVID-19-Response-Key-Messages.pdf.

64. Caroline G. Dunn, Erica Kenney, Sheila E. Fleischhacker, and Sara N. Bleich. 2020. "Feeding Low-Income Children During the Covid-19 Pandemic," *The New England Journal of Medicine*, April 30, https://www.nejm.org/doi/full/10.1056/NEJMp2005638.

65. Brooke Auxier and Monica Anderson, "As Schools Close Due to the Coronavirus, Some U.S. Students Face a Digital 'Homework Gap,'" Pew Research Center, March 16, 2020, https://www.pewresearch.org/fact-tank/2020/03/16/as-schools-close-due-to-the-coronavirus-some-u-s-students-face-a-digital-homework-gap/.

66. Kim Krisberg, "Essential Workers Facing Higher Risks During Covid-19 Outbreak: Meat Packers, Retail Workers Sickened," *The Nation's Health* 50, no. 6. August 2020, https://www.thenationshealth.org/content/50/6/1.1.

67. Laura Meckler, Valerie Strauss, and Moriah Balingit, "Plunging Into Remote Learning, Families Find Stress, Chaos and Some Surprising Wins," *The Washington Post*, March 27, 2020, https://www.washingtonpost.com/local/education/plunging-into-remote-learning-families-find-stress-chaos-and-some-surprising-wins/2020/03/27/36429de4-6f90-11ea-aa80-c2470c6b2034_story.html.

68. Many school districts arranged student and even family meal pickup at the school buildings, though distribution was a challenge (Cory Turner, "'Children Are

Going Hungry': Why Schools Are Struggling to Feed Students," *National Public Radio*, September 8, 2020), https://www.npr.org/2020/09/08/908442609/children-are-going-hungry-why-schools-are-struggling-to-feed-students.

69. Youki Terada, "Covid-19's Impact on Students' Academic and Mental Well-Being," *Edutopia*, June 23, 2020, https://www.edutopia.org/article/covid-19s-impact-students-academic-and-mental-well-being.

70. Jim Mahoney, "Three Shifts for College Counselors During and Beyond Covid-19," *Global Online Academy*, August 19, 2020, https://globalonlineacademy.org/insights/articles/three-shifts-for-college-counselors-during-and-beyond-covid-19.

71. Colette Ngo, "Student Athletes Worry the Coronavirus Pandemic Could Put Their Scholarships at Risk," *CNBC*, December 23, 2020, https://www.cnbc.com/2020/12/23/student-athletes-worry-coronavirus-could-put-their-scholarships-at-risk.html.

72. Elissa Nadworny, "'Losing a Generation': Fall College Enrollment Plummets for 1st-Year Students," *National Public Radio*, December 17, 2020, https://www.npr.org/2020/12/17/925831720/losing-a-generation-fall-college-enrollment-plummets-for-first-year-students.

73. Greta Anderson, "A Generation Defined by the Pandemic," *Inside Higher Ed*, October 15, 2020, https://www.insidehighered.com/news/2020/10/15/students-continue-be-stressed-about-college-their-futures.

74. Sasha Aslanian, "Some Small Colleges Are Closing Their Doors for Good Amid Pandemic," *Marketplace*, August 20, 2020, https://www.marketplace.org/2020/08/20/some-small-colleges-closing-for-good-covid19/.

75. Jim Soland, Megan Kuhfeld, Beth Tarasawa, Angela Johnson, Erik Ruzek, and Jing Lu, "The Impact of Covid-19 on Student Achievement and What It May Mean for Educators," Brookings Institution, May 27, 2020, https://www.brookings.edu/blog/brown-center-chalkboard/2020/05/27/the-impact-of-covid-19-on-student-achievement-and-what-it-may-mean-for-educators/.

76. Jon Valant and Daniel A. Newark, "The Politics of Achievement Gaps: U.S. Public Opinion on Race-Based and Wealth-Based Differences in Test Scores," *Educational Researcher* 46, no. 6 (2016): 1–16 (online first).

77. Ibid.

78. For a critique of this rationale, see Jonathan Kozol, *The Shame of the Nation: The Restoration of Apartheid Schooling in America* (New York: Three Rivers Press, 2005). Kozol notes that "some people who [are reluctant to throw money at failing schools], while they live in wealthy districts where schools are funded at high levels, don't send their children to these public schools but choose instead to send them to expensive private day-schools.... so they may be spending over $60,000 on their children's education every year. Yet here I am one night, a guest within their home, and dinner has been served and we are having coffee now; and this entirely likable, and generally sensible, and beautifully refined and thoughtful person looks me in the eyes and asks me whether you can really buy your way to better education for the children of the poor" (p. 57).

79. Dorie Turner, "School Voucher Bills Flood GOP-Led Statehouses," August 2, 2011, http://www.edchoice.org/Newsroom/News/AP-School-Voucher-Bills-Flood-GOP-led-Statehouses.aspx.

80. Kevin Huffman, "A Rosa Parks Moment for Education," *Washington Post*, January 31, 2011, http://www.washingtonpost.com/wp-dyn/content/article/2011/01/30/AR2011013003556.html.

81. In stark contrast to what happened to Ms. Williams-Bolar is the treatment by celebrities who were caught cheating to get their children admission to elite colleges (Annie Lowrey, "Her Only Crime Was Helping Her Kids," *The Atlantic*, September 13, 2019, https://www.theatlantic.com/ideas/archive/2019/09/her-only-crime-was-helping-her-kid/597979/).

82. Teachers unions and progressive activists, while moved by the film, feel that it represented teachers and teachers' unions, rather than larger systemic pressures, as obstacles to quality education. Further, they argue that charter schools are not all successful. Dana Goldstein, "Grading 'Waiting for Superman,'" *Nation*, September 23, 2010, http://www.thenation.com/article/154986/grading-waiting-superman.

83. Kate Zernike, "Condemnation of Charter Schools Exposes a Rift Over Black Students," *New York Times*, August 20, 2016, http://www.nytimes.com/2016/08/21/us/blacks-charter-schools.html.

84. Goldstein, "Grading 'Waiting for Superman.'"

85. Williams-Bolar has dedicated herself to social justice issues, speaking and organizing, as well as working as a teacher's assistant in the Akron public schools (Annie Lowrey, "Her Only Crime Was Helping Her Kids").

Chapter 5: Crime and Criminal Justice

1. James Madison, "Federalist 51: The Structure of the Government Must Furnish the Proper Checks and Balances Between the Different Departments," https://www.congress.gov/resources/display/content/The+Federalist+Papers#TheFederalist Papers-51.

2. Sha Wallace Stepter, "A Combat Veteran and a Veteran of the Streets Deal with PTSD," *KALW Public Radio*, November 11, 2013, http://kalw.org/post/combat-veteran-and-veteran-streets-deal-ptsd#stream/0.

3. Although they comprise only 9 percent of the US population, veterans accounted for 18 percent of all suicides in 2014. Leo Shane III and Patricia Kime, "New VA Study Finds 20 Veterans Commit Suicide Each Day," *Military Times*, July 7, 2016, http://www.militarytimes.com/story/veterans/2016/07/07/va-suicide-20-daily-research/86788332/.

4. http://www.veteranshealingveterans.com.

5. Ibid.

6. Robert Costa, Lindsey Bever, J. Fredom du Lac, and Sari Horwitz, "Church Shooting Suspect Dylann Roof Captured amid Hate Crime Investigation," *Washington Post*, June 18, 2015, https://www.washingtonpost.com/news/morning-mix/wp/2015/06/17/white-gunman-sought-in-shooting-at-historic-charleston-african-ame-church/?postshare=2131434616717681&utm_term=.59049c4e168f.

7. Dustin Waters and Mark Berman, "Dylann Roof Found Guilty on All Counts in Charleston Church Massacre Trial," *Washington Post*, December 15, 2016, https://www.washingtonpost.com/news/post-nation/wp/2016/12/15/jurors-begin-deliberating-in-charleston-church-shooting-trial/?utm_term=.0614333c3472.

8. Jessica Lussenhop, "US Election 2016: Trump and His Central Park Five Defiance," *BBC News*, October 12, 2016, http://www.bbc.com/news/election-us-2016-37614095.

9. Ibid.

10. David K. Shipler, "Why Do Innocent People Confess?" *New York Times*, February 23, 2012, http://www.nytimes.com/2012/02/26/opinion/sunday/why-do-innocent-people-confess.html.

11. Herbert L. Packer, "Two Models of the Criminal Process," *University of Pennsylvania Law Review* 113, no. 1 (1964). Available at http://scholarship.law.upenn.edu/penn_law_review/vol113/iss1/1.

12. Ibid.

13. In fact, there have been some notable recent rulings that permit exceptions to the Exclusionary Rule. For example, in *United States v. Herring* (2009) *and Hudson v Michigan* (2006), the US Supreme Court, in 5-4 decisions, argued that police officers' conduct was informed by a level of professionalism such that the exclusionary rule ought to only apply when there is explicit proof of malicious intent or reckless conduct

on the part of the police (Richard M. Re. 2014. "The Due Process Exclusionary Rule," *Harvard Law Review* 127, no. 7: 1893–1966.

14. http://eji.org.

15. Ted Conover, "'Just Mercy,' by Bryan Stevenson," *New York Times*, October 17, 2014, https://www.nytimes.com/2014/10/19/books/review/just-mercy-by-bryanstevenson.html.

16. Tim Adams, "Bryan Stevenson: 'America's Mandela,'" *Guardian*, February 1, 2015, https://www.theguardian.com/us-news/2015/feb/01/bryan-stevenson-americasmandela.

17. Adams, "Bryan Stevenson: 'America's Mandela.'"

18. "Bryan A. Stevenson Biography," New York University School of Law, n.d., https://its.law.nyu.edu/facultyprofiles/index.cfm?fuseaction=profile.biography& personid=20315.

19. Episode 45, "Just Mercy," http://thisiscriminal.com/episode-45-just-mercy-6-17-2016/.

20. Bryan Stevenson, "We Need to Talk about an Injustice," March 2012, https://www.ted.com/talks/bryan_stevenson_we_need_to_talk_about_an_injustice.

21. 430 U.S. 387 (1977).

22. Wesley Lowery, "Study Finds Police Fatally Shoot Unarmed Black Men at Disproportionate Rates," *Washington Post*, April 7, 2016, https://www.washingtonpost.com/national/study-finds-police-fatally-shoot-unarmed-black-men-at-disproportionate-rates/2016/04/06/e494563e-fa74-11e5-80e4-c381214de1a3_story.html.

23. "Trayvon Martin Shooting Fast Facts," *CNN*, February 17, 2021, https://www.cnn.com/2013/06/05/us/trayvon-martin-shooting-fast-facts.

24. "What Happened in Ferguson?" *New York Times*, August 10, 2015, http://www.nytimes.com/interactive/2014/08/13/us/ferguson-missouri-town-under-siege-after-police-shooting.html.

25. Julie Bosman and Joseph Goldstein, "Timeline for a Body: 4 Hours in the Middle of a Ferguson Street," *New York Times*, August 23, 2014, https://www.nytimes.com/2014/08/24/us/michael-brown-a-bodys-timeline-4-hours-on-a-ferguson-street.html.

26. Niraj Chokshi, "How #BlackLivesMatter Came to Define a Movement," *New York Times*, August 22, 2016, https://www.nytimes.com/2016/08/23/us/howblacklivesmatter-came-to-define-a-movement.html.

27. Daniel Victor, "Why 'All Lives Matter' Is Such a Perilous Phrase," *New York Times*, July 15, 2016, http://www.nytimes.com/2016/07/16/us/all-lives-matter-black-lives-matter.html.

28. Mark Martin, "'Blue Lives Matter' Speaks Out After Four Officers Shot in 24 Hours," *CBN News*, November 22, 2016, http://www1.cbn.com/cbnnews/us/2016/november/blue-lives-matter-speaks-out-after-four-officers-shot-in-24-hours.

29. Kimberly Kindy and Kimbriell Kelly, "Thousands Dead, Few Prosecuted," *Washington Post*, April 11, 2015, http://www.washingtonpost.com/sf/investigative/2015/04/11/thousands-dead-few-prosecuted/.

30. Chris Graves, "The Killing of George Floyd: What We Know," *Minnesota Public Radio News*, June 1, 2020, https://www.mprnews.org/story/2020/06/01/the-killing-of-george-floyd-what-we-know.

31. Brakkton Booker, "3 Men Indicted in Death of Ahmaud Arbery, Shot While He Jogged in Georgia," *National Public Radio*, June 24, 2020, https://www.npr.org/sections/live-updates-protests-for-racial-justice/2020/06/24/883050615/three-men-indicted-in-murder-of-ahmaud-arbery-killed-while-he-jogged-in-georgia.

32. "Breonna Taylor: Timeline of Black Deaths Caused by Police," *BBC News*, January 6, 2021, https://www.bbc.com/news/world-us-canada-52905408.

33. Jonah Engel Bromwich, "White and Black Police Officers Are Sharply Divided About Race, Pew Finds," *New York Times*, January 11, 2017, https://mobile.nytimes.com/2017/01/11/us/police-officers-pew-poll.html.

34. Jonah Engel Bromwich," White and Black Police Officers Are Sharply Divided About Race."

35. William T. L. Cox and Patricia G. Devine, "Experimental Research on Shooter Bias: Ready (or Relevant) Application in the Courtroom?" *Journal of Applied Research in Memory and Cognition* 5, (2016): 236–238.

36. Bob Egelko, "Why It's So Hard to Convict a Cop of Murder: Just 5 in 15 Years," *San Francisco Chronicle*, June 10, 2020, https://www.sfchronicle.com/nation/article/Why-it-s-so-hard-to-convict-a-cop-of-murder-15327778.php.

37. Amelia Thomson-DeVeaux, Nathaniel Rakich, and Likhitha Butchireddygari, "Why It's So Rare for Police Officers to Face Leagal Consequences," *FiveThirtyEight*, June 4, 2020, https://fivethirtyeight.com/features/why-its-still-so-rare-for-police-officers-to-face-legal-consequences-for-misconduct/.

38. Ibid.

39. https://blacklivesmatter.com/.

40. Deja Thomas and Juliana Menasche Horowitz, "Support for Black Lives Matter Has Decreased Since June but Remains Strong among Black Americans," Pew Research Center, September 16, 2020, https://www.pewresearch.org/fact-tank/2020/09/16/support-for-black-lives-matter-has-decreased-since-june-but-remains-strong-among-black-americans/.

41. Merriam-Webster, "The Roots of 'Radical': Getting Down to What's Under the Surface," n.d., https://www.merriam-webster.com/words-at-play/radical-word-history.

42. The full context of this remark makes clear that Trump is referring to "very fine people" who are opposed to removing Confederate statues (in contrast to those who identify with white nationalist groups), not that he found the white nationalists to be "very fine people." Nonetheless, his support for keeping statues of those who fought to maintain slavery is somewhat curious given his position as leader of the country those persons sought to defeat and from which they wished to succeed. (Angie, Drobnic Holan, "In Context: Donald Trump's 'Very Fine People on Both Sides' Transcript," Politifact, April 26, 2019.) https://www.politifact.com/article/2019/apr/26/context-trumps-very-fine-people-both-sides-remarks/.

43. Kathleen Ronayne and Michael Kunzelman, "Trump to Far-Right Extremists: 'Stand Back and Stand By,'" Associate Press, September 30, 2020, https://apnews.com/article/election-2020-joe-biden-race-and-ethnicity-donald-trump-chris-wallace-0b32339da25fbc9e8b7c7c7066a1db0f.

44. Yamiche Alcindor, "Trump Insists on Using Racist Language. Will That Approach Win Him Support?" *PBS News Hour*, July 2, 2020, https://www.pbs.org/newshour/show/trump-insists-on-using-racist-language-will-that-approach-win-him-support.

45. There are many more examples, including his embracing of birtherism (the false notion that President Barack Obama was not born in the United States), referring to African nations as "shithole countries," and telling women members of Congress who are of color to go back to where they came from (Karen Grigsby Bates, "Is Trump Really That Racist?" *National Public Radio*, October 21, 2020), https://www.npr.org/2020/10/19/925385389/is-trump-really-that-racist

46. Ed Kilgore, "Trump Is Reviving the Disgraceful Legacy of 'Law-and-Order' Politics," *New York*, June 3, 2020, https://nymag.com/intelligencer/2020/06/trump-law-and-order-politics-nixon-reagan.html.

47. Shelly Tan, Youjin Shin, and Danielle Rindler, "How One of America's Ugliest Days Unraveled Inside and Outside the Capitol," *The Washington Post*, January 9, 2021, https://www.washingtonpost.com/nation/interactive/2021/capitol-insurrection-visual-timeline/.

48. Besides a fiery in-person speech the morning of the riot, President Trump used the social media platform Twitter to instigate his supporters' anger and, after the riot turned deadly, recorded a video asking them to "go home" and telling them that they are "very special" while repeating falsehoods about the election results (Amy Sherman, "A Timeline of What Trump Said Before the Jan. 6 Capitol Riot," *Politifact*, January 11, 2021, https://www.politifact.com/article/2021/jan/11/timeline-what-trump-said-jan-6-capitol-riot/; "Trump Tells 'Very Special' Rioters to 'Go Home' While Making False Claims About Election Results," *KCRG*, January 6, 2021, https://www.kcrg.com/2021/01/06/trump-tells-very-special-rioters-to-go-home-while-making-false-claims-about-election-results/).

49. Tessa Berenson, "Donald Trump Impeached a Second Time in Historic House Vote," *Time*, January 13, 2021, https://time.com/5928988/donald-trump-impeached-second-time/.

50. Melissa Block, "Can the Forces Unleashed by Trump's Big Election Lie Be Undone?" *National Public Radio*, January 16, 2021, https://www.npr.org/2021/01/16/957291939/can-the-forces-unleashed-by-trumps-big-election-lie-be-undone.

51. Martin Pengelly and Richard Luscombe, "'Complicit in Big Lie': Republican Senators Hawley and Cruz Face Calls to Resign," *The Guardian*, January 10, 2021, https://www.theguardian.com/us-news/2021/jan/10/capitol-attack-republican-senators-josh-hawley-ted-cruz-face-resign.

52. Dahlia Lithwick, "Why Republicans Are Still Holding Onto the Big Lie," *Slate*, February 26, 2021, https://slate.com/news-and-politics/2021/02/republicans-cpac-stolen-election-lie.html.

53. Amy Gardner, "How Trump Drove the Lie That the Election Was Stolen, Undermining Voter Trust in the Outcome," *The Washington Post*, December 20, 2020, https://www.washingtonpost.com/politics/trump-election-voter-trust/2020/12/20/00282aa6-407a-11eb-8db8-395dedaaa036_story.html.

54. Kelly Welch. 2007. "Black Criminal Stereotypes and Racial Profiling," *Journal of Contemporary Criminal Justice* 23, no. 3: 276–288.

55. Morgan Chalfant, "Trump: 'The Only Way We're Going to Lose This Election Is If the Election Is Rigged,'" *The Hill*, August 17, 2020, https://thehill.com/homenews/administration/512424-trump-the-only-way-we-are-going-to-lose-this-election-is-if-the.

56. William Cummings, Joey Garrison, and Jim Sergent, "By the Numbers: President Donald Trump's Failed Efforts to Overturn the Election," *USA Today*, January 6, 2021, https://www.usatoday.com/in-depth/news/politics/elections/2021/01/06/trumps-failed-efforts-overturn-election-numbers/4130307001/.

57. Aaron Blake, "The Most Remarkable Rebukes of Trump's Legal Case: From the Judges He Hand-Picked," *The Washington Post*, December 14, 2020, https://www.washingtonpost.com/politics/2020/12/14/most-remarkable-rebukes-trumps-legal-case-judges-he-hand-picked/.

58. Kenya Evelyn, "Capitol Attack: The Five People Who Died," *The Guardian*, January 8, 2021, https://www.theguardian.com/us-news/2021/jan/08/capitol-attack-police-officer-five-deaths.

59. Doha Madani and Ali Gostanian, "Man Holding Confederate Flag in Capitol During Pro-Trump Riot Turns Himself In," *NBC News*, January 14, 2021, https://www.nbcnews.com/news/us-news/man-holding-confederate-flag-capitol-during-pro-trump-riot-turns-n1254307.

60. Kristin Romey, "Decoding the Hate Symbols Seen at the Capitol Insurrection," *National Geographic*, January 12, 2021, https://www.nationalgeographic.com/history/article/decoding-hate-symbols-seen-at-capitol-insurrection.

61. "U.S. Saw Summer of Black Lives Matter Protests Demanding Change," *U.S. News & World Report*, December 7, 2020, https://www.usnews.com/news/top-news/articles/2020-12-07/us-saw-summer-of-black-lives-matter-protests-demanding-change.

62. Rachel Hartigan, "Was the Assault on the Capitol Really 'Unprecedented?' Historians Weigh In," *National Geographic*, January 8, 2021, https://www.nationalgeographic.com/history/article/historians-on-the-unprecedented-chaos-in-congress.

63. Joel Achenbach, "In 1814, British Forces Burned the U.S. Capitol," *The Washington Post*, January 6, 2021, https://www.washingtonpost.com/history/2021/01/06/british-burned-capitol-1814/.

64. Drew Kann, "5 Facts Behind America's High Incarceration Rate," *CNN*, April 21, 2019, https://www.cnn.com/2018/06/28/us/mass-incarceration-five-key-facts/index.html.

65. E. Ann Carson, "Prisoners in 2018," Bureau of Justice Statistics, US Department of Justice, April 2020, https://www.bjs.gov/content/pub/pdf/p18.pdf.

66. Danielle Kaeble and Mariel Alper, "Probation and Parole in the United States, 2017–18," Bureau of Justice Statistics, US Department of Justice, August 2020, https://www.bjs.gov/content/pub/pdf/ppus1718.pdf.

67. E. Ann Carson, "Prisoners in 2018."

68. John Gramlich, "Black Imprisonment Rate in the U.S. Has Fallen by a Third Since 2006," Pew Research Center, May 6, 2020, https://www.pewresearch.org/fact-tank/2020/05/06/share-of-black-white-hispanic-americans-in-prison-2018-vs-2006/.

69. Danielle Kaeble and Mariel Alper, "Probation and Parole in the United States, 2017–18."

70. John Gramlich, "Black Imprisonment Rate in the U.S. Has Fallen by a Third Since 2006."

71. E. Ann Carson, "Prisoners in 2018."

72. Snejana Farberov, "Chicago Decriminalizes Possession of Small Amounts of Pot," *Daily Mail*, June 27, 2012, http://www.dailymail.co.uk/news/article-2165805/Chicago-decriminalizes-possession-small-amounts-pot-caught-puffing-joint-arrested.html?ito=feeds-newsxml. With respect to racial disparities in misdemeanor drug arrests in New York City, see Andrew Golub, Bruce D. Johnson, and Eloise Dunlap, "The Race/Ethnicity Disparity in Misdemeanor Marijuana Arrests in New York City," *Criminology and Public Policy* 6, no. 1 (2007): 131–164.

73. Marc Mauer and David Cole, "Five Myths About Americans in Prison," *Washington Post*, June 17, 2011, http://www.washingtonpost.com/opinions/five-myths-about-incarceration/2011/06/13/AGfIWvYH_story.html. For updated data relating to this trend, see C. Eugene Emery, Jr., "Van Jones Claim on Drug Use, Imprisonment Rates for Blacks, Whites Is Mostly Accurate," *Politifact*, July 13, 2016, http://www.politifact.com/punditfact/statements/2016/jul/13/van-jones/van-jones-claim-drug-use-imprisonment-rates-blacks/.

74. More than five million Americans are prohibited from voting because they have been convicted of a felony. In 11 states, individuals lose voting rights forever after being convicted. In other states, voting rates are regained or can be bought back after certain conditions are met. Two states (Maine and Vermont) allow citizens to vote while incarcerated. (Christopher Uggen, Ryan Larson, Sarah Shannon, and Arleth Pulido-Nava, "Locked Out 2020: Estimates of People Denied Voting Rights Due to Felony Convictions," The Sentencing Project, October 30, 2020: https://www.sentencingproject.org/publications/locked-out-2020-estimates-of-people-denied-voting-rights-due-to-a-felony-conviction/.)

75. One in sixteen African Americans of voting age have lost the right to vote because of a felony conviction. That figure is nearly four times the rate of other races and ethnicities. Ibid.

76. Racial disparities in pretrial release decisions for drug offenders have been found as well. Tina L. Freiburger, Catherine D. Marcum, and Mari Pierce, "The Impact of Race on the Pretrial Decision," *American Journal of Criminal Justice* 35 (2010): 76–86.

77. Office of Justice Programs, "Statistical Briefing Book," US Department of Justice, November 16, 2020, https://www.ojjdp.gov/ojstatbb/crime/ucr.asp?table_in=2.

78. These data are difficult to collect, but see, for example, Magnus Lofstrom, Daniel Morales Campos, and Brandon Martin, "African Americans Are Notably Overrepresented in Police Stops," Public Policy Institute of California, August 13, 2020, https://www.ppic.org/blog/african-americans-are-notably-overrepresented-in-police-stops/; Marisol Bello and Kevin Johnson, "Racial Profiling Debate Not Over," *USA Today*, July 23, 2009, http://www.usatoday.com/news/nation/2009-07-22-racial_N.htm; Gene Callahan and William Anderson, "The Roots of Racial Profiling: Why Are Police Targeting Minorities for Traffic Stops?" http://Reason.com, August–September 2001, http://reason.com/archives/2001/08/01/the-roots-of-racial-profiling; Will Guzzardi, "Illinois State Police Racial Bias: New Studies Show Trend of Discrimination Continued Last Year," *Huffington Post*, July 13, 2011, http://www.huffingtonpost.com/2011/07/13/illinois-state-police-rac_n_897551.html; University of Minnesota Law School, *Racial Profiling Data Collection Status Report*, 2000, http://www1.umn.edu/irp/publications/ARB/ARB%20.html; and the Racial Profiling Data Collection Resource Center at Northeastern University, http://www.racialprofilinganalysis.neu.edu.

79. Researchers have found that Americans disproportionately fear being subject to violent crime (or street crime), as opposed to white-collar crime, even though white-collar crime results in greater financial losses. See Randall A. Gordon et al., "Perceptions of Blue-Collar and White-Collar Crime: The Effect of Defendant Race on Simulated Juror Decisions," *Journal of Social Psychology* 128, no. 2 (1998): 191–197; Kristy Holtfreter et al., "Public Perceptions of White-Collar Crime and Punishment," *Journal of Criminal Justice* 36, no. 1 (2008): 50–60; Jeffrey Reiman and Paul Leighton, *The Rich Get Richer and the Poor Get Prison*, 9th ed. (Upper Saddle River, NJ: Prentice Hall, 2009); Robert L. Young, "Perceptions of Crime, Racial Attitudes, and Firearms Ownership," *Social Forces* 64, no. 2 (1985): 473–486. See also David O. Friedrichs, *Trusted Criminals: White Collar Crime in Contemporary Society*, 4th ed. (Belmont, CA: Wadsworth, 2010); Stuart A. Scheingold, *The Politics of Street Crime: Criminal Process and Cultural Obsession* (Philadelphia: Temple University Press, 1991). It is worth noting that there have historically been racial disparities with respect to presidential pardons as well, with white convicts nearly four times more likely to be pardoned than persons of color (Dafna Linzer and Jennifer LaFleur, "Presidential Pardons Heavily Favor Whites," *Propublica*, December 3, 2011, http://www.propublica.org/article/shades-of-mercy-presidential-forgiveness-heavily-favors-whites).

80. In the winter of 2013, Supreme Court Justice Sonia Sotomayor publicly criticized a prosecutor who questioned an African American defendant as follows: "You've got African Americans, you've got Hispanics, you've got a bag full of money. Does that tell you—a light bulb doesn't go off in your head and say, this is a drug deal?" Sotomayor called the statement "pernicious in its attempt to substitute racial stereotype for evidence." Lawrence Hurley, "Sonia Sotomayor Condemns Prosecutor's Racially Charged Question," *Huffington Post*, February 25, 2013, http://www.huffingtonpost.com/2013/02/25/sonia-sotomayor-prosecutor_n_2759273.html.

81. Peter Dreier, "How the Media Compound Urban Problems," *Journal of Urban Affairs* 27, no. 2 (2005): 193–201; Robert Elias, "Official Stories: Media Coverage of American Crime Policy," *Humanist* 54, no. 1 (1994): 5–10; Steve Macek, *Urban Nightmares: The Media, the Right, and the Moral Panic Over the City* (Minneapolis: University of Minnesota Press, 2006).

82. Justin T. Pickett, Ted Chiricos, Kristin M. Golden, and Marc Gertz, "Reconsidering the Relationship between Perceived Neighborhood Racial Composition and Whites' Perceptions of Victimization Risk: Do Racial Stereotypes Matter?" *Criminology* 50, no. 1 (2012): 145–186.

83. Matthew Cella and Alan Neuhauser, "Race and Homicide in America, by the Numbers," *U.S. News and World Report*, September 29, 2016, http://www.usnews.com/news/articles/2016-09-29/race-and-homicide-in-america-by-the-numbers.

84. Alfred S. Regnery, "Black on Black Crime: Blame It on the System and Ignore the Evidence," *Breitbart*, May 24, 2016, http://www.breitbart.com/big-government/2016/05/24/black-black-crime-blame-system-ignore-evidence/.

85. In February 2012 Trayvon Martin, an African American teenager, was shot by a neighborhood watch captain who was white and Latino in Sanford, Florida. The case put racial profiling in the spotlight. Research related to such profiling became salient because studies have demonstrated that people are more likely to assume that an object in the hand of an African American is a gun than if the same poorly seen object is held by someone who is white (Malcolm Ritter, "Trayvon Martin Case: Study Shows Holding a Gun May Make You Think Others Are Too," *Huffington Post*, March 20, 2012, http://www.huffingtonpost.com/2012/03/20/trayvon-martin-case-study_n_1368524.html, citing Jessica K. Witt and James R. Brockmole, "Action Alters Object Identification: Wielding a Gun Increases the Bias to See Guns," *Journal of Experimental Psychology* 38, no. 5 (2012): 1159–1167). See also Joshua Correll, Geoffrey R. Urland, and Tiffany A. Ito, "Event-Related Potentials and the Decision to Shoot: The Role of Threat Perception and Cognitive Control," *Journal of Experimental and Social Psychology* 42, no. 1 (2006): 120–128; Anthony G. Greenwald, Mark A. Oakes, and Hunter G. Hoffman, "Targets of Discrimination: Effects of Race on Responses to Weapons Holders," *Journal of Experimental and Social Psychology* 39, no. 4 (2003): 399–405; Keith B. Payne, "Prejudice and Perception: The Role of Automatic and Controlled Processes in Misperceiving a Weapon," *Journal of Personality and Social Psychology* 81, no. 2 (2001): 181–192.

86. Devah Pager, *Marked: Race, Crime, and Finding Work in an Era of Mass Incarceration* (Chicago: University of Chicago Press, 2007), cited in Seth Wessler, "Race and Recession: How Inequality Rigged the Economy and How to Change the Rules," Applied Research Center, May 2009, http://arc.org/downloads/2009_race_recession_0909.pdf, 23.

87. Devah Pager, "The Mark of a Criminal Record," *American Journal of Sociology* 108, no. 5 (2003): 937–975.

88. "Work Opportunity Tax Credit," US Department of Labor, n.d., https://www.dol.gov/agencies/eta/wotc.

89. Groups include Temporary Assistance for Needy Families (TANF) recipients, veterans, food stamp recipients, individuals living in a designated empowerment zone or rural renewal county, 16- and 17-year-olds working during the summer, disabled persons working with vocational rehabilitation referral agencies, former felons, and individuals who have recently received Supplemental Social Security Income benefits (US Department of Labor, *The Work Opportunity Tax Credit (WOTC) $olution*, 2011, http://www.doleta.gov/business/incentives/opptax/PDF/WOTC_Program_ARRA_Brochure.pdf).

90. US Department of Labor, Federal Bonding Program, 2011, http://www.bonds4jobs.com/.

91. "Workforce Investment Act," Association for Career & Technical Education, n.d., https://www.acteonline.org/workforce-investment-act/.

92. US Department of Labor, Workforce Professionals, 2011, https://www.dol.gov/agencies/eta/usworkforce.

93. Osita Nwanevu, "The Improbable Success of a Criminal-Justice Reform Bill Under Trump," *The New Yorker*, December 17, 2018, https://www.newyorker.com/news/news-desk/the-improbable-success-of-a-criminal-justice-reform-bill-under-trump.

94. Nicole Porter, "Top Trends in State Criminal Justice Reform, 2018," *Sentencing Project*, January 16, 2019, https://www.sentencingproject.org/publications/top-trends-state-criminal-justice-reform-2018/.

95. Sarah Rense, "Here Are All the States That Have Legalized Weed in the U.S.," *Esquire*, November 4, 2020, https://www.esquire.com/lifestyle/a21719186/all-states-that-legalized-weed-in-us/.

96. "State Medical Marijuana Laws," National Conference of State Legislatures, February 19, 2021, https://www.ncsl.org/research/health/state-medical-marijuana-laws.aspx.

97. For a thoughtful overview, see Jonathan Rothwell, "Drug Offenders in American Prisons: The Critical Distinction between Stock and Flow," The Brookings Institution, November 25, 2015, https://www.brookings.edu/blog/social-mobility-memos/2015/11/25/drug-offenders-in-american-prisons-the-critical-distinction-between-stock-and-flow/.

98. https://new.togetherwebake.org/.

99. Allison Aubrey, "This Bakery Offers a Second Chance for Women After Prison," *National Public Radio*, April 15, 2016, http://www.npr.org/sections/thesalt/2016/04/15/469942932/this-bakery-offers-a-second-chance-for-women-after-prison.

100. Ibid., www.togetherwebake.org.

Chapter 6: Immigration and Employment

1. US Bureau of Labor Statistics, "Employment Status of the Civilian Noninstitutional Population by Race, Hispanic or Latino Ethnicity, Sex, and Age (Table A-15)," 2009, http://www.bls.gov/web/empsit.supp.toc.htm.

2. US Bureau of Labor Statistics, "Employment Situation Summary," 2011, http://www.bls.gov/news.release/empsit.nr0.htm.

3. Corey Dade, "Government Job Cuts Threaten Black Middle Class," *National Public Radio*, May 9, 2012, http://www.npr.org/2012/05/09/152297370/government-job-cuts-threaten-black-middle-class.

4. Sylvia Allegretto and Devon Lynch, "The Composition of the Unemployed and Long-Term Unemployed in Tough Labor Markets," October, 2010, http://www.bls.gov/opub/mlr/2010/10/art1full.pdf.

5. Ibid.

6. In 2002, as a result of a suit brought by the Equal Employment Opportunity Commission, Target employees responsible for screening applicants at job fairs in the Milwaukee area admitted to routinely destroying applications from African Americans. Devah Pager, "The Use of Field Experiments for Studies of Employment Discrimination: Contributions, Critiques, and Directions for the Future," *Annals of the American Academy of Political and Social Science* 609 (2007): 104–133, at 104–105.

7. Ibid.

8. For an accessible overview of recent studies about unconscious biases that complements the scholarly articles found in the endnotes from the Introduction, see Keith Payne, "What Your Brain Won't Let You See," http://Salon.com, June 13, 2013, http://www.salon.com/2013/06/13/what_your_mind_wont_let_you_see_partner/.

9. See, for instance, Marianne Bertrand and Sendhil Mullainathan, "Are Emily and Greg More Employable than Lakisha and Jamal? A Field Experiment on Labor Market Discrimination," *American Economic Review* 94, no. 4 (2004): 991–1013.

10. Ibid., 992.

11. Laura Giuliano, David I. Levine, and Jonathan Leonard, "Manager Race and the Race of New Hires," *Journal of Labor Economics* 27, no. 4 (2009): 589–631.

12. John J. Beggs, Wayne J. Villemez, and Ruth Arnold, "Black Population Concentration and Black-White Inequality: Expanding the Consideration of Place and Space Effects," *Social Forces* 76 (1997): 65–91.

13. Matt L. Huffman and Philip N. Cohen, "Racial Wage Inequality: Job Segregation and Devaluation across U.S. Labor Markets," *American Journal of Sociology* 109, no. 4 (2004): 902–936, at 928–929.

14. See Hurbert M. Blalock, *Towards a Theory of Minority Group Relations* (New York: Wiley, 1967); Mark A. Fossett and K. J. Kiecolt., "The Relative Size of Minority Populations and White Racial Attitudes," *Social Science Research* 70 (1989): 820–835.

15. Tricia McTague, Kevin Stainback, and Donald Tomaskovic-Devey, "An Organizational Approach to Understanding Sex and Race Segregation in U.S. Workplaces," *Social Forces* 87, no. 3 (2009): 1499–1527; Kevin Stainback, Corre L. Robinson, and Donald Tomaskovic-Devey, "Race and Workplace Integration," *American Behavioral Scientist* 48, no. 9 (2005): 1200–1228; Donald Tomaskovic-Devey, *Gender and Racial Inequality at Work: The Sources and Consequences of Job Segregation* (New York: ILR Press, 1993).

16. Douglas S. Massey, "Origins of Economic Disparities: Historical Roles of Housing Segregation," in *Segregation: The Rising Costs for America*, eds. James H. Carr and Nandinee K. Kutty (New York: Routledge, 2008), 39–80.

17. On the surface, this is not an issue of race or ethnicity but of poverty. However, racial and ethnic housing segregation once again challenges us to consider the disproportionate effect on African Americans and Latinos.

18. Enterprise zones are often at the local or state levels, a similar initiative referred to as "empowerment zones" was created at the federal level ("Empowerment Zones," US Department of Housing and Urban Development, n.d., https://www.hud.gov/hudprograms/empowerment_zones). There has not been funding allocated to the federal program since 2013.

19. Don Hirasuna and Joel Michael, "Enterprise Zones: A Review of the Economic Theory and Empirical Evidence," January 2005, http://www.house.leg.state.mn.us/hrd/pubs/entzones.pdf.

20. Steve McDonald, Nan Lin, and Dan Ao, "Networks of Opportunity: Gender, Race, and Job Leads," *Social Problems* 56, no. 3 (2009): 385–402.

21. Niki T. Dickerson, "Black Employment, Segregation, and the Social Organization of Metropolitan Labor Markets," *Economic Geography* 83, no. 3 (2007): 283–307.

22. Jean McGianni Celestin, "The Jobless Rate Among Black College Graduates Is Nearly Double That of Whites. Why?" http://TheRoot.com, March 5, 2011, http://www.theroot.com/views/college-degrees-won-t-shield-blacks-unemployment; Michael Luo, "In Job Hunt, College Degree Can't Close Racial Gap," *New York Times*, November 30, 2009, http://www.nytimes.com/2009/12/01/us/01race.html.

23. Less educated Americans, however, particularly young African American men, are more likely to be burdened with additional factors that contribute to unemployment, such as incarceration and enforcement of child support laws. Harry J. Holzer, Paul Offner, and Elaine Sorensen, "Declining Employment Among Young Black Less-Educated Men: The Role of Incarceration and Child Support," *Journal of Policy Analysis and Management* 24, no. 2 (2005): 329–350.

24. "Employment Projections," US Bureau of Labor Statistics, September 1, 2020, https://www.bls.gov/emp/tables/emp-by-major-occupational-group.htm.

25. The California-based not-for-profit group Strive for College is geared toward ensuring that "every qualified, low-income high school student has the information and support necessary to enroll in their best-fit college," https://striveforcollege.org/.

26. Adam Clymer, "Jack Kemp, Star on Field and Politics, Dies at 73," *New York Times*, May 2, 2009, http://www.nytimes.com/2009/05/03/us/03kemp.html; Common Cause, "Freedom-Works," 2011, http://www.commoncause.org/site/pp.asp?b=1497377&c=dkLNK1MQIwG; James D. Gwartney, "Supply-Side Economics," in *The Concise Encyclopedia of Economics*, 2008, http://www.econlib.org/library/Enc/SupplySideEconomics.html; Andrew Malcolm, "Jack Kemp, All-Star Quarterback, Politician, Father, Dead of Cancer, 73," *Los Angeles Times*, i May 2, 2009, http://latimesblogs.latimes.com/washington/2009/05/jack-kemp-dies.html.

27. See https://www.usa.gov/jobs-and-unemployment for a list.

28. Michael W. Sherraden, "Chronic Unemployment: A Social Work Perspective," *Social Work* 30, no. 5 (1985): 403–408, at 403.

29. http://lincs.ed.gov.

30. https://proliteracy.org.

31. http://www.idealist.org.

32. http://literacychicago.org.

33. http://www.growinghomeinc.org.

34. Sandra Bynum, "Promote Adult Literacy by Teaching Reading Skills," *Volunteer Guide*, 2011, http://volunteerguide.org/volunteer/fewhours/adult-literacy.htm; Ronald Nash, "Three Kinds of Illiteracy," Center for Reformed Theology and Apologetics, 1996, http://www.reformed.org/webfiles/antithesis/index.html?mainframe=/webfiles/antithesis/v1n5/ant_v1n5_illiteracy.html; Sherraden, "Chronic Unemployment: A Social Work Perspective."

35. The American Association of Community Colleges notes that half of the students who receive a baccalaureate degree in the United States have also attended a community college along the way. "Students at Community Colleges," American Association of Community Colleges, 2011, http://www.aacc.nche.edu/AboutCC/Trends/Pages/studentsatcommunitycolleges.aspx.

36. "About MDC," Miami Dade College, n.d., https://www.mdc.edu/about/facts.aspx.

37. Ibid. See also Lizettte Alvarez, "A Community College in Florida Works to Attract the Poor and the Presidential," *New York Times*, April 29, 2011, http://www.nytimes.com/2011/04/30/us/30dade.html.

38. Lizettte Alvarez, "A Community College in Florida Works to Attract the Poor and the Presidential."

39. Karen Levesque et al., "Career and Technical Education in the United States: 1990 to 2005," National Center for Education Statistics, July 2008, http://nces.ed.gov/pubs2008/2008035.pdf, 86–94.

40. Brian Latimer, "Isa Noyola, the Translatina Activist Fighting for Immigrant Rights," *NBC News*, June 30, 2016, http://www.nbcnews.com/news/latino/translatinaactivist-isa-noyola-translatina-activist-fighting-immigrant-rights-n601641.

41. Raquel Reichard, "Woman Crush(ing the Patriarchy) Wednesday: Isa Noyola," *Latina*, January 13, 2016, http://webcache.googleusercontent.com/search?q=cache:g1XvgjY-rTkJ:www.latina.com/lifestyle/our-issues/wcw-melanie-cervantes&hl=en&gl=us&strip=1&vwsrc=0.

42. Ibid.

43. Ibid.

44. https://mijente.net/.

45. Ran Abramitzky and Leah Boustan. "Immigration in American Economic History," *Journal of Economic Literature* 55, no. 4 (2017): 1311–1345.

46. Richard A. Boswell. "Racism and U.S. Immigration Law: Prospects for Reform After '9/11?," *Journal of Gender* 7, no. 2 (2003): 315–356.

47. Abby Budiman, "Key Findings about U.S. Immigrants," Pew Research Center, August 20, 2020, https://www.pewresearch.org/fact-tank/2020/08/20/key-findings-about-u-s-immigrants/.

48. D'Vera Cohn, "How U.S. Immigration Laws and Rules Have Changed Through History," Pew Research Center, September 30, 2015, https://www.pewresearch.org/fact-tank/2015/09/30/how-u-s-immigration-laws-and-rules-have-changed-through-history/

49. Abby Budiman, "Key Findings about U.S. Immigrants."

50. Alan Gomez, "Number of Undocumented Immigrants in U.S. Stays Same for 6th Year," *USA Today*, September 20, 2016, http://www.usatoday.com/story/news/world/2016/09/20/illegal-immigration-united-states-mexico-asia-africa/

90735292/; Jeffrey Passel and D'Vera Cohn, "Unauthorized Immigrant Population: National and State Trends, 2010," Pew Hispanic Center, 2011, http://www.pewhispanic.org/2011/02/01/unauthorized-immigrant-population-brnational-and-state-trends-2010/; Julia Preston, "Illegal Immigrants Number 11.5 Million," *New York Times*, March 24, 2012, http://www.nytimes.com/2012/03/24/us/illegal-immigrants-number-11-5-million.html.

51. Jennifer Guglielmo and Salvatore Salerno, eds., *Are Italians White? How Race Is Made in America* (New York: Routledge, 2003); Noel Ignatiev, *How the Irish Became White* (New York: Routledge, 2009).

52. The word "Latinx" is increasingly used to refer to people whose heritage is traced to Latin America. The term originated as a way to push back against gender binaries inherent in the Spanish language (and society at large). It is embraced by many but rejected by others (Luis Noe-Bustamante, Lauren Mora, and Mark Hugo Lopez, "About One-in-Four U.S. Hispanics Have Heard of Latinx, But Just 3% Use It," Pew Research Center, August 11, 2020, https://www.pewresearch.org/hispanic/2020/08/11/about-one-in-four-u-s-hispanics-have-heard-of-latinx-but-just-3-use-it/).

53. José Luis Morin, "Latinas/os and US Prisons: Trends and Challenges," *Latino Studies* 6 (2008): 11–34.

54. President Donald Trump both benefitted from and perpetuated negative stereotypes of Hispanic Americans, from his first remarks as a presidential candidate in 2015 through his term in office (David A. Graham, Adrienne Green, Cullen Murphy, and Parker Richards, "An Oral History of Trump's Bigotry," *The Atlantic*, June 2019, https://www.theatlantic.com/magazine/archive/2019/06/trump-racism-comments/588067/). However, he earned a greater-than-expected share of the Latino vote in some areas in both the 2016 and 2020 elections (Amelia Thomson-DeVeaux, Geoffrey Skelley, and Laura Bronner, "What We Know About How White and Latino Americans Voted in 2020," *FiveThirtyEight*, November 23, 2020, https://fivethirtyeight.com/features/what-we-know-about-how-white-and-latino-americans-voted-in-2020/).

55. An August 2011 poll revealed that 40 percent of Americans believe that illegal immigrants take jobs away from US citizens, but 49 percent believe that they perform jobs that US citizens will not do. Rasmussen, "49% Say Illegal Immigrants Perform Jobs U.S. Citizens Won't Do," Rasmussen Reports, August 25, 2011, http://www.rasmussenreports.com/public_content/politics/current_events/immigration/49_say_illegal_immigrants_perform_jobs_u_s_citizens_won_t_do.

56. "Jobs That Americans Won't Do," *Christian Science Monitor*, September 1, 2009, http://www.csmonitor.com/Commentary/the-monitors-view/2009/0901/p08s01-comv.html.

57. Cord Jefferson, "How Illegal Immigration Hurts Black America," http://TheRoot.com, February 10, 2010, http://www.theroot.com/views/how-illegal-immigration-hurts-black-america.

58. Henry Fernandez and Jennifer A. Jones, "Black People Think Trump's Immigration Policies Are Wrong and Will Vote Accordingly," *Morning Consult*, July 22, 2019, https://morningconsult.com/opinions/black-people-think-trumps-immigration-policies-are-wrong-and-will-vote-accordingly/.

59. Maeve Reston, "Brown Signs California Dream Act," *Los Angeles Times*, July 26, 2011, http://articles.latimes.com/2011/jul/26/local/la-me-brown-dream-act-20110726.

60. Kevin Loria, "DREAM Act Stalled, Obama Halts Deportations for Young Illegal Immigrants," *Christian Science Monitor*, June 15, 2012, http://www.csmonitor.com/USA/Politics/2012/0615/DREAM-Act-stalled-Obama-halts-deportations-for-young-illegal-immigrants-video.

61. "The Dream Act, DACA, and Other Policies Designed to Protect Dreamers," American Immigration Council, August 27, 2020, https://www.americanimmigrationcouncil.org/research/dream-act-daca-and-other-policies-designed-protect-dreamers.

62. Ibid.

63. "Preserving and Fortifying Deferred Action for Childhood Arrivals (DACA),"" *The White House*, January 20, 2021, https://www.whitehouse.gov/briefing-room/presidential-actions/2021/01/20/preserving-and-fortifying-deferred-action-for-childhood-arrivals-daca/.

64. Laura Litvan and Erik Larson, "Dreamers, DACA and Biden's First Try on Immigration," *The Washington Post*, January 25, 2021, https://www.washingtonpost.com/business/dreamers-daca-and-bidens-first-try-on-immigration/2021/01/22/06bd1c1e-5cdb-11eb-a849-6f9423a75ffd_story.html.

65. A surge of anti-Asian hostilities occurred during the Covid-19 pandemic, with President Trump repeatedly referred to as the "China Flu," the "Wuhan Flu," and even the "Kung Flu" (Alana Wise, "White House Defends Trump's Use of Racist Term to Describe Coronavirus," *National Public Radio*, June 22, 2020, https://www.npr.org/2020/06/22/881810671/white-house-defends-trumps-use-of-racist-term-to-describe-coronavirus).

66. C. N. Le, "Employment and Occupational Patterns," Asian-Nation: The Landscape of Asian America, August 25, 2011, http://www.asian-nation.org/employment.shtml. It is worth noting that the Covid-19 crisis hit Asian workers in the United States particularly hard, since many were either essential low-wage workers or, on the other end of the economic divide, owned businesses that were disproportionately affected by public health processes related to the virus (Stephen Gandel, "Asian Americans are Falling Behind White Workers in the Job Market," *CBS News*, September 4, 2020, https://www.cbsnews.com/news/asian-americans-unemployment-rate-august-jobs-report/).

67. Ruth Igielnik, "70% of Americans Say U.S. Economic System Unfairly Favors the Powerful," Pew Research Center, January 9, 2020, https://www.pewresearch.org/fact-tank/2020/01/09/70-of-americans-say-u-s-economic-system-unfairly-favors-the-powerful/.

68. "Problems and Priorities," http://PollingReport.com, 2011, http://www.pollingreport.com/prioriti.htm.

69. By November 2016, in the heat of a presidential election, only 14 percent of Americans named the economy as the most important problem facing America. It was, however, the most frequently mentioned item in the open-ended question. "Economy, Elections Top Problems Facing U.S.," *Gallup*, November 17, 2016, http://www.gallup.com/poll/197786/economy-elections-top-problems-facing.aspx?g_source=Politics.

70. "Most Important Problem," *Gallup*, n.d., https://news.gallup.com/poll/1675/most-important-problem.aspx.

71. Daniel Halper, "Poll: Workers Want Less Regulation," *Weekly Standard*, March 30, 2011, http://www.weeklystandard.com/blogs/poll-workers-want-less-regulation_556014.html; John McCormick and Alison Vekshin, "Wall Street Despised in Poll Showing Most Want Regulation (Update 1)," Bloomberg, March 24, 2010, http://www.bloomberg.com/apps/news?pid=newsarchive&sid=a4nQoiYaj2ag.

72. Elle Reeve, "These Are the Democratic Socialists Backing Bernie Sanders," *CNN*, February 29, 2020, https://www.cnn.com/2020/02/28/politics/young-democratic-socialists-bernie-sanders/index.html.

73. Frank Newport, "Public Opinion Review: Americans' Reactions to the Word 'Socialism,'" *Gallup*, March 6, 2020, https://news.gallup.com/opinion/polling-matters/287459/public-opinion-review-americans-word-socialism.aspx.

Chapter 7: Health

1. Maslow's hierarchy of needs has been updated to reflect changes in psychology over the past 50 years. "Self-actualization" has been replaced at the top of the pyramid along with mate acquisition, mate retention, and parenting (Tom Jacobs, "Maslow's

Pyramid Gets a Makeover," *Miller-McCune*, June 22, 2010, http://www.miller-mccune.com/culture/maslows-pyramid-gets-a-makeover-20682/); Douglas T. Kenrick et al.," Renovating the Pyramid of Needs: Contemporary Extensions Built upon Ancient Foundations," *Perspectives on Psychological Science* 5, no. 3 (2010): 292–314; Rick Nauert," Updated Maslow's Pyramid of Needs," *PsychCentral*, August 23, 2010, http://psychcentral.com/news/2010/08/23/updated-maslows-pyramid-of-needs/17144.html.

2. Nauert, "Updated Maslow's Pyramid of Needs."

3. For instance, two recent studies showed that individuals who are diagnosed with cancer have a better chance of survival if they have private health insurance than those who do not. They are diagnosed earlier and lived longer than those who had no insurance, or even those who were covered by Medicaid. Michelle Andrews, "Studies Link Cancer Patients' Survival Time to Insurance Status," *National Public Radio*, September 16, 2016, http://www.npr.org/sections/health-shots/2016/09/16/494139538/studies-link-cancer-patients-survival-time-to-insurance-status.

4. Uwe E. Reinhardt, "A 'Government Takeover' of Health Care?" *New York Times*, February 26, 2010, http://economix.blogs.nytimes.com/2010/02/26/a-government-takeover-of-health-care/. While remaining neutral on the value of the bill, the nonpartisan organization PolitiFact called the "government takeover" language the "lie of the year" in 2010, since the government is only minimally involved and private insurers will gain millions of new customers. Bill Adair and Angie Drobnic Holan, "PolitiFact's Lie of the Year: 'A Government Takeover of Health Care,'" http://PolitiFact.com, December 16, 2010, http://www.politifact.com/truth-o-meter/article/2010/dec/16/lie-year-government-takeover-health-care/.

5. US Department of Health and Human Services, "20 Million People Have Gained Health Insurance Coverage Because of the Affordable Care Act, New Estimates Show," March 3, 2016, http://www.hhs.gov/about/news/2016/03/03/20-million-people-have-gained-health-insurance-coverage-because-affordable-care-act-new-estimates.

6. "Chart Book: Accomplishments of the Affordable Care Act," Center on Budget and Policy Priorities, March 19, 2019, https://www.cbpp.org/research/health/chart-book-accomplishments-of-affordable-care-act.

7. Particularly in both 2016 and 2020, candidates in the Democratic Party nomination contests argued for a "Medicare for All" approach, which would approximate the national health-care systems in other industrialized democracies (Alice Miranda Ollstein, "Medicare for All," *Politico*, February 19, 2020, https://www.politico.com/2020-election/candidates-views-on-the-issues/health-care/medicare-for-all/.

8. Eunice Lee, "Donald Trump Vows Again to Repeal Obamacare," *U.S. News & World Report*, November 2, 2016, http://www.usnews.com/news/politics/articles/2016-11-02/donald-trump-vows-again-to-repeal-obamacare.

9. In 2017, Congress voted to repeal the portion of the act that provided a financial penalty to those who do not carry health insurance (Sy Mukherjee, "The GOP Tax Bill Repeals Obamacare's Individual Mandate. Here's What That Means For You," *Fortune*, December 20, 2017, https://fortune.com/2017/12/20/tax-bill-individual-mandate-obamacare/).

10. Paul Demko, "Court Voids Obamacare Mandate—But Not the Whole Law," *Politico*, December 18, 2019, https://www.politico.com/news/2019/12/18/court-finds-obamacare-mandate-unconstitutional-sends-case-back-to-lower-court-087389. The United States Supreme Court heard a case related to the Affordable Care Act in November of 2020, but the decision was not handed down as of the writing of this edition. Observers noted that the questions and comments from the justices seemed to signal that the program would be upheld (Robert Barnes, Ann E. Marimow, Amy Goldstein, and Paige Winfield Cunningham, "Supreme Court Appears Ready to Uphold Affordable Care Act Over Latest Challenge from Trump, GOP," *The Washington Post*, November 10, 2020, https://www.washingtonpost.com/politics/2020/11/10/scotus-hearing-aca-live-updates/).

11. Jennifer Tolbert and Kendal Orgera, "Key Facts About the Uninsured Population," Kaiser Family Foundation, November 6, 2020, https://www.kff.org/uninsured/issue-brief/key-facts-about-the-uninsured-population/#:~:text=However%2C%20beginning%20in%202017%2C%20the,2016%20to%2010.9%25%20in%202019.

12. For example, see Philip Klein, "The Myth of the 46 Million," *American Spectator*, March 20, 2009, http://spectator.org/archives/2009/03/20/the-myth-of-the-46-million.

13. Andy Miller, "Census Bureau Report Shows Slight Increase in Uninsured in 2008," *WebMD*, September 10, 2009, http://www.webmd.com/healthy-aging/news/20090910/more-americans-have-no-health-insurance; Joshua Norman, "Report: 59 Million Americans Lack Health Care," http://CBSNews.com, November 10, 2010, http://www.cbsnews.com/stories/2010/11/10/health/main7040408.shtml; Jennifer Pifer-Bixler, "Study: 86.8 Million Americans Uninsured over Last Two Years," *CNN*, March 4, 2009, http://articles.cnn.com/2009-03-04/health/uninsured.epidemic.obama_1_families-usa-health-insurance-health-coverage.

14. Jennifer Tolbert and Kendal Orgera, "Key Facts About the Uninsured Population."

15. US Department of Health and Human Services, "Medicaid Eligibility: Overview," Centers for Medicare and Medicaid Services, http://www.medicaid.gov/AffordableCareAct/Provisions/Eligibility.html.

16. http://Medicare.gov, "Medicare Basics," 2008, http://www.medicare.gov/Pubs/pdf/11034.pdf.

17. Douglas Conway, "Adults Age 26 Had Highest Uninsured Rate Among All Ages, Followed by 27-Year-Olds," US Census Bureau, October 26, 2020, https://www.census.gov/library/stories/2020/10/uninsured-rates-highest-for-young-adults-aged-19-to-34.html#:~:text=People%20in%20this%20age%20group,0.4%20percentage%20points%20to%2015.6%25.

18. "Uninsured Rates for the Nonelderly by Race and Ethnicity," Kaiser Family Foundation, n.d., https://www.kff.org/uninsured/state-indicator/nonelderly-uninsured-rate-by-raceethnicity/?currentTimeframe=0&sortModel=%7B%22colId%22:%22Location%22,%22sort%22:%22asc%22%7D.

19. David B. Rivkin and Lee A. Casey, "Mandatory Insurance Is Unconstitutional," *Wall Street Journal*, September 18, 2009, http://online.wsj.com/article/SB10001424052970204518504574416623109362480.html; Kevin Sack, "Federal Judge Rules That Health Law Violates Constitution," *New York Times*, January 31, 2011, http://www.nytimes.com/2011/02/01/us/01ruling.html; Adam Liptak, "Supreme Court Upholds Health Care Law, 5–4, in Victory for Obama," *New York Times*, June 28, 2012, http://www.nytimes.com/2012/06/29/us/supreme-court-lets-health-law-largely-stand.html.

20. Sy Mukherjee, "The GOP Tax Bill Repeals Obamacare's Individual Mandate. Here's What That Means For You."

21. Peter Sullivan, "Analysis: ObamaCare Market Stable and Profitable Despite Loss of Individual Mandate," *The Hill*, January 6, 2020, https://thehill.com/policy/healthcare/476916-analysis-obamacare-market-stable-and-profitable-despite-loss-of-individual.

22. CHIRP Los Angeles, "20 Million People Have Gained Health Insurance Coverage Because of the Affordable Care Act, New Estimates Show," http://www.chirpla.org/news/20-million-people-have-gained-health-insurance-coverage-because-affordable-care-act-new.

23. Greg R. Alexander and Carol C. Korenbrot, "The Role of Prenatal Care in Preventing Low Birth Weight," *Future of Children* 5, no. 1 (1995): 103–120; Jane Huntington and Frederick A. Connell, "For Every Dollar Spent: The Cost-Savings Argument for Prenatal Care," *New England Journal of Medicine* 331 (1994): 1303–1307.

24. Maria G. Gonzalez, "Factors Affecting Prenatal Care in Rural, Low-Income Neighborhoods," Poster presented at the SUNY Undergraduate Research Conference, 2015, http://digitalcommons.brockport.edu/surc/2015/schedule/297/. Julie A. Gazmararian

et al., "Prenatal Care for Low-Income Women Enrolled in a Managed-Care Organization," *Obstetrics & Gynecology* 94, no. 2 (1999): 177–184.

25. Michael D. Kogan et al., "Racial Disparities in Reported Prenatal Care Advice from Health Care Providers," *American Journal of Public Health* 84, no. 1 (1994): 82–88.

26. Jann L. Murray and Merton Bernfield, "The Differential Effect of Prenatal Care on the Incidence of Low Birth Weight Among Blacks and Whites in a Prepaid Health Care Plan," *New England Journal of Medicine* 319 (1988): 1385–1391.

27. Andrew J. Healy et al., "Early Access to Prenatal Care: Implications for Racial Disparity in Perinatal Mortality," *Obstetrics & Gynecology* 107, no. 3 (2006): 625–631.

28. Greg R. Alexander, Michael D. Kogan, and Sara Nabukera, "Racial Differences in Prenatal Care Use in the United States: Are Disparities Decreasing?" *American Journal of Public Health* 92, no. 12 (2002): 1970–1975.

29. More recent studies continue to reflect racial and ethnic disparities. For instance, one study in a California high-risk clinic found such differences in expectant mothers with respect to such factors as appointment attendance, diabetes, illicit drug use, smoking, and psychiatric diagnosis. Melanie Thomas, Anna Spielvogel, Frances Cohen, Susan Fisher-Owens, Naomi Stotland, Betsy Wolfe, and Martha Shumway, "Maternal Differences and Birth Outcome Disparities: Diversity within a High-Risk Prenatal Clinic," *Journal of Racial and Ethnic Health Disparities* 1, no. 1 (2014): 12–20. A separate focus group study found that structural barriers to accessing prenatal care included access to transportation, insurance, negative attitudes about prenatal care, and overall psychosocial stress. Mary C. Mazul, Trina C. Salm Ward, and Emmanuel M. Ngui, "Anatomy of Good Prenatal Care: Perspectives of Low Income African-American Women on Barriers and Facilitators to Prenatal Care," *Journal of Racial and Ethnic Health Disparities* (2016): 1–8 (online first).

30. Anne K. Driscoll and Danielle M. Ely. 2020. "Effects of Changes in Maternal Age Distribution and Maternal Age-Specific Infant Mortality Rates on Infant Mortality Trends: United States, 2000–2017," *National Vital Statistics Reports* 69, no. 5: 1–17, https://www.cdc.gov/nchs/data/nvsr/nvsr69/NVSR-69-05-508.pdf.

31. Rob Picheta, "Black Newborns More Likely to Die When Looked After by White Doctors," *CNN*, August 20, 2020, https://www.cnn.com/2020/08/18/health/black-babies-mortality-rate-doctors-study-wellness-scli-intl/index.html.

32. A study published in 2016 found "limited opportunities and experiences of institutional racism in both accessing and receiving prenatal care" resulted in adverse birth outcomes (Jeanne L. Alhusen, Kelly Bower, Elizabeth Epstein, and Phyllis Sharps. 2016. "Racial Discrimination and Adverse Birth Outcomes: An Integrative Review," *Journal of Midwifery and Women's Health* 61, no. 6: 707–720).

33. "White Children More Likely to Receive CT Scans Than Hispanic or African-American Children," *Science Codex*, August 6, 2012, http://www.sciencecodex.com/white_children_more_likely_to_receive_ct_scans_than_hispanic_or_africanamerican_children-96136.

34. David Seith and Courtney Kalof, "Who Are America's Poor Children? Examining Health Disparities by Race and Ethnicity," National Center for Children in Poverty, Columbia University, 2011, http://www.nccp.org/publications/pdf/text_1032.pdf.

35. Michael Marmot, "The Influence of Income on Health: Views of an Epidemiologist," *Health Affairs* 21, no. 2 (2002): 31–46.

36. David R. Williams and Pamela Braboy Jackson, "Social Sources of Racial Disparities in Health," *Health Affairs* 24, no. 2 (2005): 325–334.

37. Centers for Disease Control and Prevention, "Breast Cancer Rates by Race and Ethnicity," September 28, 2010, http://www.cdc.gov/cancer/breast/statistics/race.htm.

38. Martha Hostetter and Sarah Klein, "In Focus: Reducing Racial Disparities in Health Care by Confronting Racism," The Commonwealth Fund, September 27, 2018, https://www.commonwealthfund.org/publications/2018/sep/focus-reducing-

racial-disparities-health-care-confronting-racism; see also Roxanne Nelson, "Racial Disparities in Breast Cancer Survival Are Most Apparent in Advanced Stages," *Medscape Medical News*, August 14, 2007, http://www.medscape.com/viewarticle/561377; "Disparities in Healthcare Quality Among Minority Women: Findings from the 2011 National Healthcare Quality and Disparities Reports," Agency for Healthcare Research and Quality, October 2012, http://www.ahrq.gov/qual/nhqrdr11/nhqrminority women11.pdf.

39. "Disparities in Healthcare Quality Among Minority Women."

40. Martha Hostetter and Sarah Klein, "In Focus: Reducing Racial Disparities in Health Care by Confronting Racism."

41. Ronica N. Rooks et al., "Racial Disparities in Health Care Access and Cardiovascular Disease Indicators in Black and White Older Adults in the Health ABC Study," *Journal of Aging and Health* 20, no. 6 (2008): 599–614.

42. Keith C. Norris and Lawrence Y. Agodoa, "Unraveling the Racial Disparities Associated with Kidney Disease," *Kidney International* 68 (2005): 914–924.

43. Sarah Bounse and Debra Miller, "Racial Disparities Among AIDS Diagnoses: A Regional Analysis," Council of State Governments, August 17, 2011, http://knowledgecenter.csg.org/drupal/content/racial-disparities-among-aids-diagnoses-regional-analysis.

44. Dawn M. Bravata et al., "Racial Disparities in Stroke Risk Factors: The Impact of Socioeconomic Factors," *Stroke* 36 (2005): 1507–1511.

45. Agency for Healthcare Research and Quality, "Diabetes Disparities Among Racial and Ethnic Minorities," November 2001, http://www.ahrq.gov/research/diabdisp.pdf; Luisa N. Borrell et al., "Perception of General and Oral Health in White and African American Adults: Assessing the Effect of Neighborhood Socioeconomic Conditions," *Community Dentistry and Oral Epidemiology* 32, no. 5 (2004): 363–373.

46. Carrie N. Klabunde et al., "Trends and Black/White Differences in Treatment for Nonmetastatic Prostate Cancer," *Medical Care* 36, no. 9 (1998): 1337–1348; Kathryn E. Richert-Boe et al., "Racial Differences in Treatment of Early-Stage Prostate Cancer," *Urology* 71, no. 6 (2007): 1172–1176.

47. Centers for Disease Control and Prevention, *CDC Health Disparities and Inequalities Report: United States, 2011*, Morbidity and Mortality Weekly Report, January 14, 2011, http://www.cdc.gov/mmwr/pdf/other/su6001.pdf.

48. Ibby Caputo, "Poverty Impacts Developing Brains," *WGBH News*, April 4, 2013, http://www.wgbhnews.org/post/poverty-impacts-developing-brains.

49. Ibid.

50. Rachel Ann Reimer, Meg Gerrard, and Frederick X. Gibbons, "Racial Disparities in Smoking Knowledge Among Current Smokers: Data from the Health Information National Trends Surveys," *Psychology Health* 25, no. 8 (2010): 943–959. Further, recent research suggests that African Americans who live in more segregated communities are more likely to die from lung cancer than are African Americans who live in more integrated communities. Sabrina Tavernise, "Segregation Linked in Study with Lung Cancer Deaths," *New York Times*, January 16, 2013, http://www.nytimes.com/2013/01/17/health/study-links-segregation-and-lung-cancer-deaths-in-blacks.html.

51. Kellie E. Barr et al., "Race, Class, and Gender Differences in Substance Abuse: Evidence of Middle-Class/Underclass Polarization Among black Males," *Social Problems* 40, no. 3 (2003): 314–327.

52. Ricky N. Bluthenall, Jerry O. Jacobson, and Paul L. Robinson, "Are Racial Differences in Alcohol Treatment Completion Associated with Racial Differences in Treatment Modality Entry? Comparison of Outpatient Treatment and Residential Treatment in Los Angeles County, 1998 to 2000," *Alcoholism: Clinical and Experimental Research* 31, no. 11 (2007): 1920–1926.

53. Barr et al., "Race, Class, and Gender Differences in Substance Abuse"; National Institute on Drug Abuse, "Strategic Plan on Reducing Health Disparities," July 2004, http://www.nida.nih.gov/PDF/HealthDispPlan.pdf.

54. Borrell et al., "Perception of General and Oral Health."

55. Andrew A. Zekeri, "African American College Students' Perceptions of Psycho-social Factors Influencing Racial Disparities in Health," *College Student Journal* 40, no. 4 (2006): 901–915.

56. Very early in his presidency, Joe Biden pledged to address environmental racism, signing an executive order that directly addressed relief for communities disproportionately affected by pollution (Rebecca Hersher, "Hope and Skepticism as Biden Promises to Address Environmental Racism, Connecticut Public Radio, January 29, 2021, https://www.wnpr.org/post/hope-and-skepticism-biden-promises-address-environmental-racism).

57. Robert D. Bullard, ed., *Unequal Protection: Environmental Justice and Communities of Color* (San Francisco: Sierra Club Books, 1997).

58. Robert D. Bullard et al., "Toxic Wastes and Race at Twenty: 1987–2007," United Church of Christ Justice and Witness Ministries, 2007, http://www.ucc.org/assets/pdfs/toxic20.pdf.

59. David Pace, "Blacks, Poor Most Likely to Breathe Polluted Air," December 14, 2005, http://www.deseretnews.com/article/635168651/blacks-poor-most-likely-to-breathe-polluted-air.html.

60. Miranda R. Jones, Ana V. Diez-Roux, Anjum Hajat, Kiarri N. Kershaw, Marie S. O'Neill, Eliseo Guallar, Wendy S. Post, Joel D. Kaufman, and Ana Navas-Acien, "Race/Ethnicity, Residential Segregation, and Exposure to Ambient Air Pollution: The Multi-Ethnic Study of Atherosclerosis (MESA)," *American Journal of Public Health* 104, no. 11 (2014): 2130–2137.

61. Merrit Kennedy, "Lead-Laced Water in Flint: A Step-by-Step Look at the Makings of a Crisis," *National Public Radio*, April 20, 2016, http://www.npr.org/sections/thetwo-way/2016/04/20/465545378/lead-laced-water-in-flint-a-step-by-step-look-at-the-makings-of-a-crisis.

62. Ibid.

63. "What Is Lupus?" Lupus Foundation of America, October 20, 2020, https://www.lupus.org/resources/what-is-lupus.

64. "Lupus Facts and Statistics," Lupus Foundation of America, October 6, 2016, https://www.lupus.org/resources/lupus-facts-and-statistics#:~:text=The%20Lupus%20Foundation%20of%20America,have%20a%20form%20of%20lupus.

65. "What Is Lupus?"

66. "Racial and Ethnic Bias in Health Care," Lupus Foundation of America, August 13, 2020, https://www.lupus.org/resources/racial-and-ethnic-bias-in-health-care.

67. "Covid-19 Pandemic Widens Disparities Among People with Rheumatic Diseases, Lupus," Lupus Foundation of America, July 14, 2020, https://www.lupus.org/news/covid19-pandemic-widens-disparities-among-people-with-rheumatic-diseases-lupus.

68. Agency for Toxic Substances and Disease Registry, ATSDR Case Studies in Environmental Medicine: Principles of Pediatric Environmental Health, U.S. Department of Health and Human Services, February 15, 2012, https://www.atsdr.cdc.gov/csem/ped_env_health/docs/ped_env_health.pdf.

69. Roman Bystrianyk, "Learning and Developmental Disabilities Linked to Environmental Toxins," *Health Sentinel*, September 25, 2008, http://www.healthsentinel.com/joomla/index.php?option=com_content&view=article&id=2442; Dan Orzech, "Chemical Kids: Environmental Toxins and Child Development," *Social Work Today* 7, no. 2 (2007): 37, http://www.socialworktoday.com/archive/marapr2007p37.shtml; Jiyeon Park, Ann P. Turnbull, and H. Rutherford Turnbull, "Impacts of Poverty on

Quality of Life in Families of Children with Disabilities," *Exceptional Children* 68, no. 2 (2002): 151–170.

70. Joseph Ruzich, "Special Education Programs Begin to Feel Budget Pinch," *Chicago Tribune*, March 8, 2011, http://articles.chicagotribune.com/2011-03-08/news/ct-x-s-special-ed-cuts-0309-20110309_1_special-education-students-with-severe-disabilities-teachers-end; Ronald J. Sider, "Making Schools Work for the Rich and Poor," *Christian Century*, August 25, 1999, 802–809, http://www.religion-online.org/showarticle.asp?title=702.

71. Beth Harry and Mary G. Anderson, "The Disproportionate Placement of African American Males in Special Education Programs: A Critique of the Process," *Journal of Negro Education* 63, no. 4 (1995): 602–619; Carla O'Connor, Carla and Sonia DeLuca Fernandez, "Race, Class, and Disproportionality: Reevaluating the Relationship Between Poverty and Special Education Placement," *Educational Researcher* 35, no. 6 (2006): 6–11.

72. Kisha Holden, Brian McGregor, Poonam Thandi, Edith Fresh, Kameron Sheats, Allyson Belton, Gail Mattox, and David Satcher, "Toward Culturally Centered Integrative Care for Addressing Mental Health Disparities Among Ethnic Minorities," *Psychological Services* 11, no. 4 (2014): 357–368.

73. The World Health Organization reports that "three-quarters of the worlds' neuropsychiatric disorders are in low-income or low-middle income countries" and that depression is significantly undertreated in poorer nations. Tina Rosenberg, "Fighting Depression, One Village at a Time," *New York Times*, July 18, 2012, http://opinionator.blogs.nytimes.com/2012/07/18/fighting-depression-one-village-at-a-time/. For the full report, see *Scaling Up Care for Mental, Neurological, and Substance Use Disorders*, World Health Organization, 2008, http://apps.who.int/iris/bitstream/10665/43809/1/9789241596206_eng.pdf. See also US Department of Health and Human Services. *Mental Health: Culture, Race, and Ethnicity—A Supplement to Mental Health: A Report of the Surgeon General* (Rockville, MD: Center for Mental Health Services, 2001), http://www.surgeongeneral.gov/library/mentalhealth/cre/sma-01-3613.pdf.

74. Liam Downey and Marieke Van Willigen, "Environmental Stressors: The Mental Health Impacts of Living Near Industrial Activity," *Journal of Health and Science Behavior* 46, no. 3 (2005): 289–305.

75. Norm Oliver, "Understanding Health Disparities: Race, Class, or Both?" Oliver's Twist, 2009, http://healthdisparities.virginia.edu/2009/05/13/race_class_or_both/.

76. Liam Downey, "US Metropolitan-Area Variation in Environmental Inequality Outcomes," *Urban Studies* 44, no. 5–6 (2007): 953–977.

77. These issues are further complicated by a growing body of research that addresses health disparities through the lens of the social construction of race (rather than treating race as a biological construction as it relates to health and medicine). See, for instance, Martin Donohoe, ed., *Public Health and Social Justice Reader* (San Francisco: Jossey-Bass, 2012); Camera Phyllis Jones et al., "Using 'Socially Assigned Race' to Probe White Advantages in Health Status," *Ethnicity & Disease* 18, no. 4 (2008): 496–504; Jesse Daniels and Amy J. Schulz, "Constructing Whiteness in Health Disparities Research," in *Gender, Race, Class, and Health*, eds. Amy J. Schulz and Leith Mullings (San Francisco: Jossey-Bass, 2005), 89–127. For recent work on the broader notion of race as a social construct, see Anne Fausto-Sterling's review of books by Richard C. Francis (*Epigenetics: The Ultimate Mystery of Inheritance*), Ann Morning (*The Nature of Race: How Scientists Think and Teach about Human Difference*), and Dorothy Roberts (*Fatal Invention: How Science, Politics, and Big Business Re-create Race in the Twenty-first Century*) in the May–June 2012 issue of *Boston Review*, http://www.bostonreview.net/BR37.3/anne_fausto-sterling_biology_race.php.

78. Erin White, "Whites Tend to Sleep Better Than Asians, Blacks, and Hispanics: Study Shows Differences in Length, Quality of Sleep, and Daytime Sleepiness by Race," Northwestern University, June 13, 2012, http://www.northwestern.edu/newscenter/stories/2012/06/carnethon-sleep-race.html.

79. Serge Brand et al., "High Exercise Levels are Related to Favorable Sleep Patterns and Psychological Functioning in Adolescents: A Comparison of Athletes and Controls," *Journal of Adolescent Health* 46, no. 2 (2010): 133–141.

80. See Kathleen McCann, "Ongoing Study Continues to Show That Extra Sleep Improves Athletic Performance," American Academy of Sleep Medicine, 2008, http://www.aasmnet.org/Articles.aspx?id=954; Elizabeth K. Gray and David Watson, "General and Specific Traits of Personality and Their Relation to Sleep and Academic Performance," *Journal of Personality* 70, no. 2 (2002): 177–206; Mickey T. Trockel, Michael D. Barnes, and Dennis L. Egget, "Health-Related Variables and Academic Performance Among First-Year College Students: Implications for Sleep and Other Behaviors," *Journal of American College Health* 49, no. 3 (2000): 125–131; Harvard University Medical School, "Why Sleep Matters," http://healthysleep.med.harvard.edu/healthy/matters.

81. "Obese by Race and Ethnicity," Kaiser Family Foundation, n.d., https://www.kff.org/other/state-indicator/adult-obesity-by-re/?currentTimeframe=0&sortModel=%7B%22colId%22:%22Location%22,%22sort%22:%22asc%22%7D

82. David S. Freedman, "Obesity—United States, 1988–2008," Centers for Disease Control and Prevention, January 14, 2011, https://www.cdc.gov/mmwr/preview/mmwrhtml/su6001a15.htm#:~:text=From%201976%2D%2D1980%20to,by%20sex%20and%20age%20group.

83. "Prevalence of Childhood Obesity in the United States," Centers for Disease Control and Prevention, February 11, 2021, https://www.cdc.gov/obesity/data/childhood.html#:~:text=Prevalence%20of%20Childhood%20Obesity%20in%20the%20United%20States&text=For%20children%20and%20adolescents%20aged,to%2019%2Dyear%2Dolds.

84. Ibid.

85. US Department of Agriculture, "Food Security in the United States: Definitions of Hunger and Food Security," November 15, 2010, http://www.ers.usda.gov/briefing/foodsecurity/labels.htm#new_labels.

86. "Facts about Poverty and Hunger in America," n.d., https://www.feedingamerica.org/hunger-in-america/facts.

87. Ibid.

88. US Department of Agriculture, "National School Lunch Program Fact Sheet," March 20, 2019, https://www.fns.usda.gov/nslp/nslp-fact-sheet.

89. In some areas, such as Chicago, school meals were not limited to children during the Covid-19 pandemic ("School Meals and Nutrition," Chicago Public Schools, n.d., https://www.cps.edu/services-and-supports/school-meals-and-nutrition/).

90. Kenzi Abou-Sabe, Cynthia McFadden, Jake Whitman, and Kevin Monahan, "Food Banks Struggling to Feed Hungry During Covid Look Forward to Biden's Fixes to SNAP Program," *NBC News*, February 7, 2021, https://www.nbcnews.com/news/us-news/food-banks-struggling-feed-hungry-during-covid-look-forward-biden-n1256874.

91. "Delivering Food and Services," Feeding America, n.d., https://www.feedingamerica.org/our-work/food-bank-network.

92. Amy Goldstein, "Hunger a Growing Problem in America, USDA Reports," *Washington Post*, November 17, 2009, http://www.washingtonpost.com/wp-dyn/content/article/2009/11/16/AR2009111601598.html; "Soup Kitchens," in *Encyclopedia of Food and Culture*, ed. Solomon H. Katz, vol. 3; Gale Cengage, http://eNotes.com, August 26, 2006, http://www.enotes.com/food-encyclopedia/soup-kitchens.

93. "Cheap Eats for Hard Times: The Five Most Unhealthful Fast Food 'Value Menu' Items," The Cancer Project, Winter 2008, http://www.cancerproject.org/PDFs/Five%20 Worst%20Value%20Menu%20Items%20Report.pdf; Mary Kane, "The Real Value of the Fast Food 'Dollar Menu' in a Recession," *Washington Independent*, May 12, 2009, http://washingtonindependent.com/42485/the-real-value-of-the-fast-food-dollar-menu-in-a-recession.

94. "If You Build It, They May Not Come," *Economist*, July 7, 2011, http://www.economist.com/node/18929190. For food deserts in the United States, visit the USDA's interactive map at https://www.ers.usda.gov/data-products/food-access-research-atlas/.

95. Andrew Soergel, "Millions of Food Desert Dwellers Struggle to Get Fresh Groceries," *U.S. News & World Report*, December 7, 2015, http://www.usnews.com/news/articles/2015/12/07/millions-of-food-desert-dwellers-struggle-to-get-fresh-groceries.

96. Appalachia Service Project, *An Overview of Poverty in Appalachia*, 2009, http://asphome.org/learn_about_appalachia/overview_of_poverty.

97. Pew Research Center, "Beyond Distrust: How Americans View Their Government," November 23, 2015, http://www.people-press.org/2015/11/23/2-general-opinions-about-the-federal-government/.

98. Carolyn Lochhead, "Fat Fight Turns to a New Front: School Lunches," *Houston Chronicle*, February 10, 2010, http://www.chron.com/news/houston-texas/article/Fat-fight-turns-to-a-new-front-school-lunches-1711419.php.

99. "First Travel-Related Case of 2019 Novel Coronavirus Detected in United States," Centers for Disease Control and Prevention, January 21, 2019, https://www.cdc.gov/media/releases/2020/p0121-novel-coronavirus-travel-case.html

100. "Timeline—In His Own Words: Trump and the Coronavirus," *Reuters*, October 2, 2020, https://www.reuters.com/article/us-health-coronavirus-usa-trump-comments/timeline-in-his-own-words-trump-and-the-coronavirus-idUSKBN26N0U5.

101. Trump would later admit to journalist Bob Woodward that he knew that the virus was highly contagious but sought not to cause panic in the public ("Trump Deliberately Played Down Virus, Woodward Book Says," *BBC*, September 10, 2020, https://www.bbc.com/news/world-us-canada-54094559).

102. "COVID-19 Racial and Ethnic Health Disparities," Centers for Disease Control and Prevention, December 10, 2020, https://www.cdc.gov/coronavirus/2019-ncov/community/health-equity/racial-ethnic-disparities/increased-risk-illness.html.

103. Ibid.

104. Ibid.

105. Lily Rubin-Miller, Christopher Alban, Samantha Artiga, and Sean Sullivan, "COVID-19 Racial Disparities in Testing, Infection, Hospitalization, and Death: Analysis of Epic Patient Data," Kaiser Family Foundation, September 16, 2020, https://www.kff.org/coronavirus-covid-19/issue-brief/covid-19-racial-disparities-testing-infection-hospitalization-death-analysis-epic-patient-data/.

106. Sandro Galea et al., "Estimated Deaths Attributable to Social Factors in the United States," *American Journal of Public Health* 101, no. 8 (2011): 1456–1465, quote 1462.

107. The limit is $2,839 per month for a family of four ("SNAP Eligibility," US Department of Agriculture, December 31, 2020, https://www.fns.usda.gov/snap/recipient/eligibility).

108. Supplemental Nutrition Assistance Program, Food and Nutrition Service, November 9, 2012, http://www.fns.usda.gov/pd/34SNAPmonthly.htm.

109. Lauren Hall, "A Closer Look at Who Benefits from SNAP: State-by-State Fact Sheets," Center on Budget and Policy Priorities, January 12, 2021, https://www.cbpp.org/research/food-assistance/a-closer-look-at-who-benefits-from-snap-state-by-state-fact-sheets#Alabama.

110. Philip Rucker, "Gingrich Promises to Slash Taxes, Calls Obama 'Food Stamp President,'" *Washington Post*, May 13, 2011, http://www.washingtonpost.com/politics/gingrich-promises-to-slash-taxes-calls-obama-food-stamp-president/2011/05/13/AF9Q602G_story.html.

111. Jessie Daniels, "Newt Gingrich Calls President Obama 'Food Stamp President,' Bristles at Charges of Racism," *Racism Review*, May 15, 2011, http://www.racismreview.com/blog/2011/05/15/newt-food-stamp-president/.

112. The effects of race-based political messages need not be related to any intent. See Charlton D. McIlwain and Stephen M. Caliendo, *Race Appeal: How Candidates Invoke Race in U.S. Political Campaigns* (Philadelphia: Temple University Press, 2011).

Chapter 8: Gender

1. The Lilly Ledbetter Fair Pay Act of 2009 extends the amount of time a person has to file an equal-pay discrimination lawsuit, http://www.gpo.gov/fdsys/pkg/PLAW-111publ2/html/PLAW-111publ2.htm.

2. October 16, 2012, Debate Transcript, Commission on Presidential Debates, http://www.debates.org/index.php?page=october-1-2012-the-second-obama-romney-presidential-debate.

3. Susana Schrobsdorff, "Romney's Binders: The Meme Women Love to Hate," *Time*, October 19, 2012, http://ideas.time.com/2012/10/19/romneys-binders-the-meme-women-love-to-hate/.

4. Reports immediately after the debate suggested that the story was not even accurate. A Boston-based journalist noted that a bipartisan interest group, MassGAP, which was formed before the 2002 gubernatorial election, put more women in leadership positions in the Massachusetts government. That group compiled the "binder" and presented it to Governor Romney. David S. Bernstein, "Mind the Binder," *(Boston) Phoenix*, October 16, 2012, http://blog.thephoenix.com/BLOGS/talkingpolitics/archive/2012/10/16/mind-the-binder.aspx.

5. Leila Schochet, "The Child Care Crisis is Keeping Women Out of the Workforce," Center for American Progress, March 28, 2019, https://www.americanprogress.org/issues/early-childhood/reports/2019/03/28/467488/child-care-crisis-keeping-women-workforce/.

6. There is a rich scholarly literature on the politics of housework. See, for instance, Sampson Lee Blair and Daniel T. Lichter, "Measuring the Division of Household Labor: Gender Segregation of Housework Among American Couples," *Journal of Family Issues* 12, no. 1 (1991): 91–113; Mick Cunningham, "Influences of Women's Employment on the Gendered Division of Household Labor over the Life Course: Evidence from a 31-Year Panel Study," *Journal of Family Issues* 28, no. 3 (2007): 422–444; Roderic Beaujot and Jianye Liu, "Models of Time Use in Paid and Unpaid Work," *Journal of Family Issues* 7 (2005): 924–946; Theodore N. Greenstein, "Gender Ideology and Perceptions of the Fairness of the Division of Household Labor: Effects on Marital Quality," *Social Forces* 74, no. 3 (1996): 1029–1042; Michael Braun et al., "Perceived Inequality in the Gendered Division of Household Labor," *Journal of Marriage and Family* 70, no. 5 (2008): 1145–1156.

7. For a discussion of attempts in Great Britain to improve flexible time policies for both men and women, see Amelia Gentelman, "Rebalancing Child-Care Equations," *New York Times*, November 20, 2012, http://www.nytimes.com/2012/11/21/world/europe/21iht-letter21.html.

8. Carolyn B. Maloney and Charles E. Schumer, *Women and the Economy 2010: 25 Years of Progress but Challenges Remain*, US Congress Joint Economic Committee,

August 2010, http://www.jec.senate.gov/public/?a=Files.Serve&File_id=8be22cb0-8ed0-4a1a-841b-aa91dc55fa81. See also Liza Mundy, "Women, Money, and Power," *Time*, March 26, 2012, http://www.time.com/time/magazine/article/0,9171,2109140,00.html.

9. Leila Schochet, "The Child Care Crisis is Keeping Women Out of the Workforce."

10. While this conceptualization is still prevalent, there is notable criticism of its limitations. Some writers have argued that the binary distinction relating to sex is also socially constructed, and consequently the convenient sex-gender binary is not an adequate tool for understanding that construction (Diane Richardson, "Conceptualizing Gender," in *Introducing Gender and Women's Studies*, eds. Diane Richardson and Victoria Robinson, 3rd ed. [New York: Palgrave Macmillan, 2007], 3–19).

11. Celeste Mora, "What Is the Singular They, and Why Should I Use It?" *Grammerly Blog*, May 12, 2020, https://www.grammarly.com/blog/use-the-singular-they/.

12. Similarly, the term *heterosexism* (or *heteronormativity*) refers to the hegemonic norm that leads individuals to assume that people are heterosexual unless they know otherwise. For instance, sex-segregated restrooms are grounded in the premise that everyone is heterosexual; otherwise, there is little point in ensuring that men and women do not see one another in a state of undress. There is nothing particularly malicious or individualistic about this tendency, or the fact that most laws centering on couples are rooted in similar assumptions. The more common term *homophobia* refers to resentment, animosity, or hatred of folks who are not heterosexual. Such individual-level attitudes are rooted in heterosexism to the extent that the belief that heterosexuals are normal and those who are not are deviant, but the constructs should be considered separately.

13. For an interesting discussion about the difference between sexism and misogyny in the context of an Australian dictionary's decision to shift the definition of the latter to include "entrenched prejudice against women" (rather than only hatred of them), see Naomi Wolf et al., "Sexism and Misogyny: What's the Difference?" *Guardian*, October 17, 2012, http://www.guardian.co.uk/commentisfree/2012/oct/17/difference-between-sexism-and-misogyny. *New York Times* columnist Nicholas Kristof has struggled with the difference between these concepts and how each contributes to violence against women in a global context. Nicholas D. Kristof, "Misogyny vs. Sexism," *New York Times*, April 7, 2008, http://kristof.blogs.nytimes.com/2008/04/07/misogyny-vs-sexism/.

14. Olga Khazan, "The Lasting Harm of Trump-Style Sexism," *Atlantic*, November 4, 2016, http://www.theatlantic.com/science/archive/2016/11/how-trump-style-words-hurt/506456/; Jia Tolentino, "Donald Trump's Unconscious, Unending Sexism," *New Yorker*, October 10, 2016, http://www.newyorker.com/culture/jia-tolentino/donald-trumps-unconscious-unending-sexism.

15. Franklin Foer, "Donald Trump Hates Women: It's the One Position He's Never Changed," http://Slate.com, March 24, 2016, http://www.slate.com/articles/news_and_politics/politics/2016/03/donald_trump_has_one_core_philosophy_misogyny.html; Michael Barbaro and Megan Twohey, "Crossing the Line: How Donald Trump Behaved with Women in Private," *New York Times*, May 14, 2016, http://www.nytimes.com/2016/05/15/us/politics/donald-trump-women.html.

16. For comprehensive lists of Donald Trump's sexist and misogynistic comments, see Ritu Prasad, "How Trump Talks About Women—And Does It Matter?" *BBC News*, November 29, 2019, https://www.bbc.com/news/world-us-canada-50563106; Nina Easton, "The History of Donald Trump's Insults to Women," *Fortune*, August 9, 2015, http://fortune.com/2015/08/09/trump-insult-women-history/; Claire Cohen, "Donald Trump Sexism Tracker: Every Offensive Comment in One Place," *Telegraph(UK)*, November 9, 2016, http://www.telegraph.co.uk/women/politics/donald-trump-

sexism-tracker-every-offensive-comment-in-one-place/; and Libby Nelson, "Donald Trump's History of Misogyny, Sexism, and Harassment: A Comprehensive Review," http://Vox.com, October 12, 2016, http://www.vox.com/2016/10/8/13110734/ donald-trump-leaked-audio-recording-billy-bush-sexism.

17. David A. Fahrenthold, "Trump Recorded Having Extremely Lewd Conversation About Women in 2005," *Washington Post*, October 8, 2016, https://www.washingtonpost. com/politics/trump-recorded-having-extremely-lewd-conversation-about-women-in-2005/2016/10/07/3b9ce776-8cb4-11e6-bf8a-3d26847eeed4_story.html.

18. Lorraine Ali, "'Such a Nasty Woman': Trump's Debate Dig Becomes a Feminist Rallying Cry," *Los Angeles Times*, October 20, 2016, http://www.latimes. com/entertainment/tv/la-et-nasty-woman-trump-clinton-debate-janet-jackson-20161020-snap-story.html.

19. ABC News Analysis Desk and Paul Blake, "Election 2016 National Exit Poll Results and Analysis," *ABC News*, November 9, 2016, http://abcnews.go.com/Politics/ election-2016-national-exit-poll-results-analysis/story?id=43368675.

20. "Exit Polls," http://CNN.com, November 23, 2016, http://www.cnn.com/ election/results/exit-polls.

21. Ibid.

22. Although Hillary Clinton won more than 2 million more votes than Donald Trump, she fell short of an Electoral College victory, which is the mechanism by which presidents are chosen in the United States. Gabriel Debenedetti, Kyle Cheney, and Nolan D. McCaskill, "Clinton's Lead in the Popular Vote Surpasses 2 Million," http://Politico.com, November 23, 2016, http://www.politico.com/story/2016/11/ clinton-lead-popular-vote-2016-231790.

23. Susan Chira, "Vote Highlighted a Gender Gap, with Both Sides Feeling They've Lost Ground," *New York Times*, November 9, 2016, http://www.nytimes. com/2016/11/10/us/politics/gender-gap-campaign.html.

24. Senator Harris unsuccessfully ran for the Democratic Party nomination, along with many other women (most of whom were also US Senators). Much discussion centered on the way sexism was at work during that nominating contest, as well ("Was It Sexism?" *Politico*, March 6, 2020, https://www.politico.com/news/magazine/2020/03/06/ what-will-it-take-for-american-to-elect-a-woman-president-122644).

25. Erin Delmore, "This Is How Women Voters Decided the 2020 Election," *NBC News*, November 13, 2020, https://www.nbcnews.com/know-your-value/feature/how-women-voters-decided-2020-election-ncna1247746.

26. Ibid.

27. Famously, so-called "gender reveal parties," which can feature creative explosions of pink or blue dust, have led to injuries and deaths in recent years (Rosie Blunt, "The Dangers—Physical and Psycological—of Gender Reveal Parties," *BBC News*, October 30, 2019, https://www.bbc.com/news/world-us-canada-50207452).

28. Homa Khaleeli, "Jessica Valenti: Pioneering Blogger Whose Online Activism Dragged Feminism into the 21st Century," *Guardian*, March 7, 2011, http://www. guardian.co.uk/books/2011/mar/08/jessica-valenti-100-women.

29. https://jessicavalenti.medium.com/.

30. "A Big Think Interview with Jessica Valenti," *Big Think*, December 21, 2009, http://bigthink.com/ideas/17880.

31. Ibid.

32. "Interview with Jessica Valenti: Feminist Writer and Founder of http://Feministing. com," *The Daily Femme!* June 16, 2010.

33. The effects of such messages can be observed in (and are then reinforced by) much of reality television programming. For a thorough treatment, see Jennifer L. Pozner, *Reality Bites Back: The Troubling Truth About Guilty Pleasure TV* (Berkeley, CA: Seal Press, 2010).

34. The literature—both scholarly and popular—is extensive in this area. See, for example, Lori Baker-Sperry and Liz Grauerholz, "The Pervasiveness of the Feminine Beauty Ideal in Children's Fairy Tales," *Gender & Society* 17, no. 5 (2003): 711–726; Elizabeth Bell, Lynda Haas, and Laura Sells, eds., *From Mouse to Mermaid: The Politics of Film, Gender and Culture* (Bloomington: Indiana University Press, 2008); Donald Haase, ed., *Fairy Tales and Feminism: New Approaches* (Detroit: Wayne State University Press, 2004); U. C. Knoepflmacher, *Ventures into Childland: Victorians, Fairy Tales, and Femininity* (Chicago: University of Chicago Press, 1998); Karen E. Rowe, "Feminism and Fairy Tales," *Women's Studies: An Interdisciplinary Journal* 6, no. 3 (1979): 237–257; Ella Westland, "Cinderella in the Classroom: Children's Responses to Gender Roles in Fairy-tales," *Gender and Education* 5, no. 3 (1993): 237–249.

35. Amy Siskind, "How Feminism Became the F-Word," *The Daily Beast*, January 11, 2009, http://www.thedailybeast.com/articles/2009/01/11/how-feminism-became-the-f-word.html.

36. For a study about how men and women come to embrace feminism, see Rebecca L. Warner, "Does the Sex of Your Child Matter? Support for Feminism Among Women and Men in the United States and Canada," *Journal of Marriage and Family* 5, no. 4 (1991): 1051–1056.

37. For a thoughtful, concise overview of different aspects of feminism, see Jarrah Hodge, "Feminisms 101," *Gender Focus*, November 13, 2010, http://www.gender-focus.com/tag/types-of-feminism/.

38. Martha Rampton, "The Three Waves of Feminism," *Pacific* 41, no. 2 (2008), http://www.pacificu.edu/magazine_archives/2008/fall/echoes/feminism.cfm.

39. Ibid.

40. Laura Mulvey, "Visual Pleasure and Narrative Cinema," *Screen* 16, no. 3 (1975): 6–18, http://imlportfolio.usc.edu/ctcs505/mulveyVisualPleasureNarrativeCinema.pdf.

41. An interesting element of this is the notion of the Bechdel Test, which is "a measure of women's dialogue in films" that considers the degree to which women are functioning as a central presence (see, for instance, Scott Selisker. 2015. "The Bechdel Test and the Social Form of Character Networks," *New Literary History* 46, 3: 505–523).

42. For a thoughtful, accessible elaboration on this dynamic, see Susan J. Douglas, "Girls 'n' Spice: All Things Nice?" in *Mass Politics: The Politics of Popular Culture*, ed. Daniel M. Shea (New York: St. Martin's/Worth, 1999), 45–48.

43. For examples of work that highlights the gaps in second wave feminist thought, see, for instance, Patricia Hill Collins, "The Social Construction of Black Feminist Thought," *Signs* 14, no. 4 (1989): 745–773; Patricia Hill Collins, *Black Feminist Thought: Knowledge, Consciousness, and the Politics of Empowerment* (New York: Routledge, 1999); Alma M. Garcia, ed., *Chicana Feminist Thought: The Basic Historical Writings* (New York: Routledge, 1997).

44. For example, black women are disproportionately underrepresented in corporate America. A recent study found that black women in that context face more criticism than do white women or black men: what the authors refer to as "double jeopardy." Ashleigh Shelby Rosette and Robert W. Livingston, "Failure Is Not an Option for Black Women: Effects of Organizational Performance on Leaders with Single Versus Dual-Subordinate Identities," *Journal of Experimental Social Psychology* 48, no. 5 (2012): 1162–1167.

45. Susan Thistle, *From Marriage to the Market: The Transformation of Women's Lives and Work* (Berkeley: University of California Press, 2006).

46. "Women in the Workforce—United States: Quick Take," *Catalyst*, October 14, 2020, https://www.catalyst.org/research/women-in-the-workforce-united-states/.

47. Elizabeth Ty Wilde, Lily Batchelder, and David T. Ellwood, "The Mommy Track Divides: The Impact of Childbearing on Wages of Women of Differing Skill Levels," National Bureau of Economic Research Working Paper no. 16582,

December 2010, http://www.nber.org/papers/w16582; Rebecca Korzec, "Working on the 'Mommy-Track': Motherhood and Women Lawyers," *Hastings Women's Law Journal* 8 (1997): 117–126; Mary C. Noonan and Mary E. Corcoran, "The Mommy Track and Partnership: Temporary Delay or Dead End?" *Annals of the American Academy of Political and Social Science* 596, no. 1 (2004): 130–150; E. Jeffrey Hill et al., "Beyond the Mommy Track: The Influence of New-Concept Part-Time Work for Professional Women on Work and Family," *Journal of Family and Economic Issues* 25, no. 1 (2004): 121–136; Paula England, "Gender Inequality in Labor Markets: The Role of Motherhood and Segregation," *Social Politics* 12, no. 2 (2005): 264–288.

48. Paternity leave is common in many European democracies, but not in the United States. Lisa Belkin, "Should Fathers Get Paid Paternity Leave?" *New York Times*, January 28, 2010, http://parenting.blogs.nytimes.com/2010/01/28/paid-paternity-leave-in-britain/; Jens Hansegard, "For Paternity Leave, Sweden Asks If Two Months Is Enough," *Wall Street Journal*, July 31, 2012, http://online.wsj.com/article/SB10000872396390444226904577561100020336384.html. Although the Family and Medical Leave Act of 1993 allows fathers to take up to 12 weeks away from work without being fired, that time is unpaid, and few families can afford to take advantage of it. "Leave Benefits: Family & Medical Leave Act," US Department of Labor, http://www.dol.gov/dol/topic/benefits-leave/fmla.htm#.ULjwauOe8f8.

49. In 2013, Facebook chief operating officer Sheryl Sandberg wrote a best-selling book designed to encourage women and men to think differently about the oft repeated rallying cry of the second-wave feminist movement that women can "have it all" (at the office and at home). In *Lean In*, Sandberg describes the current state of women in corporate America and encourages both women and men to work together in both settings for greater gender equity.

50. See Kim V. L. England, "Suburban Pink Collar Ghettos: The Spatial Entrapment of Women?" *Annals of the Association of American Geographers* 83, no. 2 (2005): 225–242; Joseph H. Michalski, "Resource Structuralism and Gender Economic Inequality," *Michigan Sociological Review* 18 (2004): 23–63; England, "Gender Inequality in Labor Markets"; Tony Tam, "Sex Segregation and Occupational Gender Inequality in the United States: Devaluation or Specialized Training?" *American Journal of Sociology* 102, no. 6 (1997): 1652–1692.

51. Sarah Anderson, "Five Charts that Show Why We Need to Tackle Gender Justice and Poverty Together," Institute for Policy Studies, May 17, 2018, https://ips-dc.org/five-charts-show-need-tackle-gender-justice-poverty-together/.

52. Grant Suneson, "What Are the 25 Lowest Paying Jobs in the US? Women Usually Hold Them," *USA Today*, April 4, 2019, https://www.usatoday.com/story/money/2019/04/04/25-lowest-paying-jobs-in-us-2019-includes-cooking-cleaning/39264277/.

53. Olga Alonso-Villar and Coral del Rio Otero, "The Occupational Segregation of Black Women in the United States: A Look at Its Evolution from 1940 to 2010," ECINEQ, Society for the Study of Economic Inequality, Working Paper 304, 2015, http://econpapers.repec.org/paper/inqinqwps/ecineq2013-304.htm.

54. Ben Casselman, "Why Women Are No Longer Catching Up to Men on Pay," http://FiveThirtyEight.com, August 19, 2016, http://fivethirtyeight.com/features/why-women-are-no-longer-catching-up-to-men-on-pay/.

55. Johanna Brenner, "Feminist Political Discourses: Radical Versus Liberal Approaches to the Feminization of Poverty and Comparable Worth," *Gender & Society* 1, no. 4 (1987): 447–465; Martha E. Gimenez, "The Feminization of Poverty: Myth or Reality?" *Critical Sociology* 25, no. 2–3 (1999): 336–351.

56. Robin Bleiweis, Diana Boesch, and Alexandra Cawthorne Gaines, "The Basic Facts about Women in Poverty," Center for American Progress, August 3, 2020, https://www.americanprogress.org/issues/women/reports/2020/08/03/488536/

basic-facts-women-poverty/#:~:text=In%20the%20United%20States%2C%20 more,or%2021.4%20million%E2%80%94were%20women.

57. Keiser Family Foundation, "Medicaid's Role for Women," Kaiser Family Foundation, March 28, 2019, https://www.kff.org/womens-health-policy/fact-sheet/medicaids-role-for-women/.

58. Robin Bleiweis, Diana Boesch, and Alexandra Cawthorne Gaines, "The Basic Facts about Women in Poverty."

59. Amanda Fins, "National Snapshot: Poverty Among Women & Families, 2019," National Women's Law Center, n.d., https://nwlc-ciw49tixgw5lbab.stackpathdns.com/wp-content/uploads/2019/10/PovertySnapshot2019.pdf.

60. Samuel Stebbins and Thomas C. Frohlich, "The Poverty Rates for Every Group in the U.S.: From Age and Sex to Citizenship Status," *USA Today*, November 6, 2019, https://www.usatoday.com/story/money/2019/11/06/united-states-poverty-rate-for-every-group/40546247/.

61. Richard R. Peterson, *Women, Work, and Divorce* (Albany: State University of New York Press, 1989); Teresa A. Mauldin, "Economic Consequences of Divorce or Separation Among Women in Poverty," *Journal of Divorce and Remarriage* 14, no. 3–4 (1991): 163–178; James B. McLindon, "Separate but Unequal: The Economic Disaster of Divorce for Women and Children," *Family Law Quarterly* 21 (1987–1988): 351–409; Terry J. Arendell, "Women and the Economics of Divorce in the Contemporary United States," *Signs* 13, no. 1 (1987): 121–135.

62. "Poverty Among Americans Aged 65 and Older," Congressional Research Service, July 1, 2019, https://fas.org/sgp/crs/misc/R45791.pdf.

63. Tim Lemke, "How Much is the Average Social Security Check?" *The Balance*, January 9, 2021, https://www.thebalance.com/how-much-is-the-average-social-security-check-4774723.

64. Ibid.

65. Teresa Ghilarducci, Martha Susana Jaimes, and Anthony Webb, "Old-Age Poverty: Single Women & Widows & a Lack of Retirement Security," Schwartz Center for Economic Policy Analysis, August 2018, https://www.economicpolicyresearch.org/images/Retirement_Project/Single-Women-Widows-PN-edited-12.21-final.pdf.

66. Cathleen D. Zick and Ken Smith, "Patterns of Economic Change Surrounding the Death of a Spouse," *Journal of Gerontology: Social Sciences* 46, no. 6 (1991): 310–320. For a concise review of the literature on this topic, see Youngae Lee and Jinkook Lee, "The Poverty of Widows: How Do They Become the Poor?" Ohio State University, http://paa2006.princeton.edu/papers/61592.

67. MacLeod, Darrell Montero, and Alan Speer, "America's Changing Attitudes Toward Welfare and Welfare Recipients, 1938–1995," *Journal of Sociology & Social Welfare* 26, no. 2 (1999): 175–186; "83% Favor Work Requirement for Welfare Recipients," Rasmussen Reports, July 18, 2012, http://www.rasmussenreports.com/public_content/business/jobs_employment/july_2012/83_favor_work_requirement_for_welfare_recipients.

68. See Beth Reingold and Adrienne R. Smith, "Welfare Policymaking and Intersections of Race, Ethnicity, and Gender in U.S. State Legislatures," *American Journal of Political Science* 56, no. 1 (2012): 131–147.

69. Alexis Benveniste, "The Fortune 500 Now Has a Record Number of Female CEOs: A Whopping 38," *CNN*, August 4, 2020, https://www.cnn.com/2020/08/04/business/fortune-500-women-ceos/index.html.

70. For example, see Christopher F. Karpowitz, Tali Mendelberg, and Lee Shaker, "Gender Inequality in Deliberative Participation," *American Political Science Review* 106, no. 3 (2012): 533–547; and Katty Kay and Claire Shipman, "The Confidence Gap," *Atlantic*, May 2014, http://www.theatlantic.com/magazine/archive/2014/05/the-confidence-gap/359815/.

71. Margaret Wente, "Gender Parity Trumps Excellence in Science?"*(Toronto) Globe and Mail*, November 25, 2012, http://www.theglobeandmail.com/commentary/gender-parity-trumps-excellence-in-science/article5610999/. Consider, too, this recent report that pinpoints the college-level STEM gender gap to one course: Calculus I. The study showed that men and women lost confidence in their math skills equally in that course, but women were far more likely to be discouraged as a result. Jessica Ellis, Bailey K. Fosdick, and Chris Rasmussen, "Women 1.5 Times More Likely to Leave STEM Pipeline After Calculus Compared to Men: Lack of Mathematical Confidence a Potential Culprit," *PLOS One*, July 13, 2016, http://journals.plos.org/plosone/article?id=10.1371%2Fjournal.pone.0157447.

72. Andrea Pitzer, "U.S. Eugenics Legacy: Ruling on Buck Sterilization Still Stands," *USA Today*, June 24, 2009, http://usatoday30.usatoday.com/news/health/2009-06-23-eugenics-carrie-buck_N.htm.

73. Martha Waggoner, "No Money for Forced Sterilization Victims in North Carolina," *Huffington Post*, June 20, 2012, http://www.huffingtonpost.com/2012/06/27/no-money-for-forced-steri_n_1630417.html.

74. Melissa Schettini Kearney and Phillip B. Levine, "Why Is the Teen Birth Rate in the United States So High and Why Does It Matter?" National Bureau of Economic Research Working Paper no. 17965, March 2012, http://www.nber.org/papers/w17965.

75. Napp Nazworth, "Wheaton College, Catholic University Jointly Sue over Birth Control Mandate," *Christian Post*, July 18, 2012, http://www.christianpost.com/news/wheaton-college-catholic-university-jointly-sue-over-birth-control-mandate-78491/.

76. In the summer of 2020, the US Supreme Court upheld two Trump Administration rules that allowed exemptions for organizations to refrain from offering reproductive health care to women for moral or religious reasons (Katie Keith, "Supreme Court Upholds Broad Exemptions to Contraceptive Mandate—For Now," *Health Affairs*, July 9, 2020, https://www.healthaffairs.org/do/10.1377/hblog20200708.110645/full/.

77. At least in the Catholic case, there is ostensibly a double standard, as drugs such as Viagra that help men with impotence are considered acceptable for health insurers to provide. Church leaders note that such medicines, unlike contraceptives, do not violate Church doctrine because they can be used for procreation. Julie Rovner, "Why Catholic Groups' Health Plans Say No to Contraceptives, Yes to Viagra," *National Public Radio*, February 13, 2012, http://www.npr.org/blogs/health/2012/02/13/146822713/why-catholic-groups-health-plans-say-no-to-contraceptives-yes-to-viagra.

78. Sascha Cohen, "A Brief History of Sexual Harassment in America before Anita Hill," *Time*, April 11, 2016, https://time.com/4286575/sexual-harassment-before-anita-hill/.

79. "Sexual Harassment," U.S. Equal Employment Opportunity Commission, n.d., https://www.eeoc.gov/sexual-harassment

80. Sascha Cohen, "A Brief History of Sexual Harassment in America before Anita Hill."

81. Gurvinder Gill and Imran Rahman-Jones, "Me Too Founder Tarana Burke: Movement Is Not Over," *BBC*, July 9, 2020, https://www.bbc.com/news/newsbeat-53269751.

82. Metoomvmt.org.

83. Timesupnow.org.

84. Alix Langone, "#MeToo and Time's Up Founders Explain the Difference Between the 2 Movements—And How They're Alike," *Time*, March 22, 2018, https://time.com/5189945/whats-the-difference-between-the-metoo-and-times-up-movements/.

85. Glenn Kessler, "Brett Kavanaugh and Allegations of Sexual Misconduct: The Complete List," *The Washington Post*, September 27, 2018, https://www.washingtonpost.com/politics/2018/09/27/brett-kavanaugh-allegations-sexual-misconduct-complete-list/.

86. Deloitte, "The Economic Costs of Sexual Harassment in the Workplace," March 2019, https://www2.deloitte.com/content/dam/Deloitte/au/Documents/Economics/deloitte-au-economic-costs-sexual-harassment-workplace-240320.pdf.

87. Megan Kelly Reid, "A Disaster on Top of a Disaster: How Gender, Race, and Class Shaped the Housing Experiences of Displaced Hurricane Katrina Survivors" (PhD diss., University of Texas, 2011), 58–59, http://repositories.lib.utexas.edu/bitstream/handle/2152/ETD-UT-2011-05-2926/REID-DISSERTATION.pdf.

88. Ibid., 51.

89. For a comprehensive overview of the statistics in this area, see Christianne Corbett, Catherine Hill, and Andresse St. Rose, *Where the Girls Are: The Facts About Gender Equity in Education* (Washington, DC: American Association of University Women, 2008), http://www.aauw.org/research/where-the-girls-are. For a thorough review of the scholarly literature, see Claudia Buchmann, Thomas A. DiPrete, and Anne McDaniel, "Gender Inequalities in Education," *Annual Review of Sociology* 34 (2008): 319–337. For a discussion of differentials with respect to science, technology, and mathematics, see Roland G. Fryer Jr. and Steven D. Levitt, "An Empirical Analysis of the Gender Gap in Mathematics," National Bureau of Economic Research Working Paper no. 15430, October 2009, http://www.nber.org/papers/w15430; Glenn Ellison and Ashley Swanson, "The Gender Gap in Secondary School Mathematics at High Achievement Levels: Evidence from the American Mathematics Competitions," National Bureau of Economic Research Working Paper no. 15238, August 2009; Ismael Ramos and Julia Lambating, "Risk Taking: Gender Differences and Educational Opportunity," *School Science and Mathematics* 96, no. 2 (1996): 94–98, http://www.nber.org/papers/w15238; Gijsbert Stoet and David C. Geary, "Can Stereotype Threat Explain the Gender Gap in Mathematics Performance and Achievement?" *Review of General Psychology* 16, no. 1 (2012): 93–102.

90. The biological element of this is not straightforward. The suggestion that biology is at work is not necessarily sexist. Such evidence of intrinsic skills does not suggest that one sex is "smarter" than the other but rather that there may be developmental differences that manifest in abilities being formed at different rates, particularly at very young ages. The way that we react to those tendencies can create environmental effects that will be important as children grow and develop cognitively. See Buchmann, DiPrete, and McDaniel, "Gender Inequalities in Education," 323–324, for a review.

91. Tamar Lewin, "Boys Are No Match for Girls in Completing High School," *New York Times*, April 19, 2006, http://www.nytimes.com/2006/04/19/education/19graduation.html. However, as noted in Chapter 4, there are significant racial gaps in high school graduation rates.

92. Mark Hugo Lopez and Ana Gonzalez-Barrerra, "Women's College Enrollment Gains Leave Men Behind," Pew Research Center, March 6, 2014, http://www.pewresearch.org/fact-tank/2014/03/06/womens-college-enrollment-gains-leave-men-behind/.

93. Buchmann, DiPrete, and McDaniel, "Gender Inequalities in Education."

94. National Center for Education Statistics, "SAT Scores," US Department of Education, n.d., https://nces.ed.gov/fastfacts/display.asp?id=171; see also Martha Groves, "SAT's Gender Gap Widening," *Los Angeles Times*, August 29, 2001, http://articles.latimes.com/2001/aug/29/news/mn-39684; American Physical Society, "Fighting the Gender Gap: Standardized Tests Are Poor Indicators of Ability in Physics," *AJPS News* 5, no. 5 (1996), http://www.aps.org/publications/apsnews/199607/gender.cfm.

95. National Center for Education Statistics, "SAT Scores"; this gap has persisted for decades, see Jonathan Wai et al., "Sex Differences in the Right Tail of Cognitive Abilities: A 30 Year Examination," *Intelligence* 38 (2010): 412–423. Recent work suggests that the gap may be attributable partly to test anxiety. See Brenda Hannon, "Test Anxiety and Performance-Avoidance Goals Explain Gender Differences in SAT-V, SAT-M, and Overall SAT Scores," *Personality and Individual Differences* 53, no. 7 (2012): 816–820.

96. For a concise review of this literature, see Akira Miyake et al., "Reducing the Gender Achievement Gap in College Science: A Classroom Study of Values Affirmation," *Science* 330, no. 6008 (2010): 1234–1237. One recent study suggests that there

is some inertia related to this trend. Specifically, high-performing students in the sciences were more likely to take more science classes and pursue STEM majors in science classes early in their college careers. See Scott E. Carrell, Marianne E. Page, and James E. West, "Sex and Science: How Professor Gender Perpetuates the Gender Gap," *Quarterly Journal of Economics* 125, no. 3 (2010): 1101–1144.

97. Kate Beckman, "The Gender Pay Gap Starts at the Entry Level and Affects Graduates from All Universities, Data Shows," *Ripplematch*, August 27, 2019, https://ripplematch.com/journal/article/the-gender-pay-gap-starts-at-the-entry-level-and-affects-graduates-from-all-universities-a424a192/; see also Christianne Corbett and Catherine Hill, *Graduating to a Pay Gap* (Washington, DC: American Association of University Women, 2012), http://www.aauw.org/research/graduating-to-a-pay-gap/.

98. Dani Matias, "New Report Says Women Will Soon Be Majority of College-Educated U.S. Workers," *National Public Radio*, June 20, 2019, https://www.npr.org/2019/06/20/734408574/new-report-says-college-educated-women-will-soon-make-up-majority-of-u-s-labor-f.

99. U.S. Census Bureau, "Women Now at the Head of the Class, Lead Men in College Attainment," October 7, 2015, http://blogs.census.gov/2015/10/07/women-now-at-the-head-of-the-class-lead-men-in-college-attainment/?cid=RS23.

100. Mark J. Perry, "Women Earned Majority of Doctoral Degrees in 2019 for 11th Straight Year and Outnumbmer Men in Grad School 141 to 100," American Enterprise Institute, October 15, 2020, https://www.aei.org/carpe-diem/women-earned-majority-of-doctoral-degrees-in-2019-for-11th-straight-year-and-outnumber-men-in-grad-school-141-to-100/.

101. Ibid.

102. "Incarcerated Women and Girls," *The Sentencing Project*, November 24, 2020, https://www.sentencingproject.org/publications/incarcerated-women-and-girls/.

103. Aleks Kajstura, "Women's Mass Incarceration: The Whole Pie 2019," *Prison Policy Initiative*, October 29, 2019, https://www.prisonpolicy.org/reports/pie2019women.html.

104. Ibid.

105. E. Ann Carson, "Prisoners in 2019," US Department of Justice, October 2020, https://www.bjs.gov/content/pub/pdf/p19.pdf, Table 5 (p. 9).

106. Ibid.

107. "Incarcerated Women and Girls."

108. Kara Gotsch, "Families and Mass Incarceration," *The Sentencing Project*, April 24, 2018, https://www.sentencingproject.org/publications/6148/#:~:text=Welfare's%20CW360%2C2%2B0.-,In%20the%20United%20States%20mothers%20and%20fathers%20go%20to%20prison,Health%20Measurement%20Initiative%2C%202016).

109. "Children Who Had a Parent Who Was Ever Incarcerated by Race and Ethnicity in the United States," The Annie E. Casey Foundation, n.d., https://datacenter.kidscount.org/data/tables/9734-children-who-had-a-parent-who-was-ever-incarcerated-by-race-and-ethnicity#detailed/1/any/false/1648,1603/10,11,9,12,1,13/18995,18996.

110. Geneva Brown, "The Wind Cries Mary: The Intersectionality of Race, Gender, and Reentry: Challenges for African-American Women," *Journal of Civil Rights and Economic Development* 24, no. 4 (2010): 625–648. For a historical treatment of African American women in the criminal justice system, see Paula C. Johnson, "At the Intersection of Injustice: Experiences of African American Women in Crime and Sentencing," *Journal of Gender & the Law* 41, no. 1 (1995): 1–76. For an analysis of links between the broader prison industrial complex and race and gender, see Angela Y. Davis and Cassandra Shaylor, "Race, Gender, and the Prison Industrial Complex: California and Beyond," *Meridians* 2, no. 1 (2001): 1–25, http://www.jstor.org/stable/pdfplus/40338793.pdf. For a discussion of the relationship between motherhood and crime, see Dorothy E. Roberts, "Motherhood and Crime," *Social Text* 42 (1995): 99–123.

111. Quoted in Philip Cohen, "Single Moms Can't Be Scapegoated for the Murder Rate Anymore," *Atlantic*, November 26, 2012, http://www.theatlantic.com/sexes/archive/2012/11/single-moms-cant-be-scapegoated-for-the-murder-rate-anymore/265576/.

112. Ibid.

113. For a discussion of the importance of such factors, see Reuben M. Baron and David A. Kenny, "The Moderator-Mediator Variable Distinction in Social Psychological Research: Conceptual, Strategic, and Statistical Considerations," *Journal of Personality and Social Psychology* 51, no. 6 (1986): 1173–1182.

114. "October 16, 2012 Debate Transcript," Commission on Presidential Debates.

115. For a broad overview, see Ellen Annandale and Kate Hunt, eds., *Gender Inequalities in Health* (Philadelphia: Open University Press, 2000), http://www.mheducation.co.uk/openup/chapters/0335203647.pd.

116. *Roe v. Wade* (1973) 410 US 113, http://www.law.cornell.edu/supct/html/historics/USSC_CR_0410_0113_ZS.html.

117. Erik Eckholm, "Push for 'Personhood' Amendment Represents New Tack in Abortion Fight," *New York Times*, October 25, 2011, http://www.nytimes.com/2011/10/26/us/politics/personhood-amendments-would-ban-nearly-all-abortions.html.

118. Rachel Roth, *Making Women Pay: The Hidden Costs of Fetal Rights* (Ithaca, NY: Cornell University Press, 2003). In 2012 five Republican presidential hopefuls signed pledges to support the notion of fetal personhood. Keith Ashley, "Personhood Republican Presidential Candidate Page," *Personhood USA*, December 15, 2011, http://www.personhoodusa.com/blog/personhood-republican-presidential-candidate-pledge. A flurry of other legislative and judicial activity has swirled about in the past few years, as well. Laura Bassett, "On International Women's Day, Congress Debates Measure to Limit Reproductive Rights," *Huffington Post*, March 8, 2012, http://www.huffingtonpost.com/2012/03/08/international-womens-day-congress-abortion_n_1332143.html; "Three Rulings Against Women's Rights," *New York Times*, July 31, 2012, http://www.nytimes.com/2012/08/01/opinion/three-rulings-against-womens-rights.html.

119. Fluke was nominated for *Time* magazine's Person of the Year Award in 2012. Kate Pickert, "Who Should Be TIME's Person of the Year 2012? The Candidates: Sandra Fluke, *Time*, November 26, 2012, http://www.time.com/time/specials/packages/article/0,28804,2128881_2128882_2129176,00.html. See also Leslie Marshall, "No Fluke that Sandra's on *Time's* List," *U.S. News & World Report*, November 28, 2012, http://www.usnews.com/opinion/blogs/leslie-marshall/2012/11/28/sandra-fluke-belongs-on-times-person-of-the-year-list.

120. Aaron Blake, "Todd Akin, GOP Senate Candidate: 'Legitimate Rape' Rarely Causes Pregnancy," *Washington Post*, August 19, 2012, http://www.washingtonpost.com/blogs/the-fix/wp/2012/08/19/todd-akin-gop-senate-candidate-legitimate-rape-rarely-causes-pregnancy/.

121. Michael R. Crittenden, "Mourdock's Rape Remark Sets Off Firestorm," *Wall Street Journal*, Washington Wire, October 24, 2012, http://blogs.wsj.com/washwire/2012/10/24/mourdocks-rape-remark-touches-off-firestorm/.

122. Valerie A. Earnshaw et al., "Maternal Experiences with Everyday Discrimination and Infant Birth Weight: A Test of Mediators and Moderators Among Young, Urban Women of Color," *Annals of Behavioral Medicine*, August 28, 2012, as reported by Christine Kearney, "Discrimination Can Lead to Low Birth Weight in Babies," *Medical News Today*, August 27, 2012, http://www.medicalnewstoday.com/articles/249507.php.

123. Jason L. Cummings and Pamela Braboy Jackson, "Race, Gender, and SES Disparities in Self-Assessed Health, 1974–2004," *Research on Aging* 30, no. 2 (2008): 137–168.

124. Bailey K. Sanders and Danielle M. Thomsen, "A Record Number of Women Are Serving in Congress. That's Good News for Constituents," *The Washington Post*, January 26, 2021, https://www.washingtonpost.com/politics/2021/01/26/record-number-women-are-serving-congress-thats-good-news-constituents/.

125. Karpowitz, Mendelberg, and Shaker, "Gender Inequality in Deliberative Participation"; see also Tali Mendelberg and Christopher F. Karpowitz, "More Women, but Not Nearly Enough," *New York Times*, November 8, 2012, http://campaignstops.blogs.nytimes.com/2012/11/08/more-women-but-not-nearly-enough/.

126. Patricia Scott Schroeder, "Women's Leadership: Perspectives from a Recovering Politician," in *The Difference "Difference" Makes: Women and Leadership*, ed. Deborah L. Rhode (Stanford, CA: Stanford University Press, 2003), 85.

127. "Phyllis Schlafly," *Eagle Forum*, http://www.eagleforum.org/about/bio.html.

128. Ibid. The direct link to the online radio broadcasts is http://www.eagleforum.org/radio/index.html.

129. Andrea Sachs, "Phyllis Schlafly at 84," *Time*, April 7, 2009, http://www.time.com/time/nation/article/0,8599,1889757,00.html.

130. Ibid.

131. "Are Conservative Women Like Sarah Palin Feminists? Phyllis Schlafly Says 'No,'" *The Daily Caller*, February 14, 2011, http://dailycaller.com/2011/02/14/are-conservative-women-like-sarah-palin-feminists-phyllis-schlafly-says-no/.

132. "Phyllis Schlafly," *Eagle Forum*.

133. Sachs, "Phyllis Schlafly at 84."

134. Ibid.

135. Rosalind S. Helderman, "Conservative Activist Phyllis Schlafly Defends Akin," *Washington Post*, August 20, 2012, http://www.washingtonpost.com/blogs/post-politics/wp/2012/08/20/conservative-activist-phyllis-schlafly-defends-akin/.

136. "ERA: A Brief Overview," http://EqualRightsAmendment.org, http://www.equalrightsamendment.org/overview.htm.

137. "In the States," The Equal Rights Amendment: Unfinished Business for the Construction, http://www.equalrightsamendment.org/states.htm.

138. Alex Cohen and Wilfred U. Codrington, "The Equal Rights Amendment Explained," Brennan Center for Justice, January 23, 2020, https://www.brennancenter.org/our-work/research-reports/equal-rights-amendment-explained.

139. Danielle Kurtzleben, "House Passes the Equality Act: Here's What It Would Do," *National Public Radio*, February 24, 2020, https://www.npr.org/2021/02/24/969591569/house-to-vote-on-equality-act-heres-what-the-law-would-do.

Chapter 9: Affirmative Action

1. John David Skrentny, *The Ironies of Affirmative Action: Politics, Culture, and Justice in America* (Chicago: University of Chicago Press, 1996).

2. Terry H. Anderson, *The Pursuit of Fairness: A History of Affirmative Action* (New York: Oxford University Press, 2004); Anderson, "The Strange Career of Affirmative Action," *South Central Review* 22, no. 2 (2005): 110–129; Carl E. Brody, "A Historical Review of Affirmative Action and the Interpretation of Its Legislative Intent by the Supreme Court," *Akron Law Review* 29 (1996): 291–337; Ira Katznelson, *When Affirmative Action Was White: An Untold History of Racial Inequality in Twentieth-Century America* (New York: Norton, 2005).

3. Brody, "Historical Review of Affirmative Action."

4. James W. Button and Barbara A. Rienzo, "The Impact of Affirmative Action: Black Employment in Six Southern Cities," *Social Science Quarterly* 84, no. 1 (2003):

1–14, as cited in Faye J. Crosby, Aarti Iyer, and Sirinda Sincharoen, "Understanding Affirmative Action," *Annual Review of Psychology* 57 (2006): 585–611.

5. For an in-depth study of affirmative action in higher education admission, see William Bowen and Derek Bok, *The Shape of the River: Long-Term Consequences of Considering Race in College and University Admissions* (Princeton: Princeton University Press, 2000).

6. Steven N. Durlauf, "Affirmative Action, Meritocracy, and Efficiency," *Politics, Philosophy, and Economics* 7, no. 2 (2008): 131–158; H. Roy Kaplan, "Racial Inequality and 'Meritocracy': A Closer Look," *Racism Review*, April 22, 2011, http://www.racismreview.com/blog/2011/04/22/racial-inequality-and-meritocracy-a-closer-look/.

7. "Clarence Thomas," The Oyez Project, http://www.oyez.org/justices/clarence_thomas; Ariane de Vogue, "'Silent' Justice Outspoken on Affirmative Action," *ABC News*, September 30, 2007, http://abcnews.go.com/TheLaw/story?id=3667079; Maureen Dowd, "Could Thomas Be Right?" *New York Times*, June 25, 2003, http://www.nytimes.com/2003/06/25/opinion/could-thomas-be-right.html?src=pm.

8. 438 US 265, http://www.law.cornell.edu/supct/html/historics/USSC_CR_0438_0265_ZS.html.

9. US Commission on Civil Rights, "The Commission, Affirmative Action, and Current Challenges Facing Equal Opportunity in Education," March 2003, http://www.usccr.gov/aaction/ccraa.htm, n7.

10. 539 US 244, http://www.law.cornell.edu/supct/html/02-516.ZS.html.

11. 539 US 306, http://www.law.cornell.edu/supct/html/02-241.ZS.html.

12. The scale used for ranking was 150 points; a score of 100 was needed to guarantee admission. Twelve points were awarded to applicants who had a perfect score on the Scholastic Aptitude Test (SAT), three points for an outstanding essay, and twenty points for being a scholarship athlete. A perfect grade point average was worth eighty points. Walter E. Williams, "Affirmative Action or Racism," George Mason University, January 27, 2003, http://econfaculty.gmu.edu/wew/articles/03/aa.html.

13. CJ Libassi, "The Neglected College Race Gap: Racial Disparities Among College Completers," Center for American Progress, May 23, 2018, https://www.americanprogress.org/issues/education-postsecondary/reports/2018/05/23/451186/neglected-college-race-gap-racial-disparities-among-college-completers/. See also Meredith Kolodner, "College Degree Gap Grows Wider Between Whites, Blacks and Latinos," *The Hechinger Report*, January 7, 2016, http://hechingerreport.org/25368-2/.

14. 570 US (2013), https://www.supremecourt.gov/opinions/12pdf/11-345_l5gm.pdf.

15. "New York, 13 Other States Back Affirmative Action Policy," *(Memphis) Commercial Appeal*, August 14, 2012, http://nydailyrecord.com/2012/08/14/ny-13-other-states-back-affirmative-action-policy/.

16. Richard Sander and Stuart Taylor Jr., "Why the Court Wants to Try Again," *Washington Post*, September 30, 2012, http://www.washingtonpost.com/opinions/supreme-court-wants-another-shot-at-affirmative-action/2012/09/30/82cd260e-0b28-11e2-bb5e-492c0d30bf6_story.html.

17. 579 US (2016) https://www.supremecourt.gov/opinions/15pdf/14-981_4g15.pdf.

18. *Students for Fair Admissions v. President & Fellows of Harvard College*, No. 19-2005 (1st Cir. 2020), https://www.bloomberglaw.com/public/desktop/document/StudentsforFairAdmissionsvPresidentFellowsofHarvardDocketNo190200?1614523838.

19. The petitioners are seeking review by the US Supreme Court (Scott Jaschik, "Appeals Court Backs Harvard on Affirmative Action," *Inside Higher Ed*, November 16, 2020, https://www.insidehighered.com/admissions/article/2020/11/16/appeals-court-backs-harvard-affirmative-action).

20. Ibid.

21. In the wake of *Fisher*, some affirmative action advocates shifted their attention to socioeconomic status and away from race as a direct consideration. Bill Keller, "Affirmative Reaction," *New York Times*, June 9, 2013, http://www.nytimes.com/2013/06/10/opinion/keller-affirmative-reaction.html. It is important to keep in mind, though, that considering income would have a different result than considering wealth. Using zip codes might achieve the desired result (given the robust economic and racial segregation in the United States) without violating constitutional principles relating to white students' civil rights (David Leonhardt, "The Liberals Against Affirmative Action," *New York Times*, March 9, 2013, http://www.nytimes.com/2013/03/10/sunday-review/the-liberals-against-affirmative-action.html).

22. Sam Barr, "Weighing In: Class-Based Affirmative Action Good, but Arguments Against Race-Based Affirmative Action Still Bad," *Harvard Political Review*, December 11, 2010, http://hpronline.org/hprgument/weighing-in-class-based-affirmative-action-good-but-arguments-against-race-based-affirmative-action-still-bad/.

23. Bowen and Bok, *Shape of the River*, chap. 2.

24. Thomas R. Marshall, *Public Opinion and the Supreme Court* (Boston: Unwin Hyman, 1989); Jeffrey Rosen, "Affirmative Action and Public Opinion," *New York Times*, May 23, 2011, http://www.nytimes.com/roomfordebate/2011/05/22/is-anti-white-bias-a-problem/affirmative-action-and-public-opinion; "Sandra Day O'Connor," *Oyez Project*, http://www.oyez.org/justices/sandra_day_oconnor; Peter Schmidt, "Sandra Day O'Connor Revisits and Revives Affirmative-Action Controversy," *Chronicle of Higher Education*, January 14, 2010, http://chronicle.com/article/Sandra-Day-OConnor-Revisit/63523/.

25. Faye J. Crosby et al., "Affirmative Action: Psychological Data and the Policy Debates," *American Psychologist* 58, no. 2 (2003): 93–115.

26. Barbara F. Reskin, *The Realities of Affirmative Action in Employment* (Washington, DC: American Sociological Association, 1998).

27. The full text of the bill as amended is available at http://www.eeoc.gov/laws/statutes/titlevii.cfm.

28. In this case, the Court ruled that ostensibly race-neutral policies (such as an IQ test and the requirement of holding a high school diploma at a time when far fewer African Americans than whites did so) that are not directly related to the job to be performed are unconstitutional if they cause a "disparate impact" on a protected class of citizens, according to Title VII of the Civil Rights Act of 1964. 401 US 424, http://www.law.cornell.edu/supct/html/historics/USSC_CR_0401_0424_ZO.html.

29. In this case, twenty firefighters (nineteen of whom were white) who had passed a test for promotion sued the city of New Haven, Connecticut, for invalidating the results of the test because no African Americans qualified for promotion. The city claimed that it did so out of fear of a lawsuit by the black firefighters. The Court ruled, in a 5–4 decision, that the city violated Title VII of the Civil Rights Act of 1964 by denying promotions to the twenty firefighters who earned them by passing the test. 557 US. Available at https://www.law.cornell.edu/supct/cert/07-1428.

30. Crosby et al., "Affirmative Action," 94–95.

31. But see the recent final rule on affirmatively furthering fair housing from the US Department of Housing and Urban Development, July 15, 2016, https://www.gpo.gov/fdsys/pkg/FR-2015-07-16/pdf/2015-17032.pdf.

32. For a thorough and accessible analysis of the persistence of the racial homeownership gap, see Courtney Connley, "Why the Homeownership Gap Between White and Black Americans is Larger Today Than It Was Over 50 Years Ago," *CNBC*, August 21, 2020, https://www.cnbc.com/2020/08/21/why-the-homeownership-gap-between-white-and-black-americans-is-larger-today-than-it-was-over-50-years-ago.html.

33. Frank Newport, "Affirmative Action and Public Opinion," *Gallup*, August 7, 2020, https://news.gallup.com/opinion/polling-matters/317006/affirmative-action-public-opinion.aspx.

34. Nikki Graf, "Most Americans Say Colleges Should Not Consider Race or Ethnicity in Admissions," Pew Research Center, February 25, 2019, https://www.pewresearch.org/fact-tank/2019/02/25/most-americans-say-colleges-should-not-consider-race-or-ethnicity-in-admissions/.

35. Frank Newport, "Most in U.S. Oppose Colleges Considering Race in Admissions," *Gallup*, July 8, 2016, http://www.gallup.com/poll/193508/oppose-colleges-considering-race-admissions.aspx.

36. David C. Wilson et al., "Affirmative Action Programs for Women and Minorities: Expressed Support Affected by Question Order," *Public Opinion Quarterly* 72, no. 3 (2008): 514–522.

37. Richard J. Hill, "Minorities, Women, and Institutional Change: Some Administrative Concerns," *Sociological Perspectives* 26, no. 1 (1983): 17–28; Tim Wise, "Is Sisterhood Conditional? White Women and the Rollback of Affirmative Action," *NWSA Journal* 10, no. 3 (1998): 1–26.

38. Lawrence Bobo, "Race, Interests, and Beliefs about Affirmative Action," *American Behavioral Scientist* 41, no. 7 (1998): 985–1003; David A. Kravitz and Judith Platania, "Attitudes and Beliefs About Affirmative Action: Effects of Target and of Respondent Sex and Ethnicity," *Journal of Applied Psychology* 78, no. 6 (1993): 928–938; Linda J. Sax and Marisol Arredondo, "Student Attitudes Toward Affirmative Action in College Admissions," *Research in Higher Education* 40, no. 4 (1999): 439–459; but see Dawn Michelle Baunach, "Attitudes Toward Gender-Based Affirmative Action," *Sociological Focus* 35, no. 4 (2002): 345–362.

39. Baunach, "Attitudes Toward Gender-Based Affirmative Action"; Sax and Arredond, "Student Attitudes Toward Affirmative Action in College Admissions"; Dara Z. Strolovitch, "Playing Favorites: Public Attitudes Toward Race-and Gender-Targeted Anti-discrimination Policy," *NWSA Journal* 10, no. 3 (1998): 27–53.

40. James R. Kluegel and Eliot R. Smith, "Affirmative Action Attitudes: Effects of Self-Interest, Racial Affect, and Stratification Beliefs on Whites' Views," *Social Forces* 61, no. 3 (1983): 797–824; Amy C. Steinbugler, Julie E. Press, and Janice Johnson Dias, "Gender, Race, and Affirmative Action: Operationalizing Intersectionality in Survey Research," *Gender & Society* 20, no. 6 (2006): 805–825; Steven A. Tuch and Michael Hughes, "Whites' Racial Policy Attitudes in the Twenty-First Century: The Continuing Significance of Racial Resentment," *Annals of the American Academy of Political and Social Science* 634 (2011): 134–152. Other demographic characteristics have also been found to affect attitudes about affirmative action. For instance, one study found that working women who have daughters are more likely to support affirmative action programs for women than do those who do not, though there was no such effect for men with daughters. Anastasia H. Prokos, Chardie L. Baird, and Jennifer Reid Keene, "Attitudes About Affirmative Action for Women: The Role of Children in Shaping Parents' Interests," *Sex Roles* 62 (2010): 347–360.

41. "Proposition 209: Text of Proposed Law," 1996, http://vigarchive.sos.ca.gov/1996/general/pamphlet/209text.htm.

42. In November 2020, California voters had an opportunity to reverse Prop 209 by passing Prop 16. Advocates hoped that voters in a state that was more diverse than it was in 1996 would do so, yet 56.5 percent of voters said "no" (even as 64.7 percent voted for Joe Biden for president on the same ballot) (Scott Jaschik, "Why Did Prop 16 Fail?" *Inside Higher Ed*, November 9, 2020, https://www.insidehighered.com/admissions/article/2020/11/09/experts-discuss-failure-californias-proposition-16.

43. Naomi Zevloff, "After Colorado Loss, Ward Connerly May Pull the Plug on Affirmative-Action Bans," *Colorado Independent*, November 7, 2008, http://coloradoindependent.

com/14617/ward-connerly-may-pull-the-plug. For an overview of plebiscite measures to eliminate affirmative action, see Jessica Larson and Stephen Menendian, "Anti-Affirmative Action Ballot Initiatives," Kirwan Institute for the Study of Race and Ethnicity, Ohio State University, 2008, http://www.kirwaninstitute.osu.edu/reports/2008/12_2008_AntiAffirmativeActionBallotInitiatives.pdf.

44. Justin Miller, "Ballot Wording Called Fair," *Michigan Daily*, January 9, 2006, http://www.michigandaily.com/content/ballot-wording-called-fair.

45. In *Gratz* v. *Bollinger* (the undergraduate program case), Jennifer Gratz and Patrick Hamacher brought suit; in *Grutter* v. *Bollinger* (the law school program case), Barbara Grutter brought suit. All three litigants are white, and two of the three (at least one in each case) are female.

46. Legal Information Institute, "Strict Scrutiny," 2010, http://www.law.cornell.edu/wex/strict_scrutiny.

47. For this reason, the Court's upholding of the University of Michigan Law School's policy is particularly noteworthy in *Grutter*.

48. Reverend Jackson has been a vocal supporter of affirmative action policies. He drafted a statement after attending oral arguments for the University of Michigan cases at the US Supreme Court in 2003, which can be read here: http://www.inmotionmagazine.com/opin/supreme.html.

49. https://www.projectonfairrepresentation.org/; see also Morgan Smith, "One Man Standing Against Race-Based Laws," *New York Times*, February 23, 2012, http://www.nytimes.com/2012/02/24/us/edward-blum-and-the-project-on-fair-representation-head-to-the-supreme-court-to-fight-race-based-laws.html.

50. https://www.projectonfairrepresentation.org/.

51. Stephanie Mencimer, "Meet the Brains Behind the Effort to Get the Supreme Court to Rethink Civil Rights," *Mother Jones*, March/April 2016, http://www.motherjones.com/politics/2016/04/edward-blum-supreme-court-affirmative-action-civil-rights; "Meet the Supreme Court Matchmaker: Edward Blum," *NBC News*, June 11, 2013, http://usnews.nbcnews.com/_news/2013/06/11/18750240-meet-the-supreme-court-matchmaker-edward-blum; and Morgan Smith, "One Man Standing Against Race-Based Laws," *New York Times*, February 23, 2012, http://www.nytimes.com/2012/02/24/us/edward-blum-and-the-project-on-fair-representation-head-to-the-supreme-court-to-fight-race-based-laws.html.

52. Bowen and Bok, *Shape of the River*.

53. See, for instance, Cornel West, *Race Matters* (New York: Vintage, 1993).

54. James P. Sterba, *Affirmative Action for the Future* (Ithaca, NY: Cornell University Press, 2009).

Conclusion: The Space Between Power and Powerlessness

1. Steve Wyche, "Colin Kaepernick Explains Why He Sat During National Anthem," http://NFL.com, August 27, 2016, http://www.nfl.com/news/story/0ap3000000691077/article/colin-kaepernick-explains-why-he-sat-during-national-anthem.

2. Josh Levin, "Colin Kaepernick's Protest Is Working," http://Slate.com, September 12, 2016, http://www.slate.com/articles/sports/sports_nut/2016/09/colin_kaepernick_s_protest_is_working.html.

3. Ibid.

4. For some examples of vulgar responses, see Nancy Armour, "How National Anthem Protests Bring Out Worst in People," *USA Today*, September 25, 2016, http://www.usatoday.com/story/sports/columnist/nancy-armour/2016/09/25/colin-kaepernick-anthem-protests-backlash-social-media-emails/91076216/.

5. Des Bieler, "Colin Kaepernick Responds to Justice Ruth Bader Ginsburg's Criticism of Anthem Protests," *Washington Post*, October 12, 2016, https://www.washingtonpost.com/news/early-lead/wp/2016/10/12/colin-kaepernick-responds-to-justice-ruth-bader-ginsburgs-criticism-of-anthem-protests/?utm_term=.d86f55be7c48.

6. Ariane de Vogue, "Ruth Bader Ginsburg Apologizes to Colin Kaepernick After Criticizing Anthem Protest," http://CNN.com, October 14, 2016, http://www.cnn.com/2016/10/14/politics/ruth-bader-ginsburg-apologizes-colin-kaepernick/.

7. George A. Lakoff, *The Political Mind: A Cognitive Scientist's Guide to Your Brain and Its Politics* (New York: Penguin, 2009); Drew Westen, *The Political Brain: The Role of Emotion in Deciding the Fate of the Nation* (New York: Public Affairs, 2007).

8. Though religious leaders such as Jim Wallis (who is white) and William Barber II (who is black) are pushing for poverty to be considered a values issue (John Leland, "One More 'Moral Value': Fighting Poverty," *The New York Times*, January 30, 2005, https://www.nytimes.com/2005/01/30/politics/one-more-moral-value-fighting-poverty.html; John Eligon, "From Policing to Climate Change: A Sweeping Call for a 'Moral Revolution,'" *The New York Times*, June 20, 2020, https://www.nytimes.com/2020/06/20/us/poor-peoples-campaign-platform.html).

9. Dara Z. Strolovitch, "A More Level Playing Field or a New Mobilization of Bias? Interest Groups and Advocacy for the Disadvantaged," in *Interest Group Politics*, eds. Allan J. Cigler and Burdett A. Loomis, 7th ed. (Washington, DC: CQ Press, 2007), 101.

10. Andrew Darnton and Martin Kirk, *Finding Frames: New Ways to Engage the UK Public in Global Poverty*, UK Department for International Development, January 2011, http://www.findingframes.org/.

11. Child Labor Public Education Project, "Child Labor in U.S. History," http://www.continuetolearn.uiowa.edu/laborctr/child_labor/about/us_history.html.

Index

CEOs 48; incarceration 125, 178; Medicaid recipients 172; as "minority" in US 30; occupational segregation 171; poverty 53, 172–173; prenatal care 148; support for Donald Trump 166; support for Hillary Clinton 166; underrepresentation of 36; wage gap 47, 133–134, 170–172, 177
Women, Infants, and Children program 173

Woods, Thomas Jr. 65
Workforce Reinvestment Act 127
Work Opportunity Tax Credit 126

Yassky, David 24
Yes Means Yes: Visions of Female Sexual Power and a World Without Rape (Valenti) 167

Zimmerman, George 119–120